Sharing Data and Models
in Software Engineering

Sharing Data and Models in Software Engineering

Tim Menzies

Professor of Computer Science, North Carolina State University

Ekrem Kocagüneli

Software Development Engineer, Microsoft, Redmond, USA

Leandro Minku

Research Fellow II, Centre of Excellence for Research in Computational
Intelligence and Applications (CERCIA), University of Birmingham, UK

Fayola Peters

PostDoctoral Researcher at LERO, the Irish Software Engineering
Research Center, University of Limerick, Ireland

Burak Turhan

Professor of Software Engineering, University of Oulu, Finland

AMSTERDAM • BOSTON • HEIDELBERG • LONDON
NEW YORK • OXFORD • PARIS • SAN DIEGO
SAN FRANCISCO • SINGAPORE • SYDNEY • TOKYO

Morgan Kaufmann is an imprint of Elsevier

Acquiring Editor: Todd Green
Developmental Editor: Lindsay Lawrence
Project Manager: Vijayaraj Purushothaman
Designer: Mark Rogers

Morgan Kaufmann is an imprint of Elsevier
225 Wyman Street, Waltham, MA 02451, USA

British Library Cataloguing in Publication Data
A catalogue record for this book is available from the British Library

Library of Congress Cataloging-in-Publication Data
A catalog record for this book is available from the Library of Congress

ISBN: 978-0-12-417295-1

ELSEVIER   Book Aid International   Working together to grow libraries in developing countries

www.elsevier.com • www.bookaid.org

For information on all MK publications visit our website at *www.mkp.com*

Why this book?

If you cannot—in the long run—tell everyone what you have been doing, your doing has been worthless.

Erwin Schrodinger (Nobel Prize winner in physics)

Research has deserted the individual and entered the group. The individual worker find the problem too large, not too difficult. (They) must learn to work with others.

Theobald Smith (American pathologist and microbiologist)

Foreword

During the last decade, there have been several thriving research conferences on data mining and software engineering. Two of them, called MSR and PROMISE, both happened to meet at the International Conference on Software Engineering. Due to some cosmic quirk of scheduling, MSR and PROMISE often meet at the same time, in the same corridor, sometimes even in the next room. But both events had full schedules so we rarely made it to each other sessions.

At that time, I was involved in MSR (the Mining Software Repositories conference) while the authors of this book were mostly involved in PROMISE. Naturally, we were very curious about each other. It soon became clear that there was much our two communities could learn from each other. The following is my valiant attempt to capture the differences; to misquote George Box, I hope my model is more useful than it is wrong:

- For the most part, the MSR community was mostly concerned with the *initial collection* of data sets from software projects.
- Meanwhile, the PROMISE community emphasized the analysis of the data *after it was collected.*

You could easily retort that most MSR people analyzed their data with Statistics and ML, and many PROMISE people did spend time in data collection; and you would be right to some extent, of course. But where PROMISE was different and unique was its *analysis of the analysis* of data. Most MSR papers were not concerned with a repeated analysis of data explored by a prior paper [369]. On the other hand, the PROMISE people routinely posted all their data on a public repository and their new papers would reanalyze old data, in an attempt to improve that analysis. In fact, I used to joke with one of the authors of this book (who is an Australian) that "PROMISE. Australian for repeatability" (apologies to the Fosters Brewing company).

As a result, the different conferences grew different strengths. MSR papers kept finding novel software artifacts from which we extract findings about software projects. That work is documented in successive proceedings of the MSR Conference, and I am told in an upcoming book, following this one: *The Art and Science of Analyzing Software Data*, Morgan Kaufmann, 2015, which I look forward to reading.

Meanwhile, the PROMISE people lead the charge in many areas of analysis including learning transferable lessons from one project to another. Such transfers can be remarkably difficult, and the usual result was that models that worked on one project rarely worked on another [218, 463]. Yet, from 2009, it was the PROMISE community that found ways to uncover the relevant parts of one project's data that could be applied to another [222, 226, 356, 427]. Other work [366] showed that under some accounting principles, transferred prediction models actually do quite well. This has lead to richer interactions between MSR and PROMISE people[291, 298, 462]; as time passes, the directions of these two conferences grow less distinct.

In any case, this book documents transfer learning, and the many other analysis methods developed as part of the PROMISE project. The book's central theme is how to *share* what has been learned by data science from software projects. This is an important idea since all too often, data science novices think that their work stops when they generate a model. Nothing could be further from the truth. *Data science is about __conversations__, not just conclusions*. If results are not shared, they can be quickly forgotten.

The results that are most useful are those that are shared, discussed, debated, and used to guide further analysis.

Learning data mining algorithms is a challenging problem. There are many excellent texts that can teach you the ABCs, but what comes after that? This book takes what I'd call the "PROMISE approach" to that problem: take some data sets and analyze them many times in many different ways. *The effort estimation and defect prediction problems explored in this text are good laboratory problems*; i.e. nontrivial tasks that require mastery of intricate data mining methods That is, for readers with the interest in teaching, researching, or practicing software data science, these authors offer a pretty explicit, provocative (and yet very useful) challenge: *Go ahead, make our day. Try to learn models that outperform ours.*

In conclusion, I want to stress that the lesson of PROMISE is that *open science is good science*. All the results of this book were generated, very quickly, by a small community who routinely shared their tools, their data, and their methods. All the data required to reproduce, improve, or even refute all the conclusions of this book is available in the PROMISE repository http://openscience.us/repo. All the tools used in the book are based on open source toolkits, freely available for download to your computer. Try it all out! Beat them at their own game! And then, join these authors at the annual PROMISE conference to share your ideas (and while you're there, do attend MSR as well).

Prof. Prem Devanbu
Computer Science,
University of California,
Davis, California, USA,
June 10, 2014

Contents

List of Figures

INTRODUCTION

Before we begin: for the very impatient (or very busy) reader, we offer an executive summary in Section 1.3 and statement on next directions in Chapter 25.

1.1 WHY READ THIS BOOK?

NASA used to run a Metrics Data Program (MDP) to analyze data from software projects. In 2003, the research lead, Kenneth McGill, asked: "What can you learn from all that data?" McGill's challenge (and funding support) resulted in much work. The MDP is no more but its data was the seed for the PROMISE repository (Figure 1.1). At the time of this writing (2014), that repository is the focal point for many researchers exploring data science and software engineering. The authors of this book are long-time members of the PROMISE community.

When a team has been working at something for a decade, it is fitting to ask, "What do you know <u>now</u> that you did not know <u>before</u>?" In short, we think that *sharing* needs to be studied much more, so this book is about *sharing ideas* and how *data mining can help that sharing*. As we shall see:

- Sharing can be very useful and insightful.
- But sharing ideas is not a simple matter.

The bad news is that, usually, ideas are shared very badly. The good news is that, based on much recent research, it is now possible to offer much guidance on how to use data miners to share.

This book offers that guidance. Because it is drawn from our experiences (and we are all software engineers), its case studies all come from that field (e.g., data mining for software defect prediction or software effort estimation). That said, the methods of this book are very general and should be applicable to many other domains.

1.2 WHAT DO WE MEAN BY "SHARING"?

To understand "sharing," we start with a story. Suppose two managers of different projects meet for lunch. They discuss books, movies, the weather, and the latest political/sporting results. After all that, their conversation turns to a shared problem: how to better manage their projects.

Why are our managers talking? They might be friends and this is just a casual meeting. On the other hand, they might be meeting in order to gain the benefit of the other's experience. If so, then their discussions will try to *share their experience*. But what might they share?

FIGURE 1.1

The PROMISE repository of SE data: http://openscience.us/repo.

1.2.1 SHARING INSIGHTS

Perhaps they wish to share their *insights* about management. For example, our diners might have just read Fred Brooks's book on *The Mythical Man Month* [59]. This book documents many aspects of software project management including the famous Brooks' law which says "adding staff to a late software project makes it later."

To share such insights about management, our managers might share war stories on (e.g.) how upper management tried to save late projects by throwing more staff at them. Shaking their heads ruefully, they remind each other that often the real problems are the early lifecycle decisions that crippled the original concept.

1.2.2 SHARING MODELS

Perhaps they are reading the software engineering literature and want to share *models about software development*. Now "models" can be mean different things to different people. For example, to some object-oriented design people, a "model" is some elaborate class diagram. But models can be smaller, much more focused statements. For example, our lunch buddies might have read Barry Boehm's *Software Economics* book. That book documents a power law of software that states that larger software projects take exponentially longer to complete than smaller projects [34].

Accordingly, they might discuss if development effort for larger projects can be tamed with some well-designed information hiding.[1]

(Just as an aside, by *model* we mean any succinct description of a domain that someone wants to pass to someone else. For this book, our models are mostly quantitative equations or decision trees. Other models may more qualitative such as the rules of thumb that one manager might want to offer to another—but in the terminology of this chapter, we would call that more *insight* than *model*.)

1.2.3 SHARING DATA

Perhaps our managers know that general models often need tuning with local data. Hence, they might offer to share *specific project data* with each other. This data sharing is particularly useful if one team is using a technology that is new to them, but has long been used by the other. Also, such data sharing is become fashionable amongst data-driven decision makers such as Nate Silver [399], or the evidence-based software engineering community [217].

1.2.4 SHARING ANALYSIS METHODS

Finally, if our managers are very experienced, they know that it is not enough just to share data in order to share ideas. This data has to be summarized into actionable statements, which is the task of the data scientist. When two such scientists meet for lunch, they might spend some time discussing the tricks they use for different kinds of data mining problems. That is, they might share *analysis methods for turning data into models*.

1.2.5 TYPES OF SHARING

In summary, when two smart people talk, there are four things they can share. They might want to:

- share models;
- share data;
- share insight;
- share analysis methods for turning data into models.

This book is about *sharing data* and *sharing models*. We do not discuss sharing insight because, to date, it is not clear what can be said on that point. As to sharing analysis methods, that is a very active area of current research; so much so that it would premature to write a book on that topic. However, for some state-of-the-art results in sharing analysis methods, the reader is referred to two recent articles by Tom Zimmermann and his colleagues at Microsoft Research. They discuss the very wide range of questions that are asked of data scientists [27, 64] (and many of those queries are about exploring data *before* any conclusions are made).

---

[1] N components have $N!$ possible interconnections but, with information hiding, only $M_1 < N$ components connect to some other $M_2 < N$ components in the rest of the system, thus dramatically reducing the number of connections that need to be built, debugged, and maintained.

1.2.6 CHALLENGES WITH SHARING

It turns out that sharing data and models is not a simple matter. To illustrate that point, we review the limitations of the models learned from the first generation of analytics in software engineering.

As soon as people started programming, it became apparent that programming was an inherently buggy process. As recalled by Maurice Wilkes [443] speaking of his programming experiences from the early 1950s:

> It was on one of my journeys between the EDSAC room and the punching equipment that hesitating at the angles of stairs the realization came over me with full force that a good part of the remainder of my life was going to be spent in finding errors in my own programs.

It took several decades to find the experience required to build a size/defect relationship. In 1971, Fumio Akiyama described the first known "size" law, saying the number of defects D was a function of the number of lines of code; specifically

$$D = 4.86 + 0.018 * loc$$

Alas, nothing is as simple as that. Lessons come from experience and, as our experience grows, those lessons get refined/replaced. In 1976, McCabe [285] argued that the number of lines of code was less important than the complexity of that code. He proposed "cyclomatic complexity," or $v(g)$, as a measure of that complexity and offered the now (in)famous rule that a program is more likely to be defective if

$$v(g) > 10$$

At around the same time, other researchers were arguing that not only is programming an inherently buggy process, its also inherently time-consuming. Based on data from 63 projects, Boehm [34] proposed in 1981 that linear increases in code size leads to *exponential* increases in development effort:

$$effort = a \times KLOC^b \times \prod_i (Em_i \times F_i) \tag{1.1}$$

Here, a, b are parameters that need tuning for particular projects and Em_i are "effort multiplier" that control the impact of some project factor F_i on the effort. For example, if F_i is "analysts capability" and it moves from "very low" to "very high," then according to Boehm's 1981 model, Em_i moves from 1.46 to 0.71 (i.e., better analysts let you deliver more systems, sooner).

Forty years later, it is very clear that the above models are true only in certain narrow contexts. To see this, consider the variety of software built at the Microsoft campus, Redmond, USA. A bird flying over that campus would see dozens of five-story buildings. Each of those building has (say) five teams working on each floor. These $12 * 5 * 5 = 300$ teams build a wide variant of software including gaming systems, operating systems, databases, word processors, etc. If we were to collect data from this diverse set of projects, then it would be

- A sparsely populated set of observations within a much large space of possible software projects;
- About a very diverse set of activities;
- That are undertaken for an ever-changing set of tasks;
- Using an ever-evolving set of programs and people.

Worse still, all that data would be about software practices at one very large commercial company, which may not apply to other kinds of development (e.g., agile software teams or government development labs or within open source projects).

With that preamble, we now ask the reader the following question:

> Is it likely that any single model holds across all the $12 * 5 * 5 = 300$ software projects at Microsoft (or to other organizations)?

The premise of this book is that the answer to this questions is "NO!!"; that is, if we collect data from different software projects, we will build different models and none of them may be relevant to any other (but stay calm, the next section offers three automatic methods for managing this issue).

There is much empirical evidence that different software projects produce different models [190, 218, 280]. For example, suppose we were learning a regression model for software project effort:

$$effort = \beta_0 + \beta_1 x_1 + \beta_2 x_2 + \cdots$$

To test the generality of this model across multiple projects, we can learn this equation many times using different subsets of the data. For example, in one experiment [291], we learned this equation using 20 different $(2/3)rds$ random samples of some NASA projects. As shown in Figure 1.2, the β parameters on the learned effort models vary tremendously across different samples. For example, "vexp" is "virtual machine experience" and as shown in Figure 1.2 its β_i value ranges from -8 to -3.5. In fact, the signs of five β_i coefficients even changed from positive to negative (see "stor," "aexp," "modp," "cplx," "sced").

Defect models are just as unstable as effort models. For example, Zimmermann et al. [463] learned defect predictors from 622 pairs of projects $\langle project_1, project_2 \rangle$. In only 4% of pairs, the defect predictors learned in $project_1$ worked in $project_2$. Similar findings (of contradictory conclusions in defect prediction) concern the use of object-oriented metrics. Turhan [291] reviewed the conclusions of 28 studies that discuss the effectiveness of different object-oriented metrics for predicting defects. In Figure 1.3:

- A "+" indicates a metric is significantly correlated to detects;
- A "−" means it was found to be irrelevant to predicting defects;
- And white space means that this effect was not explored.

Note that for nearly all metrics except for "response for class," the effects differ wildly in different projects.

For the manager of a software project, these instabilities are particularly troubling. For example, we know of project managers who have made acquisition decisions worth tens of millions of dollars based on these β_i coefficients; i.e., they decided to acquire the technologies that had most impact on the variables with largest β_i coefficients. Note that if the β_i values are as unstable as shown in Figure 1.2, then the justification for those purchases is not strong.

Similarly, using Figure 1.3, it is difficult (to say the least) for a manager to make a clear decision about, for example, the merits of a proposed coding standard where maximum depth of inheritance is required to be less than some expert-specified threshold.

1.2.7 HOW TO SHARE

The above results suggest that there are little to no shareable general principles in human activities such as building software:

- We cannot share models without tuning them with data.
- The best models for different domains may be different.

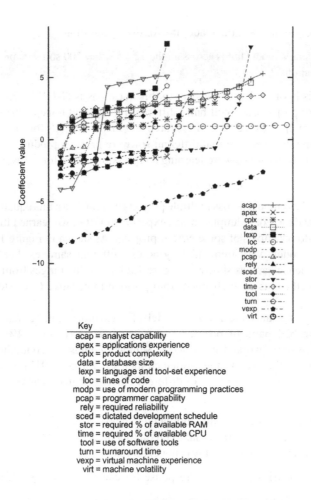

Key
acap = analyst capability
apex = applications experience
cplx = product complexity
data = database size
lexp = language and tool-set experience
loc = lines of code
modp = use of modern programming practices
pcap = programmer capability
rely = required reliability
sced = dictated development schedule
stor = required % of available RAM
time = required % of available CPU
tool = use of software tools
turn = turnaround time
vexp = virtual machine experience
virt = machine volatility

FIGURE 1.2

Instability in effort models: sorted β_i values from local calibration on 20*(66%) samples of NASA93 data. From [302]. Coefficients learned using Boehm's recommended methods [34]. A greedy backward selection removed attributes with no impact on estimates (so some attributes have less than 20 results). From [291].

- And even if not, if we dare to tune someone else's model with data, then this may be unwise because not all data is relevant outside of the context where it was collected.

But this book is not a council of despair. Clearly, it is time to end the Quixotic quest for one and only one model for diverse activities like software engineering. Also, if *one* model and *one* data source are not enough, then it is time to move to *multiple* data sources and *multiple* models.

Ref.	CBO	RFC	LCOM	DIT	NOC	WMC	# Projects	Type
[343]	+	+	+	−	−	+	6	6 versions of rhino (Java)
[1]	+	+	+	−	−	+	12	Student
[8]	+	+	−				1	Commercial telecom
[24]	+	+	−	+	+	+	8	Student
[53]	+	+	−	+	+	+	8	Student
[54]	+	+	+	+	−		1	Commercial: lalo (C++)
[65]		+		+	+		1	Commercial: telecom C++
[114]				+	−		1	Commercial Java word proc.
[112]	+	−	−	−	−	−	1	Telecom C++
[415]	−	+		−	−	+	3	3 C++ subsystems, commercial
[454]	+	+	+	−	+	+	1	Java commercial
[409]	+			+		+	1	Commercial C++ and Java
[460]	+	+	+	−	+	+	1	kcl-nasa
[152]	+	+	+	+	−	+	1	Open source: mozilla
[179]	+	+	+			+	1	Java (sap) commercial
[388]	+	+	+	+	+	+	3	Eclipse 2.0, 2.1, 3.0
[132]	−	+	+	−	−	+	8	Student
[417]		+	+	+	+		2	Sales and cd-selection system
[97]		−		−	−	−	1	Commercial telecom C++
[185]	+	+	+	−	−	+	5	Commercial telecom C++
[116]	+	+		−	−	+	1	Open source: jdt
[387]	+	+		−	−	+	2	Eclipse 2.0, 2.1
[401]	+	+	−	−	−	+	1	kcl-nasa
[144]				+	−		1	Commercial Java xml editor
[113]	−	−	−	−	−	−	1	Commercial telecom C++
[416]	−					−	0	Student
[451]	+	+	−	−	−	+	1	kcl-nasa
[410]		+		+	+		2	Commercial C++
Total +	18	20	11	11	8	17		
Total −	4	3	7	14	16	4	Key:	Strong consensus (over 2/3rds)

Total percents: "*" denotes majority conclusion in each column

	CBO	RFC	LCOM	DIT	NOC	WMC
+	64%	71%	39%	39%	29%	61%
−	14%	11%	25%	50%	57%	14%

Key:
Strong consensus (over 2/3rds)
Some consensus (less than 2/3rds)
Weak consensus (about half)
No consensus

FIGURE 1.3

Instability in defect models: studies reporting significant ("+") or irrelevant ("−") metrics verified by univariate prediction models. Blank entries indicate that the corresponding metric is not evaluated in that particular study. Colors comment on the most frequent conclusion of each column. CBO, coupling between objects; RFC, response for class (# methods executed by arriving messages); LCOM, lack of cohesion (pairs of methods referencing one instance variable, different definitions of LCOM are aggregated); NOC, number of children (immediate subclasses); WMC, # methods per class. From [291].

1.3 WHAT? (OUR EXECUTIVE SUMMARY)
1.3.1 AN OVERVIEW

The view of this book is that, when people meet to discuss data, that discussion needs automatic support tools to handle multiple models and multiple data sources. More specifically, for effective sharing, we need three kinds of automatic methods:

1. Although not all shared data from other sites is relevant, *some of it is*. The trick is to have the right *relevancy filter* that shares just enough of the correct data.
2. Although not all models move verbatim from domain to domain, it is possible to automatically build many models, then *assess what models work best* for a particular domain.
3. It is possible and useful to automatically form committees of models (called ensembles) in which *different models can debate and combine their recommendations*.

This book discusses these kinds of methods. Also discussed will be

- Methods to increase the amount of shared data we can access. For example, *privacy algorithms* will be presented that let organizations share data without divulging important secrets. We also discuss *data repair* operators that can compensate for missing data values.
- Methods to make best use of that data via *active learning* (which means learning the fewest number of most interesting questions to ask, thus avoiding needless data collection).

1.3.2 MORE DETAILS

Like a good cocktail, this book is a mix of parts—two parts introductory tutorials and two parts technical details:

- *Part I* and *Part II* are short introductory notes for managers and technical developers. These first two parts would be most suitable for *data scientist rookies*.
- *Part III* (Sharing Data) and *Part IV* (Sharing Models) describe leading edge methods taken from recent research papers. The last two parts would be more suitable for *seasoned data scientists*.

As discussed in Part I, it cannot be stressed highly enough that understanding organizational issues is just as important as understanding the data mining technology. For example, it is impossible to scale up data sharing without first addressing issues of confidentiality (the results of Chapter 16 show that such confidentiality is indeed possible, but more work is needed in this area). Many existing studies on software prediction systems tend to concentrate on *achieving the "best" model* fitting to a given task. The importance of another task—providing insights—is frequently overlooked.

When seeking insight, it is very useful to "shrink" by reducing it to just the essential, content (this simplifies the inspection and discussion of that data). There are sound theoretical reasons for believing that many data sets can be extensively "shrunk" (see Chapter 15). For methods to accomplish that task, see the data mining pruning operators of Chapter 10 as well as the CHUNK and PEEKING and QUICK tools of Chapter 12, Chapter 15, and Chapter 17.

One aspect of our work that is different than many other researchers is our willingness to "go inside" the data miners. It is common practice to use data miners as "black boxes." Although much good work can be done that way, we have found that the more we use the data miners, the more we want to adjust how they function. Much of the above chapters can be summarized as follows:

- Here's the usual way people use the data miners . . .
- . . . and here's a new way that leads to better predictions.

Based on our experience, we would encourage more experimentation on the internals of these data miners. The technology used in those miners is hardly static. What used to be just regression and classifiers is now so much more (including support vector machines, neural networks, genetic algorithms, etc.). Also, the way we use these learners is changing. What used to be "apply the learners to the data" is now transfer learning (Chapter 13 and Chapter 14), active learning (Chapter 18), ensemble learning (Chapter 20, Chapter 21, and Chapter 22), and so on. In particular, we have seen that ensembles can be very powerful and versatile tools. For instance, we show in Chapter 20, Chapter 21, Chapter 22, and Chapter 24 that their power can be extended from static to dynamic environments, from single to multiple goals/objectives, from within-company to transfer learning. We believe that ensembles will continue to show their value in future research.

Another change is the temporal nature of data mining. Due to the dynamism and uncertainty of the environments where companies operate, software engineering is moving toward dynamic adaptive automation. We show in this book (Chapter 21) that the effects of environment changes in the context of software effort estimation, and how to benefit from updating models to reflect the current context of software companies. Changes are part of software companies' lives and are an important issue to be considered in the next research frontier of software prediction systems. The effect of changes in other software prediction tasks should be investigated, and we envision the proposal of new approaches to adapt to changes in the future.

More generally, we offer the following caution to industrial data scientists:

> An elementary knowledge of machine learning and/or data mining may be of limited value to a practitioner willing to make a career in the data science field.

The practical problems facing software engineering, as well as the practicalities of real-world data sets, often require a deep understanding of the data and tailoring the right learners and algorithms to it. The tailoring can be done through augmenting a particular learner (like augmenting nearest-neighbor algorithm in TEAK, discussed in Chapter 14) or integrating the power of multiple algorithms into one (like a QUICK ensembling together a selected group of learners, as discussed in Chapter 18). But in every tailoring scenario, a practitioner will be required to justify his decisions and choices of algorithms. Hence, rather than an elementary knowledge, a deeper understanding of the algorithms (as well as their on-the-field-experience notes through books like this one) is a must for a successful practitioner in data science.

The last part of the book addresses *multiobjective optimization*. Similarly, when a software engineer is planning the development of a software, he/she may be interested in minimizing the number of defects, the effort required to develop the software, and the cost of the software. The existence of *multiple goals* and *multiobjective optimizers* thus profoundly affects data science for software engineering. Chapter 23 explains the importance of goals in model-based reasoning, and Chapter 24 presents an approach that can be used to consider different goals.

1.4 **HOW TO READ THIS BOOK**

This book covers the following material:

Part I: Data Mining for Managers: The success of an industrial data mining project depends on those technical matters as well as some very important organizational matters. This first section describes those organizational issues.

Part II: Data Mining: A Technical Tutorial: Discusses data mining for software engineering (SE) applications; several data mining methods that form the building blocks for advanced data science approaches for software engineering. For example, in this book, we apply those methods to numerous applications of data mining for SE, including software effort estimation and defect prediction.

Part III: Sharing Data: In this part, we discuss methods for moving data across organizational boundaries. The topics covered here include how to find learning contexts then how to learn across contexts (for cross-company learning); how to handle missing data; privacy; active learning; as well as privacy issues.

Part IV: Sharing Models: In this part, we discuss how to take models learned from one project and adapt and apply them to others. Topics covered here include ensemble learning; temporal learning; and multiobjective optimization.

The chapters of Parts I and II document a flow of ideas while the chapters of Parts III and IV were written to be mostly self-contained. Hence, for the reader who likes skimming, we would suggest reading all of Parts I and II (which are quite short) then dipping into any of the chapters in Parts III and IV, according to your own interests.

To assist in finding parts of the book that most interest you, this book contains several *roadmaps*:

- See Chapter 2 for a roadmap to *Part I: Data Mining for Managers*.
- See the start of Chapter 7 for a roadmap to *Part II: Data Mining: A Technical Tutorial*.
- See Chapter 11, Section 11.2, for a roadmap to *Part III: Sharing Data*.
- See Chapter 19 for a roadmap to *Part IV: Sharing Models*.

1.4.1 DATA ANALYSIS PATTERNS

As another guide to readers, from Chapter 12 onwards each chapter starts with a short summary table that we call a *data analysis pattern*:

Name:	The main technical method discussed in this chapter.
Also known as:	Synonyms, related terms.
Intent:	The goal.
Motivation:	Background.
Solution:	Proposed approach.
Constraints:	Issues that complicate the proposed approach.
Implementation:	Technical details.
Applicability:	Case studies, results.
Related to:	Pointers to other chapters with related work.

1.5 BUT WHAT ABOUT . . .? (WHAT IS *NOT* IN THIS BOOK)

1.5.1 WHAT ABOUT "BIG DATA"?

The reader may already be curious about one aspect of this book—there is very little discussion "big data." That is intentional. While the existence of large CPU farms and vast data repositories enables some novel analyzes, much of the "big data" literature is concerned with systems issues of handling terrabytes of data or thousands of co-operating CPUs. Once those systems issues are addressed, business users are still faced with the same core problems of how to share data and models and insight from one project to another. This book addresses those core problems.

1.5.2 WHAT ABOUT RELATED WORK?

This book showcases the last decade of research by the authors, as they explored the PROMISE data http://openscience.us/repo. Hundreds of other researchers, from the PROMISE community and elsewhere, have also explored that data (see the long list of application areas shown in Section 7.2). For their conclusions, see the excellent papers at

- *The Art and Science of Analyzing Software Data*, Morgan Kaufmann Publishing, 2015, in press.
- The PROMISE conference, 2005: http://goo.gl/KuocfC. For a list of top-cited papers from PROMISE, see http://goo.gl/ofpGl2.
- The Mining Software Repositories conference, 2004: http://goo.gl/FboMVw.
- As well as many other SE conferences.

One aspect of our work that is different than many other researchers is our willingness to "go inside" the data miners. It is common practice to use data miners as "black boxes." While much good work can be done that way, we have found that the more we use the data miners, the more we want to adjust how they function.

1.5.3 WHY ALL THE DEFECT PREDICTION AND EFFORT ESTIMATION?

For historical reasons, the case studies of this book mostly relate to predicting software defects from static code and estimating development effort. From 2000 to 2004, one of us (Menzies) worked to apply data mining to NASA data. At that time, most of NASA's data related to reports of project effort or defects. In 2005, with Jelber Sayyad, we founded the PROMISE project on reusable experiments in SE. The PROMISE repository was seeded with the NASA data and that kind of data came to dominate that repository.

That said, there are three important reasons to study defect prediction and effort estimation. First, they are important tasks for software engineering:

- Every software project needs a budget and *very bad things* happen when that budget is inadequate for the task at hand.
- Every software project has bugs, which we hope to reduce.

Second, another reason to explore these two tasks is that there are *open science* problems. That is, all the materials needed for the reader to repeat, improve, or even refute any part of this book are online:

- For data sets, see the PROMISE repository http://openscience.us/repo.
- For freely available data mining toolkits, download tools such as "R" or WEKA from http://www. r-project.org or http://www.cs.waikato.ac.nz/ml/weka (respectively).
- For tutorials on those tools, see e.g., [444] or some of the excellent online help forums such as http://stat.ethz.ch/mailman/listinfo/r-help or http://list.waikato.ac.nz/mailman/listinfo/wekalist, just to name a few.

Third, effort estimation and defect prediction are excellent *laboratory problems*; i.e., nontrivial tasks that require mastery of intricate data mining methods. In our experience, we have found that the data mining methods used for these kinds of data apply very well to other kinds of problems.

Hence, if the reader has ambitions to become an industrial or academic data scientist, we suggest that he or she try to learn models that *outperform the results shown in this book* (or, indeed, the hundreds of other published papers that exploring the PROMISE effort or defect data).

1.6 WHO? (ABOUT THE AUTHORS)

The authors of this text have worked real-world data mining with clients for many years. Ekrem Kocagüenli worked with companies in Turkey to build effort estimation models. Dr Kocagüenli now works at Microsoft, Redmond, on deriving operational intelligence with the Bing Ads team. Burak Turhan has an extensive data mining consultancy with Turkish and Finnish companies. Tim Menzies and Fayola Peters have been mining data from NASA projects since 2000. Dr Menzies has also been hired by Microsoft to conduct data mining studies on gaming data. Leandro Minku worked on data mining at Google during a six-month internship in 2009/2010 and has been collaborating with Honda on optimization.

Further, this team of authors has extensive experience in data mining, particularly in the area of software engineering. Tim Menzies is a Professor in Computer Science (WVU) and a former Software Research Chair at NASA where he worked extensively on their data sets. In other industrial work, he developed code in the 1980s and 1990s in the Australian software industry. After that, he returned to academia and has published 200+ refereed articles, many in the area on data mining and SE. According to academic.research.microsoft.com, he is one the top 100 most cited researchers in software engineering, in the last decade (out of 80,000+ authors). His research includes artificial intelligence, data mining and search-based software engineering. He is best known for his work on the PROMISE open source repository of data for reusable software engineering experiments. He received his PhD degree from New South Wales University, Australia. For more information visit http://menzies.us.

Ekrem Kocagüenli received his PhD from the Lane Department of Computer Science and Electrical Engineering, West Virginia University. His research focuses on empirical software engineering, data/model problems associated with software estimation and tackling them with smarter machine learning algorithms. His research provided solutions to industry partners like Turkcell, IBTech (subsidiary of Greece National Bank); he also completed an internship at Microsoft Research Redmond in 2012. His work was published at important software engineering venues such as *IEEE TSE*, *ESE* and *ASE* journals. He now works at Microsoft, Redmond, exploring data mining and operational intelligence metrics on advertisement data.

Leandro L. Minku is a Research Fellow II at the Centre of Excellence for Research in Computational Intelligence and Applications (CERCIA), School of Computer Science, the University of Birmingham (UK). He received his PhD degree in Computer Science from the University of Birmingham (UK) in 2010, and was an intern at Google Zurich for six months in 2009/2010. He was the recipient of the Overseas Research Students Award (ORSAS) from the British government and several scholarships from the Brazilian Council for Scientific and Technological Development (CNPq). Dr Minku's research focuses on software prediction models, search-based software engineering, machine learning in changing environments, and ensembles of learning machines. His work has been published at internationally renowned venues such as ICSE, IEEE TSE, ACM TOSEM, and IEEE TKDE. He was invited to give a keynote talk and to join conference steering committees.

Fayola Peters is a Research Fellow at LERO, the Irish Software Engineering Research Center (Ireland). Along with Mark Grechanik, she is the author of one of the two known algorithms (presented at ICSE12) that can privatize algorithms while still preserving the data mining properties of that data.

Burak Turhan is a Full Professor of Software Engineering at the Department of Information Processing Science at the University of Oulu, Finland. Before taking his current position, Dr Turhan was a Research Associate in the Software Engineering Group, Institute for Information Technology, National Research Council Canada. Prof. Turhan's research and teaching interests in software engineering are focused on empirical studies of software quality and programmer productivity, software analytics through the application of machine learning and data mining methods for defect and cost modeling, and mining software repositories for grounded decision making, as well as agile/lean software development with a special focus on test-driven development. He has published 70+ articles in international journals and conferences, invited for and organized panels and talks, and offered academic and industrial courses at all levels on these topics. He served in various positions for the academic community, e.g., steering committee member, chair, TPC member for 30+ academic conferences; reviewer and editorial board member for 15+ scientific journals; external reviewer and expert for national research councils and IT-related legal cases. He has been involved in 10+ national and international research projects and programs and conducted research in collaboration with leading (multi-)national companies. For more information and details please visit http://turhanb.net.

1.7 **WHO ELSE? (ACKNOWLEDGMENTS)**

The authors gratefully acknowledge the contribution of the international PROMISE community who have motivated our work with their interest, insights, energy, and synergy.

In particular, the authors would like to thank the founding members of the PROMISE conference's steering committee who have all contributed significantly to the inception and growth of PROMISE: Ayse Bener, Gary Boetticher, Tom Ostrand, Guenther Ruhe, Jelber Sayyad, and Stefan Wagner. Special mention needs to be made of the contribution of Jelber Sayyad who, in 2004, was bold enough to ask, "Why not make a repository of SE data?"

We also thank Tom Zimmermann, Christian Bird, and Nachi Nagappan from Microsoft Research, who let us waste weeks of their life to debug these ideas.

As to special mentions, *Tim Menzies* wants to especially thank the dozens of graduate students at West Virginia University who helped him develop and debug some of the ideas of this book. Dr Menzies' research was funded in part by NSF, CISE, project #0810879 and #1302169.

Ekrem Kocaguneli would like to thank Ayse Basar Bener, Tim Menzies, and Bojan Cukic for their support and guidance throughout his academic life. Dr Kocaguneli's research was funded in part by NSF, CISE, project #0810879.

Leandro Minku would like to thank all the current and former members of the projects Dynamic Adaptive Automated Software Engineering (DAASE) and Software Engineering By Automated SEarch (SEBASE), especially Prof. Xin Yao and Dr Rami Bahsoon, for the fruitful discussions and support. Dr Minku's research was funded by EPSRC Grant No. EP/J017515/1.

Fayola Peter would like to thank Tim Menzies for his academic guidance from Masters to PhD. Thanks are also deserved for members of the Modeling Intelligence Lab at West Virginia University whose conversations have sparked ideas for work contributed in this book. Dr Peter's research was funded in part by NSF, CISE, project #0810879 and #1302169.

Burak Turhan would like to give special thanks to Junior, Kamel, and the Silver-Viking for their role in the creation of this book. He would also like to acknowledge the Need for Speed (N4S) program funded by Tekes, Finland, for providing partial support to conduct the research activities leading to the results that made their way into this book.

DATA MINING
FOR MANAGERS

RULES FOR MANAGERS

2

Most of this book describes state-of-the-art technological approaches to data mining and software engineering. But if this book only contained that material, it might give the incorrect impression that solving data mining problems is mostly a matter of applying the right technologies. This is not the case; in fact, many of the success factors for a data mining project relate to management attitudes and actions.

Hence, before presenting that technical material, we present some "rules of engagement" for anyone who is orchestrating a team of scientists and the business users funding the data mining exploring some data sets.

2.1 THE INDUCTIVE ENGINEERING MANIFESTO

The Inductive Engineering Manifesto was a 2011 document describing some of the rules of thumb used by data scientists at Microsoft Research [298]. That document characterized the difference between academic and industrial data mining. These differences were systematized into the following seven principles:

1. *Users before algorithms.* Data mining algorithms are only useful in industry if users fund their use in real-world applications. The user perspective is vital to inductive engineering. The space of models that can be generated from any data set is very large. If we understand and apply user goals, then we can quickly focus an inductive engineering project on the small set of most crucial issues.
2. *Broad skill set, big toolkit.* Successful inductive engineers routinely try multiple inductive technologies. To handle the wide range of possible goals, an inductive engineer should be ready to deploy a wide range of tools. Note that the set of useful inductive technologies is large and constantly changing. So use tools supported by a large ecosystem of developers who are constantly building new learners and fixing old ones.
3. *Live with the data you have.* You go mining with the data you have, not the data you might want or wish to have at a later time. Because we may not have control over how data is collected, it is wise to cleanse the data prior to learning. For example, before learning from a data set, conduct instance or feature selection studies to see what spurious data can be removed.
4. *Plan for scale.* In any industrial application, the data mining method is repeated multiple times to answer an extra user question, make some enhancement, and/or bug fix to the method, or to deploy it to a different set of users. That is, for serious studies, to ensure repeatability, the entire analysis should be automated using some high-level scripting language.
5. *Early feedback.* Continuous and early feedback from users allows needed changes to be made as soon as possible and without wasting heavy up-front investment. Prior to conducting very elaborate studies, try applying very simple tools to gain rapid early feedback.

6. *Be open-minded.* Its unwise to enter into an inductive study with fixed hypotheses or approaches, particularly for data that has not been mined before. Do not resist exploring additional avenues when a particular idea does not work out. We advise this because data likes to surprise; initial results often change the goals of a study when business plans are based on issues irrelevant to local data.

7. *Do smart learning.* Important outcomes are riding on your conclusions. Make sure that you check and validate them. There are many such validation methods such as repeat the analysis N times on, say, 90% of the available data, then check how well your conclusions hold across all those samples.

For more details on *users before algorithms*, see Chapter 3.
For more details on *broad skill set, big toolkit*, see Chapter 4.
For more details on *live with the data you have*, see Chapter 5.
For more details on *plan for scale* and *be open-minded*, see Chapter 6.

2.2 MORE RULES

The above rules are hardly a complete set of heuristics for understanding and managing a data mining project. But even this longer list of rules will need extension and clarification for any particular data mining project. So our rule #0 must be "look for other rules" that most apply to your own work.

RULE #1: TALK TO THE USERS

3

The most important rule in industrial data science is this: talk more to your users than to your algorithms.

Why is it most important? Well, the main difference we see between academic data mining research and industrial data scientists is that the former is mostly focused on algorithms and the latter is mostly focused on "users."

Note that by this term "user," we do not mean the end user of a product. Rather, we mean the community providing the data and domain insights vital to a successful project. Users provide the funding for the project and, typically, need to see a value-added benefit, very early in a project.

At one level, talking to the people who hold the purse strings is just good manners and good business sense (because it is those people who might be willing to fund future projects). As the Mercury astronauts used to say, "No bucks, no Buck Rodgers."

But there is another, more fundamental, reason to talk to business users:

- The space of models that can be generated from any data set is very large. If we understand and apply user goals, then we can quickly focus a data mining project on the small set of most crucial issues.
- Hence, it is vital to talk to users in order to leverage their "biases" for better guiding the data mining.

As discussed in this chapter, any inductive process is fundamentally biased. Hence, we need to build ensembles of opinions (some from humans, some from data miners), each biased in their own particular way. In this way, we can generate better conclusions than using some an overreliance on a single bias.

The rest of this chapter expands on this notion of "bias," as it appears in humans and data miners.

3.1 USERS BIASES

The Wikipedia page on "List of cognitive biases"[1] lists nearly 200 ways that human reasoning is systematically biased. That list includes

- Nearly a hundred decision-making, belief, and behavioral biases such as *attentional bias* (paying more attention to emotionally dominant stimuli in one's environment and neglecting relevant data).
- Nearly two dozen social biases such as the *worse than average effect* (believing that are we are worse than others at tasks that are difficult).
- Over 50 memory errors and biases such as *illusory correlation* (inaccurately remembering a relationship between two events).

---

[1] http://en.wikipedia.org/wiki/List_of_cognitive_biases.

FIGURE 3.1

Gorillas in our midst. From [408]. Scene from video used in "invisible gorilla" study. Figure provided by Daniel Simons. For more information about the study and to see the video go to www.dansimons.com or www. theinvisiblegorilla.com.

As documented by Simons and Chabris [400], the effects of these human imperfections can be quite startling. For example, in the "Gorilla in our midst" experiment, subjects were asked to count how often a ball was passed between the members of a basketball team wearing white shirts. Nearly half the subjects (48%) were so focused on "white things" that they did not notice a six-foot tall hairy black gorilla walk slowly into the game, beat its chest, then walk out (see Figure 3.1). According to Simons and Chabris, humans can suffer from "sustained in attentional blindness" (which is a kind of cognitive bias) where they do not see effects that, to an outside observer, are glaringly obvious.

The lesson here is that when humans analyze data, their biases can make them miss important effects. Therefore, it is wise to run data miners over that same data in order to find any missed effects.

3.2 DATA MINING BIASES

When human biases stop them from seeing important effects, data miners can uncover those missed effects. In fact, best results often come from *combining* the biases of the humans and data miners (i.e., the whole may be greater than any of the parts).

That kind of multilearner combination is discussed below. First, we need to review the four biases of any data miner:

1. No data miner has access to all the data in the universe. Some *sampling bias* controls which bits of the data we offer to a miner.
2. Different data miners have a *language bias* that controls what models they write. For example, decision tree learners cannot write equations and Bayesian learners cannot write out categorical rules.
3. When growing a model, data miners use a *search bias* that controls what is the next thing they add to a model. For example, some learners demand that new rules cannot be considered unless they are supported by a minimum number of examples.
4. Once a model is grown, data miners also use an *underfit bias* that controls how they prune away parts of a model generated by random noise ("underfit" is also called "overfitting avoidance").

For example, consider the task of discussing the results of data mining with management. For that audience, it is often useful to display small decision trees that fit on one slide. For example, here's a small decision tree that predicts who will survive the sinking of the *Titanic* (Hint: do not buy third-class tickets).

```
sex = male
|   class = first
|   |   age = adult : died
|   |   age = child : survived
|   class = second
|   |   age = adult : died
|   |   age = child : survived
|   class = third   : died
|   class = crew    : died
sex = female
|   class = first   : survived
|   class = second  : survived
|   class = third   : died
|   class = crew    : survived
```

To generate that figure, we apply the following biases:

- A *language bias* that generates decision trees.
- A *search bias* that does not grow the model unless absolutely necessary.
- An *underfit bias* that prunes any doubtful parts of the tree. This is needed because, without it, our trees may grow too large to show the business users.

For other audiences, we would use other biases. For example, programmers who want to include the learned model in their program have a language bias. They often prefer *decision lists*, or a list of conditions (and the *next* condition is only checked if the *last* condition fails). Such decision lists can be easily dropped into a program. For example, here is a decision list learned from the *S.S. Titanic* data:

```
(sex = female) and (class = first)  => survived
(sex = female) and (class = second) => survived
(sex = female) and (class = crew)   => survived
 => died
```

So bias is a blessing to any data miner because, if we understand it, we can tune the output to the audience. For example, our programmer likes the decision list output as it is very simple to (say) drop it into a "C" program.

```
if ((sex == "female") && (class == "first"))  return "survived"
if ((sex == "female") && (class == "second")) return "survived"
if ((sex == "female") && (class == "crew"))   return "survived"
return "died"
```

On the other hand, bias is a challenge because, the same data can generate different models, depending on the biases of the learner. This leads to the question: Is bias avoidable?

3.3 CAN WE AVOID BIAS?

The lesson of the above example (about the *Titanic*) is that, sometimes, it is possible to use user bias to inform the data mining process. But is that even necessary? Is not the real solution to avoid bias all together?

In everyday speech, bias is a dirty word. For example:

> **Judge slammed for appearance of bias**
> A Superior Court judge has barred an Ontario Court colleague from presiding over a man's trial after concluding he appeared biased against the defendant.
> **(www.lawtimesnews.com, September 26, 2011. See http://goo.gl/pQZkF).**

But bias' bad reputation is not deserved. It turns out that bias is very useful:

- Without bias, we cannot say which bits of the data matter most to us.
- That is, without bias, we cannot divide data into the bits that matter and the bits that do not.

This is important because if we cannot ignore anything, we cannot *generalize*. Why? Well, any generalization must be smaller than the thing it generalizes (otherwise we might as well just keep the original thing and ignore the generalization). Such generalizations are vital to data mining. Without generalization, all we can do is match new situations to a database of old examples. This is a problem because, if the new situation has not occurred before, then nothing is matched and we cannot make any predictions. That is, while bias can blind us to certain details, it can also let use see patterns that let us make predictions in the future.

To put that another way:

> Bias make us blind but it also let us see.

3.4 MANAGING BIASES

Bias is unavoidable, even central, to the learning process. But how to manage it?

Much of this book is concerned with automatic tools for handling bias:

- Above, we showed an example where different learners (decision tree learners and rule learners) were used to automatically generate different models for different users.
- Later in this book, we discuss state-of-the-art ensemble learners that automatically build committees of expert, each with their own particular bias. We will show that combining the different biases of different experts produces better predictions than relying exclusively on the bias of one expert.

But even without automatic support, it is possible to exploit expert biases to achieve better predictions. For example, at Microsoft, data scientists conduct "user engagement meetings" to review the results of a data mining session:

- Meetings begin with a quick presentation on the analysis method used to generate the results.
- Some sample data is then shown on the screen, at which point the more informed business users usually peer forward to check the data for known effects in that business.

- If the data passes that "sanity check" (that it contains old conclusions), the users start investigating the data for new effects.

Other measures of success of such meetings are as follows. In a good user engagement meeting

- The users keep interrupting to debate the implications of your results. This shows that (a) you are explaining the results in a way they understand, and (b) your results are commenting on issues that concern users.
- Data scientists spend more time listening than talking as the users propose queries on the sample data, or if they vigorously debate implications of the displayed data.
- At subsequent meetings, users bring their senior management.
- The users start listing more and more candidate data sources that you could exploit.
- After the meeting, the users invite you back to their desks inside their firewalls to show them how to perform certain kinds of analysis.

3.5 SUMMARY

The conclusions made by any human- or computer-based learning will be biased. When using data miners, the trick is to match the biases of the learner with the biases of the users. Hence, data scientists should talk more, and listen more, to business users in order to understand and take advantage of the user biases.

RULE #2: KNOW THE DOMAIN

4

What are the skills needed by a successful data scientist? The previous chapter made the case that such scientists need to be skilled facilitators for meetings of business users. But is anything more needed?

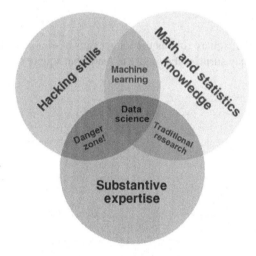

According to the famous Conway diagram (shown right), a good data scientist is part hacker, part mathematician, and part domain expert. In his comments on the diagram,[1] Conway warns that all three are essential.

Note the "danger zone" where people know enough to be dangerous but not enough to be cautious. This is the region of "lies, damned lies, and statistics" where novices report models without any real understanding of the limitations of those models or their implication for the business.

Note also the important of substantive domain expertise. Novice data scientists do not take the time to learn the context around the data they are studying. Hence, these novices can either miss important results or report spurious results.

---

[1] http://drewconway.com/zia/2013/3/26/the-data-science-venn-diagram.

4.1 CAUTIONARY TALE #1: "DISCOVERING" RANDOM NOISE

As an example of the discovery of spurious patterns, consider a data miner trying to find structures within the tick marks of Figure 4.1. Each of the squares in that figure was generated by some process that

- Reflects over the last N characters (and a random process has $N = 0$);
- Then writes either a vertical or horizontal dash.

Before reading the next paragraph, the reader is invited to decide which square in Figure 4.1 comes from a random process.

Pause.

Worked it out? In Figure 4.1, square (c) has the longer runs of identical characters; in other words, it seems the least random. It may surprise the reader to learn that square (c) was actually generated by

```
|-|-|--||-|----||-|-|-|||-          -||--|-|-||-|-||-||-|--|-|
-|-|-|||-|-||-|--|--||-|-|          --||---|--||--|-|--|-|-|--
||-|-|||||||-|---|-||---|-|-|        ---|-|-|--||-|-|||-|---|-||
|--|-|-|--|-|-||-|-|-|-|-|          --|-|-|-|--|--||-|-||-|-|-||-
-|-|-|-|-|-|-|-||-|-||-|-|--        -|-||--||-|-||-|-|-|--|-|||
-|--||-|-||-|-||-|-|---|----        |-|||||-||-|||-|-|||-||---|
|-|-|--|-|-|||-|-|-|-|||-           |-|-|-||---|--|---|-|--||-|
--|-|-|-||-|-|-|-||-|-|-|-||        -|-|||--|-||-||-|-|-|-|--|
--|-|-|-|-|-|--||--|-|--||          -|--||----|||-|-||-|-||-|-
--||-|-|--||-|-|--|||||--|          ||-|||-|-|-|||-|---|-|-||||-
-|-|-|-|-|-|-|-|-|--|-|-|---         ---||-|-|||--|-|-|---|-|--
||-----|-||-|-|-|-|-|-|-|-          |||--|--|-|-||-||-|-|-||-|
              (a)                              (b)
```

```
         -|-|||-----|-------||--|-
         -||--|||||--|--|-|||-||||
         --||----||-||-|----|--|-|
         ||-|-|-|||-||--|||-|-|||
         |-|||-|-|--||-|-|-||--|--
         ||-|--|-----|----|---||--
         ||---|---|-||||-|||||-|-|
         |---|---||-||||-|-|------
         -|---|-|||-|---||-||-|---
         |||-||----||||||-|||||---
         |-|------||----||-||-----
         -|||-|||-|--|--|-||------
                    (c)
```

FIGURE 4.1

Random, or structured, data? One of these squares was generated with each tick mark independent of the one before it (in left-to-right top-to-bottom order). From http://norvig.com/experiment-design.html.

the random process. To understand that, please consider the mathematics of random numbers. The odds of writing either character is 0.5 so the odds of writing, say, six in a row is $0.5^6 = (1/64)$. In the 312 characters of each square, we should therefore expect at least four such randomly generated structures; that is, the squares with the fewest number of long runs was generated by the least random process.

4.2 CAUTIONARY TALE #2: JUMPING AT SHADOWS

One way to avoid spurious conclusions based on random noise (such as the structures in Figure 4.1c) is to use domain knowledge. This is an important point as there are many cautionary tales about the mistakes made by data scientists who lacked that domain knowledge.

For example, in the 1990s, it was standard practice at the NASA's Software Engineering Laboratory [117] to share data with outside research groups. The only caveat was that research teams who wanted that data had to come to the lab and spend one week on domain familiarization. This policy was put in place after too many outside researchers kept making the same mistake.

- A repeated conclusion from those outsiders was that a certain class of NASA subsystems was inherently most bug prone.
- The problem with that conclusion was that, while certainly true, it missed an important factor. It turns out that that particular subsystem was the one deemed least critical by NASA. Hence, it was standard policy to let newcomers work on that subsystem in order to learn the domain.
- Because such beginners make more mistakes, it is hardly surprising that this particular subsystem saw the most errors.

Note that, for this subsystem, an ounce of domain knowledge would have been worth a ton of data mining algorithms.

4.3 CAUTIONARY TALE #3: IT PAYS TO ASK

Another cautionary tale (about the value of domain knowledge) comes from when one of the authors worked at Microsoft. During his research on the quality implications of distributed development [232], Kocagüneli, had to determine which code files were created by a distributed or centralized development process. This, in turn, meant mapping files to their authors, and then situating some author in a particular building in a particular city and country.

After six weeks of work (which was mostly spent running and debugging some very long SQL queries), it appeared that a very small number of people produced most of the core changes to certain Microsoft products.

- Initially, this result seemed very plausible as it had some precedence in the field of software engineering. In the 1970s, Fred Brooks [59] proposed organizing programming like a surgical team around one highly skilled chief programmer and other, lesser-trained support personnel.
- This "chief programmer" model is suitable when the success of a project is determined by a relatively small percent of the workforce.
- And, if this was the reality of work at Microsoft, it would mean that product quality would be most assured by focusing more on this small group.

However, the conclusions from that first six weeks of work were completely wrong. Microsoft is a highly optimized organization that takes full advantage of the benefits of auto-generated code. That generation occurs when software binaries are being built and, at Microsoft, that build process is controlled by a small number of skilled engineers. As a result, most of the files appeared to be "owned" by these build engineers even though these files are built from code provided by a very large number of programmers working across the Microsoft organization.

Now, to repeat the lesson from the last chapter, the erroneous nature of the initial conclusions was first revealed after Kocagüneli talked to his business users. That is, by showing the wrong conclusions, Kocagüneli's users were prompted to explain more of the details of the build process at Microsoft. As a result, the study could be changed and some interesting and insightful final results were generated [232].

4.4 SUMMARY

Be good at the math, be good at the programming, but also take the time to carefully understand the domain.

RULE #3: SUSPECT YOUR DATA

5

When learning from data, sometimes the best way to start is to throw most of the data away. This may be a surprising, even shocking, thing to say as most data scientists expend much effort to collect that data. However, in practice, it is wise to carefully audit and prune data, for the following reasons.

5.1 CONTROLLING DATA COLLECTION

All inductive agents (be they human or artificial) can make inductive errors, so we must employ some methods to minimize the frequency of those errors. The standard approach to this problem is to use some initial requirements at the gathering stage where the goals of the learning are defined in a careful and reflective way, as discussed in:

- Basili's Goal-Question-Metric [283] approach;
- and Easterbrook et al.'s notes on empirical SE [110].

The intent of this standard approach is to prevent spurious conclusions by (a) carefully controlling data collection and by (b) focusing the investigation on a very small space of hypotheses. Where possible, we strongly recommend this controlled approach to data collection. But what to do if such control is not possible?

5.2 PROBLEMS WITH CONTROLLED DATA COLLECTION

In practice, full control over data collection is not always possible. Collecting data comes at a cost, for example:

- Data collection should not stress the available hardware resources. For example, the transmission of that data should not crash the network. Further, the storage of that data should not exceed the free space on the hard drives.
- If humans are involved in that data collection, the effort associated with that collection must not detract from normal operations.

For these reasons, it is infeasible to collect all possible data. Worse, in our experience, it may not be possible to control data collection even for the limited amounts of information you can receive. For example, when one of us (Menzies) tried collecting data from inside NASA, he found many roadblocks to data collection. NASA makes extensive use of large teams of contractors. Data collection across those teams must navigate many layers of management from subcontractors and sub-subcontractors. This means that communication to data owners had to be mediated by up to a dozen account managers, all of whom may have many higher priority tasks to perform. Hence, very little data was ever transferred to Menzies. Further, when data was transferred, there were very few knowledgeable humans available who could discuss the content of that data.

Even when restricted to within one organization, data collection can also be complicated and exorbitantly expensive. Jairus Hihn reports the $1.5 million NASA spent in the period 1987-1990 to understand the historical records of all their software. In that study, five NASA analysts (including Hihn) worked half-time to fully document 200 records describing NASA's software development experience. NASA analysts traveled around the country to interview contractors and collect meta-knowledge about a spreadsheet of 200 rows and less than 30 columns. At the end of this process, the analysts wrote four fat volumes (300+ pages each) reporting their conclusions. Hihn reported that this exercise has never been repeated because it was so expensive [173].

Consequently, in many cases, a data scientist must

Live with the data you have: You go mining with the data you have—not the data you might want or wish to have at a later time.

Hence, the task of the data scientist is to make the most of the data at hand, and not wait for some promised future data set that might never arrive.

5.3 RINSE (AND PRUNE) BEFORE USE

We may not have control over how data is collected, so it is wise to cleanse the data prior to learning. Happily, a standard result is that given a table of data, 80-90% of the rows and all but the square root of the number of columns can be deleted before comprising the performance of the learned model [71, 155, 221, 234]. That is, even in dirty data sets it is possible to isolate and use "clean" sections. In fact, as we show below, removing rows and columns can actually be beneficial to the purposes of data mining.

5.3.1 ROW PRUNING

The reader may be puzzled by our recommendation to prune most of the rows of data. However, such pruning can remove outliers that confuse the modeling process. It can also reveal the essential aspects of a data sets:

- The goal of data mining is to find some principle from the past that can applied to the future.
- If data are examples of some general principle, then there should be multiple examples of that principle in the data (otherwise we would not have the examples required to learn that principle).
- If rows in a table of data repeat some general principle, then that means that many rows are actually just echoes of a smaller number of underlying principles.
- This means, in turn, that we can replace N rows with $M < N$ *prototypes* that are the best exemplars of that underlying principle.

5.3.2 COLUMN PRUNING

The case for pruning columns is slightly more complex.

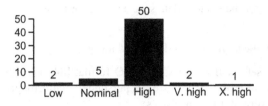

FIGURE 5.1

Distribution of software complexity *cplx* within the *na60* data set. From [75].

Undersampling. The number of possible influences on a project is quite large and, usually, historical data sets on projects for a particular company are quite small. Hence, a variable that is *theoretically* useful may be *practically* useless. For example, Figure 5.1 shows how, at one NASA site, nearly all the projects were rated as having a *high* complexity (see Figure 5.1).

Therefore, this data set would not support conclusions about the interaction of, say, extra highly complex projects with other variables. A learner would be wise to subtract this variable (and a cost modeling analyst would be wise to suggest to their NASA clients that they refine the local definition of "complexity").

Reducing Variance. Miller offers an extensive survey of column pruning for linear models and regression [316]. That survey includes a very strong argument for column pruning: the variance of a linear model learned by minimizing least squares error decreases as the number of columns in is decreased. That is, the fewer the columns, the more restrained are the model predictions.

Irrelevancy. Sometimes, modelers are incorrect in their beliefs about what variables effect some outcome. In this case, they might add irrelevant variables to a database. Without column pruning, a model learned from that database might contain these irrelevant variables. Anyone trying to use that model in the future would then be forced into excessive data collection.

Noise. Learning a model is easier when the learner does not have to struggle with fitting the model to confusing noisy data (i.e., when the data contains spurious signals not associated with variations to projects). Noise can come from many sources such as clerical errors or missing data. For example, organizations that only build word processors may have little data on software projects with high reliability requirements.

Correlated Variables. If multiple variables are tightly correlated, then using all of them will diminish the likelihood that either variable attains significance. A repeated result in data mining is that pruning away some of the correlated variables increases the effectiveness of the learned model (the reasons for this are subtle and vary according to which particular learner is being used [155]).

5.4 ON THE VALUE OF PRUNING

This section offers a case study about the benefits of row and column pruning in software effort estimation. The interesting thing about this example is that pruning dramatically improved the predictions from the model, especially for the smaller data sets. That is, for these data sets, the paradoxical result is this:

- The *less* data you have, the *more* you need to throw away.

This study [75] uses data sets in Boehm's COCOMO format [34, 42]. That format contains 15-22 features describing a software project in terms of its personnel, platform, product and use in a project. In this study, the projects were of difference sizes:

- For example, the largest data set had 160 projects;
- And the smallest had around a dozen.

Feature reduction was performed on all these data sets using a *column pruner* called WRAPPER. This WRAPPER system calls for some "wrapped" learner (in this case, linear regression) on some subset of the variables. If the results look promising, WRAPPER then grows that subset till the performance stops improving. Initially, WRAPPER starts with subsets of size one (i.e., it tries every feature just on its on).

Figure 5.2 shows how many columns were thrown away from each data set (all the data sets are sorted on the *x*-axis sorted left to right, largest to smallest). In that figure, the solid and dotted lines of show the number of columns in our data sets *before* and *after* pruning:

- In the original data sets, there were 22 attributes. For the largest data set shown on the left-hand side of Figure 5.2, WRAPPER did *nothing at all* (observe how the red and green lines fall to the same left-hand side point; i.e., WRAPPER kept all 22 columns).
- However, as we sweep from left to right, largest data set to smallest, we see that WRAPPER threw away *more columns from the smaller data sets* (with one exception—see the *p02* data set, second from the right).

This is a strange result, to say the least; the smaller data sets were pruned the most. This result raises the question: Is the pruning process faulty?

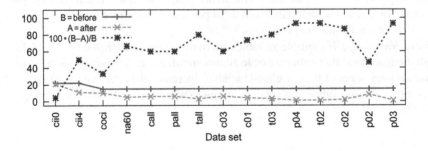

FIGURE 5.2

Column pruning with WRAPPER. Data sets are sorted along the *x*-axis, largest to smallest. The blue line (dark gray in print versions) shows the percentage of the columns discarded by WRAPPER from each data set. From [75].

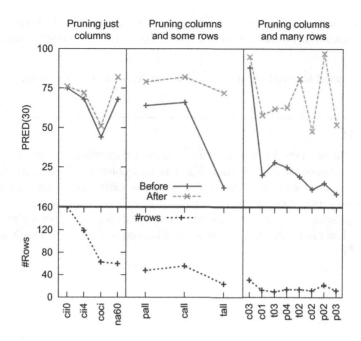

FIGURE 5.3

Effects on PRED(30) of different pruning methods. Data sets are sorted along the x-axis largest to smallest. This figure shows mean values in 30 repeated experiments where the learned model was tested on rows not seen during training. From [75].

To test that, we computed the "PRED(30)" results using all columns and just the reduced set of columns. This PRED(30) error message is defined as follows:

- *PRED(30)* = the percent of estimates that were within 30% of actual.
- For example, a PRED(30) = 50% means that half the estimates are within 30% of the actual.

The PRED(30) results associated with the pruned data sets are shown in Figure 5.3:

- The Solid lines on Figure 5.3 show the mean PRED(30) seen in 30 trials using *all the columns*. These are the baseline results for learning cost models *before* applying any pruning method.
- The dotted lines show the mean PRED(30) seen *after* automatic column pruning.
- The difference between the solid and the dotted lines is the improvement produced by pruning.

The key observation from this result is that if you start with *less* data, then the *more* columns you throw away, the *better* the final predictions. Why is this so? The answer comes from the mathematics of curve fitting:

- A model is a *fit* of some shape to a set of data points.
- Each feature is a *degree of freedom* along which the shape can move.

- If there are more degrees of freedom than original data points, then the shape can move in many directions. This means that there are multiple shapes that could be fitted to the small number of points.

That is, to clarify a model learned from a limited data source, *prune* that data source.

5.5 SUMMARY

Certainly, it is useful to manually browse data in order to familiarize yourself with the domain and conduct "sanity checks" within the data. But data may contain "islands" of interesting signals surrounded by an ocean of confusion. Automatic tools can extract those interesting humans, thus topping humans from getting confused by the data.

This notion of pruning irrelevancies is a core concept of data mining, particularly for human-in-the-loop processes. Later in this book, we offer more details on how to conduct such data pruning (see Chapters 10 and 15).

RULE #4: DATA SCIENCE IS CYCLIC

A conclusion is the place where you got tired thinking.
(Martin H. Fischer)

Data mining is inherently a cyclic activity. For example, if you are talking to your users, then any successful data mining analysis will generate conclusions *and* comments on those conclusions that require further investigation. That is, finding one pattern will prompt new questions such as "Why does that effect hold?" or "Are we sure there is no bug in step X of the method?" Each such question refines the goals of the data mining, which leads to another round of the whole data mining process.

The repetitive nature of data science implies that the data mining method is repeated multiple times to either

- Answer an extra user question;
- Make some enhancement and/or bug fix to the method;
- Or deploy the analysis to a different set of users.

This chapter discusses cyclic development in data mining and its implications for how to develop and deploy a data mining application.

6.1 THE KNOWLEDGE DISCOVERY CYCLE

In 1996, Fayyad et al. [123] noted the cyclic nature of knowledge discovery in data (KDD). Figure 6.1 summarizes their view of KDD. That figure highlights numerous significant aspects of real-world data mining:

- The "data mining" part of KDD is actually a small part of the whole process.
- Even just gaining permission to access data can be a long process requiring extensive interaction with business user groups.
- Once data is accessed, then raw data typically requires extensive manipulation before it is suitable for mining.

The general point here is that, before any learner can execute, much effort must be expended in selecting and accessing the data to process, preprocessing, and transforming it into some learnable form. And after the data mining is done, further effort is required to investigate and understand the results. That is,

Most of "data mining" is actually "data pre/postprocessing."

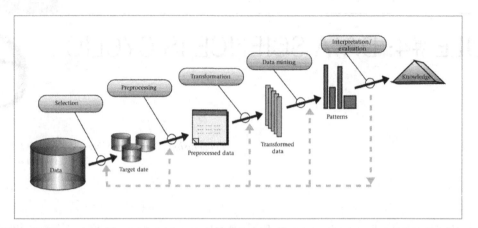

FIGURE 6.1

The Fayyad KDD cycle. From [123].

Note the dashed feedback arrows, shown in gray in Figure 6.1. In this feedback, lessons from one step tell how to improve prior work. This feedback lets users refine and mature the goals of the project. Such maturation is useful because, sometimes, the initial goals of the data mining project may not directly match the needs of the users and the content of the data. In fact, we would characterize the cyclic nature of data mining as a search to increase the overlap between the three regions shown in Figure 6.2 that describes:

1. *The questions the users care about.* This can change with feedback when (say) the users realize that their data cannot comment on "A,B,C," but might be able to comment on another set of related issues "C,D,E."
2. *The questions the data scientist cares to ask.* For example, data scientists might take the time to learn more about the domain, thus letting them pose more insightful questions.
3. *The answers that can be extracted from the data.* This can change if the data scientists work with the user to collect different kinds of data from the domain.

Novice data scientists do not understand the cyclic nature of data mining, Hence, these novices make too much use of the click-and-point GUIs seen in the data mining toolkits. Such click-and-pointing makes it hard to exactly reproduce complex prior results. Further, such clicking makes it hard to mass produce future results on new data, or small variants of existing data.

For serious studies, to ensure repeatability, the entire analysis should be automated using some high-level scripting language. To put that another way:

Thou shall not click.

That is, experts know to eschew a data miner's GUI and to code the analysis in (say) R script, MATLAB, or Bash [339] or Python.

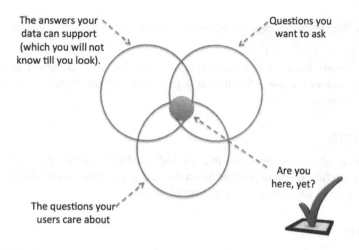

The answers your data can support (which you will not know till you look).

Questions you want to ask

Are you here, yet?

The questions your users care about

FIGURE 6.2

The questions asked, the answers available, the answers required. Data mining projects need to find the intersection between the questions being asked and the answers supported by the data.

6.2 EVOLVING CYCLIC DEVELOPMENT

In our experience, not only is data science a cyclic process, but *the cycles evolve as the project matures*. For example, consider the CRANE application developed by inductive engineers at Microsoft [86]. CRANE is a risk assessment and test prioritization tool used at Microsoft that alerts developers if the next software check-in might be problematic. CRANE makes its assessments using metrics collected from static analysis of source code, dynamic analysis of tests running on the system, and field data.

CRANE was developed in a cyclic manner, and those cycles changed as the project developed. We characterize that change as follows:

$$scout \Rightarrow survey \Rightarrow build$$

6.2.1 SCOUTING

In the *scout* phase, rapid prototyping is used to try many mining methods on the data. In this phase, experimental rigor is less important than exploring the range of user hypotheses. The other goal of this phase is to gain the interest of the users in the induction results.

It is important to stress that feedback to the users can and must appear very early in a data mining project. Users, we find, find it very hard to express what they want from their data. This is especially true if they have never mined it before. However, once we start showing them results, their requirements rapidly mature as initial results help them sharpen the focus of the inductive study. Therefore, we recommend:

> Simplicity first. Prior to conducting very elaborate studies, try applying very simple tools to gain rapid early feedback.

For example, simple linear-time column pruners, such as those discussed in the last chapter, comment on what factors are not influential in a particular domain. It can be insightful to discuss information with the users.

6.2.2 SURVEYING

In the *survey* phase, after securing some interest and goodwill amongst the user population, data scientists conduct careful experiments focusing on the user goals found during the scouting phase.

Of these three phases, the *survey* phase is closest to Figure 6.1.

6.2.3 BUILDING

In the final *build* phase, after the *survey* has found stable models of interest to the users, a systems engineering phase begins. Here, the learned models are integrated into some turnkey product that is suitable for deployment to a very wide user base.

6.2.4 EFFORT

In terms of development effort, the specific details of CRANE's development schedule are proprietary. But to give an approximate idea of the effort required for each phase, we offer the following notes.

For *greenfield applications*, which have not been developed previously:

- The development effort often takes weeks/months/years of work for *scout/survey/build* (respectively).
- The team size doubles and then doubles again after the *scout* and *survey* phases; e.g., one scout, two surveyors, and four builders (assisted by the analysis of the surveyors).

For *product line applications* (where the new effort is some extension to existing work), the above numbers can be greatly reduced when the new effort reuses analysis or tools developed in previous applications.

6.3 SUMMARY

It is unwise to enter into a data mining with fixed hypotheses or approaches, particularly for data that has not been mined before. Organize your work such that you obtain the experience that can change your mind. Deploy your data scientists to explore the domain, before prematurely committing to any particular tools. Plan to repeat a data mining study many times (and, as the project develops, mature those cycles from scout to survey to build). Finally, once you know what is going on, automate your work so you can run the study again and again (perhaps with a slightly different focus for future runs).

DATA MINING: A TECHNICAL TUTORIAL

DATA MINING AND SE

7

For our audience with a technical background, this part of the book presents some notes on

- Data mining in SE (this chapter);
- Two niche topics within data mining for software engineering:
  - Defect prediction (Chapter 8);
  - Effort estimation (Chapter 9).
- Technical details on data mining (Chapter 10).

7.1 SOME DEFINITIONS

Data mining for software engineering focuses on how to improve new and current software projects using data mined from old projects. For example,

- When managers or developers are uncertain about key decisions, data mining can be used to find prior patterns that inform current issues.
- When there are limited resources for inspection and testing, data mining can focus the available resources on just the code files that seem most error prone.

  According to Xie et al. [450], this task can be decomposed along three axes:

- *The goal*, which may include fixing bugs, finding optimizations, improving code quality, and estimating development costs, just to name a few.
- *The mining technique used.* For samples of mining methods, see this chapter and the rest of this book.
- *The input data used*, which may be many and various. For example, it might be raw source code, software binaries, configuration files, version control data, specification and/or design documents and diagrams, runtime documents such as logs and error reports, the e-mails sent by developers, and so on.

7.2 SOME APPLICATION AREAS

The following list shows some of the application areas for data mining in SE:

- Combining software product information with apps store data [164];
- Using process data to predict overall project effort [222];
- Using software process models to learn effective project changes [370];

- Using operating system logs that predict software power consumption [174];
- Using the editor logs of code to find frequently changed classes that are most bug prone [276].
- Exploring product line models to configure new applications [379];
- Mining natural language requirements to find links between components [169];
- Mining performance data [160];
- Using XML descriptions of design patterns to recommend particular designs [351];
- Using e-mail lists to understand the human networks inside software teams [31];
- Linking e-mails to source code artifacts and classifying their content [17];
- Using execution traces to learn normal interface usage patterns [148];
- Using bug databases to learn defect predictors that guide inspection teams to where the code is most likely to fail 1416 and to classify changes as clean or buggy [294];
- Using security data to identify indicators for software vulnerabilities [395];
- Using visualization to support program comprehension [439];
- Using software ontologies to enable natural language queries [447]; and
- Mining code clones to assess the implications of cloning and copy/paste in software [202].

Note that data mining and SE is a huge field and so the above list is, by its very nature, incomplete. For more examples, see the numerous articles in recent special issues on this field [462]; as well as recent conference proceedings of

- The PROMISE conference;
- The Mining Software Repositories (MSR) conference;
- The recommendation systems for software engineering conference;
- or most other current conferences or journals on software engineering.

For detailed notes on two specialized subareas of data mining in SE (which we will explore in this book), see the next two chapters.

DEFECT PREDICTION

8

Defect prediction is the study of predicting which software "modules" are defective. Here "modules" means some primitive unit of a running system such as a function or a class.

This section reviews the core motivation of that work, which is the reduction of software construction costs by an earlier detection of defects. The software in real-world systems is never written "all in one day." Rather, it is grown and new modules make extensive use of older ones. The sooner we can find and fix errors in the code, the less we will have to rework subsequent development. Also, in the agile world, code is built in staggered phases where some part of the code base is being more *developed* than *tested* while other older parts are now being *tested* more than being *developed*. Data miners can help reduce the cost of testing of older code (by focusing quality improvement activity on the sections that are most error prone) thus reducing the cost of reworking new code (that was dependent on the older, buggy code).

This chapter starts with a discussion of some of the practical considerations governing defect detection in the software life cycle. Then, we shift our focus to lightweight sampling policies. In particular, we explore one special kind: static code defect predictors.

8.1 DEFECT DETECTION ECONOMICS

Boehm and Papaccio advise that reworking software is far cheaper earlier in the life cycle than later "*by factors of 50 to 200*" [39]. This effect has been widely documented by other researchers. A panel at IEEE Metrics 2002 concluded that finding and fixing severe software problems after delivery is often 100 times more expensive than finding and fixing them during the requirements and design phase [396]. Also, Arthur et al. [11] conducted a small controlled experiment for which a dozen engineers at NASA's Langley Research Center were split into development and specialized verification teams. The same application was written with and without specialized verification teams. Figure 8.1 shows the results: (a) more issues were found using specialized verification than without; (b) the issues were found much earlier. That is, if the verification team found the *same* bugs as the development team, but found them *earlier*, the cost-to-fix would be reduced by a significant factor. For example, consider Figure 8.2 that shows the cost of quickly fixing an issue relative to leaving it for a later phase (data from four NASA projects [87]). The last line of that table reveals that delaying issue resolution even by one phase increases the cost-to-fix to $\Delta = 2, \ldots, 5$. Using this data, Dabney et al. [87] calculate that a dollar spent on verification returns to NASA, on those four projects, \$1.21, \$1.59, \$5.53, and \$10.10, respectively.

The above notes lead to one very strong conclusion: *find bugs earlier*. But how? Software assessment budgets are finite while assessment effectiveness increases exponentially with assessment effort. However, the *state space explosion problem* imposes strict limits on how much a system can be explored

43

Phase	With verification team	No verification team
Requirements	16	0
High-level design	20	2
Low-level design	31	8
Coding and user testing	24	34
Integration and testing	6	14
Totals	97	58

FIGURE 8.1

Defects found with and without specialized verification teams. From [11].

		Phase issue found					
i	Phase issue introduced	$f=1$ Requirements	$f=2$ Design	$f=3$ Code	$f=4$ Test	$f=5$ Int	$f=6$ Operations
1	Requirements	1	5	10	50	130	368
2	Design		1	2	10	26	74
3	Code			1	5	13	37
4	Test				1	3	7
5	Integration					1	3
$\Delta = \text{Mean}\left(\frac{C[f,i]}{C[f,i-1]}\right)$			5	2	5	2.7	2.8

FIGURE 8.2

Cost-to-fix escalation factors. From [87]. In this table, $C[f, i]$ denotes the cost-to-fix escalation factor relative to fixing an issue in the phase in which it was found (f) versus the phase in which it was introduced (i). The last row shows the cost-to-fix delta if the issue introduced in phase i is fixed immediately afterwards in phase $f = i + 1$.

via automatic formal methods. As to other testing methods, a *linear* increase in the confidence C that we have found all defects can take *exponentially* more effort. For example, for one-in-a-thousand defects, moving C from 90% to 94% to 98% takes 2301, 2812, and 3910 black box probes, respectively.[1] Exponential costs quickly exhaust finite resources. Standard practice is to apply the best available assessment methods on the sections of the program that the best available domain knowledge declares is most critical. We endorse this approach. Clearly, the most critical sections require the best known assessment methods. However, this focus on certain sections can blind us to defects in other areas. Therefore, standard practice should be augmented with a *lightweight sampling policy* to explore the rest of the system. This sampling policy will always be incomplete. Nevertheless, it is the only option when resources do not permit a complete assessment of the whole system.

---

[1] A randomly selected input to a program will find a fault with probability p. After N random black box tests, the chances of the inputs not revealing any fault is $(1 - p)^N$. Hence, the chances C of seeing the fault is $1 - (1 - p)^N$, which can be rearranged to $N(C, p) = \frac{log(1-C)}{log(1-p)}$. For example, $N(0.90, 10^{-3}) = 2301$.

8.2 STATIC CODE DEFECT PREDICTION

A typical, object-oriented, software project can contain hundreds to thousands of classes. In order to guarantee general and project-related fitness attributes for those classes, it is commonplace to apply some quality assurance (QA) techniques to assess the classes's inherent quality. These techniques include inspections, unit tests, static source code analyzers, etc. A record of the results of this QA is a *defect log*. We can use these logs to learn *defect predictors*, if the information contained in the data provides not only a precise account of the encountered faults (i.e., the "bugs"), but also a thorough description of static code features such as *lines of code* (LOC), complexity measures (e.g., McCabe's cyclomatic complexity [286]), and other suitable object-oriented design metrics.

For this, data miners can learn a predictor for the number of *defective* classes from past projects so that it can be applied for QA assessment in future projects. Such a predictor allows focusing the QA budget on where it might be most cost-effective. This is an important task as, during development, developers have to *skew* their QA activities toward artifacts they believe require the most effort due to limited project resources.

There are three very good reasons to study defect predictors learned from static code attributes: they are *easy to use*, *widely used*, and *useful* to use.

8.2.1 EASY TO USE

Static code attributes can be automatically and cheaply collected, even for very large systems [337]. By contrast, other methods such as manual code reviews are labor-intensive. Depending on the review methods 8-20 LOC min^{-1} can be inspected and this effort repeats for all members of the review team, which can be as large as four or six [309].

8.2.2 WIDELY USED

Many researchers use static attributes to guide software quality predictions (see the references at the back of this book). Verification and validation (V&V) textbooks [367] advise using static code complexity attributes to decide which modules are worthy of manual inspections. For several years, one of us (Menzies) worked on-site at the NASA software Independent Verification and Validation facility and he knows of several large government software contractors that will not review software modules *unless* tools like McCabe predict that they are fault prone.

8.2.3 USEFUL

A standard result for defect predictors is that they find the location of 70% (or more) of the defects in code. This is markedly higher than other currently used industrial methods such as manual code reviews.

- A panel at *IEEE Metrics 2002* [396] concluded that manual software reviews can find ≈60% of defects.[2]

---

[2] That panel supported neither Fagan claim [119] that inspections can find 95% of defects before testing nor Shull's claim that specialized directed inspection methods can catch 35% more defects that other methods [398].

- Raffo found that the defect detection capability of industrial review methods can vary from $pd = TR(35, 50, 65)\%$[3] for full Fagan inspections [118] to $pd = TR(13, 21, 30)\%$ for less-structured inspections.

The industrial experience is that defect prediction scales well to a commercial context. Defect predicting technology has been commercialized in *Predictive* [428], a defects in software projects. One company used it to manage the safety critical software for a fighter aircraft (the software controlled a lithium ion battery, which can overcharge and possibly explode). After applying a more expensive tool for structural code coverage, the company ran Predictive on the same code base. Predictive produced results consistent with the more expensive tool. But, Predictive was able to process a larger code base faster than the more expensive tool [428].

In addition, defect predictors developed at NASA [303] have also been used in software development companies outside the United States (in Turkey). When the inspection teams focused on the modules that trigger the defect predictors, they found up to 70% of the defects using just 40% of their QA effort (measured in staff hours) [420].

Finally, a subsequent study on the Turkish software compared how much code needs to be inspected using random selection versus selection via defect predictors. Using random testing, 87% of the files would have to be inspected in order to detect 87% of the defects. However, if the inspection process was restricted to the 25% of the files that trigger the defect predictors, then 88% of the defects could be found. That is, the same level of defect detection (after inspection) can be achieved using $(87 - 25)/87 = 71\%$ less effort [419].

---

[3] $TR(a, b, c)$ is a triangular distribution with min/mode/max of a, b, c.

EFFORT ESTIMATION

9

One of the earliest questions asked about SE data is "How much will it cost to develop this software?" In fact, the whole field of software engineering was founded on the economic realization that the primary cost of building software is not memory or screens or cooling systems, but rather it is the time it takes for *people to write the code* [40].

9.1 THE ESTIMATION PROBLEM

In many domains, estimating the completion time of a project is a core problem [20]. Accurate effort estimates are needed for many business tasks such as project plans, iteration plans, budgets, investment analyses, pricing processes, and bidding rounds. Over-or underestimating development effort can lead to undesirable results:

- Underestimation results in schedule and budget overruns, which may cause project cancellation.
- Overestimation hinders the acceptance of promising ideas, thus threatening organizational competitiveness.

Software effort estimation is the process of estimating the total effort necessary to complete a software project. Boehm [34, 42] takes care to distinguish between development *effort* and development *time*:

- Time counts calendar months from start to finish. Boehm states that one month of work takes 152 h (and this includes development and management tasks).
- Effort is the total number of person hours on that task; for e.g., 12 developers working for 1000 h of elapsed time require 12,000 h of effort.

Interestingly, usually we do not consider hardware costs when creating estimates. This was Barry Boehm's core insight. In the 1960s, he was asked to write a report recommending how best to improve on the state of the art in computing. The expectation was that his report would recommend further funding for new kinds of hardware. Instead, he found that the limiting factor to using computers was the effort required to program their functionality [40]. More recent studies support Boehm's conjecture that people, not hardware, are the critical factor in predicting the development effort of software:

- In 2007, a panel at the International Conference on Software Engineering discussed the role of programmers and managers in software development. Tim Lister (a coauthor of Peopleware [95]) commented that sociology beats technology in terms of successfully completing projects—a notion endorsed by the other panelists.
- After the initial software development comes software maintenance. The cost of maintenance is determined by how many bugs are in the system. A 2012 study by a game development company found that less than 1% of bugs were due to hardware issues [448].

Software costs dominate the cost of delivering and maintaining software, and software effort estimates are often wrong by a factor of four [34] or even more [204]. The (in)famous Standish report claims that this terrible track record has improved in recent years [404], but the reported improvements are so remarkable that researchers such as Magne Jorgensen doubt those findings [195]. Also, when other researchers check for those improvements in their own data, they find more evidence for poor estimation than otherwise [245].

The lesson here is that industrial managers should take great care when making their effort estimates. They should avoid practices such as rushing out an estimate or using the first number that comes to mind. Otherwise, the allocated funds may be inadequate to develop the required project. In the worst case, overrunning projects are canceled and the entire development effort is wasted. For example,

- NASA canceled its incomplete Check-out Launch Control System project after the initial $200 million estimate was exceeded by another $200 million [402].
- The ballooning software costs of JPLs Mission Science Laboratory recently forced a two-year delay [60].

9.2 HOW TO MAKE ESTIMATES

Because effort estimation is so important, it is a very active and lucrative consultancy market, particularly for large defense contractors and other government customers. It is also a very active area of research. One recent review of the research literature reported hundreds of recent papers [192], 61% of which dealt with introduction of new methods and their comparison to old ones.

Jorgensen notes that there are two standard methods for effort estimation:

- Expert-based methods that use human expertise (possibly augmented with process guidelines, checklists, and data) to generate predictions [190, 191];
- Or model-based methods that can summarize old data with data miners that make predictions about new projects [42, 307].

Also, as discussed below, there are hybrid methods that combine expert- and model-based methods.

9.2.1 EXPERT-BASED ESTIMATION

Regarding expert-based effort estimation, Jorgensen lists the following as best practices for those kind of estimates [190]:

- Evaluate estimation accuracy, but avoid high evaluation pressure;
- Avoid conflicting estimation goals;
- Ask the estimators to justify and criticize their estimates;
- Avoid irrelevant and unreliable estimation information;
- Use documented data from previous development tasks;
- Find estimation experts with relevant domain background;
- Estimate top-down and bottom-up, independently of each other;
- Use estimation checklists;
- Combine estimates from different experts and estimation strategies;

- Assess the uncertainty of the estimate;
- Provide feedback on estimation accuracy; and
- Provide estimation training opportunities.

The last two points are particularly important for the success of expert-based effort estimation [191, 194]. Passos et al. [354] report that many commercial software engineers have a habit of generalizing from their first few projects to all their future projects. Passos et al. [354] caution that this can be a major mistake:

> ...past experiences (are used) without consideration for their context.

For example, Jorgensen et al. [191] document how commercial estimation gurus rarely use lessons from past projects to improve their estimates for future projects.

For the rest of this book, we will focus less on expert-based methods and more on repeatable algorithmic approaches. There are two reasons for this. Firstly, as mentioned above, there exist some "experts" in effort estimation that based their estimates on outdated information. To guard against this, a wise manager should run some model-based method to double check those estimates (just as a sanity check).

Second, organizations may demand repeatable and auditable effort estimations (e.g., this was a requirement last decade for software effort estimates at NASA and the U.S. Department of Defense). Model-based estimates can satisfy those requirements because it is possible to rerun the models. However, the subjective nature of expert estimates make them harder to reproduce.

9.2.2 MODEL-BASED ESTIMATION

Model-based methods range in complexity from

- Relatively simple nearest neighbor methods [206];
- To the more intricate tree-learning methods, as used in CART [48];
- To even more complex search-based methods that, say, use tabu search to set the parameters of support vector regression [82].

According to Boehm [34, 42]; Chulani [77, 374]; Kemerer [204]; Stutzke [406]; Shepperd [390]; our own work [74, 75, 296]; and a tutorial at the 2006 International Conference of the International Society of Parametric Analysts [83], best practices for model-based estimation include at least the following:

- Reuse regression parameters learned from prior projects on new projects;
- Log transforms on costing data before performing linear regression to learn log-linear effort models;
- Model tree learning to generate models for nonlinear relationships;
- Stratification, i.e., given a database of past projects, and a current project to be estimated, just learn models from those records from similar projects. Some researchers recommend using domain knowledge to find similar projects. An alternate approach that can sometimes work better, is the use of automatic clustering methods to find those similar projects [291].
- Local calibration, i.e., tune a general model to the local data via a small number of special tuning parameters;
- Hold out experiments for testing the learned effort model [296];

- Assessing effort model uncertainty via the performance deviations seen during the hold out experiments;
- Variable subset selection methods for minimizing the size of the learned effort model [74, 75, 212, 316].

9.2.3 HYBRID METHODS

This separation of model-based and expert-based methods is not a strict division as some practices fall into both categories. Some research actively tries to combine the two approaches.

- Such hybrid methods are discussed elsewhere; e.g., by Valedri [430].
- Chulani and Boehm's Bayesian tuning method [77] is a hybrid expert/model-based method that allows an algorithm to carefully combine expert judgment with the available data.
- Shepperd proposes case-based reasoning (CBR) [390] as an algorithmic method for emulating expert analogical reasoning.

CBR is an algorithmic method; hence, its conclusions are repeatable and auditable. CBR seeks to emulate human recollection and adaptation of past experiences in order to find solutions to current problems. According to cognitive psychologists such as Kolodner [235] and Schank and Abelson [380], humans do not base their decisions on complex reductive analysis, but on an instantaneous survey of past experiences. To put that claim another way, according to CBR

Humans often do not <u>think</u>, they <u>remember</u>.

CBR is based purely on the direct adaptation of past cases, based on the similarity of those cases with the current situation. CBR-based systems have no explicit world model (e.g., like the process models used by Rodriguez et al. [370] or the equations used by Boehm in COCOMO). Rather, the model is implicit within the data stored about past cases. The advantage of this approach is that when this cache is updated and appended with additional cases, then a CBR system is instantly updated to the latest findings. No model needs to be generated or validated, and the same CBR algorithms can be applied to any data (i.e., no need to control domain data collection).

While this sounds complicated, in practice it is not. One advantage of these methods is that they are very simple to code. For example, Chapter 12 shows how full code for a clustering system got SE project data. That system is very short; less than 200 lines of code. With that code, finding the nearest cases to some test example would require implementing a *closest* function (which is a simple modification to the six lines of the *furthest* function shown in that chapter).

While this book makes extensive use of CBR, in terms of technical details it is sometimes more insightful to discuss *clustering*, *row pruning*, *prototypes*, and *column pruning* rather than CBR. For details on pruning and prototypes, see Chapter 10.

DATA MINING (UNDER THE HOOD)

10

The last three chapters listed *application areas* of data mining in software engineering. This chapter discusses the *internals of a data miner*. In particular, it answers the question, "Just what is data mining?"

This chapter is meant for data mining novices. Hence, our running example will be a very simple database (15 examples of "when to play golf").

10.1 DATA CARVING

According to the Renaissance artist Michelangelo di Lodovico Buonarroti Simoni:

> Every block of stone has a statue inside it and it is the task of the sculptor to discover it.

While sculptors like Michelangelo carved blocks of marble, data scientists carve into blocks of data. So, with apologies to Señor Simoni, we say:

> ~~Every~~ Some ~~stone~~ databases have ~~statue~~ a model inside and it is the task of the ~~sculptor~~ data scientist to ~~discover~~ check for it.

Enter data mining. Decades of research has resulted in many automatic ways to wield the knife that slices and refines the data. All these data miners have the following form:

1. Find the crap (where "crap" might also be called "superfluous details"); 2. Cut the crap; 3. Go to Step 1.

FIGURE 10.1

Horse, carved from stone, 15,000 BC. From goo.gl/C4byU4.

For example, here is a table of data. In this table, we are trying to predict for the goal of `play`, given a record of the weather. Each row is one example where we did or did not play golf (and the goal of data mining is to find what weather predicts for playing golf).

```
# golf data, version1.

outlook   , temp , humidity , windy , play
--------  , ---- , -------- , ----- , -----
overcast  , 64   , 65       , TRUE  , yes
rainy     , 65   , 70       , TRUE  , no
rainy     , 68   , 80       , FALSE , yes
sunny     , 69   , 70       , FALSE , yes
rainy     , 70   , 96       , FALSE , yes
rainy     , 71   , 91       , TRUE  , no
overcast  , 72   , 90       , TRUE  , yes
sunny     , 72   , 95       , FALSE , no
rainy     , 75   , 80       , FALSE , yes
sunny     , 75   , 70       , TRUE  , yes
sunny     , 80   , 90       , TRUE  , no
overcast  , 81   , 75       , FALSE , yes
overcast  , 83   , 86       , FALSE , yes
sunny     , 85   , 85       , FALSE , no
```

This chapter "cuts" into this data using a variety of pruning methods. The result will be a much smaller summary of the essential details of this data, without superfluous details.

Before that, some digressions.

- Later in this chapter, we will call the above table a *simple* data mining problem in order to distinguish it from other kinds of problems such as *text mining* or *Big Data* problems.
- We use the above table of data to illustrate some basic principles of data mining. That said, in practice, we probably need more data than shown above before daring to report any kind of conclusions to business users. Data mining is an *inductive* process that learns from examples, and the above table is probably too small to support effective induction. For a discussion on how to learn models from very small data sets, see [299].
- The following notes do not survey *all* data mining technologies; such a survey would fill many books. Rather, they focus on the technologies used frequently in this book. If the reader wants to explore further, see [107, 444].

Enough digressions; back to the tutorial on data mining. Note that the following notes describe learning algorithms that could be applied to software engineering data or, indeed, data from many other sources.

10.2 ABOUT THE DATA

Before we cut up the data, it is insightful to reflect on the structure of that data because different kinds of data miners work best on different kinds of data.

Data mining executes on *tables* of *examples*:

- Tables have one column per *feature* and one row per example.
- The columns may be *numeric* (has numbers) or *discrete* (contain symbols).
- Also, some columns are *goals* (things we want to predict using the other columns).
- Finally, columns may contain *missing values*.

For example, in *text mining*, where there is one column per word and one row per document, the columns contain many missing values (not all words appear in all documents) and there may be hundreds of thousands of columns.

While text mining applications can have many columns. *Big Data* applications can have any number of columns and millions to billions of rows. For such very large data sets, a complete analysis may be impossible. Hence, these might be sampled probabilistically.

On the other hand, when there are very few rows, data mining may fail because there are too few examples to support summarization. For such sparse tables, *nearest neighbors* methods [107] may be best that make conclusions about new examples by looking at their neighborhood in the space of old examples. Hence, such methods only need a few (or even only one) similar examples to make conclusions. This book uses nearest neighbor methods many times. For example, Chapter 13 uses them as a *relevancy filter* to find pertinent data from other organizations.

If a table has many goals, then some may be competing; e.g., it may not be possible to find a car with the twin goals of low cost and low miles per gallon. Such competing multigoal problems can be studied using a *multiobjective optimizer* like the genetic algorithms used in NSGA-II [93] or the optimizers of Chapter 24.

If a table has no goal columns, then this is an *unsupervised* learning problem that might be addressed by (say) finding clusters of similar rows using, for example, algorithms like k-means of EM [444] or the CHUNK tool of Chapter 12. An alternate approach, taken by the APRORI association rule learner [365], is to assume that every column is a goal and to look for what combinations of any values predict for any combination of any other.

If a table has one goal, this is a *supervised* learning problem where the task is to find combinations of values from the other columns that predict for the goal values. Note that for data sets with one discrete goal feature, it is common to call that goal the *class* of the data set.

Such simple tables are characterized by just a few columns and not many rows (say, dozens to thousands). Traditionally, such simple data mining problems have been explored by algorithms like C4.5 and CART [48]. However, with some clever sampling of the data, it is possible to scale these traditional learners to Big Data problems [49, 68]. C4.5 and CART are both examples of *iterative dichotomization*, which is a general divide-and-conquer strategy that splits the data, then recurses on each split. For more on *iterative dichotomization*, see below (in *contrast pruning*).

10.3 COHEN PRUNING

Now that we know what data looks like, we can cut it up.

There are many ways to prune superfluous details from a table of data. One way is to apply *Cohen pruning*:

Cohen pruning: Prune away small differences in numerical data.

For example, the users might know that they can control or measure data in some column c own to some minimum precision ϵ_c. With that knowledge, we could simplify all numerics by rounding them to their nearest ϵ_c. Without that knowledge, we might apply some domain general rule such as Cohen's rule that says values are different by a *small amount* if they differ by some fraction of the standard deviation σ. And, just to remind us all, the standard deviation of n numbers from some list X measures how much they usually differ from the mean value $X.\mu$; i.e.,

$$\sigma = \sqrt{\frac{\sum_i^n (x_i - X.\mu)^2}{n - 1}} \tag{10.1}$$

In the above table of data, the standard deviation of *temperature* and *humidity* in the above columns are $\sigma_{temperature} = 6.6$ and $\sigma_{humidity} = 10.3$ (respectively). If we round those numerics to $\sigma/2$ of those values (then round those values to the nearest integer), we get the following table:

```
# golf data, version2.
# Numerics rounded to half of the
# standard deviation in each column.

outlook  , temp , humidity , windy , play
-------- , ---- , -------- , ----- , -----
overcast , 62   , 67       , TRUE  , yes
rainy    , 66   , 72       , TRUE  , no
rainy    , 69   , 82       , FALSE , yes
sunny    , 69   , 72       , FALSE , yes
rainy    , 69   , 98       , FALSE , yes
rainy    , 72   , 93       , TRUE  , no
overcast , 72   , 93       , TRUE  , yes
sunny    , 72   , 93       , FALSE , no
rainy    , 76   , 82       , FALSE , yes
sunny    , 76   , 72       , TRUE  , yes
sunny    , 79   , 93       , TRUE  , no
overcast , 82   , 77       , FALSE , yes
overcast , 82   , 87       , FALSE , yes
sunny    , 85   , 87       , FALSE , no
```

In this case, the change is quite small but, for other data sets, Cohen pruning can avoid silly discussions about (say) 10.00111 versus 10.003112. For more on how to avoid being distracted by *small effects*, see [200, 232, 432].

One frequently asked question about Cohen pruning is how big to select a good value for ϵ. Standard values are to use $\epsilon \in \{0.3, 0.5, 0.8\} * \sigma$ for *small*, *medium*, or *large* differences within a set of numbers. Note that the justification for those values is more "engineering judgment" than "rigorous statistical argument."[1]

---

[1] For a more rigorous approach to defining ϵ, use equations 2-4 from [200] to calculate the Hedges' g measure. Then, from table 9 of that paper, use $g \leq \{0.38, 1.0, \infty\}$ to determine if some value is a *small*, *medium*, or *large* difference.

10.4 DISCRETIZATION

In theory, numbers might range from negative to positive infinity. In practice, there may be only a few important distinctions within that infinite range of values. As an example of this, consider the *age* values collected from humans. In theory, this number can range from 0 to 120 (or 0 to 200,000 if we include all *homo sapiens* from the fossil record). For most purposes it is enough to *discretize* those numbers into small bins such as *baby, infant, child, teenager, adult, old, dead*.

That is, one way to remove spurious details in a table is

Discretization pruning: prune numerics back to a handful of bins.

For example, in the above table, notice that

- Up to *temperature* = 69, nearly all the *play* variables are *yes*.
- Similarly, if we were to sort on *humidity*, we would see that up to *humidity* = 80, that $\frac{7}{8}$ of the *play* values are *play* = *yes*.

Based on the above discussion, we might use discretization to divide our numerics into two bins (*lo, hi*) at the following cuts:

- If *temperature* ≤ 69 then *temperate* = *lo* else *temperature* = *hi*.
- If *humidity* ≤ 80 then *humidity* = *lo* else *humidity* = *hi*.

This results in the following data where the numeric data has are been replaced with symbols:

```
# golf data, version 3: numerics discretized

outlook  , temp , humidity , windy , play
-------- , ---- , -------- , ----- , -----
overcast , lo   , lo       , TRUE  , yes
rainy    , lo   , lo       , TRUE  , no
rainy    , lo   , hi       , FALSE , yes
sunny    , lo   , lo       , FALSE , yes
rainy    , lo   , hi       , FALSE , yes
rainy    , hi   , hi       , TRUE  , no
overcast , hi   , hi       , TRUE  , yes
sunny    , hi   , hi       , FALSE , no
rainy    , hi   , hi       , FALSE , yes
sunny    , hi   , lo       , TRUE  , yes
sunny    , hi   , hi       , TRUE  , no
overcast , hi   , lo       , FALSE , yes
overcast , hi   , hi       , FALSE , yes
sunny    , hi   , hi       , FALSE , no
```

10.4.1 OTHER DISCRETIZATION METHODS

In the above example, discretization is reflected over some target class column in order to find useful breaks (and in the above data, *golf* is the class column). Formally speaking, the discretization of numerics based on the class variable is called *supervised discretization*. A widely used supervised discretization method is the "Fayyad-Irani" method [122] that uses information content to decide where to cut up numeric ranges. For more on the use of information content, see the next section.

The alternative to discretized supervision is *unsupervised discretization* that just reflects over the column of numbers without considering values from elsewhere. For example, in *equal-width discretization*, we round the data to the value nearest to $\frac{max-min}{bins}$. Alternatively, in *equal-frequency discretization*, we sort the numbers and divide them into *bins* of equal-sized intervals. In these approaches, a frequently asked question is how many *bins* should be used. In our experience, some small number between 2 and 16 (median 5) is often useful (and the best number for a particular data set requires some experimentation).

Rather than guess how many *bins* are required, it is possible to use the distribution of the numbers to infer where to insert the breaks. This approach, which we call MEANGAIN, recursively splits a list of numbers X into sublists Y and Z in order to isolate the larger or smaller values. This requires reflecting over $X.\mu, Y.\mu.Z.\mu$ (i.e., the mean values seen *before* and *after* each split). After sorting the numbers, we recursively divide the data X of n items at position i to generate $Y = X[1, \ldots, i]$ and $Z = Y[i + 1 \ldots, n]$. For that division, we seek the index "i" that most maximizes the expected value of the square of the differences in the means before and after the split, i.e.,

$$\arg\max_i \left(\frac{i}{n}(X.\mu - Y.\mu)^2 + \frac{n-i}{n}(X.\mu - Z.\mu)^2 \right)$$

This recursion halts when

- Either division is too small, where "small" might be less than three items in Y or Z;
- The means of the two splits differ by only a small amount; i.e., $|Y.\mu - Z.\mu| < \epsilon$. Recalling the above discussion in Section 10.3, we could set $\epsilon = 0.3\sigma$, where σ is the standard deviation of the entire column of data (note that in this procedure, ϵ is set once before starting the recursion).

If MEANGAIN is applied to the *temperature* and *humidity* columns, then we learn to break *temperature* at {69, 76} and *humidity* at {87}.

As to which discretization method is best, that is always data set dependent. But note that seemingly more sophisticated methods are not necessarily better or, indeed, lead to different conclusions. For example, in the above discussion, we eyeballed the *temperature* and *humidity* numerics and proposed breaks at *temperature* = 69 and *humidity* = 87. The rest of the chapter will use those manually generated breaks as they are not far off the breaks proposed by MEANGAIN.

For a good discussion on other discretization methods, see [105, 139, 453].

10.5 COLUMN PRUNING

Discretization can be the first step in another pruning process called *column pruning* or, more formally, *feature subset selection* [155].

A repeated observation is that most data sets have tightly correlated columns or columns containing noisy or irrelevant data [155, 234]. Consequently, in practice, N columns can often be pruned back to $\sqrt{N}$ columns (or less) without damaging our ability to mine useful patterns from that data. Hence, we recommend

Column pruning: prune away columns that are not redundant and/or noisy.

To find ignorable columns of numbers, we might apply supervised discretization and reflect on the results.

1. If discretization fails to find any breaks in the column, then that means this column does not influence the class variable (and can be ignored).
2. If discretization divides the data, and the distribution of the classes *within each break* is similar to the *original* class distribution, then dividing this column does not influence the class (and can be ignored).

This second rule can be generalized to include numeric and nonnumeric columns. Once the numerics are discretized in a table with R rows, then all the columns are divided into ranges containing $r_1, r_2, \ldots$ rows. For each range i with r_i rows,

- Let those rows have $n_1, n_2, \ldots, n_j$ examples of class $c_1, c_2, \ldots, c_j$ each with probability in the range of $p_j = n_j/r_i$.
- We can score those ranges using *entropy*, which is like the inverse of information content. Entropy measures the *disorder* of some part of the data, so *less* entropy is *better*. The *entropy* of a range r_i is

$$e_i = -\sum p_j \log_2(p_j) \tag{10.2}$$

The expected value E of the entropy of a column is the weighted sum of the entropy e_i in each of its ranges r_i; that is, $E = \sum_i e_i r_i/R$. Now the *smaller* the entropy E, the *better* that column as it means that its ranges correspond most to particular classes. If we normalize all the column entropies to $0, \ldots, 1$ for E_{min} to E_{max} then there is usually a small number of *best* columns with normalized $E < 0.25$ and many more *worse* columns that can be pruned.

The above procedure is usually called INFOGAIN [155] and has the advantage that, after the numerics have been discretized, it requires only two passes over the data. While one of the fastest known methods, other column pruners can perform better (albeit, slower). For more details, see [155, 234].

Later is this book, we present another column pruning method called CHUNK. CHUNK finds two distant rows and asks "what separates them?" by (a) drawing a line between the two rows and (b) mapping all the other points onto that line.[2] In doing so, it can be learned that some columns do not contribute to distinguishing distant rows. Such columns can then be ignored.

10.6 ROW PRUNING

Discretization can also be the first step toward pruning away irrelevant rows. This is interesting because, just as many columns can be safely pruned, so too is it possible to prune away many rows. If that surprises the reader, then consider this:

- If data contains a model then those data contain multiple examples of the relationships within that model.

---

[2] To be precise, it uses the cosine rule to project all the other points somewhat along that line. The details of that process need not concern us in this introductory chapter, but see the *fastdiv* procedure of Chapter 12 for more details.

- This means that within the R rows, there exists $P < R$ rows that are *prototypes*; i.e., best examples of different aspects of the model.

That is, another way to prune data is

> Row pruning: Prune the rows in a table back to just the prototypes.

This chapter presents two methods for finding prototypes (for a long list of many other methods, see [345]). The first way is to *cluster* the data then replace each cluster with its *centroid* (the central point of that cluster). For more on that method, see the next section on *cluster pruning*.

Another way to implement row pruning is to (slightly) modify the INFOGAIN procedure, described above. Recall that INFOGAIN calculated the entropy e_i associated with each range r_i which covered n_i rows in each column c_k. Our simple row pruner, called RANGEGAIN, uses the same information. It scores each range in each column using

$$S(c_k, r_i) = e_i(R - n_i)/R$$

where R is the total number of rows and $R = \sum_i r_i$.

Once we know the value of each range, we can then score each row using the sum of the scores S of the ranges in that row (and *smaller* scores are *better*). If we normalize all those row scores $0, \dots, 1$, min to max, then there is usually a small number of *best* rows with a normalized score $S < 0.25$ and many more *worse* rows that can be pruned.

RANGEGAIN has all the advantages and disadvantages of INFOGAIN. It is very fast (only two passes over the data) and if INFOGAIN is already available, then there is little else to implement. On the other hand, like INFOGAIN, the RANGEGAIN procedure it is not a detailed analysis of the structure of the data. Hence, other row pruners [345] might perform better (albeit slower).

Note the similarities of this row pruner to the above column pruning procedure. There are deep theoretical reasons for this: Lipowezky [262] notes that column and row pruning are similar tasks as both remove cells in the hypercube of all rows times all columns. When we prune rows or columns, it is like we are playing an accordion with the ranges. We can "squeeze in" or "pull out" that hypercube as required, which makes that range cover more or less rows and/or columns. Later in this book we will take advantage of this connection when the POP1 row pruner (in Chapter 17) is extended to become the QUICK column pruner (in Chapter 18).

If the reader wants more information on row pruning, then:

- For notes on other row pruners, see [345].
- For a discussion of a tool that uses *both* column *and* row pruning, see Chapter 15.
- For a discussion on the connection of row pruning to privacy (that uses a variant of the RANGEGAIN procedure), see Chapter 16.
- For a discussion on the connection of row pruning to clustering, see the next section.

10.7 CLUSTER PRUNING

Discretization, column pruning, and row pruning are like a fine-grained analysis of data that prunes some parts of a table of data. *Clustering* is a more coarse-grained approach that finds very large divisions in the data.

Clusters are groups of similar rows. Once those clusters are known, this can simplify how we reason over data. Instead of reasoning over R rows, we can reason over C clusters, which is very useful if there are fewer clusters than rows; i.e., $C < R$. That is, another way to remove spurious information about data is

Cluster pruning: Prune many rows down to a smaller number of clusters containing similar examples.

There are many different clustering methods [444], including the CHUNK algorithm of Chapter 12. When clustering, some *distance* function is required to find similar rows. One reason for discretizing data is that this simplifies finding those distances. First, in the case of discretized data, that distance function can be as simple as the number of column values from the same ranges. Second, a simple reverse index *from* column range *to* row id means that it is very fast to find some *row2* with some overlap to *row1*.

One other thing about clustering: it is usual to *ignore* the class variable (in this case, *play*) and cluster on the rest. If we CHUNK on those nonclass columns, then we find the following four clusters:

```
# golf data, version 4: clustered.
# Note that ''c'' is the cluster id.

c, outlook,temp,humid,wind,play
---------------------------------
1,    rainy, lo, lo,  TRUE,  no
1, overcast, lo, lo,  TRUE, yes
1, overcast, hi, lo, FALSE, yes
---------------------------------
2,    sunny, lo, lo, FALSE, yes
2,    sunny, hi, lo,  TRUE, yes
2, overcast, hi, hi,  TRUE, yes
2,    sunny, hi, hi,  TRUE,  no
---------------------------------
3, overcast, hi, hi, FALSE, yes
3,    sunny, hi, hi, FALSE,  no
3,    sunny, hi, hi, FALSE,  no
---------------------------------
4,    rainy, hi, hi,  TRUE,  no
4,    rainy, hi, hi, FALSE, yes
4,    rainy, lo, hi, FALSE, yes
4,    rainy, lo, hi, FALSE, yes
```

To find the pattern in these clusters, we ask what ranges are found in one cluster, but not the others. It turns out if you first decide a value for *humidity* and then decide a value for *outlook*, you can build a predictor for cluster membership. We will return to that point in the next section on *contrast pruning*.

The above clusters can be used to reduce the golfing data to four prototypes. For each cluster, we write one *centroid* from the majority value in each column (and if there is no clear majority, we will write "?"):

```
# golf data, version 5: clusters replaced with the centroids
# Note that ''c'' is the cluster id.

c, outlook,temp,humid, windy, play
----------------------------------
1,overcast,  lo,   lo,   TRUE, yes
2,   sunny,  hi,    ?,   TRUE, yes
3,   sunny,  hi,   hi, FALSE,  no
4,   rainy,   ?,   hi, FALSE, yes
```

That is, to a first-level approximation, we can prune the original golfing data to just four rows. Just as an aside, this kind of prototype generation is not recommended for something as small as the golfing data. However, for larger data sets with hundreds of rows or more, show in Chapter 15 that CHUNKing R rows down to $\sqrt{R}$ clusters is an effective method for defect and effort estimation.

10.7.1 ADVANTAGES OF PROTOTYPES

There are many advantages of reasoning via prototypes. For example, they are useful for handling unusual features in the data, If we collapse each cluster to one prototype (generated from the central point in that cluster), then each prototype is a report of the average effects within a cluster. If we restrict the reasoning to just those average effects, we can mitigate some of the confusing effects of noisy data.

Also, prototype-based reasoning can be faster than reasoning about all the rows [71]. For example, a common method for classifying new examples is to compare them to similar older examples. A naive approach to finding those nearest neighbor reasoning is to search through all rows. However, if we index all the rows according to their nearest prototype, then we can find quickly find nearest neighbors as follows:

1. For all prototypes, find the nearest neighbor.
2. For all rows associated with that prototype, find the nearest neighbors.

Note that Step 2 is sometimes optional. In Chapter 15, we generate effect detect predictions by extrapolating between the known effort/defect values seen in their two nearest prototypes. In that approach, once the prototypes are generated, we can ignore the original set of rows.

Other benefits of prototypes are compression, anomaly detection, and incremental model revision:

- *Compression*: Suppose we generate, say, $\sqrt{N}$ clusters and keep only say, $M = 10$ rows from each cluster. This approach means we only need to store some fraction $M/\sqrt{N}$ of the original data.
- *Anomaly detection*: When new data arrives, we can quickly search that space to find its nearest neighbors. If those "nearest neighbors" are unusually far away, then this new data is actually an anomaly as it is an example of something *not* seen during the initial clustering.
- *Incremental model revision*: If we keep the anomalies found at each prototype then if that number gets too large, that would be a signal to reflect over all those anomalies and the M examples to, say, generate new clusters around those examples and anomalies. This approach means we rarely have to reorganize all the data, which can lead to very fast local incremental updates of a model [145].

Finally, another benefit of prototype learning is implementing privacy algorithms. If we reduce R rows to (say) $\sqrt{R}$ centroids then, by definition, we are ignoring the particular details or $R - \sqrt{R}$ individuals in the data. This has implications for sharing data, while preserving confidentiality (see Chapter 16).

Note that the above benefits of using prototypes can only be achieved if the cost of finding the prototypes is not exorbitant. While some clustering methods can be very slow, tools like CHUNK run in near-linear time.

10.7.2 ADVANTAGES OF CLUSTERING

Apart from prototype generation, there are many other advantages of cluster-based reasoning. For one thing, when exploring new data sets, it is good practice to spend some initial time just looking around the data for interesting or suspicious aspects of the data. Clustering can help such an unfocused because since it reduces the data to sets of similar examples.

Also, clusters can be used to impute missing data. If a clustered row has some value missing in a column, then we might guess a probable replacement value using the most common value of the other columns in that cluster.

Further, clusters are useful for reducing uncertainty in the conclusions reached from data. Any special local effects (or outliers) that might confuse general reasoning can be isolated in their own specialized cluster [291]. Then, we can reason about those outliers in some way that is different than the rest of the data.

More generally, clustering can find regions where prediction certainty *increases* or *decreases*. Raw tables of data contain many concepts, all mixed up. If we first cluster data into regions of similar examples, then it is possible that our prediction certainty will *increase*. To see this, we apply Equation (10.2) to the original golf data with $\frac{9}{14} \approx 64\%$ examples of *play* = *yes* and $\frac{5}{14} \approx 36\%$ examples of *play* = *no*. This has entropy $e_0 = 0.94$. In the four clusters shown above (see version 4 of the golf data), the entropy of clusters 1, 2, 3, 4 are $e_{1,2,3,4} = \{0.92, 0.81, 0.92, 0.92\}$, respectively. The rows in these clusters comprise different fractions $f_{1,2,3,4} = \frac{3}{14}, \frac{4}{14}, \frac{3}{14}, \frac{4}{14}$ (respectively) of the data. From this, we can see that the expected value of entropy of these clusters is $\sum e_i f_i = 0.86$, which is less than the original entropy of 0.94. This is to say that clustering has clarified our understanding of the data by finding a better way to divide the data.

On the other hand, clustering can also find regions where prediction certainty *decreases*. Suppose our clustering had generated the following cluster:

```
# golf data, imagined cluster

outlook,temp,humid,wind,play
-------------------------
  sunny, hi, hi, FALSE,  no
  rainy, hi, hi,  TRUE,  no
  rainy, hi, hi, FALSE, yes
  rainy, lo, hi, FALSE, yes
```

The problem with the this cluster is that it is no longer clear if we are going to play golf (because the frequency of *play* = *yes* is the same as *play* = *no*). For such a cluster, Equation (10.2) tells us that the entropy is $-2 * 0.5 * \log_2(0.5) = 1$. Because this is more than $e = 0.94$, we would conclude that in this cluster the entropy is *worse* than in the original data. This is a *confusing cluster* because, if we entered this cluster, we would know *less* about what sports we play than if we just stayed with the raw data.

How to handle such *confusing clusters*? One approach is to declare them "no-go" zones and delete them. The TEAK system of Chapter 14 takes that approach: If regions of the data are found with high conclusion variance, then those regions are deleted. TEAK then runs clustering again, but this time on just the examples from the nonconfusing regions. This proves to be remarkably effective. TEAK can look into data from other organizations (or from very old prior projects) and find the small number of relevant and nonconfusing examples that are relevant to current projects.

10.8 CONTRAST PRUNING

The universe is a complex place. Any agent recording *all* their stimulation will soon run out of space to store that information. Lotus founder Mitchell Kapor once said, "Getting information off the Internet is like drinking from a fire hydrant." We should take Kapor's observation seriously. Unless we can process the mountain of information surrounding us, we must either ignore it or let it bury us.

For this reason, many animals react more to the *difference* between things rather than the *presence* of those things. For example, the neurons in the eyes of frog are most attuned to the *edges* of shapes and the *changes* in the speed of their prey [91]. As with frogs, so too with people. Cognitive scientists and researchers studying human decision making note that humans often use simple models rather than intricate ones [143]. Such simple models often list *differences* between sets of things rather than extensive *descriptions* of those things [203].

If we listen to frogs and cognitive scientists, then it seems wise to apply the following pruning method to our data:

Contrast pruning: Prune away ranges that do not contribute to differences within the data.

To illustrate this point, we use the C4.5 *iterative dichotomization* algorithm [363] to learn the distinctions between the clusters shown above (in version 4 of the golf data).

C4.5 recursively applies the INFOGAIN procedure to find the best column on which to split the data. Recall that INFOGAIN sorts the columns based on their entropy (and *lower* entropy is *better*). C4.5 then splits the data, once for every range in the column with *lowest* entropy. C4.5 then calls itself recursively on each split.

C4.5 returns a decision tree where the root of each subtree is one of the splits. For example, we applied C4.5 to version 4 of the cluster data (ignoring the *play* variable) calculating entropy using the cluster id of each row. The result is shown below:

```
# rules that distinguish different clusters
#
#                              : conclusion (all, missed)
-------------------------------------------------
humidity = lo
|    outlook = overcast : cluster1   (  2,    0)
|    outlook = rainy    : cluster1   (  1,    0)
```

```
|    outlook = sunny     : cluster2   (  2,     0)
humidity = hi
|    outlook = rainy     : cluster4   (  4,     0)
|    outlook = overcast  : cluster2   (  2,     1)
|    outlook = sunny     : cluster3   (  3,     1)
```

In this tree, indentation indicates the level of tree. Also, anything after ":" is a conclusion reached by one branch of the tree. For example, the branch in the first two rows of this tree can be read as

IF humidity = lo AND outlook = overcast THEN cluster1

Induction is not a certain process and, sometimes, we cannot fit all the data to our models. Hence, after every conclusion, ID counts *all* the examples that fell down each branch as well how many *missed* on being in the right leaf. For most of the conclusions shown above, all the examples fall down branches that place them into the correct clusters. Hence, their *missed* number is zero. However, for the last two branches, there were some issues. For example, of the three examples that match *humidity = hi and outlook = rainy*, two of them are in *cluster3* but one actually comes from *cluster2*. Hence, the numbers on this last branch are 3/1.

Here's the important point: Notice what is *not* in the above tree? There is no mention of *temperature* and *windy* because, in terms of distinguishing between structures in our data, that data is superfluous. Hence, if we were engaging business users in discussions about this data, we would encourage them to discuss issues relating to *humidity* and *outlook* before discussing issues relating to the less relevant columns of *temperature* and *wind*.

More generally, contrast pruning is a more refined version of column pruning. Contrast pruning selects the ranges that help us distinguish between different parts of the data. Whereas column pruning ranks and removes all ranges in uninformative *columns*, contrast pruning can rank *ranges* to select some parts of some of the columns.

In the case of the golf data, the contrast ranges shown in the above rules use all the ranges of *humidity* and *outlook*. But in larger data sets, a repeated result is that the contrast sets are some small subset of the ranges in a small number of columns [306]. For example, Figure 10.2 shows the 14 columns that describe 506 houses from Boston (and the last column "PRICE" is the target concept we might want to predict). If we discretize the housing pricing to {*low, medlow, medhigh, high*} then C4.5 could learn the predictor for housing prices shown in Figure 10.3. For this discussion, the details of that tree do matter. What does matter are the *details* of that tree. C4.5 is a zealous data miner that looks for numerous nuanced distinctions in increasingly smaller and specialized parts of the data. Hence, this tree mentions nearly all of the columns (all except for *ZN* and *B*).

On the other hand, if we use contrast pruning then we can generate models that are much smaller than Figure 10.3. To do this, we first assign some *weights* to the classes such that higher priced houses are increasingly more desired:

$$w_{low} = 1 w_{medlow} = 2$$

$$w_{medhigh} = 4 w_{high} = 8$$

After discretizing all numerics, we then divide the houses into {*low, medlow, medhigh, high*} and weight each range by its frequency in that range times the w_i value for that division. Those range scores are then normalized $0, \dots, 1$ and we build rules from just the top quarter scoring ranges (i.e., with

- CRIM: per capita crime rate by town
- ZN: proportion of residential land zoned for lots over 25,000 sq.ft.
- INDUS: proportion of nonretail business acres per town
- CHAS: Charles River dummy variable (=1 if tract bounds river; 0 otherwise);
- NOX: nitric oxides concentration (parts per 10 million);
- RM: average number of rooms per dwelling
- AGE: proportion of owner-occupied units built prior to 1940
- DIS: weighted distances to five Boston employment centers
- RAD: index of accessibility to radial highways
- TAX: full-value property-tax rate per $10,000
- PTRATIO: pupil-teacher ratio by town
- B: 1000 $(B - 0.63)^2$ where B is the proportion of blocks by town
- LSTAT: lower status of the population
- PRICE: Median value of owner-occupied homes.

FIGURE 10.2

Columns in the Boston *housing* table. From http://archive.ics.uci.edu/ml/datasets/Housing.

a normalized range score over 0.75). Starting with those ranges, the TAR3 contrast set learner [295] learns the following selector for houses with large resale value:

$$(12.6 \leq PTRATION < 16) \cap (6.7 \leq RM < 9.78) \tag{10.3}$$

Figure 10.4 shows the effects of this rule. The light gray/dark gray bars show the distributions of houses before/after applying RuleEquation (10.3). Note that the houses selected in the green bars are mostly 100% *high*-priced houses; in other words, the learned rule is effective for selecting desired subsets of the data.

It turns out, in many data sets, the pruning offered by contrast sets can be very large, which is to say that in many domains, there are a small number of most powerful ranges and many more ranges that are superfluous (and can be safely ignored) [306]. For example, the model learned after contrast pruning on the housing data was one line long and referenced only 2 of the 13 possible observable columns. Such succinct models are quick to read, audit, and apply. On the other hand, models learned without pruning can be more complicated to read and harder to understand; for example, see Figure 10.3.

For notes on other contrast set learners, see [342].

10.9 GOAL PRUNING

Our final pruning leverages the known goal for the learning process. For example, if the goal is to learn when we might play golf, then we could report just a summary of the data that affects that decision. That is,

Goal pruning: Prune away ranges that do not effect final decisions.

For example, what if we had the goal "what predicts for playing for golf"? This question has been made very simple, thanks to our pruning operators:

```
LSTAT <= 14.98
|   RM <= 6.54
|   |   DIS <= 1.6102
|   |   |   DIS <= 1.358: high
|   |   |   DIS > 1.358
|   |   |   |   LSTAT <= 12.67: low
|   |   |   |   LSTAT > 12.67: medlow
|   |   DIS > 1.6102
|   |   |   TAX <= 222
|   |   |   |   CRIM <= 0.06888: medhigh
|   |   |   |   CRIM > 0.06888: medlow
|   |   |   TAX > 222: medlow
|   RM > 6.54
|   |   RM <= 7.42
|   |   |   DIS <= 1.8773: high
|   |   |   DIS > 1.8773
|   |   |   |   PTRATIO <= 19.2
|   |   |   |   |   RM <= 7.007
|   |   |   |   |   |   LSTAT <= 5.39
|   |   |   |   |   |   |   INDUS <= 6.41: medhigh
|   |   |   |   |   |   |   INDUS > 6.41: medlow
|   |   |   |   |   |   LSTAT > 5.39
|   |   |   |   |   |   |   DIS <= 3.9454
|   |   |   |   |   |   |   |   RM <= 6.861
|   |   |   |   |   |   |   |   |   INDUS <= 7.87: medhigh
|   |   |   |   |   |   |   |   |   INDUS > 7.87: medlow
|   |   |   |   |   |   |   |   RM > 6.861: medlow
|   |   |   |   |   |   |   DIS > 3.9454: medlow
|   |   |   |   |   RM > 7.007: medhigh
|   |   |   |   PTRATIO > 19.2: medlow
|   |   RM > 7.42
|   |   |   PTRATIO <= 17.9: high
|   |   |   PTRATIO > 17.9
|   |   |   |   AGE <= 43.7: high
|   |   |   |   AGE > 43.7: medhigh
LSTAT > 14.98
|   CRIM <= 0.63796
|   |   INDUS <= 25.65
|   |   |   DIS <= 1.7984: low
|   |   |   DIS > 1.7984: medlow
|   |   INDUS > 25.65: low
|   CRIM > 0.63796
|   |   RAD <= 4: low (13.0)
|   |   RAD > 4
|   |   |   NOX <= 0.655
|   |   |   |   AGE <= 97.5
|   |   |   |   |   DIS <= 2.2222: low
|   |   |   |   |   DIS > 2.2222: medlow
|   |   |   |   AGE > 97.5: medlow
|   |   |   NOX > 0.655
|   |   |   |   CHAS = 0: low
|   |   |   |   CHAS = 1
|   |   |   |   |   DIS <= 1.7455: low
|   |   |   |   |   DIS > 1.7455: medlow
```

FIGURE 10.3

A decision tree to predict housing prices.

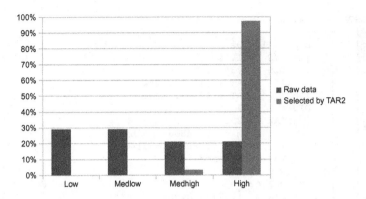

FIGURE 10.4

Distributions of houses, before and after applying RuleEquation (10.3).

1. Cohen pruning has simplified the numerics;
2. Discretization has collapsed the simplified numerics into a few ranges;
3. Clustering has found that the data falls into four groups;
4. Contrast pruning has found a minority of ranges and columns that can distinguish between those groups (which are all the ranges in *humidity* and *outlook*).

From all this pruning, we now run C4.5 looking for ways to separate the classes *play* = *yes* and *play* = *no*. For that run, we only use the ranges found in the contrast pruning:

```
# golf data, version 6
# Only discretized ranges found
# in contrasts between clusters.

outlook  , humidity , play
-------- , -------- , -----
overcast , lo       , yes
rainy    , lo       , no
rainy    , hi       , yes
sunny    , lo       , yes
rainy    , hi       , yes
rainy    , hi       , no
overcast , hi       , yes
sunny    , hi       , no
rainy    , hi       , yes
sunny    , lo       , yes
sunny    , hi       , no
overcast , lo       , yes
overcast , hi       , yes
sunny    , hi       , no
```

When given to C4.5, this yields the following tree:

```
#                      : conclusion (all, missed)
----------------------------------------------------
outlook = overcast : yes        (4,        0)
outlook = rainy    : yes        (5,        2)
outlook = sunny
|   humidity = lo  : yes        (2,        0)
|   humidity = hi  : no         (3,        0)
```

Observe how all this pruning has led to a very succinct model of golf-playing behavior. For $4 + 5 = 9$ of the rows, a single test on *outlook* is enough to make a decision. It is true that for $2 + 3 = 5$ rows, the decision making is slightly more complex (one more test for *humidity*). That said, the tree is usually very accurate.

- In three of its four branches, there are no *missed* conclusions.
- In the remaining branch, errors are in the minority (only two of five cases).

10.10 EXTENSIONS FOR CONTINUOUS CLASSES

Most of the examples in this chapter focuses on predicting for discrete classes, e.g., symbols like *play = yes* and *play = no*. Another category of learners used in this book are learners that predict for continuous classes. There are many such learners such as linear regression, support-vector machines, etc., but the one we use most is a variant of the C4.5 iterative dichotomization algorithm.

Recall that C4.5 recursively divides data on the columns whose ranges have the lowest entropy. This approach can be quickly adapted to numerical classes by switching the entropy equation of Equation (10.2) with the standard deviation equation of Equation (10.1). Like entropy, the standard deviation is *least* when we know *most* about that distribution (lower standard deviations means we have less uncertainty). This is the approach taken by the "regression tree" (RT) learners such as the CART algorithm used in Chapters 17, 18 and 22.

RTs are discussed in the next section. After that, we also review experimental methods that show how to extend single numeric predictors to multigoal tasks.

10.10.1 HOW RTs WORK

RTs are nonlinear predictive structures for problems where the target output is numeric. An example of a RT is shown in Figure 10.5. RTs can be seen as rules to separate examples based on their input features. In order to make an estimation, the leaf node most similar to the test instance in terms of input feature values is determined. This is done by following the path that matches the input features of the instance to be predicted. For example, the prediction made for a project with functional size 200 and language type 4GL using the RT from Figure 10.5 would be 2698 person-hours. Each leaf node represents a subset of the training examples used to create the tree, and the estimation given by a leaf is calculated based on these examples.

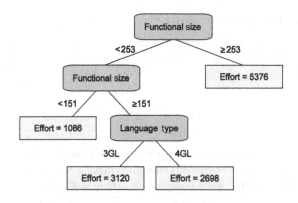

FIGURE 10.5

An example of a RT for software effort estimation, where efforts are measured in person-hours.

Note that Figure 10.5 looks similar to the decision trees discussed earlier, with one key difference. In the text above, our trees lead to predictions of *symbolic* values. In RTs, on the other hand, the goal is predicting numerics.

Several different learning algorithms can be used to create RTs. Learning consists in deciding which input features (and numeric threshold values in the case of numeric features) to make splits on, usually in a top-down and recursive way. So, first, the split at the root node is decided. Then, for each node in the next level of the tree, the split is decided in a similar way to the root node, and so on. Learning algorithms differ mainly in the way to decide which input feature (and numeric threshold value) to make the split on. New splits continue to be created until there are no input features left to split on or a certain termination criterion is met.

When making splits, RTs typically consider two different types of input features: categorical and numeric. Categorical input features are discrete and unordered. For example, the input feature *development type* could be a categorical feature that can assume values *new*, *enhancement*, or *redevelopment*. Numeric input values are continuous and ordered. For example, the input feature *functional size* could be a numeric feature that can assume any positive real value. Some RTs also consider a third type of input feature: ordinal. Ordinal input features are discrete and ordered. For example, one could consider the input feature *team expertise* and the input feature *functional size* ordinal features that can assume values *low*, *medium*, or *high*. In this section, ordinal features will be treated in the same way as categorical features. Sections 10.10.2, 10.10.3 explain a typical way to decide and make splits on categorical and numeric input features, respectively.

10.10.2 CREATING SPLITS FOR CATEGORICAL INPUT FEATURES

Splits involving categorical input features create *b* branches, where *b* is the number of possible values of the given input feature. So, when dealing with categorical input features, the splitting decision is the same as the decision of which input feature to split on. As explained previously, we will consider ordinal features as categorical features in this section. For example, consider that the input feature *functional size* can assume values *low*, *medium*, and *high*. Then, a split on this input feature would create three branches, as exemplified in Figure 10.6.

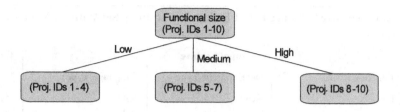

FIGURE 10.6

An example of a split at the root node using the training set from Table 10.1 and treating ordinal input features as categorical input features. The project IDs of the training examples represented by each node are shown in brackets.

The splits are made so as to separate training examples into homogeneous groups, i.e., groups with similar target outputs. In the above discussion, "homogeneity" was measured in terms of the entropy measure discussed in Section 10.5. That entropy measure is the preferred option when the target class is symbolic. On the other hand, for RTs where the target class is numeric, we will switch from entropy to variance.

Variance is used to measure homogeneity in algorithms such as REPTree [444]. A group of examples with smaller variance is considered more homogeneous. So, a split that will result in children nodes with lower overall variance than the parent node will be improving the homogeneity of the tree. The feature chosen to split on is the one that leads to the highest variance reduction from the parent to the children nodes.

Recall that the variance associated to a node S is the variance of the target outputs of the training examples associated to this node:

$$var(S) = \frac{1}{|S|} \sum_{(\mathbf{x}^{(i)}, y^{(i)}) \in S} (y^{(i)} - mean(S))^2, \qquad (10.4)$$

where $|S|$ is the number of training examples associated to the node S, $y^{(i)}$ is the target output of the ith training example $(\mathbf{x}^{(i)}, y^{(i)})$ associated to the node S, and $mean(S)$ is the average of all $y^{(i)}$:

$$mean(S) = \frac{1}{|S|} \sum_{(\mathbf{x}^{(i)}, y^{(i)}) \in S} y^{(i)}.$$

For example, let's consider the hypothetical training set given in Table 10.1. In this example, there are no numeric input features, which will be explained in Section 10.10.3. Each training example is composed of three input features: (1) *functional size*, which can assume value *low*, *medium*, or *high*; (2) *language type*, which can assume value *3GL* or *4GL*; and (3) *development type*, which can assume value *new* or *enhancement*. The output feature is the required software effort in person-hours. The variance $var(S_{root})$ associated to the root node S_{root} of the tree corresponding to this training set is calculated as follows:

$$mean(S_{root}) = \frac{1}{10} \cdot (520 + 530 + 300 + 310 + 900 + 910 + 700 + 1500 + 2000 + 1340)$$
$$= 901.$$

Table 10.1 An Illustrative Software Effort Estimation Training Set Without Numeric Input Features

Project ID	Input Feature			Target Output
	Functional Size	Development Type	Language Type	True Effort
1	Low	New	3GL	520
2	Low	Enhancement	3GL	530
3	Low	New	4GL	300
4	Low	Enhancement	4GL	310
5	Medium	Enhancement	3GL	900
6	Medium	New	3GL	910
7	Medium	New	4GL	700
8	High	Enhancement	3GL	1500
9	High	New	4GL	2000
10	High	Enhancement	4GL	1340

Note: *The project IDs are usually not used for learning.*

$$var(S_{root}) = \frac{1}{10} \cdot [(520 - 901)^2 + (530 - 901)^2 + (300 - 901)^2$$
$$+ (310 - 901)^2 + (900 - 901)^2 + (910 - 901)^2 + (700 - 901)^2$$
$$+ (1500 - 901)^2 + (2000 - 901)^2 + (1340 - 901)^2]$$
$$= 279,309.$$

The variance associated to a split on the node S based on feature a is the weighted average of the variance associated to the children nodes:

$$var(S, a) = \sum_{S_j} \frac{|S_j|}{|S|} \cdot var(S_j), \quad (10.5)$$

where $|S|$ is the number of training examples in the node S, $|S_j|$ is the number of training examples in the child node S_j of the split, and $var(S_j)$ is the variance associated to the child node S_j calculated using Equation (10.4). For example, consider that we need to decide on a split to the root node of an RT being trained on the examples from Table 10.1. In order to do so, we will need to calculate the variance associated to all possible splits on this node, i.e., the split based on functional size, the split based on development type, and the split based on language type. The variance $var(S_{root}, fs)$ associated to the split on functional size (*fs*) is calculated as follows:

$$var(S_{root,fs=low}) = \frac{1}{4} \cdot [(520 - 415)^2 + (530 - 415)^2 + (300 - 415)^2 + (310 - 415)^2]$$
$$= 12,125.$$
$$var(S_{root,fs=medium}) = \frac{1}{3} \cdot [(900 - 837)^2 + (910 - 837)^2 + (700 - 837)^2]$$
$$= 9356.$$

$$var(S_{root,fs=high}) = \frac{1}{3} \cdot [(1500 - 1613)^2 + (2000 - 1613)^2 + (1340 - 1613)^2]$$

$$= 79,022.$$

$$var(S_{root},fs) = \frac{4}{10} \cdot 12,125 + \frac{3}{10} \cdot 9356 + \frac{3}{10} \cdot 79,022$$

$$= 31,363.$$

The variance reduction generated by a split on node S based on feature a is the difference between the variance associated to the parent node (calculated using Equation (10.4)) and the variance associated to the split (calculated using Equation (10.5)):

$$var\_reduction(S, a) = var(S) - var(S, a). \tag{10.6}$$

For instance, the variance reduction of the split on the root node based on the feature functional size in the example above is $279,309 - 31,363 = 247,946$. The variance reductions resulting from splits on development type and language type are $279,309 - 279,084 = 225$ and $279,309 - 278,468 = 841$, respectively. As the split with the highest variance reduction is the chosen one, functional size would be chosen for the split, as shown in Figure 10.6.

The splits on each of the nodes in the next level of the tree would be decided recursively, similar to the above. For instance, the split on the node with project IDs 1-4 would be decided between development type and language type. The variance associated to this node is 12,125. The variance associated to the split on development type is 12,100, and the variance associated to the split on language type is 25. As the split on language type produces the highest variance reduction, this feature would be chosen for the split, as shown in Figure 10.7. The whole tree generated using the examples from Table 10.1 is shown in Figure 10.8.

10.10.3 SPLITS ON NUMERIC INPUT FEATURES

When making a split based on a categorical input feature, the number of branches corresponds to the number of all possible values of the input feature. Using the same strategy for numeric input features

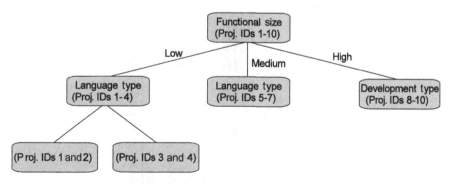

FIGURE 10.7

An example of a further split using the training set from Table 10.1. The project IDs of the training examples represented by each node are shown in brackets.

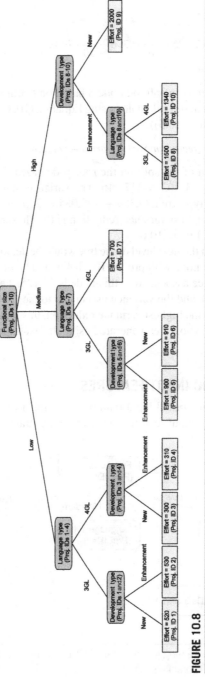

FIGURE 10.8

An example of RT produced using the training set from Table 10.1. The project IDs of the training examples represented by each node are shown in brackets.

would be infeasible, as the number of possible values would be too high. So, how to make splits based on numeric input features?

In most algorithms, splits involving numeric input features create two branches only: one for input values smaller than a certain threshold value and the other one for input values equal to or greater than this threshold value. An example of that is shown in Figure 10.5 and the beginning of Section 20.3. So, when dealing with numeric input features, it is necessary to decide not only which input feature to split on, but also which threshold value to use. Given a certain input feature being considered for the split, this is commonly done by first sorting the values of this feature assumed by all training examples in the node to be split. Then, the variance reduction (using Equation (10.6)) that a split with threshold in the midpoint between each neighboring value is calculated.

For example, consider that a certain node S to be split contains the training examples with IDs 2, 3, 4, 7, and 9, and that we are considering the split on the input feature functional size. Different from Section 10.10.2, functional size is a numeric input feature in this example. Table 10.2 shows the training examples sorted by functional size. There are four different possible split points based on this input feature: between 13 and 15 (threshold value 14), 15 and 150 (threshold value 82.5), 150 and 160 (threshold value 155), and 160 and 165 (threshold value 162.5).

The variance reduction of each of these four possible splits is computed based on Equation (10.6), similar to Section 10.10.2. For instance, the (rounded) variance reduction associated to the threshold value 14 is calculated as follows:

$$var(S) = \frac{1}{5} \cdot [(6-304)^2 + (10-304)^2 + (496-304)^2 + (510-304)^2 + (500-304)^2]$$
$$= 58,591.$$

$$var(S_{fs<14}) = \frac{1}{1} \cdot (6-6)^2$$
$$= 0.$$

$$var(S_{fs\geq14}) = \frac{1}{4} \cdot [(10-379)^2 + (496-379)^2 + (510-379)^2 + (500-379)^2]$$
$$= 45,413.$$

$$var(S, fs_{threshold=14}) = \frac{1}{5} \cdot 0 + \frac{4}{5} \cdot 45,413$$
$$= 36,330.$$

$$var\_reduction(S, fs_{threshold=14}) = 58,591 - 36,330 = 22,261.$$

Table 10.2 An Illustrative Example of Training Examples Sorted According to Functional Size

Project ID	3	2	4	7	9
Functional size	13	15	150	160	165
True effort	6	10	496	510	500

Note: *Input features different from functional size are omitted.*

The threshold value with the highest variance reduction is considered as the best threshold value for the corresponding numeric input feature on the node being analyzed. In the example above, the best threshold value for the feature functional size on node S would be 82.5. When deciding a split on a certain node, the split with the highest variance reduction among all available categorical input features and all available numeric input features with their possible threshold values is chosen. Different than categorical input features, a certain numeric input feature may be chosen for a split more than once in a single path. This is because even though a certain threshold value may have been chosen in a certain level of the tree, another threshold value could still be chosen in another level of a given path. An example of that can be seen in Figure 10.5. An example of a RT learning algorithm that makes splits as described in this section is REPTree [444], even though it uses an additional mechanism to sort input feature values a single time during the whole training procedure.

10.10.4 TERMINATION CONDITION AND PREDICTIONS

Node splits can continue to be performed until there is no input feature (or threshold value) left to split on. In this case, each leaf node will correspond to a single training example, as in Figure 10.8. The prediction made by a leaf node in this case is the target output of its corresponding training example. It is easy to see that RTs with no extra termination condition could become very large. They could also *overfit* the training examples, i.e., they would be able to make very good (perfect) estimations for the training examples, but would be unable to generalize well for new instances.

Additional termination conditions can avoid creating undesirable leaves by stopping the learning process earlier. An example of termination condition is to stop splitting a node once the number of training examples represented by this node reaches a predefined minimum value. Another example is when none of the possible splits on a node would cause variance reduction larger than a certain predefined minimum value. When such additional termination conditions are used, a certain leaf node may accommodate more than one training example. In this case, the prediction made by it can be, for example, the average target output of all its corresponding training examples.

Another way to maintain RTs with a manageable and readable size is to prune them. Examples of pruning methods will not be discussed in this book and can be found elsewhere [444].

10.10.5 POTENTIAL ADVANTAGES OF RTs FOR SOFTWARE EFFORT ESTIMATION

RTs have several features that potentially help them achieve good accuracy for software effort estimation (SEE). One feature is that RTs can be considered as local methods, whose estimations are based on training examples similar to the instance being predicted. Locality may be particularly useful for SEE because SEE data sets are usually small and heterogeneous. Algorithms that are not based on locality typically have many parameters to be learned, requiring larger data sets. Moreover, different from many of the existing local methods, RTs are created considering not only the input features of the training examples, but also the impact of the input features on the target output. So, the locality structure may group together examples that are more likely to have similar target values. This is a potential advantage over other local methods. Another potential advantage, and perhaps one of the most important ones, is that the locality structure of RTs may operate in such a way as to not only perform feature selection naturally, but also to give different importance for different features depending on the levels of the tree in which they appear. For example, if the most important feature for determining software effort is functional size, then this feature will be used for the root split of the tree. Less important features would be used in lower level splits or even not used at all. This hierarchy of features can be particularly useful for SEE, as data sets frequently have many (more and less relevant) features and few training examples. Another advantage of RTs is that their prediction rules are readable, making their estimations transparent and understandable.

10.10.6 PREDICTIONS FOR MULTIPLE NUMERIC GOALS

There is a more challenging kind of continuous class problem where rows contain multiple numeric classes. For example, a table of cars might score each example with *cost2buy* and *milesPerGallon*. For such data sets, the goal might be to learn the trade-offs between competing goals. Traditionally, this kind of problem is explored with specialized optimizers (e.g., NSGA-II [93]) but these tasks can also be addressed via data mining. In this "data mining for optimization" approach

1. Each row is split into *objectives* (a.k.a. the goals) and the decisions (things we can control or observe and that contribute to the objective).
2. Cluster the rows based on the decisions.
3. Apply contrast pruning to identify ranges in the decisions that distinguish between different clusters.
4. To score each cluster, find the expected value of each objective in that cluster.
5. For every cluster c_j with some low scores in some objective, find a nearby cluster c_j that has better scores.
6. Using the results from Step 2, build the rules Δ_{ij} that select for less c_i and more c_j rows.

The rules Δ_{ij} are candidates for nudging the rows in cluster c_i toward the scores of cluster c_j. Of course, these rules must be tested by going back to the data generating phenomenon and seeing what happens when that data generation is constrained by Δ_{ij}. As it happens, this approach has proved useful in many domains:

- Working with Martin Feather, we applied this approach to the optimization of competing goals for software designs based on a NASA requirements model. Working in rounds, we used contrast sets to generate rules that constrained how we ran the models in the next round of the reasoning. Each round produced a new data set and, hence, new contrast ranges and new rules (that were used to constrain the next round) [125].
- We recently reported results with this approach where the rules learned from contrast sets selected from data with up to half the original defects and development effort [291].
- In other work, TAR3 has been benchmarked against state-of-the-art numerical optimizers at NASA's AMES Research facility. The task there was to optimize landing trajectories of spacecraft coming in from earth orbit. In comparisons with state-of-the-art gradient descent algorithms (a quasi-Newton method that incrementally updates a Hessian approximation), TAR3 ran 30-48 times faster that the state-of-the-art optimizer, and found better solutions (much higher precision and recall of better trajectories) [141].

SHARING DATA

III

SHARING DATA

SHARING DATA: CHALLENGES AND METHODS

This book now turns to the complex issue of sharing data and models. In this part, we discuss sharing data (and the next part, starting on page 235 discusses sharing models).

Until very recently, there was much pessimism about transferring data from one software project to another. However, as we shall see, several recent results show that such sharing is possible, providing we carefully assess what data is relevant (or otherwise) to a new situation. So before showing those new results, we briefly review the long list of results warning that data sharing is very difficult. This list will motivate the rest of the chapters is this part of the book.

11.1 HOUSTON, WE HAVE A PROBLEM

In the SE literature, there are many examples where the conclusions drawn from data do not hold across multiple projects. For example, Meyers [314] argues that OO systems are less bug prone but Hatton strongly disputes that claim [168]. Also, while research at Microsoft suggests that the nature of a developer's community predicts for defects, other research at AT&T suggests that such social knowledge does not improve defect predictors [150, 349, 440]. In other work, Menzies et al. [291] show how the relationship between project factors and effort (respectively) changes dramatically between projects. Further, recalling Fig. 1.3 on page 7, that figure showed 28 studies that offer contradictory conclusions regarding the effectiveness of OO metrics for predicting defects. Finally, a recent special issue of the *Empirical Software Engineering Journal*, January 2012, documents other cases of lack of repeatable results in SE [310].

Some of these results (about how data from one project cannot work for another) are quite startling. For example, Zimmermann et al. studied 629 pairs of software development projects [463]. In only 4% of cases was a defect prediction model learned from one project useful on its pair. One of the most interesting results in the Zimmermann et al. study was from the comparison of two browsers (one open-source and one proprietary): defect models learned from the first would work on the second but *not the other way around*.

Recent papers on local inference, Menzies et al. [291] and Bettenburg et al. [28], compare models learned from all data to models learned from local clusters. They both report that better models come from small subsets of the data rather than from the entire data set. These results suggest that it is best *not* to share data; rather, it might be better to reflect more deeply on local data.

The list of SE conclusions that do not generalize goes on and on. Kitchenham et al. calls this the "cross-company" versus "within-company" problem; in other words, is it best learning from local data or learning from data shared from another project? In 2007, Kitchenham et al.'s own conclusions about the value of cross-company learning were not encouraging [218]. In their work, they found almost an equal number of studies that reported

- The accuracy of the cross-company model was the same as within-company models;
- Within-company models did better.

That is, it was like the effect was a random variable so that you were just as likely as not to be able to effectively share data.

11.2 GOOD NEWS, EVERYONE

This part of the book is an antidote to the above pessimism. It turns out that it is a mistake to share *all* the data. As discussed below:

- Very little of someone else's data may be useful to you;
- But, if we just focus on the small number of *relevant* data items, that data may be very useful for predicting aspects of your project.

Hence, when two agents share data, we need to reflect on what portions of the available data are *relevant* to some new problem. Accordingly, this part of the book explores methods and applications of such relevancy-based reasoning.

- Chapter 12 discusses the pros and cons of manual versus automatic methods for finding relevant regions. That chapter also presents sample source code for "CHUNK," a very fast automatic contextualization tool.
- Chapter 13 shows how to find local regions of data from other projects that are useful to predict defects in some current project.
- Chapter 14 shows how to prune bad local regions of data. In that work, "bad" means regions of the data that would confuse predictions (as the predictions in that region would have high variance). As discussed there, data pruned in this way produces better predictions.
- Chapter 15 goes one step further to ask: "Why do we only need to share small samples of all the data?" That chapter will appeal to certain mathematical results to design PEEKER, a prediction tool that needs only 10% (on average) of all the data.
- Chapter 16 points out that a benefit of sharing less data is that this exposes less information. This chapter explores methods to share data, while preserving the privacy of the organizations sharing the data. The chapter is an excellent example of how sharing just enough of the right kind of data can be very beneficial to software engineering.
- The last two chapters in this part of the book that discuss how to share and organize better a shareable data collection.
  - Chapter 17 shows how to fill in missing data from related information (again, the trick will be to find regions of related data).
  - Chapter 18 discusses methods to group together related data, then only seek more information on the most relevant groups.

For the purposes of historical accuracy, we note that the CHUNK code of Chapter 12 was written after we completed the other chapters. In theory, much of the processing of Chapter 13–Chapter 18 could be implemented as special cases of CHUNK. However, that claim has yet to be tested or checked by the international peer review process. Such tests and checks take many years and several generations of graduate students (as a point of reference, this book was 8 years in the making and consumed the time of three PhD students and two masters students).

That said, compared to the code used in those chapters, CHUNK is far simpler. Hence, we present CHUNK, as it might be a simple method that allows you (the reader) to quickly try the methods of Chapter 13– Chapter 18.

LEARNING CONTEXTS

In summary, this chapter proposes our first *data analysis pattern*; i.e., an abstract description of a specific data mining task. In writing these patterns, we will take care to comment on the connections between patterns from different chapters.

Name:	CHUNK
Also known as:	Contexts, contextualization, stratification, clustering, chunking.
Intent:	When sharing data, avoid applying irrelevancies from other projects.
Motivation:	Without knowledge of contexts, we cannot know what parts of old data are relevant to new projects. With contexts, data sharing between projects is enabled. Also, contexts offer other services: variance reduction, anomaly detection, building a certification envelope, incremental learning, compression, optimization of the learning algorithms.
Solution:	Applying clustering to raw data. For all items in test data, only use the nearest cluster to each item.
Constraints:	Standard clustering methods are confused by irrelevant or noisy variables. Also, naive clustering methods are very slow due to their quadratic time comparison of all pairs of items.
Implementation:	CHUNK is a near-linear time spectral learner that ignores irrelevant variables by combining raw data into an approximation to the data's eigenvectors (which it finds via a linear-time heuristic). CHUNK generates clusters by recursively dividing the data on those eigenvector approximations.
Applicability:	In theory, much of the processing of Chapter 13–Chapter 18 could be implemented as special cases of CHUNK (but see notes at the end of last chapter).
Related to:	CHUNK is a simplified and clarified version of PEEKER Chapter 15 and WHERE [291].

12.1 BACKGROUND

In any discussion about sharing data and models, sooner or later someone will argue that some data set "*X*" or model "*Y*" is not relevant to the current discussion. For example, it might be commented that

> We cannot use that data since they use *that* (e.g., an object-oriented language) while we use *this* (e.g., a functional programming language).

Such a remark is an appeal to *contextualization*; i.e., that general conclusions may not hold for particular software projects. For example, in general, it is unwise to drive a car very quickly. But in the specific case of an ambulance driver rushing a critically ill patient to a hospital, then driving very quickly is actually a very good idea.

In software engineering, there is a long history of such contextualization statements. Two founding fathers of empirical software engineering are Vic Basili and Dieter Rombach [23]. They view such contextualizations as the hallmark of mature reasoning about software engineering. For example, if they ask their students a question such as "what factors cause defects in software?," they hope for an answer of the form "well, it depends."

But the question is, depends on what? How can we find sets of related projects? That is the task of this chapter. After a brief description on manual methods, we will then discuss automatic methods for learning contexts; i.e., for learning how to divide raw data into meaningful subgroups.

In terms of the overall flow of this book, this chapter is highly significant. As discussed in the next chapter, the main method we have for sharing data and models are the contextualizations that restrain what data and models we share. In fact, nearly all the methods described in the rest of this book can be viewed as different methods for contextualization.

12.2 MANUAL METHODS FOR CONTEXTUALIZATION

Software is constructed in very many ways by very many different people, using a wide range of tools, to solve a large number of different problems. Given that diversity, not all lessons learned from one project apply to every other project. But how to define the context of a lesson learned? To put that another way, how to define when the lessons of one past project are *not* relevant to some current project?

The context problem is how to divide software projects into groups such that, in a particular subset, the lessons from one project are relevant to another. If done manually, we call this *delphi contextualization*, which is the process of asking some expert to propose project groupings. For example:

- When building his COCOMO-I software effort estimation model, Boehm divided software projects into "embedded," "semi-detached," "organic," and offered different COCOMO-I effort models for each [34].
- More recently, Petersen and Wohlin offer a rich set of dimensions for contextualizing projects ("processes," "product," "organization," etc.) [358].
- In Figure 12.1, Madachy et al. [279] applied their domain knowledge to their project data in order to define 7 operating environments and 21 application domains. Madachy et al. say that each of these $7 \times 21 = 147$ delphi contextualizations needs its own effort estimation model.

There are several problems with delphi contextualizations. First, they usually stop at the level of an individual project. This can be misleading as it is useful to sub-divide data below the level of single

	operating environment							
Application domain	Avionics	Fixed ground	Missile	Mobile ground	Shipboard	Unmanned airborne	Unmanned space	Total
Business systems		6		4	2			12
Command and control	1	41		16	35			93
Communications	4	77			17		2	100
Controls and display	8	6		2	5			21
Executive		4			3			7
Information assurance		1						1
Infrastructure		11			23			34
Maintain and diagnose	1				5			6
Mission management	42	2	3	2		1		50
Mission planning	1	17						18
Modeling and simulation		1						1
Process control		3		6	1			10
Scientific systems					3			3
Sensor processing	12	15			18			45
Simulation and modeling		19			17			36
Spacecraft BUS							9	9
Spacecraft payload							16	16
Test and evaluation		2			2			4
Tool and tool systems		6	1					7
Training				2	6			8
Weaps delivery and control	11		19		9			39
Totals	80	211	23	32	146	1	27	520

FIGURE 12.1

147 Delphi contextualizations (built from 520 US Defense Department software projects by Madachy et al. [279]).

projects. Posnett et al. [361] discuss "ecological inference"; i.e., the conceit that an empirical finding at an aggregated level (e.g., data from many projects) can apply at the disaggregated level (e.g., data from one file). They document that this conceit is widespread in the SE literature. They also conduct data mining experiments to show that they can learn better defect predictors at the file level than at the aggregate package level.

Second, it is unclear how to audit delphi contextualizations. For example, Petersen and Wohlin offer no way to learn new contextualizations for new projects.

Third, there is no agreement on which contextualizations are the "right" or the most useful ones. For example, Boehm abandoned his own contextualizations when he built the COCOMO-II model [42]. The Madachy et al. delphi contextualizations of Figure 12.1 generates such a sparse matrix that there may be insufficient historical data to learn models for most of their delphi contextualizations. Note that only $17/147 \approx 11\%$ of the cells in Figure 12.1 have more than the 10 examples required for generating the most minimal effort models.[1]

---

[1] The modeling framework used by Madachy et al. needs at least two attributes for a minimalist *local calibration* of models [34]. Valerdi [430] offers the rule of thumb that for Madachy's kind of modeling, the training data should include five examples per attribute. That is, according to Valerdi's rule, effort models require at least $2 \times 5 = 10$ examples. This is a concern as, in Figure 12.1, only 17 of the 147 contextualizations have 10 or more examples.

Fourth, as shown by the following case study, the time spent on delphi contextualizations may in fact be a waste of time. The following examples comes from Chen et al.'s work [301] on learn estimation models for software projects.

In the effort estimation community, delphi contextualization is called *stratification* (formally: the division of the *superset* of all data into *subsets* of related data [42, 78, 126, 153, 274, 296, 390, 407, 408]). In theory, stratifications containing related projects have less variation and so can be easier to calibrate. Various experiments offer some evidence for the value of stratification [42, 296, 390]. But the following, somewhat more rigorous, study raises doubt about the value of stratification (a.k.a. delphi contextualization).

Chen et al. [301] tested if more accurate estimates are generated using *all* the data or just *some* stratification. In these experiments, stratification is identified and N examples from that stratification (selected at random) are set aside as a test set. Then, we train from either

- *Treatment1 (all):* The remaining data in the stratification;
- *Treatment2 (some):* Or all data from all the stratifications (less the test set).

The learned models are then applied to the same test sets to generate results for *some* or *all* treatments (respectively). Finally, using some hypothesis test, the performance scores from these two results are checked to see if the *some* results are statistically significantly different and better than the *all* results.

This process was applied to Figure 12.2. This figure lists context variables for two effort estimation data sets from NASA. By combining the ranges of all these variables we can generate hundreds of possible stratifications. For example, *Nasa93* has the following subsets:

- All the records;
- Whether or not it is a *flight* or *ground* system;
- The *parent project* that includes the project expressed in this record;
- The NASA center where the work was conducted;
- etc.

For this study, we select stratifications to study. Given an example labeled with subsets $\{S_1, S_2, S_3, \ldots\}$ a *candidate stratification* has several properties as follows:

- It contains instances labeled $\{S_i, S_j\}$;
- The number of instances in S_j is greater than S_i; i.e., S_j is the superset and S_i is the stratification.
- S_j contains 150% (or more) records than S_i;
- S_i contains at least 20 records;

For example, the *Nasa93* data set of Figure 12.2 contains 207 stratifications that satisfy the above criteria (including one stratification containing all the records).

Now here's the important point: of the 207 stratifications explored by Chen et al. [301], only in *four* cases were results from the stratification significantly different and better. That is, in only $\frac{4}{207} \approx 2\%$ of cases was there a clear benefit in using stratifications.

This is a most puzzling result. Other studies [42, 296, 390] report success with their manual stratifications. Why did the stratifications of Chen et al. fail while other teams reported success? Perhaps the real issue in the last section was *the choice of data set*. That is, delphi localizations may be useful but just not for that particular data set.

All: selects all records from a particular source; e.g., "coc81_all".

Category: is a NASA-specific designation selecting the type of project; e.g., avionics, data capture, etc.

Dev: indicates the development methodology; e.g., div.waterfall.

DevEnd: shows the last year of the software project.

Fg: selects either "*f*" (flight) or "*g*" (ground) software.

Kind: selects records relating to the development platform; max= mainframe and mic= microprocessor.

Lang: selects records about different development languages.

Project **and** *center***:** *Nasa93* designations selecting records relating to where the software was built and the name of the project.

Mode=e: selects records relating to the *embedded* COCOMO 81 development mode; one of "organic", "embedded", or "semi-detached".

Mode=o: selects COCOMO 81 *organic* mode records.

Mode=sd: selects COCOMO 81 *semidetached* mode records.

Org: is a *cocII* designation showing what organization provided the data.

Size: is a *cocII* specific designation grouping the records into (e.g.) those around 100KLOC.

Type: selects different *coc*81 designations and include "bus" (for business application) or "sys" (for system software).

Year: is a *nasa*93 term that selects the development years, grouped into units of five; e.g., 1970,1971,1972,1973,1974 are labeled "1970".

FIGURE 12.2

Context variables for two NASA effect estimation data sets: COC81 and NASA93 (see http://goo.gl/MfzBLb and http://goo.gl/PPnUOR).

Another possibility is that *contextualization is useful, but only if is done carefully.* While manual delphi localization can sometimes be useful, often it is not (in the above study, in 98% of stratifications). There are many reasons for this. For example, when dealing with data sets that are sparse or otherwise insufficient for building models using delphi contextualization, it is necessary to ignore the barriers suggested by humans to find relevant similar data. Hence, in Figure 12.1, in order to build an estimation model, it is necessary to ignore most of the boundaries proposed by human experts in order to find enough data.

Whichever of these arguments you believe, in either case it would be useful to enhance (replace?) manual contextualization with automatically generated contextualization.

12.3 AUTOMATIC METHODS

Several recent studies [28, 170, 196, 220, 221, 226, 291, 361, 424, 452] offer strong support for automatic contextualization methods. Those studies show that supposedly general models (built using all available data) are outperformed by specialized models (built from data collected from particular parts of the data). The implications of this are staggering. Put simply, what works best *there* may not work best *here*. That is,

> Any model that is generally true across many projects may not be useful for any particular project.

This is an exciting conclusion that changes the nature of empirical SE research. Perhaps it is time to stop looking for some "holy grail" of a unifying theory or model of software engineering. Constructing software is a highly specialized task where specific people build specific products for specific reasons. It is therefore to be expected that what works here does not work there. Clearly, what is required is a new kind of data science for software engineering, one that is less focused on a model's external validity but is most focused on developing and validating "best" local models, in a cost-effective manner.[2]

12.4 OTHER MOTIVATION TO FIND CONTEXTS

The second half of this chapter offers code for quickly and automatically finding contexts in data. Before making you read all that, this section offers some additional motivation concerning *why* that code is interesting.

Our first reason for finding contexts was discussed above: it may not be wise to build trite global models from all data. Rather, it may be better to *personalize* the model to the local context.

Other reasons to divide data into small subsets are that such a division supports a very useful range of activities:

- Variance reduction.
- Anomaly detection.
- Building a certification envelope.
- Incremental learning.
- Compression.
- Optimization.
- Sharing data between projects.

The rest of this section discusses the above reasons. See also the remainder of this part of the book on sharing data for other reasons to reason about SE data, divided into multiple small contexts.

12.4.1 VARIANCE REDUCTION

Recently, for effort and defect prediction, we studied the *uncertainty* associated with model predictions. In many data sets, the predictions of models learned and applied to local contexts exhibit far less uncertainty (movement away from the median) than models learned from all data [291]. That is, the predictions found in local data are more trustworthy than those found in large sets of global data.

12.4.2 ANOMALY DETECTION

As shown below, CHUNK builds a binary tree of clusters. When new data arrives, we can run it down the tree in time $O(\log_2(N))$ to find the nearest examples seen previously. If, after doing that, we arrive at

---

[2] As to what "best" means in this context, we mean that the local model gives better conclusions; i.e., higher predictive accuracy or lower variance. For details, see Ref. [291].

a leaf cluster containing examples that are still quite a distance from the newcomer, then that newcomer is an anomaly (something we have not seen before).

12.4.3 CERTIFICATION ENVELOPES

What to do with such anomalies? One thing might be to reject them; to warn the user that the newcomer is outside of the set of examples seen previously by the learner. That is, CHUNKing can offer an *operational envelope* for a learner that warns when we should not trust its conclusions.

For another approach to learning operational envelopes that uses very different methods, see Feather et al. [124].

12.4.4 INCREMENTAL LEARNING

Another method for handling anomalies is to record a "black mark" against the leaf cluster that attracted the anomalous newcomer. If a leaf gets more than (say) 10% new black marks, then that could tell us to rerun CHUNK and our learner, just for that cluster (plus the newcomers that caused the black marks). In this way, CHUNK could be the basis for a fast *incremental learning scheme* that knows to revise just small models from tiny regions in the data.

For more on this kind of incremental learning, see Farnstrom et al. [121].

12.4.5 COMPRESSION

The flip side of anomaly detection is *compression*. To understand this, consider the core functionality of an anomaly detector; it reports what is "unusually novel." This means that an anomaly detector can also report what is "already seen." That is, as new data arrives, we can learn when to ignore it because we have already seen data like that before.

From a technical perspective, such a compression algorithm would cluster some small percent of the data, then stream over the rest. During streaming, only the new data is added to the clusters (using the incremental learning method discussed above).

In practice, the compression achieved by this method can be quite substantial. For example, Chapter 15 discusses incremental learners that ignore all but 10% of the data.

12.4.6 OPTIMIZATION

Yet another reason to CHUNK prior to learning is to *optimize that learning*. Many learning schemes take quadratic time (or more) to execute. This is a fancy way of saying that if a learner runs on only half the data, then it runs much more than twice as fast. For example, many nearest neighbor schemes require some all-pairs distance calculation. Such an $O(N^2)$ calculation can be very slow for large data sets. This can be very slow, especially if this calculation is called repeatedly deep inside the innermost loop of a program. In practice, any program working with distance calculations spends most of its time computing those measures.

On the other hand, if we CHUNK data into groups of $\sqrt{N}$, then the total runtime of that learner is now linear; i.e., much faster. As shown below, CHUNKing has very little overhead so it is a viable optimization method.

Note that CHUNK is just one of many ways to optimize the clustering process. Other methods include clustering [287], incremental stochastic k-means [381], and a range of techniques based on the triangle inequality (e.g., Hamerly [159]). It is a matter of personal preference what method you use, but the CHUNK tool shown below is very simple, scalable, and is known to be effective for SE data [291]

12.5 HOW TO FIND LOCAL REGIONS

Much of this book concerns methods for automatically finding local contextualizations. One issue with those methods is that, due to their technical intricacies, it may be hard for novices to this field to apply those methods. In fact, we know of cases where research teams have *not* applied local learning because (and this is a quote from a leading researcher in the field) "we did not have access to your local learning technology."

To encourage our preferred kind of local learning, the rest of this chapter presents an example of the kind of technology required to find local regions. To use this tool

- Call CHUNK to find groupings in the data;
- Then apply your favorite learner to those groupings.

The important point of this code is that it is simple and scalable. The following code, called CHUNK is less than 200 lines of Python and implements a linear-time clustering algorithm that finds groupings in data.

12.5.1 LICENSE

CHUNK is released under the BSD 3-clause license that allows proprietary use and allows the software released under the license to be incorporated into proprietary products. Works based on CHUNK may be released under a proprietary license as closed source software.

12.5.2 INSTALLING CHUNK

Download *chunk.py* from http://unbox.org/open/tags/sharing/chunk/1.0/chunk.py.

12.5.3 TESTING YOUR INSTALLATION

Test the code using

```
python chunk.py
```

That call will automatically run a function that recursively clusters *nasa93*. That data is from 93 NASA software projects from the years 1971-1987:

```
def nasa93():
  return [
    [1980,4,2,4,6,6,2,4,4,4,4,3,4,4,4,3,7.5,72]
   ,[1980,3,2,4,3,3,2,2,4,5,5,3,4,3,3,3,20,72]
   ,[1984,3,2,4,3,3,2,2,4,5,4,3,4,3,3,3,6,24]
   ,[1980,3,2,4,3,3,2,2,4,5,5,3,4,3,3,3,100,360]
```

```
,[1985,3,2,4,3,3,2,2,4,5,3,3,2,3,3,3,11.3,36]
,[1980,3,2,4,3,3,4,2,4,4,4,2,1,3,3,3,100,215]
# lines deleted from view
]
```

In this data, each row is one project and the first column is the year of the project. Also, the second to last column is the known size of the project (measured in thousands of lines of code). Finally, the last column is the known effort for that project (respectively). As to the other columns, these are the standard variables from the COCOMO model such as *rely* (required reliability), *data* (database size), *cplx* (product complexity), and many others (e.g., *virt, turn, acap, aexp, pcap, vexp, vecp, modp, too, sced*).

When *chunk.py* is loaded into Python, it prints the following tree. Note that the 93 projects in *nasa93* were first subdivided into two groups of 47 items. This division is repeated to find 16 leaf clusters of size five of six.

```
93
...                       # <=== [some lines omitted]
|.. 47
|.. |.. 23
|.. |.. |.. 11
|.. |.. |.. |.. 5.
|.. |.. |.. |.. 6.   #<=== clusterX
|.. |.. |.. 12
|.. |.. |.. |.. 6.
|.. |.. |.. |.. 6.
|.. |.. 24
|.. |.. |.. 12
|.. |.. |.. |.. 6.
|.. |.. |.. |.. 6.
|.. |.. |.. 12
|.. |.. |.. |.. 6.
|.. |.. |.. |.. 6.   #<=== clusterY
```

Just to show that the clustering works, we note that some of these clusters are very uniform. For example, *clusterY* contains six projects, all from 1979, and all with mostly repeated values. In the following, the columns marked *rdctsvTaApvlmTS* hold values for *rely, data, cplx, time, stor, virt, turn, acap, aexp, pcap, vexp, lexp, modp, tool, sced* (respectively). Also, if a value is the same as the one above, this is shown with a "ditto" mark, ".".

```
            year rdctsvTaApvlmTS ksloc effort
            ==== =============== ===== =====
project 88: 1979 424332233334432 9.7 = 25.2
project 89:   . ..............  8.2 =   36
project 90:   . ..............  7.7 = 31.2
project 91:   . ..............  3.5 = 10.8
project 92:   . ..............  2.2 =  8.4
project 93:   . ..............  0.9 =  8.4
```

Other clusters are more diverse. For example, *clusterX* contains data from nearly 10 years of software development. As might be expected, those projects are not all similar so there are fewer ditto marks:

```
            year rdctsvTaApvlmTS  ksloc  effort
            ==== ================ =====  ======
project 52: 1977 345332343523432    70 =  278
project 53: 1979 5.4553.55.34.4.   227 = 1181
project 54:    . 43.4424343.3253    50 =  370
project 55: 1980 34.5...43424432 177.9 = 1248
project 56: 1984 .2.36.2.433.3.3  32.5 =   60
project 57: 1986 .3.433333..3...    16 =  114
```

12.5.4 APPLYING CHUNK TO OTHER MODELS

CHUNK recursively divides data in the format of the *nasa93()* function shown above. So, to apply CHUNK to different data, write another function like *nasa93*.

Also, CHUNK needs to know some meta-knowledge about the data. For example, column of data, CHUNK needs to know the low and high value.

```
def lohi(m,x):
  if m == nasa93:
    if   x==16: return 0,1000    # range of KLOC
    elif x==0 : return 1971,1987 # years
    else      : return 1,6 # 1..6 = vlow,low,nom,
                   #          hi,vhi,xhi
  else:
    raise Exception('[%s] unknown' % m.__name__)
```

Sometimes, there is knowledge that some variables are more important than others. In the case of *nasa93*, we have no such knowledge so everything has the same weight.

```
def weight(m,x):
  if m == nasa93:
    return 1
  else:
    raise Exception('[%s] unknown' % m.__name__)
```

CHUNK groups together projects with similar decisions. To do that, CHUNK isolates those decisions (which it calls *dec*) from the objectives (which it calls *obj*).

```
def project2Slots(project = nasa93()):
  "Returns 'Slots'- a struct with named fields."
  return [Slots( dec = col[:-1],
                 obj = [col[-1]
         ]) for col in project]
```

In summary, to apply CHUNK to other data, write a new model function (like *nasa93*) then modify *lohi* and *weight* to add in the meta-knowledge. Optionally, you may also need to modify *project2Slots* to convert your model's data format into the *Slots* needed by CHUNK.

12.6 **INSIDE CHUNK**
12.6.1 **ROADMAP TO FUNCTIONS**

As shown below, *chunk* is the main function that recursively divides the data. In that division, the *dist* function reports the distance between data items (and that function is helped by *normalize* and *squaredDifferences*).

To divide the data, we use *fastdiv*, which in turn uses *twoDistantPoints* to separate the data. Note that the main *chunk* function recurses on the divisions generated by *fastdiv*. That recursion is controlled by the parameters initialized in *settings*.

After that, this code is all low-level Python tricks such as *align*, which pretty prints columns of data. Two other important tricks are the *leafs* iterator (that walks over the tree of clusters found by *chunk*) and *Slots* which is a generic Python struct that supports reading and writing to names fields.

Finally, the function *_nasa93* shows an example of how to chunk the *nasa93* data, shown above.

All these functions are detailed, below.

12.6.2 **DISTANCE CALCULATIONS**

CHUNK finds groups of similar things. But what does "similar" mean?

To answer that question, CHUNK uses the following *dist* function. This function excepts two examples *i,j* from some model *m*. It then decides *how* to compare them (the default is to use decisions *dec* collected together by *project2Slots*—see above). Next, *dist* sums the squares of the differences between each part of the example. Finally, *dist* returns the square root of that sum, normalized to the range zero to one.

```
def dist(m,i,j, how=lambda x: x.dec):
  "Euclidean distance 0 <= d <= 1 between decisions"
  d1,d2 = how(i), how(j)
  deltas, n = 0, 0
  for d,x in enumerate(d1):
    y = d2[d]
    v1 = normalize(m, d, x)
    v2 = normalize(m, d, y)
    w  = weight(m,d)
    deltas,n = squaredDifference(m,v1,v2,w,deltas,n)
  return deltas**0.5 / (n+0.0001)**0.5
```

(Aside: the last line adds in 0.0001 to avoid any divide-by-zero errors.)

12.6.2.1 *Normalize*

When computing distances, it is standard practice to *normalize* all numeric values to the range zero to one, min to max. To do that, CHUNK uses the *lohi* function described above.

```
def normalize(m,x,value) :
  if not The.normalize   : return value
  if value == The.missing : return value
```

```
if isinstance(value,str) : return value
lo, hi = lohi(m,x)
return (value - lo) / (hi - lo + 0.0001)
```

As seen above, *normalize* has some special cases. First, if some global flag has disabled normalization, we just return the unaltered value. Similarly, if we are trying to normalize some missing value or some nonnumeric value, we also return the unaltered value.

12.6.2.2 SquaredDifference

The *dist* function needs to compute the square of the differences between two values $v1,v2$ from some model *m*. It is assumed that each value is weighted; i.e., it can add up to some amount *most* to the distance measure. This is done using the *squaredDifference* function, which uses some distance heuristic first proposed by Aha [2]. For example, if in doubt, assume the maximum distance. Such doubts arise if (e.g.) we are comparing missing values.

```
def squaredDifference(m,v1,v2,most,sum=0,n=0):
  def furthestFromV1() :
    return  0 if v1 > 0.5 else 1
  if not v1 == v2 == The.missing:
    if v1 == The.missing:
      v1,v2 = v2,v1 # at the very least, v1 is known
    if isinstance(v1,str) and isinstance(v2,str):
      if v2 == The.missing or v1 != v2 :
        inc = 1
    else:
      if v2 == The.missing: v2 = furthestFromV1()
      inc = (v1 - v2)**2
  return (sum + most*inc, # sum of incs, so far
          n   + most) # sum of max incs, so far
```

Note that the *squaredDifference* function knows how to handle numerics as well as nonnumerics differently than numerics. Two nonnumerics have zero distance if they are the same (and distance is equal to max, otherwise).

12.6.3 DIVIDING THE DATA

12.6.3.1 FastDiv

With the above machinery, we can very quickly recursively divide some training data in half using *fastdiv*. This function finds the distance *c* between two distance items *west, east*. All data has some distance *a, b* to *west, east*. Using *a, b, c*, the *fastdiv* function uses the cosine rule to sort the data along where it falls on a line running from *west* to *east*. This function then returns the data, divided on the median value.

```
def fastdiv(m,data,details, how):
  ''Divide data at median of two distant items.''
  west, east = twoDistantPoints(m,data,how)
  c    = dist(m, west, east, how)
  for i in data:
    a    = dist(m,i, west, how)
```

```
  b   = dist(m,i, east, how)
  i.x = (a*a + c*c - b*b)/(2*c) # cosine rule
data = sorted(data,key=lambda i: i.x)
n    = len(data)/2
details.also(west=west, east=east, c=c, cut=data[n].x)
return data[:n], data[n:]
```

12.6.3.2 TwoDistantPoints

CHUNK is fast because it uses the linear-time "FastMap" heuristic [120] to find the *twoDistantPoints*. This heuristic starts by picking any item at random. Next, it finds the furthest item from the first pick. Finally, it finds the furthest item from the second item. Note that this is fast as it requires only one scan of the data for each pick. While the two found items may not be the most distant points, they are far enough away to guide data division.

```
def twoDistantPoints(m,data,how):
  def furthest(i):
    out,d= i,0
    for j in data:
      tmp = dist(m,i,j,how)
      if tmp > d: out,d = j,tmp
    return out
  one  = any(data)        # 1) pick any thing
  west = furthest(one)    # 2) far from thing
  east = furthest(west)   # 3) far from west
  return west,east
```

While *twoDistantPoints* looks simple, it actually offers a profound summation of important aspects of a data set. According to John Platt, this FastMap heuristic belongs to a class of algorithms that find approximations to the eigenvectors of a data set [359]. Spectral learners [201] use these eigenvectors to reason along the most important dimensions in a data set.

12.6.3.3 Settings

By applying *fastdiv* recursively, we can build a binary tree whose leaves contain similar examples. That tree generation is controlled by the following *settings*. By default, we will stop when any leaf has less than *minSize=10* or if we have recursed more that *depthMax=10* items. Also, just to make sure we get at least a few branches in the tree, we will recurse at least *minSize=2* times. Further, when we recurse, if *verbose=True*, we will trace the transversely by printing one *b4* string for each level of the recursion. Finally, when computing distances, this code uses *how=x.dec*; i.e., the decisions of each item in the data.

```
def settings(**has):
  "Return control settings for recursive descent."
  return Slots(minSize  = 10,     # min leaf size
               depthMin= 2,       # no pruning till depthMin
               depthMax= 10,      # max tree depth
               b4       = '|.. ', # indent string
               verbose = False,   # show trace info?
               how= lambda x:x.dec # how to measure distance
  ).override(has)
```

12.6.3.4 Chunk (main function)

Finally, we arrive at the main *chunk* function. This function uses the above *settings* to build a tree that recursively divides the data. The *chunk* function holds those *settings* in its *slots* variable (which is set on the first line of the function, if it is not already known). Local functions within *chunk* use these *slots* to control how the tree is built.

```python
def chunk(m,data,slots=None, lvl=0,up=None):
  "Return a tree of split data."
  slots = slots or settings()
  def tooFew() :
    return len(data) < slots.minSize
  def tooDeep():
    return lvl > slots.depthMax
  def show(suffix):
    if slots.verbose:
      print slots.b4*lvl + str(len(data)) + suffix
  tree= Slots(_up=up,value=None,_left=None,_right=None)
  if tooDeep() or tooFew():
    show(".")
    tree.value = data
  else:
    show("")
    wests,easts = fastdiv(m, data, tree, slots.how)
    if not worse(wests, easts, tree) :
      tree._left  = chunk(m, wests, slots, lvl+1, tree)
    if not worse(easts, wests, tree) :
      tree._right = chunk(m, easts, slots, lvl+1, tree)
  return tree

def worse(down1,down2,here): return False
```

Note some subtleties in the above code. First, because we use *fastdiv*, our *chunk* function is a very fast method to divide data.

Second, the function *worse* is a hook for any clever pruning you might want to add to this process (this *chunk* function only recurses on subtrees that are not *worse*). While we do not use *worse* here, this function could be used to prune subtrees that fail some test; e.g., that do not reduce the variance of the current tree.

Third, *chunk* returns a tree of *Slots* where each node contains pointers to its *_left* and *_right* kids as well as a pointer *_up* to the parent node (which, for the root node, points to *None*). Note that all leaves of this tree have empty child pointers. Such childless leaves hold the items that fall into that leaf in the *value* field.

12.6.4 SUPPORT UTILITIES

12.6.4.1 Some standard tricks

```python
import sys,math,random
sys.dont_write_bytecode = True # disable writing .pyc files
seed = random.seed      # convenient shorthand
```

```
any  = random.choice   # another convenient shorthand

def say(x):
  "Output a string, no trailing new line."
  sys.stdout.write(x)

def showd(d):
  """Catch key values to string, sorted on keys.
     Ignore hard to read items (marked with '_')."""
  return ' '.join([':%s %s' % (k,v)
                  for k,v in
                  sorted(d.items())
                  if not "_'' in k])
```

Slots is based on a Peter Norvig trick from http://norvig.com/python-iaq.html. When all you want to do is create an object that holds data in several fields, the following will do. For an example of using *Slots*, see *settings* (above).

```
class Slots():
  "Place to read/write named slots."
  id = -1
  def __init__(i,**d) :
    i.id = Slots.id = Slots.id + 1
    i.override(d)
  def override(i,d): i.__dict__.update(d); return i
  def also(i, **d) : i.override(d)
  def __eq__(i,j)  : return i.id == j.id
  def __ne__(i,j)  : return i.id != j.id
  def __repr__(i)  : return '{' + showd(i.__dict__) + '}'
```

Note that *Slots* can pretty print themselves using the *showd* function (shown above). Also, as our *Slots* have a unique *id*, we can quickly test for equality and inequality.

12.6.4.2 Tree iterators

To simplify the processing of trees, we define some iterators to return all *nodes* or just the *leafs* of the tree.

```
def nodes(t,lvl=0):
  "Iterator. Return all nodes."
  if t:
    yield lvl,t
    for t1 in [t._left,t._right]:
      for lvl1,leaf in nodes(t1,lvl+1):
        yield lvl1,leaf

def leafs(t):
  "Iterator: returns all leaf nodes."
  for lvl,node in nodes(t):
    if not node._left and not node._right:
      yield lvl,node
```

12.6.4.3 Pretty printing

The *ditto* function marks repeated entries in a column with a "..".

```python
def ditto(lst,old,mark="."):
  """Show 'mark' if an item of  lst is same as old.
     As a side-effect, update cache of 'old' values."""
  out = []
  for i,now in enumerate(lst):
    before = old.get(i,None) # get old it if exists
    out    += [mark if  before == now else now]
    old[i] = now # next time, 'now' is the 'old' value
  return out # the lst with ditto marks inserted
```

Once we "ditto" a list of lists, we have to lay it out and pretty print it for the users.

```python
def align(lsts):
  "Print, filled to max width of each column."
  widths = {}
  for lst in lsts: # pass1- find column max widths
    for n,x in enumerate(lst):
      w = len('%s' % x)
      widths[n] = max(widths.get(n,0),w)
  for lst in lsts: # pass2- print to max width
    for n,x in enumerate(lst):
      say(('%s' % x).rjust(widths[n],' '))
    print ""
  print ""
```

12.7 PUTTING IT ALL TOGETHER

The following code is an example of how to use *chunk*.

12.7.1 _nasa93

The following code initializes some globals then builds a tree of clusters from *nasa93* using *chunk*. Then, using the *leafs* iterator, this code traverses the leaf clusters of the tree to pretty prints the clusters in aligned columns (using ditto marks).

```python
The = Slots(normalize=True,missing="?")

def _chunkDemo(model=nasa93):
  seed(1)
  data   = project2Slots( model() )
  options= settings(verbose = True,
                    minSize = len(data)**0.5)
  tree   = chunk(model,  data ,options)
  eg,cid = 0,0
```

```
for lvl,leaf in leafs(tree):
  context = leaf.value
  cid += 1
  print "----| cluster",cid,"|","-"*35
  lines  = []
  dittos = {}
  for row in sorted(context,key=lambda x:x.dec[0]):
    eg += 1
    pre = ["project ", eg,": "]
    params       = ditto(row.dec,dittos)
    params[0]    = str(params[0]) + '' "
    params[-1]   = '' '' + str(params[-1])
    lines    += [pre + params + ['' = "] + row.obj]
  align(lines)

_chunkDemo()
```

Note that we override the default *settings* to offer control values that make more sense for small data sets like *nasa93* (see the *minSize* setting).

To change the default load behavior, change the last line of *chnunk.py* (which is currently *_chunkDemo()*).

12.8 USING CHUNK

There are many applications of CHUNK. As discussed in Section 12.4, there are many reasons to group together related SE data items prior to inferencing. Those reasons include variance reduction, anomaly detection, building a certification envelope, incremental learning, compression, and optimization. For other applications of grouping together related SE projects, see the next six chapters of this book.

Before going on, we offer one quick result from using CHUNK. The following result comes from a recent paper [291] that asked the question "does locality matter?" That paper asked if, pragmatically speaking, we can ignore local contexts and just apply standard learners to all available data. Specifically, that study compared the effects of using *global rules* learned from all data or *local rules* learned from small clusters found within the data. To build the *global rules*, a rule learner was applied to all the data. To build the *local rules*, the same rule learner was applied as follows:

1. Data was divided as per CHUNK: the Fastmap heuristic was applied to recursive divide the data and to generate trees of clusters.
2. *Local rules* were learned in each cluster to select for instances with least defects or effort.
3. Each cluster C_1 was asked "who do you envy"; i.e., which neighboring cluster C_2 has better defect or effort values than C_1.
4. For each C_1, C_2 pair, rules from C_2 were applied to C_1 to select some instances.

(The reader may recall that this is the *contrast pruning* method discussed in Chapter 10.)

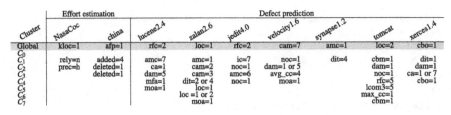

FIGURE 12.3

Rules learned to reduce effort or defects. Data sets from http://openscience.us/repo. From Ref. [291].

This study then reflected on the median m and maximum M defect or effort values seen in

- The original data, denoted m_0, M_0.
- The instances selected by the global rules, denoted m_1, M_1.
- The instances selected by the local rules, denoted m_2, M_2.

The good news was that learning local rules from CHUNKs of data was significantly advantageous.

- The median values of these samples m_0, m_1, m_2 were significantly different;
- The local rules worked best by a wide margin ($m_0 > m_1 > m_2$ and $m_1/m_2 = 1.60$);
- The global rules let more worst-case instances slip through ($M_2 > M_1$). In fact, in the average case, the instances with worst defects or effort were 256% worse after applying the global rules (compared to the local rules).

The bad news was that, as shown in Figure 12.3, the rules learned in this manner varied widely from cluster to cluster. In that figure, C_i denotes a cluster and C_0 is the cluster with best score: no rule was needed there. In this experiment, numerics were discretized into seven equal frequency bins so (e.g.) $kloc = 1$ is "set lines of code to min." The *global rules* are shown in row one of that figure; all the other rows show the *local rules*. The key thing to note in Figure 12.3 is that in nearly all cases, the local rules are different than the global rules. Also, the local rules were almost always different.

In summary: *locality matters, very much.* Different parts of SE data are best modeled by very different models. And if we reason over all the data then we generate underperforming models.

12.9 CLOSING REMARKS

This chapter has argued that SE data needs to be *contextualized* before it is shared. Manual contextualizations can be useful but can also be problematic. Automatic contextualizations, on the other hand, can easily be discovered by simple tools such as the CHUNK code shown here.

CROSS-COMPANY LEARNING: HANDLING THE DATA DROUGHT

13

In summary, this chapter proposes the following data analysis pattern:

Name:	Relevancy filtering
Also known as:	Transfer learning [352].
Intent:	Software defect prediction, when there is insufficient local information to build a software defect predictor.
Motivation:	Experiments with sharing data for defect prediction found very large false alarm rates in detectors built from shared data. This work checked if using just a small amount of *most relevant* data would allow for good local predictors.
Solution:	For each code function in some local project, find their 10 nearest neighboring functions in other projects. Combine together (rejecting repeats) all 10-nearest neighbors (NNs) for all the test suite. Train a Naive Bayes classifier on that combined data. Use that to predict defects in the functions of the local data.
Constraints:	Functions from other projects must be described using the same variables as the local functions. Also, NN methods have to scale across all the projects.
Applicability:	The research described in this chapter spawned an entire subfield of defect prediction software engineering [427]. Prior to this work, it was very unclear if data from one project could be usefully shared with another [218]. After this paper, a swarm of other papers showed that such sharing was possible for effort estimation and/or defect prediction (e.g., Refs. [222, 224, 277, 291, 338, 452]).
Related to:	The CHUNK code of Chapter 12 could be used to optimize the search for NNs used by relevancy filtering.

This chapter presents a case of contextualization for defect prediction, in a setting where a company does not track defect-related data, by demonstrating the applicability of cross-company (CC) data for building localized defect predictors. The material in this chapter is based on a journal article [427] and it was rewritten throughout to adapt the technical content for the book's target audience with significantly new introduction, motivation, and closing sections, as well as new discussions on the feasibility of the approach and possible future directions based on the review of follow-up studies.

Common attempts for defect prediction modeling assume the availability of local data (i.e., within-company predictors). In other words, building analytical models require a company to have a local data repository, where project metrics and defect information from past projects are stored. However, few companies apply defect predictors in practice and we suspect that one reason for that is the lack of local data repositories.

In order to overcome this issue, it is tempting to benefit from third-party data, e.g., public repositories (PROMISE [300]), open-source projects, and public data from other companies. But the following question rises immediately:

> When a company lacks local data, is it feasible to rely upon third-party data sources for making decisions based on the outcomes of the resulting defect predictors?

This chapter argues the case for the potential utilization of cross-company data using simple tricks from analogy-based learning to set the right "context" for cross-company defect predictors. Specifically, this chapter assesses the relative merits of cross-company (CC) versus within-company (WC) data for defect prediction, and identifies the conditions when CC models might come in handy, giving hints on how to find local regions of third-party data that are useful to predict defects in local projects. In this respect, this chapter is driven by the following set of questions:

Can CC data be useful for an organization? To address this question, we will identify the conditions under which cross-company data should be preferred to within-company data by comparing the performance of defect predictors learned from WC data to those learned from CC data.

How to cleanup CC data for local tuning? CC data includes information from many diverse projects and are heterogeneous compared to WC data. Hence, in the second analysis we will use only a "relevant" subset of the available CC data—that is, similar to WC data—and investigate the effect of data homogeneity on the defect prediction performance. We will use a relevancy filter by applying a simple NN filtering to CC data for automatically constructing a locally tuned repository.

How much local data does an organization need for a local model? In the third analysis, we will focus on WC models and determine the smallest amount of local data needed for constructing a model. We employ an incremental learning approach to WC data in order determine the number of samples in local repositories for building defect prediction models.

How trustworthy are these results? We will use only data from publicly available NASA subcontractor projects in our three analyses to answer the questions above. In order to check the external validity of our results, this last analysis replicates the first two on projects from a company that has no ties with NASA or its subcontractors: a white goods manufacturer developing software controllers for home appliances and located in another continent!

13.1 MOTIVATION

Before we dive deeper into the details of the analyses in this chapter, let's take a step back and try to answer another question: *Why study WC versus CC?*

The genesis of this work was several frustrating years working at NASA trying to collect data on new projects. This proved difficult to do, for a variety of reasons (including feuding NASA centers and contractors trying to maintain some control over the information flow to the client). Several times in that process, we asked "Is it necessary to collect new data? Can't we just apply old data"

Then, in the middle of 2007, we had an opportunity to evaluate CC data usage on a Turkish software development company. That company worked in a highly competitive market and a decrease in their bug rate of even 1% had an economic benefit to them. However, that company had no historical data with which to train its defect detectors. We therefore trained a defect detector on NASA data and applied it to the Turkish software.

Much to our surprise, that detector could "adequately" predict errors within Turkish software ("adequate" in the sense that the Turkish client looked at the code that triggered our detectors, found bugs, and was subsequently interested enough to request more studies of this nature). Based on that experience, we saw

- The business benefits in using CC data (no need to wait for local data collection);
- The adequacy of the learned detectors.

And this chapter is about the details on what we really did behind the scenes.

13.2 SETTING THE GROUND FOR ANALYSES

The analyses of this chapter use data from 10 projects tabulated in Tables 13.1, 13.2, which are available at the PROMISE repository [300]. The data consist of static code features and defect-related information. The project data are taken from software developed in different geographical locations across North America (NASA) and Turkey (SOFTLAB), so the static code features that are available for each project slightly differ. This is an important limitation for CC data studies: if you want to utilize CC data, you should gather some local data from scratch or prune the existing local data so that the same set of features are available locally. Table 13.3 lists the common features in both sources used in the analyses throughout this chapter.

Table 13.1 Descriptions of 10 Software Projects Used in This Chapter

Source	Project	Language	Description
NASA	pc1	C++	Flight software for earth orbiting satellite
NASA	kc1	C++	Storage management for ground data
NASA	kc2	C++	Storage management for ground data
NASA	cm1	C++	Spacecraft instrument
NASA	kc3	JAVA	Storage management for ground data
NASA	mw1	C++	A zero gravity experiment related to combustion
SOFTLAB	ar4	C	Embedded controller for white goods
SOFTLAB	ar3	C	Embedded controller for white goods
NASA	mc2	C++	Video guidance system
SOFTLAB	ar5	C	Embedded controller for white goods

The rows labeled "NASA" come from NASA aerospace projects while the rows labeled "SOFTLAB" come from a Turkish software company writing applications for domestic appliances. From Ref. [427].

Table 13.2 Summary of Data from 10 Software Projects of Table 13.1, Sorted in Order of Number of Functional Units

| Source | Project | (# Modules) | | | % Defective |
		Examples	Features	loc	
NASA	pc1	1,109	21	25,924	6.94
NASA	kc1	845	21	42,965	15.45
NASA	kc2	522	21	19,259	20.49
NASA	cm1	498	21	14,763	9.83
NASA	kc3	458	39	7749	9.38
NASA	mw1	403	37	8341	7.69
SOFTLAB	ar4	107	29	9196	18.69
SOFTLAB	ar3	63	29	5624	12.70
NASA	mc2	61	39	6134	32.29
SOFTLAB	ar5	36	29	2732	22.22
				4102	

From Ref. [427].

Table 13.3 Static Code Features Shared by NASA and SOFTLAB Projects

#	Feature	NASA Shared	All Shared
1	*branchcount*	X	X
2	*codeandcommentloc*	X	X
3	*commentloc*	X	X
4	*cyclomaticcomplexity*	X	X
5	*designcomplexity*	X	X
6	*halsteaddifficulty*	X	X
7	*halsteadeffort*	X	X
8	*halsteaderror*	X	X
9	*halsteadlength*	X	X
10	*halsteadtime*	X	X
11	*halsteadvolume*	X	X
12	*totaloperands*	X	X
13	*totaloperators*	X	X
14	*uniqueoperands*	X	X
15	*uniqueoperators*	X	X
16	*executableloc*	X	X
17	*totalloc*	X	X
18	*halsteadcontent*	X	
19	*essentialcomplexity*	X	
	Total	19	17

From Ref. [427].

13.2.1 WAIT . . . IS THIS REALLY CC DATA?

While NASA and SOFTLAB are one single *source* of data, there are several projects within each source. For example, NASA is really an umbrella organization used to coordinate and fund a large and diverse set of projects.

- The NASA data was collected from across the United States over a a period of five years from numerous NASA contractors working at different geographical locations.
- These projects represent a wide array of projects, including satellite instrumentation, ground control systems, and partial flight control modules (i.e., Altitude Control).
- The data sets also represent a wide range of code reuse; some of the projects are 100% new, and some are modifications to previously deployed code.

That is, even if we explore just the NASA data sets, we can still examine issues of cross- versus within-company data use. Nevertheless, using our connections with the Turkish software industry, we collected new data sets, in a format that matches that of NASA, from a Turkish white goods manufacturer. The SOFTLAB data sets ({ar3, ar4, ar5}) in Table 13.1, are the controller software for a washing machine, a dishwasher, and a refrigerator!

In summary, seven data sets in Table 13.1 are from NASA projects developed at different sites by different teams; hence, we treat each of them as if they were from seven different companies. The remaining three data sets are from a Turkish company, collected from software for domestic home appliances. Therefore, we make the assumption that we use 10 projects from 8 different companies in our analysis.

13.2.2 MINING THE DATA

In prior work we have explored a range of data mining methods for defect prediction and found that classifiers based on Bayes theorem yields better performance than rule-based methods (i.e., decision trees, oneR), for the Table 13.1 NASA data Ref. [305].[1] An extensive study by Lessmann et.al also shows that Naive Bayes performs equivalently well with 15 other methods [249]. Therefore, we find Naive Bayes as a viable choice as a classifier to use in our analysis.

In all our experiments, the data was pre-processed as follows:

- As the number of features in each data table is not consistent, we restricted our data to only the features shared by all data sets (see Table 13.3).
- Previously [305], we have observed that all the numeric distributions in the data features are exponential in nature. It is therefore useful to apply a "log-filter" to all numerics N with $\log(N)$.
- Each project in Table 13.2 contains information from many modules; the smallest unit of functionality, i.e., methods. To learn defect predictors, the project data are augmented with one dependent variable holding boolean values for "defects detected."
- Finally, the data mining task is to find combinations of static code features that predict the boolean value of the dependent variable.

---

[1] SOFTLAB data were not available at that time.

We measured the performance of the predictor using p_d, p_f, and balance. If $\{A, B, C, D\}$ are the true negatives, false negatives, false positives, and true positives (respectively) found by a defect predictor, then

$$p_d = recall = D/(B + D) \tag{13.1}$$

$$p_f = C/(A + C) \tag{13.2}$$

$$bal = balance = 1 - \frac{\sqrt{(0 - p_f)^2 + (1 - p_d)^2}}{\sqrt{2}} \tag{13.3}$$

All these values range from zero to one. Better and *larger* balances fall *closer* to the desired zone of no false alarms ($p_f = 0$) and 100% detection ($p_d = 1$).

The results were visualized using *quartile charts*. To generate these charts, the performance measures for an analysis are sorted to isolate the median and the lower and upper quartile of numbers. For example:

$$\overbrace{\{4, 7, 15, 20, 31,}^{q1} \overbrace{40}^{median}, 52, 64, \overbrace{70, 81, 90\}}^{q4}$$

In our quartile charts, the upper and lower quartiles are marked with black lines; the median is marked with a black dot; and vertical bars are added to mark the 50% percentile value. The above numbers would therefore be drawn as follows:

$$0\% \,|{-} \quad \bullet \;| \quad {-}\!\!\!- \quad |100\%$$

The Mann-Whitney U test was used to test for statistical difference between results. This nonparametric test replaces performance measure values (i.e., p_d, p_f, bal) with their rank inside the population of all sorted values. Such nonparametric tests are recommended in data mining since many of the performance distributions are non-Gaussian [96].

13.2.3 MAGIC TRICK: NN RELEVANCY FILTERING

In order to pick the most relevant data from CC sources, or to leave the irrelevant ones out, we employed a relevancy filter inspired by analogy-based learning. Our idea behind filtering is to collect similar instances together in order to construct a learning (e.g., CC) set that is homogeneous with the validation (e.g., local) set.

More formally, we try to introduce a bias in the model by using training data that are similar to the validation data characteristics. While a bias is not desired in general, it is what we seek on purpose, since in our case we can control the bias against removing the noise in CC data (i.e., extraneous factors). We simply use the k-Nearest Neighbor (k-NN) method to measure the similarity between the validation set and the training *candidates*. The similarity measure is the Euclidean distance between the static code features of validation and training candidate sets. The expected outcome of the filtering part is to obtain a subset of available CC data that shows similar characteristics to the local code culture.

The details of the NN filter are as follows: We calculate the pairwise Euclidean distances between the validation set and the *candidate* training set (i.e., all CC data). Let N be the number of validation set size. For each validation data, we pick its $k = 10$ NNs from the candidate training set.[2] Then we

[2] Caveat: We did not optimize the value of k for each project. We simply used a constant $k = 10$.

come up with a total of $10 \times N$ similar data points (i.e., module feature vectors). These $10 \times N$ samples may not be unique (i.e., a single data sample can be an NN of many data samples in the validation set). Using only unique samples, we form the training set and use a random 90% of it for training a predictor.

13.3 ANALYSIS #1: CAN CC DATA BE USEFUL FOR AN ORGANIZATION?
13.3.1 DESIGN

Our goal is to determine whether using cross-company data is beneficial for constructing defect predictors and to identify the conditions under which cross-company data should be preferred to within-company data. Our first WC-versus-CC analysis follows the pseudo code given in Table 13.4, for all seven NASA projects of Table 13.1. For each project, test sets were built from 10% of the data, selected at random. Defect predictors were then learned from

- CC data: all data from the other six projects.
- WC data: remaining 90% data of that project.

Most of the Table 13.1 data come from systems written in "C/C++" but at least one of the systems was written in JAVA. For cross-company data, an industrial practitioner may not have access to detailed

---

Table 13.4 Pseudocode for Analysis #1

```
DATA = [PC1, KC1, KC2, CM1, KC3, MW1, MC2]       // all available data
LEARNER = [Naive Bayes]                          //  defect predictor

C_FEATURES <- Find common features IN DATA
FOR EACH data IN DATA
        data = Select C_FEATURES in data         // use common features
END
REPEAT 20 TIMES
      FOR EACH data in DATA
                CC_TRAIN = DATA - data           // cross-company training data
                WC_TRAIN = random 90\% of data   // within-company training data
                TEST = data - WC_TRAIN           // shared test data

                //construct predictor from CC data
                CC_PREDICTOR = Train LEARNER with CC_TRAIN
                // construct predictor from WC data
                WC_PREDICTOR = Train LEARNER with WC_TRAIN
                //Evaluate both predictors on the same test data
                [cc_pd, cc_pf, cc_bal] = CC_PREDICTOR on TEST
                [wc_pd, wc_pf, wc_bal] = WC_PREDICTOR on TEST
      END
END
```

From Ref. [427].

meta-knowledge (e.g., whether it was developed in "C" or JAVA). They may only be aware that data, from an unknown source, are available for download from a certain url. To replicate that scenario, we will make no use of our meta-knowledge about Table 13.1.

In order to control for *order effects* (where the learned theory is unduly affected by the order of the examples), our procedure was repeated 20 times, randomizing the order of data in each project each time. In all, we ran 280 tests to compare WC-versus-CC:

$$(2 \text{ data sources}) * (20 \text{ randomized orderings}) * (7 \text{ projects})$$

For this analysis, only the features that are common in all NASA projects, a total of 19 features, are used. These features are marked in the "NASA Shared" column of Table 13.3.

13.3.2 RESULTS FROM ANALYSIS #1

Figure 13.1 shows the $\{p_d, p_f\}$ quartile charts for CC versus WC data averaged over seven NASA projects. The pattern is very clear: CC data dramatically increases *both* the probability of detection and the probability of false alarms. The p_d results are particularly striking.

For cross-company predictors:

- 50% of the p_d values are at or above 97%;
- 75% of the p_d values are at or above 83%;
- And all the p_d values are at or over 50%.

To the best of our knowledge, Figure 13.1 includes the largest p_d values ever reported from these data. However, these very high p_d values come at some considerable cost. We observe in Figure 13.1 that the median false alarm rate has changed from 29% (with WC) to 64% (with CC) and the maximum p_f rate now reaches 100%. Note that a 100% p_f rate means that all defect-free modules are classified as defective, which yields inspection of all these modules unnecessarily and contradicts with the purpose of defect prediction. However, it is not right to assess the general behavior of the CC defect predictors with such an extreme case. We mention this issue in order to clarify that high false alarm rates may be prohibitive in the practical application of defect predictors.

We explain these increases in p_d, p_f with the *extraneous factors* in CC data. More specifically, using a large training set (e.g., seven projects in Table 13.1) informs of not only the sources of errors, but also numerous irrelevancies. For example, the defect characteristics of software modules with different complexity levels or sizes may differ [239]. In this context, a complicated search algorithm's metrics

Treatment		min	Q1	median	Q3	max
p_d	CC	50	83	97	100	100
	WC	17	63	75	82	100
p_f	CC	14	53	64	91	100
	WC	0	24	29	36	73

FIGURE 13.1

Analysis #1 results averaged over seven NASA projects. Numeric results on left; quartile charts on right. "Q1" and "Q3" denote the 25% and 75% percentile points (respectively). The upper quartile of the first row is not visible as it runs from 100% to 100%; i.e., it has zero length. From Ref. [427].

Table 13.5 Summary of U-Test Results (95% Confidence): Moving from WC to CC

Group	p_d WC → CC	p_f WC → CC	Projects	|Projects|
a	increased	increased	CM1 KC1 KC2 MC2 MW1 PC1	6
b	same	same	KC3	1

For all projects' results, see Figure 13.2. From Ref. [427].

are irrelevant to the defective behavior of a simple *sum* function. There are few modules with extreme characteristics (i.e., complexity, size) in a single project, so their effect on the overall model are limited. However, when data from multiple companies are combined, the number of these extreme cases, and hence their cumulative effect on the overall model, increase significantly. Therefore, factors such as programming language constructs (i.e., object oriented vs. procedural) and project specific requirements (i.e., availability, speed) that have impacts on the module characteristics can be considered as extraneous factors.

Hence, large training sets increase the error detection rates (i.e., p_d) because there are more known sources of errors. However, they also increase the probability of false alarms (p_f) as there are more *extraneous factors* introduced to the analysis. We will test the validity of this claim in the next analysis by using the relevancy filtering trick.

13.3.3 CHECKING THE ANALYSIS #1 RESULTS

Once a *general result* is defined (e.g., defect predictors learned from CC projects dramatically increase both p_f and p_d), it is good practice to check for specific exceptions to that pattern. Table 13.5 shows a summary of results when U tests with $\alpha = 0.05$ were applied to test results from each of the seven projects, *in isolation*, and Figure 13.2 shows the $\{p_d, p_f\}$ quartile charts for Analysis #1 for each NASA project.

- For six projects, the general result holds (i.e., both (p_d, p_f) increases if defect predictors learned from CC projects are used rather than defect predictors learned from WC projects (see group a in Table 13.5).
- For one project, there is no difference in the performances of the defect predictors learned from CC and WC projects (see group b in Table 13.5).

13.3.4 DISCUSSION OF ANALYSIS #1

When practitioners use defect predictors with high false alarm rates (e.g., the 64% reported above), they must allocate a large portion of their debugging budget to the unfruitful exploration of erroneous alarms.

In our industrial work, we have sometimes seen several situations in which detectors with high false alarms are useful.

Table (cm1)

Treatment		min	Q1	median	Q3	max
p_d	CC	80	100	100	100	100
	WC	40	60	80	100	100
p_f	CC	87	91	96	96	98
	WC	24	27	33	38	47

Table (kc1)

Treatment		min	Q1	median	Q3	max
p_d	CC	82	88	94	94	100
	WC	64	73	82	85	97
p_f	CC	47	49	51	53	57
	WC	27	34	36	38	40

Table (kc2)

Treatment		min	Q1	median	Q3	max
p_d	CC	82	91	91	100	100
	WC	55	73	82	91	100
p_f	CC	57	62	64	74	81
	WC	14	24	31	33	45

Table (kc3)

Treatment		min	Q1	median	Q3	max
p_d	CC	60	80	80	80	100
	WC	40	60	80	80	100
p_f	CC	14	19	24	31	38
	WC	10	17	21	26	36

Table (mc2)

Treatment		min	Q1	median	Q3	max
p_d	CC	50	67	83	100	100
	WC	17	33	67	67	83
p_f	CC	55	64	73	73	100
	WC	0	27	36	45	73

Table (mw1)

Treatment		min	Q1	median	Q3	max
p_d	CC	75	75	100	100	100
	WC	25	50	75	75	100
p_f	CC	50	55	63	66	82
	WC	13	18	21	29	37

Table (pc1)

Treatment		min	Q1	median	Q3	max
p_d	CC	88	100	100	100	100
	WC	38	63	63	75	88
p_f	CC	89	92	93	95	99
	WC	17	25	27	30	34

FIGURE 13.2

Analysis #1 results (project-wise) for NASA projects. From Ref. [427].

- *When the cost of missing the target is prohibitively expensive.* In mission critical or security applications, the goal of 100% detection may be demanded in all situations, regardless of the cost of chasing false alarms.
- *When only a small fraction of the data is returned.* Hayes et al. call this fraction *selectivity* and offer an extensive discussion of the merits of this measure [169].
- *When there is little or no cost in checking false alarms.*

Having said that, we have shown these results to five of our user groups in the United States and Turkey and none of them could accept false alarm rates as high as 64%. Therefore, the conditions under which the benefits of CC data (high probabilities of detection) outweigh their high costs (high false alarm rates) are not common.

In summary, for most software applications, very high p_f rates like the CC results of Figure 13.1 make the predictors impractical to use. This calls for further action and not to use CC data as-is. Analysis #2 is designed for this purpose.

13.4 ANALYSIS #2: HOW TO CLEANUP CC DATA FOR LOCAL TUNING?

The results of the first analysis restricts the use of CC data to a limited domain (i.e., mission critical) and may look discouraging at first glance. In the first analysis we explained our observations with the *extraneous factors*, that the results are affected by the irrelevant factors in CC data. In this section we hypothesize this claim and test for its validity.

13.4.1 DESIGN

In this analysis, we try to construct more homogeneous *defect* data sets from CC data in an automated manner. For this purpose we use the relevancy filtering method (i.e., NN), which is described earlier. The analysis design is given in Table 13.6. For this analysis, we use all common features available in NASA projects which is a total of 19 features; marked in the NASA Shared column of Table 13.3.

13.4.2 RESULTS

If the results of Analysis #1 are due to the extraneous factors in CC data (as we suspect), then we would expect lower p_f's in NN results than CC results. And indeed, the results indicate that using NN-filtered CC data significantly decreases the false alarms compared to CC data. Yet, we observe that p_d's have also decreased. However, false alarm rates are more dramatically decreased than detection rates as seen in Figure 13.3–Figure 13.6. For example, in the *CM*1 project, the median false alarm rate decreases nearly one third, from 91% to 33%, whereas the median detection rate slightly decreases from 94% to 82%. In all cases, predictors learned from NN data dramatically reduce the high false alarm rates associated with the use of cross-company data. Often that reduction halves the false alarm rate. For example, in MW1, the median false alarm rate drops from 68% (CC) to 33% (NN).

Showing that defect predictors learned from NN-filtered CC data are significantly better than the ones learned from CC data, the ideal result would be that models based on NN-filtered can be used as a surrogate for WC data-based models. This, in turn, would mean that developers could avoid the tedious and expensive work of local data collection.

Hence, we should also investigate the relation between the NN-filtered CC data and the WC data-based defect predictors. If defect predictors learned from NN-filtered CC data outperformed the ones learned from WC data then we would expect to notice two observations:

- *Observation1:* NN would have p_d values above or equal to WC's p_d. The examples displaying *Observation*1 are shown in Figure 13.3.
- *Observation2:* NN would have p_f values below or equal to WC's p_f. The examples displaying *Observation*2 are shown in Figure 13.5.

Table 13.6 Pseudocode for Analysis #2

```
DATA = [PC1, KC1, KC2, CM1, KC3, MW1, MC2]
LEARNER = [Naive Bayes]

C_FEATURES <- Find common features IN DATA
FOR EACH data IN DATA
        data = Select C_FEATURES in data
END
REPEAT 100 TIMES
        FOR EACH data in DATA
                WC_TRAIN = random 90\% of data
                TEST = data - WC_TRAIN
                CC_TRAIN = DATA - data

        //NN-Filtering: Select k=10 neighbors for each validation data

                FOR EACH test IN TEST
                        dist = L2_DISTANCE(test, CC_TRAIN)
                        NNCC_TRAIN <- 10 Samples in CC_TRAIN with min(dist)
                END

        //Use only unique samples from the union of all selected neighbors

                NNCC_TRAIN = UNIQUE(NNCC_TRAIN)

                NNCC_PREDICTOR = Train LEARNER with NNCC_TRAIN
                CC_PREDICTOR = Train LEARNER with CC_TRAIN
                WC_PREDICTOR = Train LEARNER with WC_TRAIN
                [nncc_pd, nncc_pf, nncc_bal] = NNCC_PREDICTOR on TEST
                [cc_pd, cc_pf, cc_bal] = CC_PREDICTOR on TEST
                [wc_pd, wc_pf, wc_bal] = WC_PREDICTOR on TEST
        END
END
```

From Ref. [427].

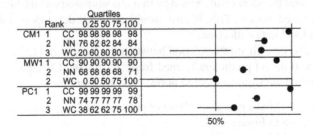

FIGURE 13.3

Analysis #2 PD results where $NN_{pd} \geq WC_{pd}$. Rankings computed via Mann-Whitney (95% confidence) comparing each row to all other rows. From Ref. [427].

	Rank		Quartiles 0	25	50	75	100
KC1	1	CC	94	94	94	94	94
	2	WC	64	76	82	85	94
	3	NN	60	64	65	66	69
KC2	1	CC	94	94	94	94	94
	2	WC	45	73	82	91	100
	2	NN	77	78	79	79	80
KC3	1	CC	81	81	81	84	84
	2	WC	20	60	80	100	100
	3	NN	60	63	65	67	70
MC2	1	CC	83	83	83	83	85
	2	WC	17	50	67	83	100
	3	NN	56	56	56	56	58

50%

FIGURE 13.4

Analysis #2 PD results for $NN_{Pd} < WC_{Pd}$. From Ref. [427].

	Rank		Quartiles 0	25	50	75	100
KC1	1	NN	22	23	24	25	27
	2	WC	26	32	35	37	43
	3	CC	59	60	60	60	60
KC2	1	NN	24	25	25	25	27
	1	WC	10	21	26	31	40
	2	CC	67	67	67	67	67
KC3	1	NN	17	18	18	19	20
	2	WC	7	17	21	26	31
	3	CC	26	27	27	27	27
MC2	1	NN	29	30	31	32	35
	2	WC	0	27	36	45	73
	3	CC	71	71	71	71	71

50%

FIGURE 13.5

Analysis #2 PF results for $NN_{Pf} \leq WC_{Pf}$. From Ref. [427].

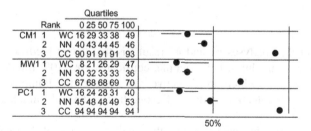

	Rank		Quartiles 0	25	50	75	100
CM1	1	WC	16	29	33	38	49
	2	NN	40	43	44	45	46
	3	CC	90	91	91	91	93
MW1	1	WC	8	21	26	29	47
	2	NN	30	32	33	33	36
	3	CC	67	68	68	69	70
PC1	1	WC	16	24	28	31	40
	2	NN	45	48	48	49	53
	3	CC	94	94	94	94	94

50%

FIGURE 13.6

Analysis #2 PF results where $NN_{Pf} > WC_{Pf}$. From Ref. [427].

Please note that the conjunction of *Observation*1 and *Observation*2 is uncommon. In fact, our results suggest that *Observation*1 and *Observation*2 are somewhat mutually exclusive:

- As shown in Figures 13.3, 13.6, the examples where NN increases the probability of detection are also those where it increases the probability of false alarms.

Hence, we cannot recommend NN as a replacement for WC. Nevertheless, if local WC data are not available, then we would recommend processing foreign CC data with NN.

13.4.3 DISCUSSIONS

In Analysis #1 we have used random samples of CC data and observed that the false alarm rates substantially increased compared to the WC models. Our new analysis shows that NN filtering of CC data removes the increased false alarm rates. Now we argue that, using NN filtering instead of using all available CC data, helps choosing training examples that are similar to the problem at hand. Thus, the irrelevant information in nonsimilar examples is avoided. However, this also removes the rich sample base and yields a slight decrease in detection rates. Mann-Whitney tests reveal that NN filtering is

- far better than random sampling cross-company data,
- and still worse than using within-company data.

The performances of defect predictors based on the NN-filtered CC versus WC data do not give necessary empirical evidence to make a strong conclusion. Sometimes NN data-based models may perform better than WC data-based models. A possible reason may be hidden in the processes that are implemented for those projects. Maybe, a group of new developers were working together for the first time and corresponding WC data included more heterogeneity, which is reduced by NN. Maybe the development methodology changed during the project, producing a different code culture. However, we do not have access to the internals of these projects that allows a discussion of these observations.

13.5 ANALYSIS #3: HOW MUCH LOCAL DATA DOES AN ORGANIZATION NEED FOR A LOCAL MODEL?

Our results of Analyses #1 and #2 reveal that WC data models are better if data are available. In this section, we will show that defect predictors can be learned from very small samples of WC data.

13.5.1 DESIGN

An important aspect of the Analyses #1 and #2 results is that defect predictors were learned using only a handful of defective modules. For example, consider a 90%/10% train/test split on $pc1$ with 1109 modules, only 6.94% of which are defective. On average, the training set will only contain $1109 * 0.9 * 6.94/100 = 69$ defective modules. Despite this, $pc1$ yields an adequate median $\{p_d, p_f\}$ result of $\{63, 27\}\%$.

Analysis #3 was therefore designed to check the smallest amount of data needed to learn defect predictors. The design is given in Table 13.7. Analysis #3 is essentially the same as the first analysis, but without the cross-company treatment. Instead, Analysis #3 took the seven NASA projects of Table 13.1 and learned predictors using

- reduced WC data: a randomly selected subset of up to 90% of each project data.

After randomizing the order of the data, training sets were built using just the first 100, 200, 300, ...data samples in the project. After training the defect predictor, its performance is tested on the remaining data samples not used in training.

Analysis #1 only used the features found in all NASA projects. For this analysis, we imposed no such restrictions and used whatever features were available in each data set.

Table 13.7 Pseudocode for Analysis #3

```
DATA = [PC1, KC1, KC2, CM1, KC3, MW1, MC2]
LEARNER = [Naive Bayes]

REPEAT 100 TIMES
 FOR EACH data IN DATA
    WC_TRAIN = random 90\% of data
       TEST = data - WC_TRAIN
       FOR i IN {100, 200, 300, $\ldots$}
           WC_TRAIN_INCREMENTAL <- Random i Examples from WC_TRAIN
           WC_INC_PREDICTOR = Train LEARNER with WC_TRAIN_INCREMENTAL
             [iwc_pd, iwc_pf, iwc_bal] = WC_INC_PREDICTOR on TEST
       END
  END
END
```

From Ref. [427].

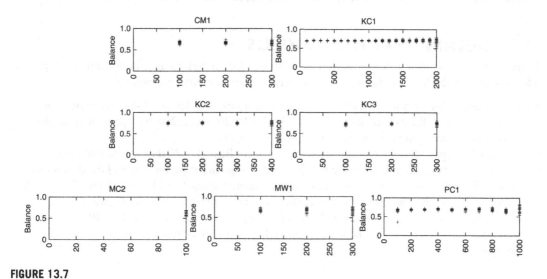

FIGURE 13.7

Analysis #3 results. Training set size grows in units of 100 examples, moving left to right over the x-axis. The MC2 results only appear at the maximum x-value as MC2 has less than 200 examples. From Ref. [427].

13.5.2 RESULTS FROM ANALYSIS #3

Equation (13.1) defined "balance" to be a combination of $\{p_d, p_f\}$ that decreases if p_d decreases or p_f increases. As shown in Figure 13.7, there was very little change in balanced performance after learning from 100, 200, 300, ... examples. Indeed, there is some evidence that learning from larger training sets had detrimental effects: the more training data, the larger the variance in the performance of the learned predictor. Observe how, in $kc1$ and $pc1$, as the training set size increases (moving right along the x-axis) the dots showing the balance performance start spreading out. We conjecture that this effect is due to the presence of occasional larger outliers in the training data (the probability of discovering these increases as the training set grows inside and, if the learner trains on them, then the resulting theory has more variance.)

The Mann-Whitney U test was applied to check the visual trends seen in Figure 13.7. For each project, all results from training sets of size $100, 200, 300 \ldots$ were compared to all other results from the same project. The issue was "how much data are enough?"; i.e., what is the minimum training set size that never lost to other training set of a larger size. Usually, that min value was quite small.

- In five projects $\{cm1, kc2, kc3, mc2, mw1\}$, min $= 100$;
- In $\{kc1, pc1\}$, min $= \{200, 300\}$ instances, respectively.

We explain the Analysis #3 results as follows. This analysis used simplistic static code features such as lines of code, number of unique symbols in the module, etc. Such simplistic static code features are hardly a complete characterization of the internals of a function. We would characterize such static code features as having *limited information content* [311]. Limited content is soon exhausted by repeated sampling. Hence, such simple features reveal all they can reveal after a small sample.

13.5.3 CHECKING THE ANALYSIS #3 RESULTS

There is also some evidence that the results of Analysis #3 (that performance improvements stop after a few hundred examples) have been seen previously in the data mining literature.

- In their discussion on how to best handle numeric features, Langley and John offer plots of the accuracy of Naive Bayes classifiers after learning on $10, 20, 40, \ldots 200$ examples. In those plots, there is little change in performance after 100 instances [189].
- Orrego [347] applied four data miners (including Naive Bayes) to 20 data sets to find the *plateau point*; i.e., the point after which there was little net change in the performance of the data miner. To find the plateau point, Oreggo used t-tests to compare the results of learning from Y or $Y + \Delta$ examples. If, in a 10-way cross-validation, there was no statistical difference between Y and $Y + \Delta$, the plateau point was set to Y. Many of those plateaus were found at $Y \leq 100$ and most were found at $Y \leq 200$. Please note that these plateau sizes are consistent with the results of Analysis #3.

13.5.4 DISCUSSION OF ANALYSIS #3

In the majority of cases, predictors learned from as little as one hundred examples perform as well as predictors learned from many more examples. This suggests that the effort associated with learning defect predictors from within-company data may not be overly large. For example, Table 13.8 estimates that the effort required to build and test 100 modules may be as little as 2.4-3.7 person-months. However, practitioners should use this approach cautiously. The populations of one hundred examples in our experiments are randomly selected from completed projects *with* stratification. Therefore, in practice, any one hundred sample may not necessarily reflect the company characteristics and constructing this initial set may take longer than expected.

Table 13.8　An Estimate of the Effort Required to Build and Test 100 Modules

100 modules may take as little as 2-4 person-months to construct. This estimate was generated as follows:

- In the *cm*1 data base, the median module size is 17 lines. 100 randomly selected modules would therefore use 1700 LOC.
- To generate an effort estimate for these modules, we used the online COCOMO [42] effort estimator (http://sunset.usc.edu/research/COCOMOII/expert_cocomo/expert_cocomo2000.html). Estimates were generated assuming 1700 LOC and the required reliability varying from very low to very high.
- The resulting estimates ranged from between 2.4 and 3.7 person-months to build and test those modules.

From Ref. [427].

13.6　HOW TRUSTWORTHY ARE THESE RESULTS?

Analyses #1-#3 were based on NASA projects. For the external validity of the conclusions of those analyses, we replicate the same analyses on SOFTLAB projects of Table 13.1.

For each SOFTLAB project, we follow the same procedure as in Analyses #1 and #2; i.e., 10% of the rows of each data set are selected at random for constructing test sets. Then, three different types of defect predictors are constructed. The first type are defect predictors trained with cross-company data (i.e., all seven NASA projects). The second type of defect predictors are trained with within-company data (i.e., random 90% rows of remaining SOFTLAB projects. Finally, the third type are defect predictors trained with NN-filtered cross-company data (i.e., *similar* rows from seven NASA projects).

The SOFTLAB projects include 29 static code features, 17 of which are common with the NASA projects. In order to simplify the comparison between these new projects and Analyses #1 and #2, we used only these shared attributes in our CC analyses. On the other hand we use all available features in WC analyses for SOFTLAB projects. In the following external validity analysis, we treated each NASA project as cross-company data for SOFTLAB projects.

Figure 13.8 shows the results:

- The p_d values for CC data increase compared to WC data with the cost of increased p_f.
- CC data shifts {Q1, median} of p_f from {5, 29} to {59, 65}.
- For CC data:
  - 25% of the p_d values are at 100%.
  - 50% of the p_d values are above 95%.
  - And all the p_d values are at or over 88%.

These results also provide evidence for the validity of our conclusions for Analysis #3. In Analysis #3, we conclude that the minimum number of instances for training a defect predictor is around $100 - 200$ data samples. Please note that three SOFTLAB projects *ar3, ar4*, and *ar5* have {63,107,36} modules, respectively. Thus, the minimum number of training samples occurs when a predictor is trained from *(ar3 + ar5)* projects. In this case, only $(63 + 36) * 0.90 = 90$ training samples are used to construct a defect predictor for the *ar4* project. Similarly, the maximum number of training samples

Overall results on SOFTLAB data

Treatment		min	Q1	median	Q3	max
p_d	CC	88	88	95	100	100
	WC	35	40	88	100	100
p_f	CC	52	59	65	68	68
	WC	3	5	29	40	42

Table (ar3)

Treatment		min	Q1	median	Q3	max
p_d	CC	88	88	88	88	88
	WC	88	88	88	88	88
p_f	CC	62	65	65	65	65
	WC	40	40	40	40	42

Table (ar4)

Treatment		min	Q1	median	Q3	max
p_d	CC	95	95	95	95	95
	WC	35	40	40	40	40
p_f	CC	52	55	56	59	60
	WC	3	3	3	5	5

Table (ar5)

Treatment		min	Q1	median	Q3	max
p_d	CC	100	100	100	100	100
	WC	88	100	100	100	100
p_f	CC	57	68	68	68	68
	WC	29	29	29	29	29

FIGURE 13.8

Analysis #1 results for the SOFTLAB projects. Overall and individual results are shown, respectively. From Ref. [427].

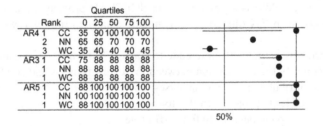

	Rank		Quartiles 0 25 50 75 100				
AR4	1	CC	35	90	100	100	100
	2	NN	65	65	70	70	70
	3	WC	35	40	40	40	45
AR3	1	CC	75	88	88	88	88
	1	NN	88	88	88	88	88
	1	WC	88	88	88	88	88
AR5	1	CC	88	100	100	100	100
	1	NN	100	100	100	100	100
	1	WC	88	100	100	100	100

50%

FIGURE 13.9

Analysis #2 PD results for the SOFTLAB projects where $NN_{p_d} \geq WC_{p_d}$. Rankings computed via Mann-Whitney (95% confidence) comparing each row to all other rows. From Ref. [427].

occurs when a predictor is trained from *(ar3 + ar4)* projects. Then $(63 + 107) * 0.90 = 153$ training samples are used to construct a defect predictor for the *ar5* project. Therefore, the WC results in Figure 13.8 are achieved using a minimum of 90 and a maximum of 153 training samples.

Figure 13.9–Figure 13.11 shows *Observation1* (i.e., $NN_{p_d} \geq WC_{p_d}$) and *Observation2* (i.e., $NN_{p_f} \leq WC_{p_f}$) for SOFTLAB projects. Please recall that these observations were mutually exclusive for NASA data. The pattern is similar in SOFTLAB projects:

- for *ar4* mutual exclusiveness hold: $NN_{p_d} \geq WC_{p_d}$ and $NN_{p_f} > WC_{p_f}$
- for *ar3* and *ar5*: $NN_{p_f} \leq WC_{p_f}$. If the observations were mutually exclusive, we would expect $NN_{p_d} < WC_{p_d}$. While this is not the case for p_d, we observe that $NN_{p_d} = WC_{p_d}$ and $NN_{p_d} \not> WC_{p_d}$ (see Figure 13.9).

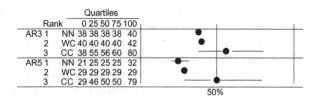

FIGURE 13.10

Analysis #2 PF results for the SOFTLAB projects for $NN_{p_f} \leq WC_{p_f}$. From Ref. [427].

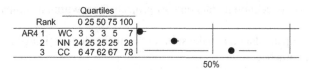

FIGURE 13.11

Analysis #2 PF results for the SOFTLAB projects for $NN_{p_f} > WC_{p_f}$. From Ref. [427].

In summary, the WC, CC, and NN patterns found in American NASA rocket software are also observed in software controllers of Turkish domestic appliances. While this is not the definitive proof of the external validity of our results, we find it a very compelling result that is reproducible in different companies.

13.7 ARE THESE USEFUL IN PRACTICE OR JUST NUMBER CRUNCHING?

While our analyses show that our defect detectors work nearly as well as standard data mining methods, it does not necessarily demonstrate that false alarm rates of around 29% are useful in an industrial context. For example, Arisholm and Briand have certain concerns on the practical usage of defect predictors [8]. They argue that if X% of the modules are predicted to be faulty and if those modules contain less than X% of the defects, then the cost of generating the defect predictor is not worth the effort.

Let us analyze the testing efforts on the MW1 project from Arisholm and Briand's point of view. For MW1, there are a total of 403 modules with 31 defective and 372 defect-free ones. CC model yields 90% p_d and 68% p_f, and one should examine 280 modules, which is around a 31% reduction in inspection efforts compared to examining all modules. Yet, we argue that 68% p_f rate is quite high and using NN we are able to reduce it to 33% along with 68% p_d. This corresponds to examining 144 modules, a reduction of 47% compared to exhaustive testing (and we assume an exhaustive test should examine 274 modules for detecting 68% defects, as Arisholm and Briand suggests).

This analysis can be extended for all projects used in this chapter. For instance, the company from which SOFTLAB data in Table 13.1 are collected is keen to use our detectors, arguing that they operate in a highly competitive market segment where profit margins are very tight. Therefore, reducing the cost of the product even by 1% can make a major difference both in market share and profits. Their applications are embedded systems where, over the last decade, the software components have taken precedence over the hardware. Hence, their problem is a software engineering problem. According to Brooks [59], half the cost of software development is in unit and systems testing. The company also believes that their main challenge is the testing phase and they seek predictors that indicate where the defects might exist *before* they start testing. Their expectation from the predictor is not to detect all defects, but to guide them to the problematic modules so that they can detect more defects in less time. Hence, any reduction in their testing efforts allows them to efficiently use their scarce resources.

An important issue worth more attention is the concern about the time required for setting up a metric program (i.e., in order to collect data for building actual defect predictors). Our incremental WC results suggest that, in the case of defect prediction, this concern may be less than previously believed. Kitchenham et al. [218] argue that organizations use cross-company data because within-company data can be so hard to collect:

- The time required to collect enough data on past projects from within a company may be prohibitive.
- Collecting within-company data may take so long that technologies change and older projects do not represent current practice.

In our analysis we observe that as few as 100 modules are enough to learn adequate defect predictors. When so few examples are enough, it is possible that projects can learn local defect predictors that are relevant to their current technology in just a few months.

Further, our experiences with our industry partners show that data collection is not necessarily a major concern. Static code attributes can be automatically and quickly collected with relatively little effort. We have found that when there is high level management commitment, it becomes a relatively simple process. For the three projects of SOFTLAB data, neither the static code attributes, nor the mapping of defects to software modules were available when the authors attempted to collect these data. These were smaller-scale projects, so it was sufficient to spend some time with the developers and going through defect reports.

13.8 WHAT'S NEW ON CROSS-LEARNING?

Following the publication of these analyses in the *Empirical Software Engineering Journal* in 2009, a critical mass of research activities in cross-learning for defect prediction has been reached. We deliberately chose to use the term cross-company, as the idea behind investigating cross-company defect predictors was inspired by Kitchenham et al.'s cross- versus within-company study on cost estimation [218]. Since 2009, other terms have been used to describe the same or slightly different concepts, e.g., cross-project [463], transfer learning [277]. In this part, we would like to provide a brief review of follow-up studies.

Yet, we will first explain the reasons that led us to conduct cross- learning research. At the time, we were simply curios about why defect prediction research failed to utilize data across projects. Was it because such an approach is useless in defect prediction context? We were optimistic about the answer, considering the problem of cost estimation, which is technically similar to defect prediction, i.e., a supervised learning problem utilizing past data.[3] Though the effectiveness of resulting models may vary, cost estimation research have made use of cross-project data for a long time. The systematic

---

[3] We should note that there are also studies using *unsupervised techniques* both for cost estimation and defect prediction; however, this is not the point behind the motivation explained here.

review comparing within-company versus cross-company cost estimation models concluded that some companies may benefit from cross-company cost estimations, while others may not [218]. Data gathered from different projects are extensively used in cost estimation studies, i.e., COCOMO models and ISBSG data set [43, 271]. However, it should be noted that the abstraction levels for cost estimation and defect prediction are different, i.e., project level and module (e.g., method, class, file) level. While a project corresponds to a single data point for cost estimation, the same level of abstraction provides many data points for defect prediction. Nevertheless, it was the idea of using data from other projects, which turned out to be applicable at least to some extent in cost estimation, that was of interest for this line of research.

Fortunately, our optimism was supported to some extent with the follow-up studies on cross-learning for defect prediction. Here we provide a discussion of cross-learning studies, which is still an emerging area with a limited number of published work—among which we have identified seven empirical studies [56, 85, 197, 265, 339, 426, 463] to discuss in this section. Our selection is not a comprehensive literature review, but the main idea is to provide pointers to as many different approaches as possible to give you, the reader, an insight about the ongoing efforts on cross-learning defect prediction. Also, we chose to focus our discussions on these studies rather than providing a general review of defect prediction literature, which is out of the scope, and we refer you to [158] for a systematic review of defect prediction studies in general. Brief descriptions and discussions on these studies are provided next, along with a summary presented in Table 13.9.

Though our work attracted lots of interest to conduct further studies, it was not the first! To the best of our knowledge, the earliest work on cross-project prediction is by Briand et al. [56], where they use logistic regression and MARS models to learn a defect predictor from an open-source project (i.e., Xpose), and apply the same model to another open-source project (Jwriter), which is developed by an identical team with different design strategies and coding standards. They observed that cross-project prediction is indeed better than a random and a simple, class size-based model. Yet, cross-project performance of the model was lower compared to its performance on the training project. They argue that cross-project predictions can be more effective in more homogeneous settings, adding that such an environment may not exist in real life. They identify the challenge as of high practical interest, and not straightforward to solve.

Zimmermann et al. considered different factors that may affect the results of cross-project predictions [463]. They categorized projects according to their domain, process characteristics and code measures. In their initial case study they ran experiments to predict defects in Internet Explorer (IE) using models trained with Mozilla Firefox and vice versa. These products are in the same domain and have similar features, but development teams employ different processes. Their results show that Firefox can predict the defects in IE successfully (i.e., 76.47% precision and 81.25% recall), however the opposite direction does not work (i.e., 4.12% recall). Zimmermann et al. then collected data from 10 additional projects and performed 622 pairwise predictions across project components. This is a slightly different approach than ours, where we constructed predictors from a common pool of cross-project data with data filtering in order to satisfy Briand et al.'s homogeneity argument. Zimmermann et al. classify a prediction as successful if precision, recall, and accuracy values are all above 75%, which results in only 21 successful predictions corresponding to a 3.4% success rate. They do not mention the performance of predictions that are below the threshold. They derive a decision tree using these prediction results to estimate expected performance from a cross-project predictor in order to guide practitioners. Decision nodes include the number of observations (i.e., data points), company, whether

Table 13.9 Summary of Selected Cross-Learning Defect Prediction Studies

References	Data Sources	Cross-Project Utilization	Findings & Summary
[56]	2 open-source projects	Train on one project and test on the other	The problem is of high practical interest. Cross-project prediction is far from straightforward. Though two systems are developed by the same team in a similar environment, available measures differ. It could work in more homogeneous environments.
[463]	28 components from 12 proprietary and open-source projects	Pairwise cross-project prediction	An important challenge for the community. Cross-project prediction is not transitive among projects. Open-source projects are strong predictors for closed-source projects. Open-source projects cannot be predicted.
[85]	two open-source and five student projects	Train with largest project and test on the remaining projects	Outlier removal and data transformation (normalization) improves prediction performance, when the transformed training and test project data show similar distributions.
[426]	13 proprietary and open-source projects	With selection of similar data points (nearest neighbor selection) from a pool of cross-project data	The significant effects observed in proprietary projects are not that clear for predicting open-source projects.
[339]	7 proprietary projects	With selection of similar data points from (nearest neighbor selection) a pool of cross-project data	Replication of [427] confirms findings.
[197]	92 versions of 38 proprietary, open-source and academic projects	Identifying clusters of similar projects and making predictions within the clusters	There exists clusters of projects, where defects in a project can be predicted by the other projects in the same cluster.
[265]	7 proprietary projects	With selection of similar data points from (genetic algorithm selection) a pool of cross-project data	Search-based (i.e., genetic algorithms) prediction models yield lower misclassification error than trivial, nonsearch-based models.

the project uses a database; and whether the project has internationalization, average churn, and relative deleted LOC. An interesting pattern in their predictions is that open-source projects are good predictors of closed-source projects; however, open-source projects can not be predicted by any other projects.

In a following study, Turhan et al. investigated whether the patterns in our previous work [427] are also observed in open-source software and analysed three additional projects [426]. Similar to Zimmermann et al., they found that the patterns they observed earlier are not easily detectable in predicting open-source software defects using proprietary cross-project data.

Cruz et al. trained a defect prediction model with an open-source project (Mylyn) and tested the performance of the same model on six other projects [85]. Before training and testing the model, they tried to obtain similar distributions in training and test samples through data transformations (i.e., power transformation). They also removed outliers in data by trimming the tails of distributions. They observed that using transformed training and test data yields better cross-project prediction performances [85].

Jureczko and Madeyski looked for clusters of similar projects in a pool of 92 versions from 38 proprietary, open-source, and academic projects [197]. Their idea is to reuse the same defect predictor model among the projects that fall in the same cluster. They used a comprehensive set of code metrics to represent the projects and compared the performances of prediction models that are trained on the same project versus other projects in the same cluster. They identify 3 statistically significant clusters (out of 10), where cross-project predictions are better than within-project predictions in terms of the number of classes that must be visited to detect 80% of the defects.

Liu et al. conducted similar experiments to [427], differing in the data selection approach [265]. They employed a search-based strategy, using genetic algorithms, to select data points from seven NASA MDP projects in order to build cross-project defect prediction models. They use 17 different machine learning methods and majority voting to build defect predictors. They consistently observe lower misclassification errors than trivial cross-project models (i.e., using all available cross-project data without data selection). They argue that single project data may fail to represent the overall quality trends, and recommend development organizations to combine multiple project repositories using their approach for exploiting the capabilities of their defect prediction models [265]. However, they do not provide a comparison with baseline within-project defect predictors.

13.8.1 DISCUSSION

Existing studies can be classified into two main categories. The first category consists of studies that apply *straightforward cross-project prediction*: a prediction model is traditionally trained on one project and then directly applied to the others [56, 85, 463]. The second category can be named as *selective cross-project prediction*: studies in this category try to select training data samples [265, 339, 426, 427], or training projects [197] that are similar to the test project such that the homogeneity condition proposed by Lionel et al. [56] is achieved. Different methods for selecting similar instances include nearest neighbor filtering [339, 426, 427], genetic algorithms [265], and clustering [197].

Almost all studies explicitly state that cross-project defect prediction is a challenge with important practical aspects. Further, they provide empirical evidence over a wide range of software systems, advocating that cross-project defect predictors can be effective. As one may intuitively expect, there are no reported cases where cross-project predictions are consistently better than within-project predictions. Considering that the idea behind cross-project prediction is to make estimates of faulty locations in projects with no history, it is a viable stop-gap choice [427] in data starving project environments.

An important practical aspect is that cross-project predictions may enable practitioners to use the available open-source project data for defect prediction [463], without making big changes in or investments to their existing processes for data collection and process improvement activities. However, it is not clear whether this is applicable to the other direction. Both Refs. [426, 463] found that cross-project prediction for open-source projects is more of a challenge than the counterpart.

It would also be worth pursuing an investigation of the same problem using other types of project metrics, e.g., code churn and noncode metrics; however, we acknowledge the difficulty of collecting required data. Finally, we should note one caveat of cross-project prediction: all projects need to have the same set of metrics in order to be able to pool data from different projects. This requires the availability of standard tools and metric sets accepted by the community.

13.9 WHAT'S THE TAKEAWAY?

The takeaway from this chapter is of practical importance: the defect detectors learned from site A *might* be useful at site B; in the absence of local data, companies can benefit from cross-company data:

- with high probability of detecting defects,
- with affordable false alarm rates,
- after a minor investment, which is to use an automated tool to collect local static code measurements.

Considering the results of our analyses, if a company lacks local data, we would suggest a two-phase approach. In phase one, that organization uses imported CC data, filtered via NN. Also, during phase one, the organization should start a data collection program to collect static code attributes. Phase two commences when there is *enough* local WC data to learn defect predictors. During phase two, the organization would switch to new defect predictors learned from the WC data.

Nevertheless, utilizing cross- data is an open challenge and further research is needed to identify methods for benefiting from and to investigate the merits of using such data.

BUILDING SMARTER TRANSFER LEARNERS

Name:	TEAK
Also known as:	TEAK could be categoried as a transfer learner or a relevancy filter. It could also be categorized as an instance-based (or case-based) reasoner.
Intent:	Generating software effort estimates, when there is insufficient local data to build an effort model.
Motivation:	Chapter 13 showed that defect prediction data can move between projects. Do the same methods work for effort estimation? And can we achieve such transfers not only between *current* projects but also between *old* and *new* projects?
Solution:	Effort estimation data sets are smaller than defect data sets (tens of examples, not hundreds). Hence, TEAK uses a different relevancy filter than discussed in Chapter 13. TEAK says that projects are *irrelevant* if they increase the uncertainty of a prediction (specifically, if they increase the variance of the actual efforts seen in near neighbors of a test instance). TEAK recursively explores subsets of project data, stopping when the subset's predictive uncertainty is greater than the superset. Also, as a preprocessor, TEAK discards project data found in subsets with very large variance in their actual effort values.
Applicability:	TEAK's irrelevancy filtering is successful for cross-company effort estimation. It is also useful for reaching back into history to find old projects that are still useful to predict the effort of current projects.
Related to:	Chapter 13 reported a "relevancy" filter for selecting useful data. TEAK is a "irrelevancy" filter that discards confusing data. Note that TEAK's recursive clustering would not scale to very large data sets (for such larger data sets, the CHUNK algorithm of Chapter 12 could be useful).

This chapter is an update to "Transfer Learning in Effort Estimation" by E. Kocaguneli, T. Menzies, and E. Mendes published in the *Journal of Empirical Software Engineering*, March 2014. This chapter is a rewrite of that paper with a book focus, throughout. Additional introductory pages have been added (with practitioners in mind). Also, additional discussion and explanatory paragraphs have been added throughout the chapter, again with practitioners in mind.

> *Yes, but that is very simple, right?*
>
> **Anonymous**

The above quote was directed to us (in a somewhat sarcastic manner) as a question during one of our presentations at the International Conference on Software Engineering (ICSE) in 2013. The attendee did not have any previous knowledge on transfer learning or on the prior research in this domain. He was under the impression that we were introducing the idea as a brand new concept (well, we wish we could, but fortunately transfer learning was already introduced before). As a concept, the attendee found the idea of transfer learning very simple and asked us to confirm it (very simple, right?). However, from our previous experience (where we tried to transfer NASA projects to the context of a proprietary company) as well as from what we have learned during the course of our research, transfer learning problems are nothing to be underestimated. There are a number of factors to consider such as:

- The consistency of the feature space, i.e., are the features of the source and target domain the same?
- If the feature space is not consistent, then how can we match different features; can we transfer all the features and all the instances?
- Or do we need to select a subset of the features and/or instances?
- If we need to select a subset of features and/or instances, then which ones should we keep?

As we will see later in this chapter, the initial transfer learning studies reported in software engineering (SE) are not very promising [218, 463]. The initial studies, which aimed to transfer the training set of an organization into the context of another organization, report compromised estimation accuracy values. In other words, those initial studies report that we can use the data of another company for our own estimation tasks, yet the performance will be much worse in comparison to using our own data. Then one might ask: "If the performance is compromised, then why should a practitioner use transfer learning in the first place?" That is a very valid question and, indeed, there would be no need for this chapter if this was still the case. However, the transfer learning studies in SE that followed the initial ones [227, 322, 427] showed that it is not a good idea to use all the instances of a data set that belongs to another company. In other words, if we are to use data from another domain (the so-called source domain, e.g., another company or another time frame), then it is best to select only the relevant instances. The relevancy should be with respect to the so-called target domain, e.g., an organization that lacks data and wants to use the data of another organization.

In this chapter, we will start with a brief introduction to the problem of transfer learning and we will use the specific problem of software effort estimation (SEE). SEE is basically a regression problem, where we define software projects via independent features and try to estimate the final duration of the project. After the introduction, we will continue with some background notes on transfer learning and introduce a transfer learning algorithm called TEAK. We will evaluate TEAK on sample data sets and provide the results. We will conclude this chapter with some takeaway lessons that one can apply to his/her own organization or domain.

14.1 WHAT IS ACTUALLY THE PROBLEM?

Finding enough training data for local estimation problems has never been easy. Every time we undertake a project that involves building an estimation method for our local organization, we will soon find ourselves looking for local data, i.e., the data of our own organization. More often than not, we will find out that the data is not there at all or that the data is there, but scattered into different databases, different documents, etc., and there is a significant cost associated with collecting the required data. In such cases, whether or not to invest in a costly data collection project is an important decision. After all, we do not even know whether the collected data will result in a successful estimation. Hence, it would be good to have an alternative solution to the lack of local data problem. Transfer learning may provide an alternative solution to this problem.

The lack of local data for estimation methods is one of the fundamental problems of estimation methods in SE [218, 427, 463]. In this chapter, we argue that finding local training data can be addressed through filtering cross-domain data (e.g., data from another organization) with appropriate methods. A company willing to use *"within-data,"* a.k.a. local data, will face the problem of considerable time and resource requirements for data collection and maintenance activities. In this chapter, local data refers to a company's own domain data or data from the same time interval (e.g., the same decade). Another problem of local data is aging, i.e., how to choose or disregard projects from older time intervals [340]. We refer to aforementioned problems of within-data as "local data issues." The benefit of being able to transfer knowledge of *"cross-data"* (the data either coming from another domain or from a different time interval) is twofold: (1) Possibility to cure the local data issues and (2) ability to identify which instances to use from past time intervals. *Instance transfer* is the process of keeping some of the relevant training instances (while discarding the others).

For the cross-domain data transfer research presented in this chapter, we use a novel transfer learning method using variance-based instance selection, called TEAK [229]. We show that the use of this method enables successful transfer of data across space (i.e., between organizations) and across time (i.e., between different time intervals). The proposed method was evaluated on the proprietary data sets of eight Web companies from the Tukutuku [289] database (for transfer between domains) as well as publicly available NASA data sets called Cocomo81and Nasa93 (for transfer between time intervals). In the experimentation, each test instance is evaluated in two different scenarios:

- In the first scenario, the test instance is allowed to be used only within training data (i.e., restricted to its own domain or time interval).
- In the second scenario, the test instance is allowed to be used cross as well as within-data (i.e., it is allowed to transfer knowledge from other domains or time intervals).

The performance of the test instances in both scenarios are compared according to eight different error measures (MAR, MER, MMRE, MdMRE, Pred(25), MBRE, MIBRE, and SA, see Section 14.4.2 for details of these performance measures) subject to the Wilcoxon test (at 95% confidence). We were able to observe that in six out of eight companies of the Tukutuku database, the instance transfer between domains enabled cross-data performance to be statistically significantly the same as the performance of within-data. To put it in other words: six out of eight companies that use data of another organization elicited results that are just as good as the results that they would have elicited, if they were to use their own data. In all cases of the transfer learning between time intervals, the within- and cross-data performance were statistically the same. The second scenario tackles the problem of cross-data borders by investigating the *selection tendency* of test instances. We define *selection tendency* to be the percentage of instances selected from within- and cross-data sources. We have found that if a test instance is allowed to use a blend of cross- and within-data sources (as in the case of the second scenario), test instances select equally likely from within- and cross-data.

14.2 WHAT DO WE KNOW SO FAR?

As the name of this section suggests, here we will briefly discuss what we know about transfer learning in SE so far, given the light of the prior research. Because we can only discuss each previous work up to a certain extent in this book, in case a concept appears to be interesting and the reader wishes to gain more insight, he/she is strongly recommended to follow up the cited work for further information.

14.2.1 TRANSFER LEARNING

A learning problem can be defined by

- a specific domain D, which consists of a feature space and a marginal distribution defining this space;
- and a task T, which is the combination of a label space and an objective estimation function.

Transfer learning allows for the training and test data to have different domains and tasks [277]. According to Jialin et al., transfer learning can be formally defined as follows [352]: Assuming we have a source domain D_S, a source task T_S, a target domain D_T, and a target task T_T; transfer learning tries to improve an estimation method in D_T using the knowledge of D_S and T_S. Note that the assumption in the above definition is that $D_S \neq D_T$ or $T_S \neq T_T$. There are various subgroups of transfer learning, which define the relationship between traditional machine learning methods and various transfer learning settings, e.g., see [352, Table 1]. SEE transfer learning experiments have the same task but different domains, which places them under the category of transductive transfer learning [10].

There are four different approaches to transfer learning [352]: instance transfer (or instance-based transfer) [134], feature representation transfer [246], parameter transfer [140] and relational knowledge transfer [315]. The transfer learning approach of the estimation method used in this chapter corresponds to instance transfer. Besides the SEE research (which is used in this chapter), the benefits of instance-transfer learning are used in various other research areas, e.g., Ma et al. use transfer learning for cross-company defect prediction, where they use a weighted Naive Bayes classifier [277]. Other research areas that benefit from instance transfer are text classification [88], e-mail filtering [457], and image classification [446].

14.2.2 TRANSFER LEARNING AND SE

Transfer learning studies in the context of SE, are not very old. For example, the earliest studies cited by Kitchenham et al. in their literature review [218] were published in 1999 and they belong to Maxwell et al. [284] and Briand et al. [55]. In other words, transfer learning studies in SE are quite new and quite frankly we probably have not even discovered the tip of the iceberg yet. As a matter of fact, up until recently, the transfer learning studies in SE were oftentimes referred to as *cross company learning*, so do not be surprised if you do not see the term transfer learning in some of the earlier papers.

We can divide the prior work on transfer learning in the context of SE into two subsets: (1) transfer learning between different organizations and (2) transfer learning between different time intervals. As we will see in the following paragraphs, most of the earlier work focuses on the first subset, i.e., the problem of transferring data of one organization to another organization. Recently, the SE community also started addressing the problems of how to transfer data from one time interval to another time interval [269, 270] or how to transfer data as the time passes (a.k.a. data set shift) [322].

The prior results on the performance of transfer learning (a.k.a. cross-company learning in SEE) are unstable. In their review, Kitchenham et al. [218] found equal evidence for and against the value of transfer learning in SEE. Out of the 10 studies reviewed by Kitchenham et al., 4 studies favored within-data, another 4 studies found that transferring data is not statistically significantly worse than within-data, and 2 studies had inconclusive results. In the field of defect prediction, Zimmermann et al. studied the use of transferring data [463]. Zimmermann et al. found that predictors performed worse when trained on cross-application data than from within-application data. From a total of 622 transfer and within-data comparisons, they report that within performed better in 618 cases. Recently, Ma et al. defined using data across other domains in the research field of defect prediction as a transfer learning problem [277]. Ma et al. propose a Naive Bayes variant, so-called transfer Naive Bayes (TNB), so as to use all the appropriate features from the training data. TNB is proposed as an alternative transfer learning method for defect prediction when there are too few training data. According to Ma et al., data transferring problem of defect prediction corresponds to an inductive transfer learning setting; where source and target tasks are the same, yet source and target domains are different. The inductive transfer learning methods are summarized as either instance transfer or feature transfer [181]. The current literature of transfer learning in defect prediction as well as SEE focuses on instance transfer.

Turhan et al. compared defect predictors learned from transferred or within-data [427]. Like Zimmermann et al. [463], they found that transferring *all* data leads to poor estimation method performance (very large false alarm rates). However, after *instance selection* pruned away irrelevant data during transfer learning, they found that the estimators built on transferred data were equivalent to the estimators learned from within-data [427]. Motivated by Turhan et al. [427], Kocaguneli et al. [227] used *instance selection* as a preprocessor for a study of transfer learning in SEE, where test instances are allowed to use only transferred or only within-data. In a limited study with three data sets, they found that through instance selection, the performance differences in the predictors trained on transferred or within-data were not statistically significant. This limited study was challenged by Kocaguneli et al. in another study that uses eight different data sets [222]. The results were identical: performance differences of within- and transferred data are not statistically significant.

Transfer learning between different time intervals has been paid very little attention in SEE. In [270] Lokan and Mendes found out by using chronological sets of instances that time frame divisions of instances did not affect prediction accuracy. In [269], they found out that it is possible to suggest a window size of a time frame of past instances, which can yield performance increase in estimation. They also note that the size of the window frame is data set dependent. Recently, Minku and Yao pointed out an important issue with the SEE transfer learning studies [322], which is that SEE is a *class of online learning tasks*; they have investigated several scenarios, testing different approaches designed for nonchanging as well as changing environments in the context of CC learning. Their findings indicated that CC subsets may be beneficial or detrimental, depending on the moment in time. The algorithm reported in their work can benefit from time dependence and can perform better than WC data when using CC data [322]. The research and the method provided in this chapter builds on the prior findings to provide evidence of knowledge transfer through both space and time.

14.2.3 DATA SET SHIFT

Turhan offers a formal treatment for this problem of "context change" in SE [425]. He discusses *data set shift*, which appears when training and test joint distributions are different.[1] Turhan investigates different types of data set shift issues as proposed by Storkey [405]:

- Covariate shift: The covariates in test and train sets differ.
- Prior probability shift: The prediction model is found via Bayes' Rule, yet the distribution of the dependent variable differs for training and test sets.
- Sample selection bias: The training and test sets are selected from populations with different characteristics, e.g., the training set coming from a higher maturity level company is used on a test set of a lower maturity level company.
- Imbalanced data: Certain event (or class) types of interest are rarer compared to other events (or classes).
- Domain shift: The cases where the method of measurement (e.g., performance measures, size measures) changes between training and test conditions.
- Source component shift: Parts of data come from different sources with particular characteristics in varying sizes, e.g., data sets whose instances are collected in different companies or time frames.

Turhan continues his discussion by introducing techniques to handle data set shift problems in SE, which are grouped under two main groups: Instance-based techniques and distribution-based techniques. The former group of techniques aim at handling instances (through outlier removal [427], relevancy filtering [222], or instance weighting [455]); whereas the latter group of techniques aim at regulating the distribution of instances to train and test sets (through stratification [425], cost curves [186], and mixture models [7]).

Quoting from Storkey: "Data set shift and transfer learning are very related." Transfer learning deals with the cases where there are multiple training scenarios that are partially related and are used to predict in one specific scenario. For example, in the case of our research, multiple training scenarios are either data from different companies (transfer of data in space) or data from different time frames (transfer of data in time). Data set shift is the specific case, where there are only two scenarios (training and test sets) and one of them has no training targets [405]. Turhan's mapping of the data set shift types to SE is an excellent example of specific transfer learning issues that are becoming imminent.

In the context of SEE, Lokan and Mendes, as well as Minku and Yao, investigated the data set shift problem [270, 322]. The work of Lokan and Mendes posed the question of whether it is better to use all the available past data as the training set or whether it is better to use a subset (window) of past projects. They employed data from the ISBSG database, and their findings showed that using a window can significantly improve estimation accuracy, when compared to using the entire training set. Furthermore, they also point out that the size of the window (i.e., the number of projects to be included as the training set) plays an important role in the estimation accuracy and it is data set dependent [270]. Minku and Yao's work observes the SEE problem as a class of online learning problems, where the environment is changing [322]. Their results show that the estimation accuracy when using CC data is

---

[1] Note that the literature contains numerous synonyms for data set shift including "concept shift" or "concept drift," "changes of classification," "changing environments," "contrast mining in classification learning," "fracture points," and "fractures between data." We will use the term as defined in the above text.

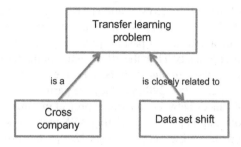

FIGURE 14.1

Prior cross company studies are specific cases of transfer learning, which is very closely related to the data set shift problem. From Ref. [224].

dependent on time, i.e., the CC subsets can be either beneficial or detrimental to estimation accuracy, depending on the moment in time.

In this chapter, we provide a more general treatment of the transfer learning and propose that our earlier work that we called "cross company learning" [222] as well as specific data set issues are in fact particular cases of transfer learning (see Figure 14.1). One of the main ideas of this research is that separate problems of cross company and time frame estimation are problems of transfer learning, and the data set shift problem is closely related to transfer learning. Hence, instead of proposing different solutions for each specific case of each specific problem, we should be looking for general transfer learning solutions that work for multiple cases in both problem types. Strictly speaking, data set shift and transfer learning problems are not subsets of one another, yet they are closely related. Hence, we believe that CC studies in SE can benefit considerably from both domains (transfer learning and data set shift).

The data set shift problem differs from the transfer learning problem in the sense that it refers to a nonstationary learning problem [466], where the core assumption is that future involves uncertainty. The main distinction is the fact that the source of a future target instance is not known with certainty, i.e., data cannot be simply decomposed into two disjoint sets and learned with two separate models [466]. The idea of transfer learning is to assume the two data sets have different distributions, yet one of them may be used to aid the other; whereas, in the case of data set shift, the changes are detected and adapted to new distributions (instead of the mere use of the other data set).

14.3 AN EXAMPLE TECHNOLOGY: TEAK

TEAK is an example of a transfer learning method that is a *variance-based* instance selector, which discards training data associated with regions of high dependent variable (effort) variance [229]. TEAK is based on the locality principle, which states that "Instances that are close to one another in space according to a distance measure (e.g., Euclidean distance measure) are similar instances and should have similar dependent variable values (hence the low variance)." A high-variance region, where similar instances have very different effort values (hence, the high variance) violates the locality assumption and is pruned away by TEAK [229].

TEAK is built on a standard analogy-based estimation (ABE) technique called ABE0. Hence, before we continue with the details of TEAK, we will provide some notes on the ABE methods. ABE methods generate their estimates by using a database of past projects. For a *test* project, ABE methods retrieve analogies from a database of past projects. Then the effort values of the retrieved analogies are adapted into an estimate. We use ABE methods in this study because they are widely investigated methods in the literature [70, 199, 206, 227, 229, 259, 290] and they are particularly helpful for transfer learning studies as they are based on distances between individual project instances.

There are a high number of design options concerning ABE methods such as the distance measure for nearness [290], adaptation of analogy effort values [290], row processing [70, 206], column processing [206, 259], and so on. For example, Keung et al. show that the number of different design options can easily lead to more than 6000 ABE variants [207]. Here we define ABE0 that is a *baseline* ABE method that combines the methods used in Kadoda & Shepperd [199], Mendes et al. [290], and Li et al. [259]. ABE0 executes the following steps:

- Input a database of past projects.
- For each test instance, retrieve k similar projects (analogies).
  - For choosing k analogies, use a similarity measure.
  - Before calculating similarity, scale independent features to 0-1 interval so that higher numbers do not dominate the similarity measure.
  - Use a feature weighting scheme to reduce the effect of less informative features.
- Adapt the effort values of the k nearest analogies to come up with the effort estimate.

ABE0 uses the Euclidean distance as a similarity measure, detailed in Equation (14.1), where w_i corresponds to feature weights applied on independent features. The ABE0 framework does not favor any features over the others; therefore, each feature has equal importance in ABE0, i.e., $w_i = 1$. For adaptation, ABE0 takes the median of k projects:

$$\text{Distance} = \sqrt{\sum_{i=1}^{n} w_i (x_i - y_i)^2} \qquad (14.1)$$

TEAK augments ABE0 with instance selection and an indexing scheme for filtering relevant training examples. In summary, TEAK is a two-pass system:

- Pass 1 prunes training instances implicated in poor decisions (instance selection);
- Pass 2 retrieves closest instances to the test instance (instance retrieval).

In the first pass, training instances are combined using greedy agglomerative clustering (GAC), to form an initial cluster tree that we call GAC1; e.g., see Figure 14.2. Level zero of GAC1 is formed by leaves, which are the individual project instances. These instances are greedily combined (combine the two closest instances) into tuples to form the nodes of upper levels. The variance of the effort values associated with each subtree (the performance variance) is then recorded and normalized: $min \ldots max$ to $0 \ldots 1$. The high variance subtrees are then pruned, as these are the subtrees that would cause an ABE method to make an estimate from a highly variable instance space. Hence, pass one prunes subtrees with a variance in the vicinity of $rand() * \alpha\%$ of the maximum variance seen in any tree, where $rand()$ gives a normal random value from 0-1 interval. After some experimentation, we found that $\alpha = 10$ leads to estimates with lowest errors.

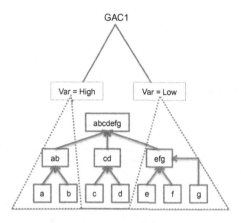

FIGURE 14.2

A sample GAC tree with regions of high and low variance (dashed triangles). GAC trees may not always be binary. For example, here leaves are odd numbered, hence node "g" is left *behind*. Such instances are pushed *forward* into the closest node in the higher level. For example, "g" is pushed forward into the "e+f" node to make "e+f+g" node. From Ref. [224].

The leaves of the remaining subtrees are the *survivors* of pass one. They are filtered to pass 2 where they are used to build a second GAC tree (GAC2). GAC2 is generated in a similar fashion to GAC1, then it is traversed by test instances that are moved from root to leaves. Unlike GAC1, this time variance is a decision criterion for the movement of test instances: If the variance of the current tree is larger than its subtrees, then continue to move down; otherwise, stop and retrieve the instances in the current tree as the analogies. TEAK is a form of ABE0, so its adaptation method is the same, in other words, take the median of the analogy effort values. A simple visualization of this approach is given in Figure 14.3.

We use TEAK in this chapter as a sample transfer learning method because, as shown by the leave-one-out experiments of Kocaguneli et al. [229], its performance is comparable to other commonly used effort estimators including neural networks (NNet) and linear regression (LR). For a complete analysis of TEAK compared to NNet, LR, and various ABE0 methods, please refer to [229, Figure 7]. Figure 14.4 can be interpreted as follows:

- The columns $k = 1, 2, 4, 8, 16$ denote variants of standard ABE0 where estimates are generated from the k-th nearest neighbors.
- The column $k = best$ denotes a variant of ABE0 where k was chosen by an initial preprocessor that chose a best k value after exploring the training data.
- The columns LR and NNet refer to LR and neural nets.

The black triangles in Figure 14.4 mark when an estimator was one of the top-ranked methods for a particular data set. Ranking was accomplished via the *win-loss* calculation. See Section 14.4.2 for details of *win-loss* calculation. The key feature of Figure 14.4 is that TEAK always performed better than the other ABE0 methods, and usually performed better than neural nets. TEAK's only near-rival was LR but, as shown in the LR columns, TEAK was ranked top nearly twice as much as LR.

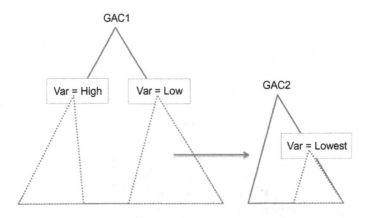

FIGURE 14.3

Execution of TEAK on two GAC trees, where the tree on the left is GAC1 of Figure 14.2 and the one on the right is GAC2. The instances in the low-variance region of GAC1 are selected to form GAC2. Then the test instance traverses GAC2 until no decrease in effort variance is possible. Wherever the test instance stops is retrieved as the subtree to be used for adaptation (var=lowest labeled, dashed triangle of GAC2). From Ref. [224].

	TEAK	LR	NNet	$k=best$	Simple ABE0				
					$k=1$	$k=16$	$k=2$	$k=4$	$k=8$
MdMRE									
Cocomo81	▲	▲							
Cocomo81e	▲	▲							
Cocomo81o	▲	▲							
Nasa93		▲							
Nasa93c2		▲							
Nasa93c5									
Desharnais	▲	▲							
Sdr	▲								
ISBSG-Banking	▲								
Count	6	3	0	0	0	0	0	0	0
Pred(25)									
Cocomo81	▲								
Cocomo81e	▲		▲						
Cocomo81o	▲								
Nasa93		▲							
Nasa93c2		▲							
Nasa93c5	▲	▲							
Desharnais		▲							
Sdr	▲								
ISBSG-Banking	▲								
Count	5	3	1	0	0	0	0	0	0
MAR									
Cocomo81	▲	▲							
Cocomo81e	▲	▲							
Cocomo81o	▲	▲							
Nasa93		▲							
Nasa93c2		▲							
Nasa93c5									
Desharnais	▲	▲							
Sdr	▲								
ISBSG-Banking	▲								
Count	6	3	0	0	0	0	0	0	0

FIGURE 14.4

Results from 20 repeats of a leave-one-out experiment, repeated for the performance measures of MdMRE, Pred(25), and MAR. Black triangles mark when an estimator was one of the top-ranked methods for a particular data set (where ranking was computed via *win-loss* from a Wilcoxon test, 95% confidence). The *Count* rows show the number of times a method appeared as the top-performing variant. The results of this figure come from Ref. [229].

14.4 THE DETAILS OF THE EXPERIMENTS

The goals of the experiments carried out in this chapter can be summarized as follows:

1. Compare the performance of TEAK when trained from just within-data versus when trained from a combination of cross- and within-data.
2. The *retrieval tendency* goals question the tendency of a *within* test instance to retrieve *within* or *cross* data. In other words, given the chance that a test instance had access to *within*- and *cross*-data at the same time, what percentage of every subset would be retrieved into k analogies used for estimation?

The first goal challenges the findings from older publicly available SEE data sets on the proprietary data sets of eight different contemporary Web development companies. This is quite important, as the results pertaining to our first goal can give the practitioners an idea about how well cross-data studies may perform in their actual settings. The second goal challenges our assumptions regarding the definition of cross-data, i.e., is it right to draw a border and say some data is cross or within based on single features like the company name? The results regarding the second goal are indicators for practitioners regarding which factors to consider and which factors to ignore when using cross-data.

14.4.1 PERFORMANCE COMPARISON

With regard to performance comparison we have two settings: *within*- and *cross*. In the *within*-data setting, onlythe *within*-source is used as the data set, and a testing strategy of leave-one-out cross-validation (LOOCV) is employed.

Cross data setting uses one instance at a time (because we use LOOCV) from the *within* data as the test set and the *combination of remaining within instances and all the cross* data as the training set. In this setting TEAK derives an estimate for each test instance by adapting the analogies of the training set. Ultimately, we end up with T predictions adapted from the training set. Finally, the performances under *within*- and *cross*-data settings are compared. For that purpose, we use both mere performance values as well as win-tie-loss statistics.

14.4.2 PERFORMANCE MEASURES

There are multiple performance measures (a.k.a. error measures) used in SEE, which all aim to measure the success of a prediction. In this research, we use a total of eight performance measures. For example, the absolute error (AE) is the absolute difference between predicted and the actual values:

$$AE_i = |x_i - \hat{x}_i| \tag{14.2}$$

(where $x_i, \hat{x}_i$ are the actual and the predicted values (respectively) for test instance i). We use a summary of AE through taking the mean of AE, which is known as mean absolute error (MAE).

The magnitude of relative error (a.k.a. MRE) measure is a very widely used performance measure for selecting the best effort predictor from a number of competing software prediction models[133, 390]. MRE measures the error ratio between the actual effort and the predicted effort and is expressed by the following equation:

$$\text{MRE}_i = \frac{|x_i - \hat{x}_i|}{x_i} = \frac{\text{AE}_i}{x_i} \tag{14.3}$$

A related measure is MER (magnitude of error relative to the estimate [133]):

$$\text{MER}_i = \frac{|x_i - \hat{x}_i|}{\hat{x}_i} = \frac{\text{AE}_i}{\hat{x}_i} \tag{14.4}$$

The overall average error of MRE can be derived as the mean or median magnitude of relative error (MMRE and MdMRE, respectively) measure:

$$\text{MMRE} = mean(allMRE_i) \tag{14.5}$$

$$\text{MdMRE} = median(allMRE_i) \tag{14.6}$$

A common alternative to MMRE is PRED(25), which is defined as the percentage of successful predictions falling within 25% of the actual values, and can be expressed as follows, where N is the data set size:

$$\text{PRED(25)} = \frac{100}{N} \sum_{i=1}^{N} \begin{cases} 1 \text{ if MRE}_i \le \frac{25}{100} \\ 0 \text{ otherwise} \end{cases} \tag{14.7}$$

For example, PRED(25) = 50% implies that half of the estimates fall within 25% of the actual values [390].

Other performance measures used here are mean balanced relative error (MBRE) and the mean inverted balanced relative error (MIBRE), both suggested by Foss et al. [133]:

$$\text{MBRE}_i = \frac{|\hat{x}_i - x_i|}{min(\hat{x}_i, x_i)} \tag{14.8}$$

$$\text{MIBRE}_i = \frac{|\hat{x}_i - x_i|}{max(\hat{x}_i, x_i)} \tag{14.9}$$

The above mentioned performance measures are selected due to their wide use in the SEE research. However, none of these error measures are devoid of problems. For instance, MRE-based error measures have been criticized due to their asymmetry [133]. This criticism applies to MMRE, MdMRE, and Pred(25). A recent study by Shepperd et al. provides a good discussion of the error measures [393]. In their study, Shepperd et al. propose a new unbiased error measure called standardized accuracy (SA), which is based on the MAE. SA's equation is as follows:

$$\text{SA} = 1 - \frac{\text{MAE}_{P_i}}{\overline{\text{MAE}_{P_0}}} \tag{14.10}$$

MAE_{P_i} is defined to be the MAE of the estimation method P_i. $\overline{\text{MAE}_{P_0}}$ is the mean of a large number of (in our case 1000) random guessing. In the random guessing procedure, a training instance is randomly chosen with equal probability from the training set (with replacement) and its effort value is used as the estimate of the test instance. SA gives us an idea of how good an estimation method is in comparison to random guessing. Since the term MAE_{P_i} is in the nominator, the higher the SA values, the better an estimation method.

In this chapter we evaluate different SEE methods using the *win-loss* calculation of Figure 14.5. According to the pseudocode of Figure 14.5, we first check if two distributions i, j are statistically

```
win_i = 0, tie_i = 0, loss_i = 0
win_j = 0, tie_j = 0, loss_j = 0
if Wilcoxon(Perf_i, Perf_j) says they are the same then
    tie_i = tie_i + 1;
    tie_j = tie_j + 1;
else
    if mean or median(Perf_i) < median(Perf_j) then
        win_i = win_i + 1
        loss_j = loss_j + 1
    else
        win_j = win_j + 1
        loss_i = loss_i + 1
    end if
end if
```

FIGURE 14.5

Pseudocode for win-tie-loss calculation between methods *i* and *j* w.r.t. performance measures *Perf_i* and *Perf_j*. If *Perf_i* and *Perf_j* are measures like MMRE, MdMRE, or MAR, lower values are better; whereas for performance measures like Pred(25), higher values are better.

different according to the Wilcoxon test. In our experimental setting, i, j are arrays of performance measure results coming from two different methods. If they are not statistically different, then they are said to *tie* and we increment tie_i and tie_j. On the contrary, if they are different, we update win_i, win_j and $loss_i, loss_j$ after a numerical comparison of performance measures. The related pseudocode is given in Figure 14.5. In order to reduce any possible bias due to a particular experimental setting, for every experiment 20 runs are made.

14.4.3 RETRIEVAL TENDENCY

For retrieval tendency experiments we mark every *within* and *cross* instance in the training set and let the test instance choose analogies from the training data set of within- and cross-data instances. Note that retrieved analogies are the unique training instances in the lowest-variance region of GAC2 (see Figure 14.3). In this setting, our aim is to see what percentage of *within* and *cross* subsets would appear among retrieved *k* analogies. The retrieval percentage is the average (over all test instances) ratio of instances retrieved in analogies to the total size of the training set:

$$\text{Percentage} = \frac{\text{Number of retrieved analogies}}{\text{Training set size}} \times 100 \qquad (14.11)$$

14.5 RESULTS
14.5.1 PERFORMANCE COMPARISON

Comparing the performance of within- and cross-data is the first goal of this experimentation. Due to space constraints and also in order to make the results more readable, we equally divided the domain transfer results of the Tukutuku subsets into two figures: Figures 14.6, 14.7. The time interval transfer results of Cocomo81 and Nasa93 are provided in Figures 14.9, 14.10, respectively.

Data set	W			MAR	
	Win	Tie	Loss	W	C
tuku1	8	12	0	27.8	55.9
tuku2	20	0	0	6.1	60.6
tuku3	20	0	0	661.7	2577.6
tuku4	2	18	0	104.5	177.4
tuku5	0	20	0	305.8	315.4
tuku6	8	12	0	25.8	42.7
tuku7	2	18	0	542.7	551.6
tuku8	1	19	0	87.6	103.0

Data set	W			MMRE	
	Win	Tie	Loss	W	C
tuku1	9	11	0	0.9	3.1
tuku2	20	0	0	1.1	20.6
tuku3	20	0	0	0.3	0.9
tuku4	2	18	0	0.4	5.5
tuku5	0	19	1	2.9	1.0
tuku6	5	15	0	0.3	0.7
tuku7	3	17	0	1.2	1.0
tuku8	0	20	0	0.9	0.8

Data set	W			MdMRE	
	Win	Tie	Loss	W	C
tuku1	8	12	0	0.6	1.0
tuku2	20	0	0	0.7	10.2
tuku3	20	0	0	0.2	1.0
tuku4	2	18	0	0.3	0.9
tuku5	0	19	1	0.9	0.8
tuku6	5	15	0	0.3	0.4
tuku7	3	17	0	0.6	0.7
tuku8	0	20	0	0.4	0.6

Data set	W			Pred(25)	
	Win	Tie	Loss	W	C
tuku1	6	10	4	0.4	0.1
tuku2	18	0	2	0.1	0.2
tuku3	20	0	0	0.7	0.4
tuku4	2	18	0	0.5	0.5
tuku5	1	19	0	0.2	0.2
tuku6	5	15	0	0.4	0.4
tuku7	3	17	0	0.2	0.3
tuku8	0	20	0	0.4	0.4

FIGURE 14.6

Performance comparison of within (**W**) and cross (**C**) data w.r.t. four of eight different performance measures: MAR, MMRE, MdMRE, Pred(25). Win, tie, loss values are w.r.t. **W**. Last two columns are the actual performance measure values of **W** and **C**. From Ref. [224].

Figure 14.6 shows a uniformity of results. The tie values are very high for five out of eight companies (tuku1, tuku4-to-7), which means that cross-data performance is as good as within-data performance. The high tie values are also reflected in the actual error measures. See that the values of the error measures (the last two columns of Figure 14.6) for within (**W**) and cross (**C**) data sources are very close to one another for tuku1 and tuku-4-to-7. For 1 company, tuku8, within- and cross-data performance depends on the error measure: According to all error measures except MMER, the within- and cross-performances are very close, whereas for MMRE the within-data performance appears to be better. For 2 companies out of 8 (tuku2 and tuku3), the within-data performance is dominantly better than cross-data performance with a win value of 20. Remember from Section 14.3 that TEAK performs 20 times

Data set	W			MMER	
	Win	Tie	Loss	W	C
tuku1	0	20	0	1.0	1.2
tuku2	0	20	0	1.6	0.8
tuku3	20	0	0	0.3	58.2
tuku4	0	20	0	4.9	4.9
tuku5	6	14	0	2.3	8.2
tuku6	8	12	0	0.4	2.5
tuku7	6	14	0	5.1	9.2
tuku8	14	6	0	0.7	2.5

Data set	W			MBRE	
	Win	Tie	Loss	W	C
tuku1	6	14	0	1.4	3.8
tuku2	20	0	0	2.2	20.6
tuku3	20	0	0	0.3	58.2
tuku4	1	19	0	4.9	9.7
tuku5	0	20	0	4.6	8.5
tuku6	6	14	0	0.4	2.8
tuku7	5	15	0	5.7	9.6
tuku8	2	18	0	1.2	2.7

Data set	W			MIBRE	
	Win	Tie	Loss	W	C
tuku1	2	18	0	0.5	0.6
tuku2	17	3	0	0.5	0.8
tuku3	20	0	0	0.2	0.9
tuku4	1	19	0	0.4	0.8
tuku5	0	20	0	0.6	0.6
tuku6	6	14	0	0.3	0.4
tuku7	4	16	0	0.5	0.6
tuku8	3	17	0	0.4	0.5

Data set	W			SA	
	Win	Tie	Loss	W	C
tuku1	8	12	0	0.2	−0.7
tuku2	20	0	0	−0.0	−10.3
tuku3	20	0	0	0.0	−2.7
tuku4	2	18	0	0.4	0.1
tuku5	0	20	0	0.1	0.0
tuku6	8	12	0	0.2	−0.5
tuku7	2	18	0	0.3	0.3
tuku8	1	19	0	−0.1	−0.4

FIGURE 14.7

Performance comparison of within (represented with **W**) and cross (represented with **C**) data w.r.t. four of eight different performance measures: MMER, MBRE, MIBRE, SA.

LOOCV, hence the total of win, tie, and loss values for each data set subject to each error measure amounts to 20. The reason for 20 LOOCV repeats is to remove the bias due to the random pruning step of TEAK.

Figure 14.7 shows the within- and cross-data performance of TEAK for the error measures of MMER, MBRE, MIBRE, and SA. The reading of Figure 14.7 is exactly the same as Figure 14.6, i.e., it shows the win, tie, and loss values according to four error measures as well as the actual error measure values. The general pattern we have observed from four error measures in Figure 14.6 is also visible in Figure 14.7. In relation to the error measures MBRE, MIBRE, and SA, in six data sets (tuku1, tuku2, tuku4-to-7) cross and within performances are the same. According to the MMER, within performance is better than the cross performance for two data sets: tuku3 and tuku8.

Data set	MAR			MMRE			MdMRE			Pred(30)		
	Win	Tie	Loss	Win	Tie	Loss	Win	Tie	Loss	Win	Tie	Loss
cocomo81e	0	20	0	0	16	4	4	16	0	4	16	0
cocomo81o	0	20	0	2	18	0	2	18	0	2	18	0
cocomo81s	18	2	0	15	5	0	15	5	0	13	5	2
nasa93_center_1	0	20	0	0	20	0	0	20	0	0	20	0
nasa93_center_2	4	16	0	2	18	0	2	18	0	2	18	0
nasa93_center_5	0	20	0	0	12	8	8	12	0	8	11	1
desharnaisL1	11	9	0	9	11	0	9	11	0	9	11	0
desharnaisL2	0	20	0	0	20	0	0	20	0	0	20	0
desharnaisL3	0	20	0	2	18	0	2	18	0	2	18	0
finnishAppType1	0	20	0	0	20	0	0	20	0	0	20	0
finnishAppType2345	0	20	0	0	17	3	0	17	3	0	17	3
kemererHardware1	0	0	20	0	0	20	0	0	20	0	0	20
kemererHardware23456	0	20	0	0	20	0	0	20	0	0	20	0
maxwellAppType1	6	14	0	1	19	0	1	19	0	0	19	1
maxwellAppType2	0	18	2	0	19	1	0	19	1	0	19	1
maxwellAppType3	0	20	0	1	19	0	1	19	0	1	19	0
maxwellHardware2	0	20	0	0	20	0	0	20	0	0	20	0
maxwellHardware3	0	20	0	0	20	0	0	20	0	0	20	0
maxwellHardware5	0	20	0	0	20	0	0	20	0	0	20	0
maxwellSource1	6	14	0	1	19	0	1	19	0	1	19	0
maxwellSource2	0	20	0	0	20	0	0	20	0	0	20	0

FIGURE 14.8

Summary of prior TEAK results [221] on 21 public data sets. For 19 data sets, cross and within-data performances are the same (note high tie values). For only two data sets (highlighted), within-data performance is better than cross.

The aforementioned results support the prior results reported by Kocaguneli et al. [222], where they have used 21 public data sets from a PROMISE data repository. A summary of their results on 21 public data sets is provided in Figure 14.8. As can be seen in Figure 14.8, Kocaguneli et al. use four error measures and identify only two data sets (gray highlighted rows) for which within-data performance is worse than cross company. For $21 - 2 = 19$ data sets, cross-data performance is statistically significantly the same as that of within company.

Figures 14.9, 14.10 show the performance results of transfer learning in time intervals for Cocomo81 and Nasa93. For Cocomo81, two within sources are defined: projects developed from 1960 to 1975 (called coc-60-75) and projects developed from 1976 onward (called coc-76-rest). Similarly, the subsets of Nasa93 are projects from 1970 to 1979 (called nasa-70-79) and projects from 1980 onward (called nasa-80-rest). In both Figures 14.9, 14.10, the tie values are quite high with the smallest tie value of 16. Note that in neither of the two figures is there a highlighted row, which means that in none of the time interval instance transfer experiments was there a case where TEAK failed to transfer instances between different time intervals. The implications of within- and cross-data experiments through instance transfer in time intervals are important for practitioners. Transfer learning results on Cocomo81 and Nasa93 subsets show that instance transfer methods, such as TEAK, may help

Data set	W			MAR	
	Win	Tie	Loss	W	C
coc-60-75	0	20	0	1181.0	1194.1
coc-76-rest	0	20	0	383.6	385.5

Data set	W			MMRE	
	Win	Tie	Loss	W	C
coc-60-75	0	19	1	2.3	1.2
coc-76-rest	0	20	0	1.9	1.6

Data set	W			MdMRE	
	Win	Tie	Loss	W	C
coc-60-75	0	19	1	0.9	0.9
coc-76-rest	0	20	0	0.8	0.8

Data set	W			Pred(25)	
	Win	Tie	Loss	W	C
coc-60-75	0	19	1	0.1	0.0
coc-76-rest	0	20	0	0.1	0.1

Data set	W			MMER	
	Win	Tie	Loss	W	C
coc-60-75	0	20	0	34.4	47.6
coc-76-rest	0	20	0	8.9	8.8

Data set	W			MBRE	
	Win	Tie	Loss	W	C
coc-60-75	1	19	0	35.9	48.1
coc-76-rest	0	20	0	10.2	9.7

Data set	W			MIBRE	
	Win	Tie	Loss	W	C
coc-60-75	0	19	1	0.8	0.7
coc-76-rest	0	20	0	0.6	0.6

Data set	W			SA	
	Win	Tie	Loss	W	C
coc-60-75	0	20	0	0.3	0.2
coc-76-rest	0	20	0	0.2	0.2

FIGURE 14.9

Performance comparison of Cocomo81 subsets for transfer learning in time. From Ref. [224].

organizations use aged data sets. Figures 14.9, 14.10 fundamentally show that decades of time difference can be crossed with the help of instance transfer.

The results of this research on proprietary data sets combined with the prior results of public data sets [222] give us a broader picture of the cross-data performance. By using instance transfer methods, such as TEAK, we have

- five out of eight proprietary data sets;
- 19 out of 21 public data sets;

where the performance difference between within- and cross-data is not statistically significant. This shows us that from a total of $21 + 8 = 29$ public and proprietary data sets, cross-data performs as well as within-data for $5 + 19 = 24$ cases. Also, by using TEAK for transfer learning between time intervals, we have two data sets subject to eight error measures ($2 \times 8 = 16$ cases), where cross-data performance is always the same as within-data performance.

Data set	W			MAR	
	Win	Tie	Loss	W	C
nasa-70-79	0	20	0	640.0	744.5
nasa-80-rest	4	16	0	339.6	377.6

Data set	W			MMRE	
	Win	Tie	Loss	W	C
nasa-70-79	0	20	0	3.8	2.2
nasa-80-rest	4	16	0	1.1	2.0

Data set	W			MdMRE	
	Win	Tie	Loss	W	C
nasa-70-79	0	20	0	0.7	0.8
nasa-80-rest	4	16	0	0.6	0.7

Data set	W			Pred(25)	
	Win	Tie	Loss	W	C
nasa-70-79	0	20	0	0.2	0.2
nasa-80-rest	4	16	0	0.3	0.2

Data set	W			MMER	
	Win	Tie	Loss	W	C
nasa-70-79	4	16	0	2.3	4.4
nasa-80-rest	0	20	0	2.7	2.5

Data set	W			MBRE	
	Win	Tie	Loss	W	C
nasa-70-79	2	18	0	5.6	5.9
nasa-80-rest	2	18	0	3.2	4.0

Data set	W			MIBRE	
	Win	Tie	Loss	W	C
nasa-70-79	2	18	0	0.6	0.6
nasa-80-rest	2	18	0	0.5	0.6

Data set	W			SA	
	Win	Tie	Loss	W	C
nasa-70-79	0	20	0	0.2	0.1
nasa-80-rest	4	16	0	0.2	0.1

FIGURE 14.10

Performance comparison of Nasa93 subsets for transfer learning in time. From Ref. [224].

14.5.2 INSPECTING SELECTION TENDENCIES

The second goal of our experimentation is to observe the selection tendencies of the test instances. Figure 14.11 shows what percentage of instances are selected from within-data sources (diagonal cells) as well as cross-data sources (off diagonal cells) in transfer learning experiments between domains. The first column of Figure 14.11 shows the within-data sources (eight different companies) as well as their sizes in parentheses. The second column shows the number of analogies retrieved from GAC2 on average over 20 runs. For each row, the columns *tuku1-to-8* show how the number of analogies in the second column is distributed to each data source. The values outside the parenthesis in each cell of columns *tuku1-to-8* are the number of analogies selected from that data source; the percentage value of that number w.r.t. the first column is given inside the parenthesis. Figures 14.12, 14.13 show the selection tendency of test instances for Cocomo81 and Nasa93 time interval transfer learning experiments. These figures are structured in the same manner as Figure 14.11.

The selection tendency values of Tukutuku, Cocomo81, and Nasa93 subsets provide us with suggestions regarding how much data a test instance uses from within- and cross-data sources during the domain and time interval transfer of instances. From the selection tendency figures, we can identify two findings:

Data set	# of Analogies	tuku1	tuku2	tuku3	tuku4	tuku5	tuku6	tuku7	tuku8
tuku1(14)	5.8	0.5(3.6)	1.0(7.1)	0.1(0.7)	0.1(0.7)	0.4(2.9)	0.4(2.9)	1.7(12.1)	1.6(11.4)
tuku2(20)	11.0	1.1(5.5)	1.6(8.0)	0.3(1.5)	0.8(4.0)	0.7(3.5)	0.7(3.5)	2.7(13.5)	3.1(15.5)
tuku3(15)	7.3	0.9(6.0)	1.3(8.7)	0.4(2.7)	0.2(1.3)	0.8(5.3)	0.2(1.3)	1.5(10.0)	1.9(12.7)
tuku4(6)	6.7	0.6(10.0)	1.5(25.0)	0.2(3.3)	0.3(5.0)	0.2(3.3)	0.7(11.7)	1.2(20.0)	2.0(33.3)
tuku5(13)	9.3	2.4(18.5)	1.4(10.8)	0.3(2.3)	0.5(3.8)	0.5(3.8)	0.4(3.1)	1.3(10.0)	2.4(18.5)
tuku6(8)	8.9	0.7(8.8)	1.6(20.0)	0.2(2.5)	0.7(8.8)	0.7(8.8)	0.7(8.8)	1.8(22.5)	2.6(32.5)
tuku7(31)	7.8	1.2(3.9)	1.3(4.2)	0.3(1.0)	0.5(1.6)	0.6(1.9)	0.1(0.3)	1.7(5.5)	2.1(6.8)
tuku8(18)	6.9	1.1(6.1)	1.1(6.1)	0.3(1.7)	0.3(1.7)	0.7(3.9)	0.3(1.7)	1.3(7.2)	1.8(10.0)

FIGURE 14.11

The amount of instances selected from within- and cross-company data sets. The first column is the subset names and their sizes in parenthesis. The second column is the average number of retrieved instances in GAC2. The following columns show the number of analogies from each particular subset, in parenthesis the percentage values of these numbers w.r.t. the first column are given. From Ref. [224].

Data set	# of Analogies	coc-60-75	coc-76-rest
coc-60-75 (20)	3.6	0.8 (4.1)	2.8 (6.4)
coc-76-rest (43)	4.5	1.3 (6.6)	3.2 (7.4)

FIGURE 14.12

Instances selected from within- and cross-company data sets of Cocomo81. From Ref. [224].

Data set	# of Analogies	nasa-70-79	nasa-80-rest
nasa-70-79 (39)	7.3	2.6 (6.6)	4.7 (8.7)
nasa938089 (54)	9.5	3.2 (8.2)	6.3 (11.7)

FIGURE 14.13

Instances selected from within- and cross-company data sets of Nasa93.

Finding #1: See the second columns of Figure 14.11–Figure 14.13 that only a very small portion of all the available data (cross and within) is transferred as useful analogies. This finding points to the importance of: instance transfer, a.k.a filtering and estimation methods like TEAK that are capable of transferring relevant analogies between domains and time intervals. The low number of instances selected are also supported by relevant literature: Chang's prototype generators [70] replaced training sets of size $T = (514, 150, 66)$ with prototypes of size $N = (34, 14, 6)$ (respectively). That is, prototypes may be as few as $\frac{N}{T} = (7, 9, 9)\%$ of the original data. Note that these values are close to how many instances were retrieved in the above results.

Finding #2: When we compare the diagonal and off-diagonal percentages, we see that the values are very close. This is consistent with what Kocaguneli et al. had reported from public data sets [222]. The second finding bears some importance concerning the definition of cross-data. It shows that defining cross-data on the basis of a single feature (e.g., w.r.t. a particular company) is misguided. It also shows that prior findings of domain transfer experiments on the public data sets [222] are stable for proprietary data sets as well as for time interval transfer. TEAK, being an instance transfer method using all features to transfer analogies, selects close amounts of instances from each data source.

To better observe how close within- and cross-data percentages are, we plot the percentage values of within- and cross-data sources of Tukutuku subsets in Figure 14.14a and b, respectively. Figure 14.14a and b are basically the plots of diagonal and off-diagonal percentage values of Figure 14.11. We see from Figure 14.14a and b that the maximum and minimum percentages of within- and cross-data selection are very close. To align these percentages, we took the percentile values from 0th percentile to 100th percentile with increments of 10. The resulting percentiles are shown in Figure 14.14c. See in Figure 14.14c that within- and cross-data have similar percentile values, i.e., the selection tendencies from within- and cross-sources are very close to one another. Note that percentage and percentile plots are unnecessary for Figures 14.12, 14.13, as the closeness of within- and cross-data selection percentages of Cocomo81 and Nasa93 subsets can easily be verified with manual inspection: For Cocomo81 subsets the biggest percentage difference is $6.6 - 4.1 = 2.5\%$; for Nasa93 subsets it is $11.7 - 8.2 = 3.5\%$.

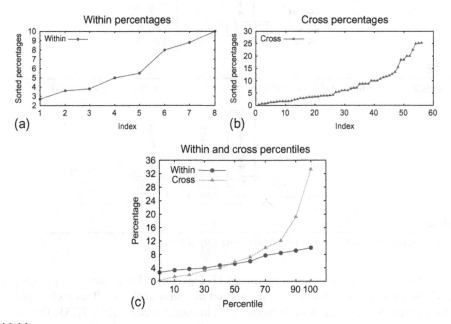

FIGURE 14.14

Percentages of retrieved instances (a.k.a. analogies) from within (a) and cross (b) data sets. The percentage values come from Figure 14.11. Within company percentages are the gray-highlighted diagonal cells, whereas cross company percentages are the remaining off-diagonal cells. The percentile graph (c) shows the percentiles of (a) and (b). From Ref. [224].

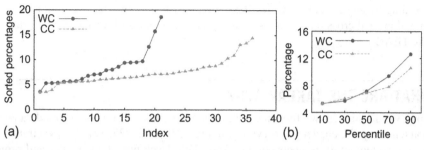

FIGURE 14.15

Percentages and percentiles of instances retrieved by TEAK from within- and cross-data sets as given by Kocaguneli et al. [222]. Note the similarity of the percentile plot of this figure to that of Figure 14.14.

Figure 14.15 is taken from our manuscript published as part of the research presented in this chapter, regarding the selection tendency experiments on the public data sets [222]. In the performance experiments, we have seen the similarity between the results of this research and that of Kocaguneli et al. in terms of performance. Comparison of Figure 14.15 to Figure 14.14 shows that the similarity of results are also valid in terms of the selection tendencies. See in particular the percentile values of Figures 14.14, 14.15 that transfer learning between domains of proprietary data sets and public data sets have similar selection tendencies.

14.6 DISCUSSION

Based on the majority of the companies in the domain-transfer-learning experiments (depending on the error measure, five or six companies out of eight) the cross-data performance is the same as the within-data performance. In terms of time interval transfer learning, in *all* of the cases, within- and cross-data performances were statistically the same. This shows us that instance transfer methods like TEAK that filter cross-data can help transfer learning between domains and time intervals so that cross-data can perform as well as within-data. However, for a minority of the companies in the domain transfer learning experiments, the cross-data performance may be far from satisfactory. The reason for the difference of these companies may be hidden in their within-data quality, but this statement is just our speculation. For concrete reasons leading to failure of cross-data in certain companies, further research is needed on the features defining within- and cross-data borders.

Another interesting fact is that error measures can result in different conclusions. For example, see in Figures 14.6, 14.7 that cross-data performance for the company tuku8 depends on error measures. This disagreement may cause different companies to make different conclusions depending on the particular error measures they are using.

Note that in the experiments of this chapter, the cross borders are defined by same-area (Web) companies or same time interval projects. Different companies and different time intervals may mean different geographical locations; possibly different development languages or development methodologies. Such single features are deemed to define cross-data borders that hinder knowledge transfer. However, the selection tendencies of the test instances are in disagreement with defining cross borders according to single features. Given the option, test instances select training instances equally likely from within- and cross-data sources by using all the features of a data set via instance transfer methods like TEAK.

14.7 **WHAT ARE THE TAKEAWAYS?**

In this chapter we questioned two fundamental problems of cross-data usage: cross-data performance and selection tendency. We challenged previous findings [218, 222, 227, 427, 463] via transfer learning experiments on contemporary projects coming from Web development companies and projects from different time periods. Our findings are in agreement with the prior results. Regarding cross-data performance between domains, our analysis showed that cross-data performance is indistinguishable from within-data performance for the majority (five or six out of eight, depending on the error measure) of the data sets. However, a minority of companies (two out of eight) are better off using their own within-data. Practitioners should also be warned that for some cases, different error measures lead to different conclusions. Our recommendations to practitioners regarding the cases of conflicting error measures are

- to use a number of different error measures;
- and to make their decisions based on:
  - either the agreement of the majority of the error measures
  - or the particular error measure favoring their priorities.

The selection tendency results showed that the definitions of cross and within-data based on single features like company name or time interval may be handled with instance transfer methods. Our results show that test instances select both from within- and cross-data sources. The meaning of this result is that the most similar project(s) to the one currently being estimated is not necessarily within the same company or time interval, but it may be in a cross-data set collected on the other side of the world in another time period. This research shows that instance transfer methods like TEAK can make it possible for companies to automatically prune away irrelevant projects and transfer knowledge from relevant training data.

SHARING LESS DATA (IS A GOOD THING)

Name:	PEEKER
Intent:	Find the smallest, most useful portion of a data set.
Motivation:	Chapters 13, 14 showed that it is possible to share data between software projects. Potentially, those results could motivate massive data collection across every software project. Before wasting energy on massive disk drives, it is responsible to ask if all data needs to be stored?
Solution:	Cluster the data. Replace each cluster with its centroid. Also, rank all variables and discard 75% of the lower-scoring variables. These generate a new *reduced* data set with one row for each centroid and one column per unpruned variables. The reduced data set can contain as little as 1% of the original data, while still supporting predictions comparable to those that can be generated using all the data (via state-of-the-art data miners).
Applicability:	The experiments of this chapter show that PEEKER's tiny summary of data generates defect predictions that are at least as good as those found by more elaborate methods (running on all the data).
Related to:	This code described in this chapter uses a (slightly) more complicated version of Chapter 12 system.

This chapter is a summary and extension of a Masters thesis "Data Carving: Identifying and Removing Irrelevancies in the Data" by Vasil Papakroni, Computer Science, West Virginia University, 2013. It has not been previously published.

> The computing scientists main challenge is not to get confused by the complexities of (their) own making.
>
> **E.W. Dijkstra**

In the age of big data, data centers, and cloud storage, it is now possible to access exabytes (10^{28} bytes or more) of data. However, as soon as one team wants to share *useful* data with another, the task changes. Rather than sharing large amounts of possibly noisy information, it can be more useful to *just just share the small parts that matter.*

Why share less data? For one thing, it is the mark of the rookie to demand a full inspection of all aspects of all parts of all the data. Novice data scientists obsess on all effects (no matter how small) found in all parts of the data. Insight is lost as these amateur analysts generate an endless stream of complex charts and spurious statistics. For example:

- Once upon a time, we supervised a graduate student who proudly presented a 300-page draft of a masters thesis. The last 200 pages of this document was all dense tables of data, printed in a five-point font size.
- The student was asked, "What does all that data mean?" When no succinct answer was forthcoming, we told the student to remove those tables.
- The student protested and asked, "How will people know what I have done?" We replied that *collecting data* is very different then *sharing data*, and it is not necessarily useful for all the collected data to be shared.[1]

The rest of this chapter makes the case for the benefits of reasoning from less data. We advocate a two-layered approach to data collection and usage:

- Layer1: Big data storage for the collected data;
- Layer2: Big discussion over a summary of the most relevant data.

While Layer1 is what needs to be *stored*; it is Layer2 that should be *shared* and discussed. Layer2 can be very small; for example, in the main example of this chapter, we show one summary table that is 98% smaller than the original data sets. In this smaller space, business users can easily explore and refine their ideas. This will naturally lead to additional queries about different aspects of the data that, in turn, will lead to more queries to Layer1 (the big data storage).

Many texts address the Layer1 storage for big data [441] but few discuss the discussion benefits of sharing Layer2. Hence, this text will focus on Layer2.

15.1 CAN WE SHARE LESS DATA?

As discussed in Chapters 4, 5, one motivation for sharing less data is that much data is redundant, noisy, or irrelevant. For example:

---

[1] Our colleagues who teach composition at university have an analogous mantra: *just because something took a long time to write, does not mean it should take a long time to read.*

- If a model can be generated from a table of data, then that table contains enough examples to learn that model.
- That is, many rows are actually echoes of a smaller number of underlying effects called *prototypes* [71].
- One way to share less data if only share a small number of prototypes.

Another way to share less data is to share fewer columns. Figure 15.1 offers a mathematical argument that, in the expected case, models can only use a small number of columns (if it were

Consider the standard Euclidean distance measure from the origin to some point in n dimensions $x = \{x_1, x_2, \ldots, x_n\}$: $d = \sqrt{\sum_i^n x_i^2}$. Note that this d is the radius of some sphere so, at first glance, this equation seems to say that more dimensions means more volume (as new dimension $n' > n$ adds more to $\sum_i^{n'}$).

But that first glance is misleading. For modeling, we must generalize from related examples. If "related" means "nearby" then it is important to check what happens if we increase the number of dimensions n, while keeping d constant. For the special case where $x_i = x_j$, we can rewrite the above equation as $d = \sqrt{n x_i^2}$. To see how to change x_i for some constant d, we rearrange our equation to $x_i = \sqrt{d^2/n}$. Note how, in this equation, x_i must decrease as n increases; i.e., we must decrease the gap x_i between any two instances (i.e., their distance along any single dimension). And as this gap shrinks, it becomes less likely to find new examples in that reduced space.

There is another way to see how *increasing* the number of dimensions can *decrease* the space where we can find related examples. Consider the volume of an n-dimensional sphere. The volume of an $n = 2$-dimensional sphere of radius r (otherwise known as a "circle") is $V_2 = \pi r^2$. If that circle grows into $n = 3$ dimensions, it becomes a sphere with volume $V_3 = \frac{4}{3}\pi r^3$. More generally, the volume of an n-dimensional sphere is $V_n = V_{n-2}\frac{2\pi r^2}{n}$. That is, to compute a volume of an n-dimensional sphere, go back two dimensions then multiply that by the factor $\frac{2\pi r^2}{n}$.

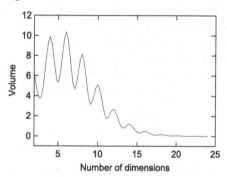

A curious feature of the V_n expression is when $n > 2\pi r^2$, the volume starts decreasing. For example, shown above is the volume of the unit sphere (with $r = 1$), as the number of dimensions increases. Note that the volume in which we can find related examples shrinks to zero after about 15 dimensions.

In summary, what this math shows is that that the repeatable effects that we can summarize into a model are either low-dimensional or so rare that they are no longer repeatable. To say that another way, models are either simple or unsupportable.

FIGURE 15.1

Why most models are low-dimensional.

otherwise, there would not be enough data to cover all the possible values of all the columns). That is, if we were so foolish as to try to build high-dimensional models, we would fail as the region where we can find related examples would become vanishingly small. Note that this is often called the *curse of dimensionality*:

> When the dimensionality increases, the volume of the space increases so fast that the available data becomes sparse. This sparsity is problematic for any method that requires statistical significance. In order to obtain a statistically sound and reliable result, the amount of data needed to support the result often grows exponentially with the dimensionality.
>
> **http://en.wikipedia.org/wiki/Curse_of_dimensionality**

Note this curse can also be a blessing:

- Because it is impossible to find the data to support bigger models, then all we need ever do is build small ones;
- Which, in turn, means that we might be able to build those small models for just a little data;
- Which also means that we need only share small amounts of data.

There is much empirical evidence that just because a data set has n columns, we need not use them all. Numerous researchers have examined what happens when a data miner deliberately ignores some of the columns in the training data. For example, the experiments of Ron Kohavi and George John show that, on numerous real-world datasets, over 80% of columns can be ignored. Further, ignoring those columns doesn't degrade the learner's classification accuracy (in fact, it sometimes even results in small improvements [234]).

Further, if we combine both prototype and column selection, the net result can be a dramatic reduction in the complexity of the data. Figure 15.2 shows 22 rows and 6 columns that summarize a larger data set with hundreds of rows and dozens of columns.[2] This table is a summary of Figure 15.3 (and the columns of that table are described in Figure 15.4). The larger data set describes the defects seen in the 400+ classes of an open-source JAVA application

Note how the size reduction of this data is quite large:

- The original data set had 21 columns, 426 rows, and $21 \times 426 = 8946$ cells.
- The summary has 6 columns, 21 rows, and $6 \times 21 = 126$ cells.
- That is, our summary has $\frac{126}{8946} \approx 1\%$ of the the original data.

A concern with making such a short summary is that some information has been lost. To check that, at the end of this chapter we show a comparison between defect prediction in the larger data set (using state-of-the-art methods including Random Forests [51]) with predictions using a very simple method (extrapolating between the two nearest clusters). In that comparison, the predictions from the summary were found to be no different than those using state-of-the-art methods on the full data set (because the original data had some spurious noise that was removed by the centroid generation process).

---

[2] It turns out there are very many ways to implement prototype and column pruning [155, 345]. The example of Figure 15.2 was generated using two linear-time methods, discussed later in this chapter: (i) PEEKING2 clusters the data, then prints one centroid per cluster; (ii) INFOGAIN prunes columns whose values tend not to isolate either the defective or nondefective classes.

Centroid	lcom3	ce	rfc	cbm	loc	Defect rate
0	2	0.75	1.94	0	4.25	0.22
1	0.97	3.19	14.2	1.06	66.5	0.42
2	0.83	3.91	19.46	3.49	102	0.86
3	1.31	2	8	0.51	30	0.29
4	1.74	1.38	6.88	0.50	12.6	0
5	1.03	3.43	18.3	1.14	77.1	0.71
6	0.60	2.71	14.7	0.86	101	0.43
7	1.19	1	4.50	0	32.4	0.50
8	0.82	5.24	25	2.76	171	0.76
9	0.80	4.71	34	3.46	282	1
10	1.26	3.08	14.54	0.38	48.5	0.15
11	0.85	1.69	8.62	1	80.4	0.23
12	0.93	7.75	33.2	1.75	185	0.83
13	0.80	3.75	27.8	2.17	271	0.75
14	0.80	6.90	47.9	2.90	458	0.90
15	0.78	4.33	22.2	3.13	115	0.92
16	0.75	8.39	48.7	2.39	261	0.78
17	0.84	2.71	17.9	0.79	674	0.46
18	0.79	3.72	34.5	2.17	662	0.83
19	0.79	16.6	82	1.67	508	0.78
20	0.82	5.33	54.9	2.22	722	1
21	0.82	20.5	122	4.13	1324	0.87

FIGURE 15.2

PEEKING2's summary of Figure 15.3.

The only way larger data sets can be summarized to smaller ones is if there is some superfluous details in the larger set. Hence, before we can advocate such summarizations we must first offer a measure of *data set simplicity* and *only* summarize the simpler data. Figure 15.5 offers *intrinsic dimensionality* as such a measure and applies it to 10 data sets with 21 columns of data. As shown in that figure, the intrinsic dimensionality of our data sets can be very small indeed. It is hardly surprising that such an intrinsically low-dimensional data set can be summaries in half a dozen columns and a few dozen rows.

15.2 USING LESS DATA

To see how we might use the reduced data of Figure 15.2 to quickly make decisions, we highlight three different kinds of clusters:

- Find the nearest cluster to some current situation, which we call *now*.
- Find a close cluster with some desired property, which we call *envied*.
  - For the data of Figure 15.2, *envied* might mean a close cluster with *less defects*.
- Find another close cluster with some undesired property, which we call *feared*.
  - For example, such a feared cluster might have *more defects*.

cdd	id	lcom3	ce	rfc	cbm	loc	max_cc	wmc	cbo	amc	dam	lcom	mfa	npm	avg_cc	cam	dit	moa	ca	ic	noc	defect
0	11	2								4									4			0
0	17	2			4																	0
0	32	2			4																	0
0	28	2			5					1									1			0
0	89	2			7																	0
0	57	2			10					2									2			1
0	13	2	1	1	1		1		9					1	1	1			9			0
0	37	2	1	1	1		1		1					1	1	1			1			0
0	41	2	1	1	1		1		3					1	1	1			3			0
0	43	2	1	1	1		1		4					1	1	1			3			0
0	12	2	1	1	1		1		8					1	1	1			7			0
0	16	2	1	1	1		1		4					1	1	1			3			0
0	36	2	1	1	1		1		2					1	1	1			2			1
0	36	2	1	1	1		1		7					1	1	1			6			0
0	37	2	1	1	1		1		2					1	1	1			1			0
0	39	2	1	1	1		1		5					1	1	1			4			0
0	8	2	2	6		1	1		3							1			1			0
0	26	2	2	5		1	1		4		1	1				1			1			0
0	80	2	2	4		1			3							1			1			0
0	12	2	2	2	2	2	5				1		2	1	7				5			0
0	40	2	2	2	2	2	5				1		2	1	7				5			0
0	14	2	2	13		1	4	7				1	1		1				3			1
0	67	2	2	6		1	7	5				1	1		1				6			0
0	24	2	2	6		1	2	5				1	1		1				1			0
0	18	2	2	4		1	2	3				1	1		1						1	0
0	37	2	2	2		2	2				1		2	1	1				2			1
0	14	2	4	4		4	6					6		4	1				6			0
0	22	2	4	4		4	3					6		4	1	7			3			0
0	88	2	4	4		4	2					6		4	1	4			1			1
0	43	2	4	4		4	5					6		4	1	5			4			0
0	98	2	4	12		2	3		4.50		1	1			6				1			0
0	19	2	4	12		2	3		4.50		1	1		2	6				1			1
0	31	2	4	8		3	5		1.67		3		3	67	7				4			1
0	21	2	4	4		4	6				6	4	1		6				5			1
0	30	2	4	4		4	3				6	4	1		5				1			0
0	11	2	4	4		4	3	4	1.33		3	3		67	8				1			1
1	419	82		13		62	1	12	18	3.83		42		12	83	71	1		18		2	0
1	111	1.13	3	13		64	1	9	5	5.89		36	30	9	78	26	2		2			0
1	42	1.13	3	13		62	1	9	5	5.67		36	30	9	78	26	2		2			1
1	135	1.13	3	13		62	1	9	5	5.67		36	30	9	78	26	2		2			0
1	277	1.13	3	13		62	1	9	5	5.67		36	30	9	78	26	2		2			0
1	341	1.13	3	13		62	1	9	5	5.67		36	30	9	78	26	2		2			1
1	369	1.13	3	13		62	1	9	5	5.67		36	30	9	78	26	2		2			1
1	29	1.13	3	13		60	1	9	5	5.33	33	36	30	9	78	26	2		2			0
1	4	1.13	3	13		59	1	9	5	5.33		36	30	9	78	26	2		2			0
1	99	1.13	3	13		58	1	9	5	5.33		36	30	9	78	26	2		1			0
1	179	1.13	3	13		58	1	9	4	5.33		36	30	9	78	26	2		1			0
1	432	1.13	3	13		58	1	9	4	5.33		36	30	9	78	26	2		1			0
1	46	85	3	13	2	83	2	10	4	7	33	3	50	9	90	23	2	2	1			0
1	86	72	4	13	2	69	1	10	6	5.70	50	3	47	10	80	30	3		2	1		1
1	316	17	2	14	1	85	7	7	4	11	1	9	69	7	1.43	43	3		2	1		0
1	112	1.11	3	14		67	1	10	5	5.40	33	45	27	10	80	25	2		2			1
1	176	1.11	3	14		67	1	10	5	5.40	33	45	27	10	80	25	2		2			1
1	141	1.11	3	14		63	1	10	5	5	33	45	27	10	80	25	2		2			0
1	125	1.11	3	14		59	1	10	6	4.60	33	45	27	10	80	25	2		3			1
1	370	1.11	3	14		57	1	10	4	4.40	33	45	27	10	80	25	2		1			1
1	348	92	4	14		66	1	11	11	4.45		41	64	11	91	33	3	1	7		1	1
1	431	61	4	14		71	3	10	6	5.90	1	19		6	1.30	33	1	2	3		2	0
1	227	2	4	14	2	67	1	6	7	117		15	56	6	67	33	2	3	1	1		0
1	118	1		15		86	3	5	1	16		3			1.60	67	1					0
1	406	1.11	4	15		59	1	10	6	4.60	33	45	27	10	80	25	2		2			0
1	82	1.14	4	15	4	60	2	8	5	6.38		28	65	6	88	33	2		1	1		1
1	228	1.14	4	15	4	60	2	8	6	6.38		28	65	6	88	33	2		1	1		1
1	250	1.14	4	15	4	60	2	8	5	6.38		28	65	6	88	33	2		1	1		1
1	295	1.14	4	15	4	60	2	8	5	6.38		28	65	6	88	33	2		1	1		1
1	22	43		16	1	66	2	8	11	7.13	1	22	81	8	75	35	4		11	1	4	0
1	152	85	4	16	2	86	1	11	5	6.45	75	21	44	11	82	26	2		2	1	1	1
1	315	1.13	4	16	4	71	2	9	5	6.78		36	61	7	89	31	2		1	1		1
1	262	1.13	4	16	4	70	2	9	11	6.67		36	63	7	89	31	3		8	1	1	1
1	134	1.13	4	16	4	67	2	9	7	6.33		36	61	7	89	31	2		3	1	1	1
1	147	33	6	16		82	3	4	6	19.25		4		4	1.25	42	1		1			0
1	136	25	3	17		85	1	11	7	6.55	1	9		11	64	52	1		4			1
2	27			1		11		4	7	27.7	1			3	1.2	5			2			0
2	58	89		1		11		7	5	15.1	3		7	6	71	3			2			0
2	6	83		1		10	1	6	9	7	2	4	1	80	2				2			1
2	14	83		1		10	1	6	9		3	5	8	1.1	2				2			1

...

(362 lines removed)

FIGURE 15.3

The first 80 examples of the POI-3.0 data set (362 examples omitted). From openscience.us/repo. Empty cells denote "0." This data forms 37 clusters, three of which are shown above (the gray rows show clusters zero and two). See Figure 15.4 for an explanation of column names.

amc	Average method complexity	E.g., number of JAVA byte codes
avg_cc	Average McCabe	Average McCabe's cyclomatic complexity seen in class
ca	Afferent couplings	How many other classes use the specific class.
cam	Cohesion amongst classes	Summation of number of different types of method parameters in every method divided by a multiplication of number of different method parameter types in whole class and number of methods.
cbm	Coupling between methods	Total number of new/redefined methods to which all the inherited methods are coupled
cbo	Coupling between objects	Increased when the methods of one class access services of another.
ce	Efferent couplings	How many other classes is used by the specific class.
dam	Data access	Ratio of the number of private (protected) attributes to the total number of attributes
dit	Depth of inheritance tree	
ic	Inheritance coupling	Number of parent classes to which a given class is coupled (includes counts of methods and variables inherited)
lcom	Lack of cohesion in methods	number of pairs of methods that do not share a reference to an instance variable.
locm3	Another lack of cohesion measure	If m, a are the number of *methods, attributes* in a class number and $\mu(a)$ is the number of methods accessing an attribute, then $lcom3 = ((\frac{1}{a}\sum_j^a \mu(a_j)) - m)/(1 - m)$.
loc	Lines of code	
max_cc	Maximum McCabe	Maximum McCabe's cyclomatic complexity seen in class
mfa	Functional abstraction	Number of methods inherited by a class plus number of methods accessible by member methods of the class
moa	Aggregation	Count of the number of data declarations (class fields) whose types are user defined classes
noc	Number of children	
npm	Number of public methods	
rfc	Response for a class	Number of methods invoked in response to a message to the object.
wmc	Weighted methods per class	
defect	Defect	Binary class. Indicates whether any defect is reported to a post-release bug-tracking system.

FIGURE 15.4

OO measures used in our defect data sets.

- Find a set of *what2do* and *what2avoid* rules by calculating the contrasting delta as follows:
  - *what2do = envied - now*; i.e., the changes that select for *less defects*;
  - *what2avoid = feared - now*; i.e., the changes that select for *more defects*.

For instance, Figure 15.6 shows the nearest cluster to one row of Figure 15.2. We label this cluster as *now*. Figure 15.7 reports that 39% of the examples used to form that cluster had defects. The nearest cluster to *now* that we *envy* has slightly fewer defects (35%). Of more interest are

- The slightly more remote cluster (called *lessDefects2*), with half the defect rate to *now* (18%);
- The two clusters (*moreDefects1,moreDefects2*) where defect rates are nearly double to *now* (64% and 76%).

Levina and Bickel report that it is possible to simplify seemingly complex data: "...the only reason any methods work in very high dimensions is that, in fact, the data are not truly high-dimensional. Rather, they are embedded in a high-dimensional space, but can be *efficiently summarized in a space of a much lower dimension*... [251]." Their tool for finding the shape of that lower dimensionality space is the *correlation dimension* that measures how

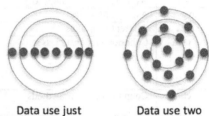

(a) Data use just one dimension. (b) Data use two dimensions.

many more items are found if we explore a progressively larger space. For example, in the figure at right, the "A" data only uses one-dimension while the data of "B" is spread out across more dimensions. As we explore a progressively larger circle in "A" we can only ever find linearly more items. However, in "B," as r increases, we can find up to r^2 more items (as "B" uses more dimensions than "A").

Therefore, to find the underlying dimensionality of a data set with n items, we plot the radius r against the number of items found at distance within r:

$$C(r) = \frac{2}{n(n-1)} \sum_{i=1}^{n} \sum_{j=i+1}^{n} \begin{cases} 1, & \text{if } \mathrm{dist}(x_i, x_j) < r. \\ 0, & \text{otherwise.} \end{cases}$$

In astrophysics [251], it is standard to report the intrinsic dimension as the maximum slope of the plot $log(C(r))$ versus $log(r)$. These plots show those slopes for 10 data sets that use the 21 columns of Figure 15.4. In the charts, each plot is marked with its intrinsic dimensionality. All these values are much less than one; in other words, much less than the 21 columns of the original data set. That is, it should be possible to reduce these data sets to a much smaller number of underlying data points.

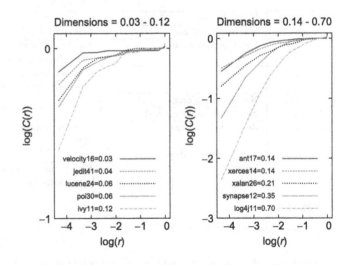

FIGURE 15.5

Intrinsic dimensionality.

If users are willing to refactor their code, they could make changes to avoid the feared *moreDefects* and to target the envied *lessDefects* examples. Figure 15.7 shows the *what2do* to drive *now* toward the envied *lessDefect* clusters and *what2avoid* to dodge the feared *moreDefects* cluster. The best recommendation, in *what2do₂*, is increase *lcom3* and *cam*, which, as Figure 15.4 tells us, relate to

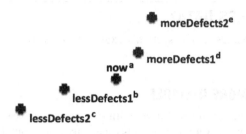

FIGURE 15.6

"Now," "less defects," and "more defects" clusters from the summarized data of POI3.

cluster/rule	rfc	lcom3	loc	cam	amc	defect_rate
a = now	1	6	1	4	1	0.39
b = envied	1	5	1	4	1	0.35
c = envied_2	1	9	1	5	1	0.18
d = feared	1	5	1	5	1	0.64
e = feared_2	2	4	1	4	1	0.76
what2do = b - a	0	-1	0	0	0	-0.04
what2do_2 = c - a	0	3	0	1	0	-0.21
what2avoid = d - a	0	-1	0	1	0	0.25
what2Avoid_2 = e - a	1	-2	0	0	0	0.37

FIGURE 15.7

Contrast-set learning from Figure 15.6. For an explanation of the column names, see Figure 15.4. Please note that the values shown in this table are not raw column values (except the last column) but discrete levels derived from applying a 10 equal-width bins discretization.

the cohesion within each class. So, in this case, this contrast study has a very simple business-level summary:

> Programmers may need to improve the cohesion of the classes in the system.

This summary prunes away a large number of possible factors, letting users focus their discussions on the small number of remaining factors. These factors may not be causal (learners cannot distinguish true causality from mere correlation), but they are at least candidates for action in a domain. In our view, managers should think of contrast set rule learning as a tool to discover alternative solutions to improve the software quality (and such alternatives could be discussed in a data engagement meeting).

Another way to look at this style of analysis is that it supports *hypothesis generation* and *hypothesis pruning*:

- *Hypothesis generation:* When it is not known what options are available, Figure 15.7 can offer an initial set of possible actions that could be discussed and developed by users.
- *Hypothesis pruning:* When a team is debating a large set of options, a team leader can guide the discussion away from options not supported by the data; i.e., those that do not appear in Figure 15.7.

15.3 WHY SHARE LESS DATA?

Stepping back from the specifics of last section's example, are there more general reasons to favor summary-based reasoning?

15.3.1 LESS DATA IS MORE RELIABLE

When talking about computer systems, Edsger Dijkstra once said "Simplicity is prerequisite for reliability." What's true about software in general is especially true about data mining algorithms. The simpler the data, the fewer the possible mistakes (as less than can be computed). On the other hand, the more complex the learning scheme, the more skill is required by the operator to (e.g.) select the right parameters for the right kernel for a support vector machine.

Recent results highlight the problem of excessive complexity in our data miners. Hall et al. [157] reviewed data mining work for software defect prediction. They report that "models performing comparatively well are relatively simple techniques that are easy to use and well understood. . ., e.g., Naive Bayes and Logistic regression." That is, our supposedly better data miners are not producing better models.[3] This is an important point as Martin Shepperd [391] reports that even supposed experts are making poor use of these data mining tools. Using data from the Hall et al. study, he found an alarmingly large variance in the performance of models generated by different research teams even when they are applying the same data miners to the same data. Shepperd pessimistically summarizes this result as

It doesn't matter what you do but it does matter who does it!

In this context, it is interesting to note that once data has been simplified into small tables like Figure 15.2, then further inference becomes very simple indeed (as evidence of that, note that the recommendations generated in Section 15.2 were generated via a simple processing of subtracting two rows). Therefore, one reason to share less data is to simplify the inference required to mine that data.

15.3.2 LESS DATA IS FASTER TO DISCUSS

The last section argued that we should share and use less data in data mining since that simplifies the processing requirements of a data miner. But that is not the whole story. Data is read by two audiences:

- Automatic algorithms;
- Humans, making decisions about that data.

One reason to share less data is to better support humans who want to make conclusions from that data. This is an important issue since, at some stage, a group of business users will have to convene to *interpret the results* (e.g., to decide if it is wise to deploy the results as a defect reduction method within an organization). These business users are now demanding that data mining tools be augmented with tools to support business-level interpretation of that data. For example, at a recent panel on software analytics at ICSE12, industrial practitioners lamented the state of the art in data mining and software engineering [313]. Panelists commented that prediction is all well and good, but what about decision

---

[3] A similar conclusion, that in practice in has become hard to improve our results with better data miners, was also made by the Dejaeger et al. review of data mining in effort estimation [94].

making? That is, these panelists are more interested in the interpretations that follow the mining, rather than just the mining. The problem with interpretataion is that it is time-consuming and expensive:

- When commissioning an effort model, Ricardo Valerdi [431] reconciles expert opinions with domain data using model-based Bayesian tuning. While a strong proponent of this approach, he concedes that "(it is) extremely time consuming when large sample sizes are needed." For example, Valerdi once recruited 40 experts to three panel sessions to review an effort model. Each panel took three hours so, on total, this study required $3 \times 3 \times 40/7.5 = 48$ days to complete. Valerdi remarks on the problem on reasoning over too much data. He notes that "more columns increase the explanatory power of the model, but too many make the model too complex to use and difficult to calibrate." There are also cost implications for using too many columns. He offered the heuristic that training data needs 5 to 10 examples per column; i.e., the fewer the columns, the less is required for calibration. That is, if we can reduce the size of the training data, that would increase our confidence in the learned model.
- Valerdi's comments on discussing data are echoed by Brendon Murphy [333] from Microsoft (UK). He comments that the high cost of interpretation implies that there is never enough time to review all the defect data or all the models generated by the data miners. Hence, he is very interested in methods that reduce the number of columns and rows of data that need to be discussed with users. These reduction methods are a black art. In a personnel communication, he notes that while experts can rapidly identify some key columns and examples, novices are far less successful at this task. He cautions that such experts are in short supply.

Since data reduction is so important, and since (as Murphy says) there are so few people that can do it properly, we explore automatic reduction methods (such as those that generated Figure 15.2) in order to simplify the task of humans analyzing the data.

15.3.3 LESS DATA IS EASIER TO PROCESS

Another reason to share and use less data is that it addresses certain systems issues associated with data mining. For example, in the above, conclusions were made in the summarization table by extrapolating between neighbors. This is a *case-based reasoning* technique [2]. The main advantage of CBR is its conceptual simplicity (new conclusions are made by looking at nearby older examples). On the other hand CBR has certain drawbacks:

- The *memory* required to store the examples.
- The *slow runtimes* associated with finding the nearby examples.
- The conclusions can be damaged by *noise or outliers* in the training data.
- All the cases are needed to make inferences, so it is hard to deploy a CBR tool without *violating the privacy* of the individuals and organizations described in the data.

It turns out that if we apply CBR to the summary space, then we can address the above issues:

- If we reason over the summaries, then we use *less memory* and *run faster*. Not only is using the summaries faster but generating those summaries need not be a time-consuming process (we will see below that the methods for building the summaries take linear time).
- As to the influence of *noise and outliers*, the clustering and pruning process used to make Figure 15.2 tends to smooth out the effect of distracting signals. This means that if original larger

data contains outliers and noise, then it is better to reason over the summaries than the original data. Hence, as discussed above, it is possible to find better predictions in the summary than in the original data.[4]

- As to *privacy* concerns, observe how no individual record in the full data survives into the summary data of Figure 15.2. That is, this summarization process makes individual identification very difficult (for more on the issue of privacy and data mining, see Chapter 16).

15.4 HOW TO FIND LESS DATA

Turning now to the "how" of generating data summaries, this section discusses how to generate short summaries like Figure 15.2 from larger data sets like Figure 15.3.

There are many ways to reduce the number of rows and columns in a data set [155, 345, 345]. The most direct way (and the slowest) is to label each row and column with a binary flag *use* ∈ *{yes,no}*, then try all combinations of 2^C columns with 2^R rows. This is a large search space (to say the least) but it has been known to work on some data sets [259].

If it is expected that only a few rows and columns will be selected, then some forward select search might be faster. In this approach, we grow the *used* set from smaller to larger if the smaller seemed to be useful. This is the approach used in the WRAPPER column selector [234].

Other "filter"-based methods propose some initial ordering to the columns or rows, then the rows and columns are then explored in that fixed order. The literature describes many such column filters [155] and row filters [345, 356]. Some filters run very quickly since they quickly propose an fixed linear ordering of the columns, which can be explored in linear or logarithmic time (using a binary chop procedure).

The general trade-off in this area of research is speed versus quality:

- The slower the selection process, the better the selections and the higher the quality of the predictions from the selected subsets. For example, WRAPPER is generally viewed as the best (but slowest) column selector [155].
- The faster the selection, the simpler the inference and the implementation. Also, simpler methods scale to larger data sets.

For data sets with low intrinsic dimensionality, the slower column selectors may be an unnecessary use of the CPU. Figure 15.2 was generated using the linear-time column and row selectors discussed below. We make no claim that the following is the best way to perform row and column selection.[5] Rather, we just note that the following is a fast method for producing summaries in which there is no apparent information loss.

---

[4] To be completely accurate, the summaries do not always generate better predictions than the longer data. That said, usually, the summaries perform as well or better than using all the data (results generated from 20 data sets relating to effort and defect prediction). And even when the predictions were worse in the summary, they were not much worse; see the end of this chapter.

[5] Indeed, several of the following decisions were determined by "engineering judgment," which is a euphemism for "it seemed like a good idea at the time." For example, we recursively cluster the data into four regions since that was not hard to implement. Also, we halt that recursion when we arrive at less than $2 \times \sqrt{N}$ of the original N examples. Finally, when doing column selection, we just keep the top 25% of columns, as sorted by INFOGAIN.

15.4.1 INPUT

The PEEKING2 row selector accepts as inputs tables of data such as Figure 15.3. The only hard requirement is that the data is *classified*; i.e., one column contains some quality measurement. In the case of the data used in the following experiment, that quality measure is a binary value that indicates if a class is found defective or not.

PEEKING2's processing divides into the following three steps:

1. Optionally, prunes uninteresting columns using the INFOGAIN measure described below.
2. Recursively partitions N examples into four sets, stopping when it finds a *final* partition, i.e., one with less than $2 \times \sqrt{N}$ examples.
3. Builds one centroid from the mean values of columns from the examples in each final partition.

To estimate INFOGAIN, all columns are discretized using the Fayyad-Iranni algorithm [122]. As shown in Figure 15.8, INFOGAIN rejects a column, if in the subset of examples selected according to its values there is little change to the class distribution seen in the entire data set. PEEKING2 rejects all but the columns with the top 25% INFOGAIN, which is scored as follows. If the frequencies of examples associated with the two possible class values (nondefective, detective modules) are respectively f_1 and f_2, then $H(D) = -\sum_{c=1}^{2} f_c \log f_c$ and

$$\text{INFOGAIN}(D, A) = H(D) - \sum_{v \in A} \frac{|D_{A=v}|}{|D|} H(D_{A=v})$$

Columns	Entropy	Information Gain
lcom3	0.68	0.27
ce	0.70	0.25
rfc	0.70	0.24
cbm	0.72	0.23
loc	0.74	0.21
max_cc	0.74	0.21
wmc	0.75	0.20
cbo	0.75	0.19
amc	0.76	0.19
dam	0.76	0.18
lcom	0.77	0.18
mfa	0.77	0.18
npm	0.80	0.15
avg_cc	0.80	0.15
cam	0.81	0.13
dit	0.89	0.06
moa	0.91	0.04
ca	0.93	0.01
ic	0.95	0.00
noc	0.95	0.00

FIGURE 15.8

Using INFOGAIN: columns of the POI-3.0 data set, from the PROMISE repository, sorted on infogain. PEEKING2 rejects the bottom 75% of these columns.

where D is the set of all examples, $D_{A=v}$ is the set of examples with column A equal to v, and A is a given independent column.

PEEKING2 recursively partitions the examples into a dendogram (tree of clusters). The instance space is initially projected on the two dimensions of the greatest variability using the FASTMAP heuristic [120], which is similar to principal component analysis (PCA). FASTMAP defines the direction of the greatest variability to be a line drawn between the two most distant points in the examples. This line approximates the first component of PCA, but it is generated in much faster time (linear time for FASTMAP, quadratic time for PCA). The second dimension is defined by drawing a perpendicular line to the first dimension. Studies showed the effectiveness of FASTMAP for software engineering data [291]. The FASTMAP heuristic works as follows:

- Pick any example Z at random.
- Find the example X farthest from Z.
- Find the example Y farthest from X.
- For all examples E, find the distance a, b to X, Y.
- Find the distance $c = \text{dist}(X, Y)$.

For this study, we used a standard Euclidean measure:

$$\text{dist}(E1, E2) = \sqrt{\sum_i (E1_i - E2_i)^2}$$

From the cosine rule, we can now project E onto the line $\overline{XY}$ at $x = (a^2 + c^2 - b^2)/(2c)$. Then after finding x, Pythagoras is used to find $y = \sqrt{a^2 - x^2}$. Once these (x, y) values are calculated for each example, the instance space is partitioned into four sets (two for each dimension), separating the data above and below the median x and median y value.[6]

Figure 15.9 shows the instance space of POI-3.0 data set projected on the two dimensions found by FASTMAP. Gray and dark gray points denote nondefective and defective modules, respectively (the larger the mark, the greater percent of each). The 442 original examples are shown at the top and the summarized data is shown at the bottom. The picture in the middle demonstrates how the projected space is recursively partitioned by the median values of x and y dimensions.

Two important details:

- PEEKING2 clusters on the *independent* columns (i.e., everything but the last line of Figure 15.4). It then keeps statistics on the distribution of the dependent column(s) added to those centroids (in our case, the rate of defective modules per centroid).
- To use the clusters to make predictions on new data, PEEKING2 finds the distance d_1 and d_2 to the two nearest centroids from the new data. Each centroid then "votes" on the test example and that vote is weighted by the distance of the test to the centroid; i.e., $w_i = 1/d_i$. These weights are normalized, so the final tally is

---

[6] PEEKING2 is slightly more complex than the CHUNK system of Chapter 12. CHUNK divides the data in one dimension, that recurses on two halves of that one dimension. PEEKING2 divides data on two dimensions then recurses on the four quarters defined by the two halves of each of its two dimensions.

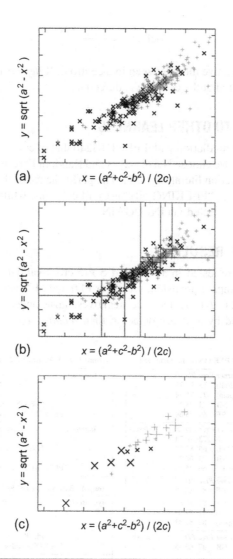

FIGURE 15.9

Pruning 442 examples from the POI-3.0 data set of the PROMISE repository. (a) (top): Raw data projected into a 2-D (x, y) plane by FASTMAP. Gray, dark gray points denote nondefective, defective modules (respectively). (b) (middle): The final partitions found by PEEKING2: each contains no more than $2 \times \sqrt{442} \approx 40$ examples. (c) (bottom): Each final partition is replaced with its centroid. The size of each mark is in proportion to the *purity* of the respective cluster.

$$\text{defects} = \frac{\sum_{i=1}^{2} r_i w_i}{\left(\sum_i w_i\right)}$$

where r_i is the rate of defective modules seen in a centroid. If *defects* is over some threshold (currently, 0.5) then we predict the example is defective.

15.4.2 COMPARISONS TO OTHER LEARNERS

This section compares defect prediction with PEEKING2 to that of commonly used data miners (Naive Bayes and Random Forests). We choose Naive Bayes and Random Forests because these classifiers are often used in the defect prediction literature [157]. The performance of these classifiers was compared to two versions of PEEKING2. "PEEKING(all)" uses all columns, while "PEEKING(infogain)" just uses the top 25% of columns selected via INFOGAIN.

15.4.3 REPORTING THE RESULTS

All these four classifiers were tested in a stratified 5×5 cross-validation scheme using the data of Figure 15.10. Our results compare precision, recall (or PD) and "F" measures results for PEEKING2 and other learners. If $\{A, B, C, D\}$ are the true negatives, false negatives, false positives, and true positives (respectively) found by a binary detector, then *recall* is $p_d = \frac{D}{B+D}$, *precision* is $\frac{D}{C+D}$, and

Group 1 - Both versions of PEEKING2 perform well

ivy-1.1	Learner	Prec	PD	F	Rank
	PEEKING2(all)	75	83	78	1
	PEEKING2(infogain)	73	75	74	2
	NB	73	75	71	2
	RF	69	75	69	2

lucene-2.4	Learner	Prec	PD	F	Rank
	RF	73	76	74	1
	PEEKING2(all)	65	83	73	2
	NB	75	68	71	3
	PEEKING2(infogain)	66	75	70	4

poi-3.0	Learner	Prec	PD	F	Rank
	RF	84	86	85	1
	NB	87	82	84	1
	PEEKING2(all)	81	84	83	2
	PEEKING2(infogain)	82	82	83	2

ant-1.7	Learner	Prec	PD	F	Rank
	NB	47	65	55	1
	PEEKING2(all)	67	42	52	2
	PEEKING2(infogain)	69	42	51	2
	RF	61	45	50	3

Group 2 - Only PEEKING2 with infogain performs well

xerces-1.4	Learner	Prec	PD	F	Rank
	RF	94	95	95	1
	PEEKING2(infogain)	90	98	93	2
	PEEKING2(all)	82	93	87	3
	NB	94	80	86	4

Group 3 - Only PEEKING2 on all features performs well

xalan-2.6	Learner	Prec	PD	F	Rank
	NB	74	72	73	1
	RF	73	66	70	2
	PEEKING2(all)	71	62	68	3
	PEEKING2(infogain)	74	59	65	4

log4j-1.1	Learner	Prec	PD	F	Rank
	NB	67	62	67	1
	PEEKING2(all)	75	57	62	2
	RF	67	57	62	2
	PEEKING2(infogain)	71	50	56	3

Group 4 - Both versions of PEEKING2 do not perform well

synapse-1.2	Learner	Prec	PD	F	Rank
	NB	60	59	61	1
	RF	64	53	58	1
	PEEKING2(all)	56	50	55	2
	PEEKING2(infogain)	65	41	52	3

jedit-4.1	Learner	Prec	PD	F	Rank
	NB	61	62	63	1
	PEEKING2(all)	71	38	50	2
	RF	59	44	50	2
	PEEKING2(infogain)	67	31	38	3

velocity-1.6	Learner	Prec	PD	F	Rank
	NB	56	60	59	1
	RF	58	50	55	2
	PEEKING2(infogain)	54	33	40	3
	PEEKING2(all)	50	27	35	4

FIGURE 15.10

Experimental results. RF=Random Forest; NB=Naive Bayes; Prec=precision; PD=recall; *F*=f-measure.

the *f-measure* is $F = \frac{2 \times p_d \times \text{prec}}{p_d + \text{pred}}$. A good defect predictor must achieve high values of probability of detection and precision in the same time. However, increasing one of the measures comes at the cost of decreasing the other. Consequently, we use the *f*-measure as the most important measure in our analysis, because it takes into consideration both the probability of detection and precision of the defect predictor.

Figure 15.10 sorts all classifiers by the median of their *f*-measures seen across the 25 results generated by our cross-validation experiment (and *higher* numbers are *better*). In the following, when we say that a classifier performs "almost as well" or "close" to another, we mean that the median *f*-measure is less than 5% or 2% different, respectively.

The column *Rank* in Figure 15.10 compares the populations of *f*-measures of all classifiers within each data set. The classifiers are sorted in decreasing order according to their median *f*-measure. The classifier with the highest *f*-measure was sorted at rank $i = 1$. For the remaining classifiers (sorted into positions $i > 1$), classifier i was ranked the same as $i + 1$ if their *f*-measures are statistically insignificantly different (Wilcoxon, 95% confidence).

Figure 15.10 groups our results as follows:

- Group1 (4 data sets): Both versions of PEEKING2 performs close or better than Naive Bayes, Random Forests;
- Group2 (1 data set): Only PEEKING2(infogain) performs close to Naive Bayes or Random Forests;
- Group3 (2 data sets): Only PEEKING2(all) performs almost as well as Naive Bayes or Random Forests.
- Group4 (3 data sets): PEEKING2 performance was not close to the other classifiers.

15.4.4 DISCUSSION OF RESULTS

We note that in two of the Group4 data sets, all our classifiers were unsuccessful in achieving more than 2/3rds *Prec* or *PD* (see the VELOCITY-1.6 and SYNAPSE-1.2 results). Rather than cherry-pick our results, we leave those data sets in this chapter. However, it is unfair to assess one classifier on data that challenges all classifiers. Hence, the following summary is based on the eight data sets where at least one classifier achieved more than 2/3rds *Prec* or *PD*:

- In 7/8 of the data, at least one version of PEEKING2 performed almost as well as the standard classifiers.
- For 6/8 of our data, PEEKING2(all) applied to the full set of columns performed nearly as well as anything else.
- For 5/8 of our data, using column selection PEEKING(infogain) performed almost as anything else.
- In 4/8 of our data, at least one version of PEEKING2 outperformed Random Forests.

From these results, we note that selecting columns with INFOGAIN is usually useful, but not always. We suggest running PEEKING2 twice (once with and once without column selection) and use the version that gives the largest *f*-measure. INFOGAIN is very fast (less than 0.2 s for any of the data used here) so even if this dual run is repeated in 5×5 cross-val, this recommendation would take just a few seconds to apply.

From the above, we say that PEEKING2 did not always perform worse despite working on very small summaries of the data. In fact, it some cases, it actually out-performed other standard learners routinely used for defect prediction. That is, measured in terms of classifying software defects from static code columns, reasoning over the summaries is not considered harmful. In fact, often, it may produce better predictions than those seen in the original data.

15.5 WHAT'S NEXT?

We have shown in this chapter that small insightful summaries can be built from larger data sets. In the examples shown here, for data sets with very low intrinsic dimensionality, that up to 98% of the cells in a table of data can be ignored without damaging out ability to make conclusions from that data.

Returning to the start of this chapter, we recommend handling data into two layers:

- Layer1: Big data storage for the collected data;
- Layer2: Big discussion over a summary of the most relevant data.

Our claim was that Layer1 is what needs to be *stored* while the smaller Layer2 is what should be *shared* and discussed. Note that while we list these two layers as separate entities, they may interact in the following manner.

In order to handle very large data sets, and to recognize changing patterns, in the data, we are experimenting with using Layer2 as an interactive summary of the Layer1. Our approach is a variant of Farnstrom et al.'s incremental clusterer [121] that

- Builds its centroids on the first α examples.
- For each cluster, keep the two distant points found via FASTMAP.
- It then streams over the remaining data, checking for *aliens*; i.e., examples that are more than $\beta \times \text{dist}(X, Y)$ away from current centroids.
- Nonaliens are added to their nearest centroid (where they update the class distributions of that centroid).
- But If we see more than $\gamma \times \alpha$ aliens in a cluster, we call PEEKING2 on that data to create additional centroids.

Our results in this area are preliminary, but using $\alpha = 10,000, \beta = \gamma = 0.1$ seems promising. For example, one simple thing to do in the above rig is to identify outliers (these would be the *aliens* described in the last paragraph). That is, using this rig, we can not only make predictions via incremental summarization of very large data sets, we can also recognize what clusters are "polluted" with so many aliens that they should not be used for predictions.

HOW TO KEEP YOUR DATA PRIVATE

16

Name:	CLIFF&MORPH
Also known as:	CLIFF is an *instance selector* that can be used as an instance-based selector (or case-based) reasoner. MORPH is an *instance mutator* and can also be categorized as a *noise injector*.
Intent:	The combination of CLIFF&MORPH is used as a privacy algorithm for software defect prediction when there is insufficient local data to build a defect predictor.
Motivation:	There are promising results with cross-company defect prediction (CCDP), however CCDP requires data sharing, which raises privacy concerns. Can minimizing the data with CLIFF and privatizing the remaining data with MORPH maintain the promising results while providing adequate privacy?
Solution:	For defect data, CLIFF seeks those instances that best predict for the target class. For each class value ("defective" and "nondefective") we measure the frequency of an attribute value for one class value versus the other class value(s). We call these measures ranks and calculate them for each attribute value. We then find the products of these ranks for each instance, and those instances with the lowest ranks are discarded. MORPH's goal is to minutely change the values of data to protect it while keeping it useful for defect prediction.
Applicability:	CLIFF&MORPH was successful for CCDP: that is, with these tools, we can privatize data while keeping it useful.
Related to:	The research described in this chapter is the first known for privacy in CCDP. It shows that data can be made private and remain useful. This is especially important in a field of study such as CCDP, where data sharing is a requirement.

This chapter is an update to "Balancing Privacy and Utility in Cross-Company Defect Prediction" by F. Peters, T. Menzies, L. Gong, and H. Zhang, which was published in the *IEEE Transactions on Software Engineering*, August 2013. This chapter extends that work with a practitioner focus. Sections 16.2–16.5 expand on topics such as "what is privacy-preserving data publishing?" and a review of how and why the background knowledge of an attacker can be integrated as a part of privacy measures.

16.1 MOTIVATION

Data sharing is the enemy of privacy preservation. In the wrong hands shared data can lead to an individual's identity being stolen, loans and health insurance coverage can be denied, and an individual can become a victim of financial fraud. However, in the right hands, terrorists can be identified, scientists find treatments that work better than others, and doctors are aided in treatment and diagnostic decisions. So, to minimize the problems that can be caused by attackers (those seeking to gain confidential knowledge about individuals), the new and active fields of privacy preserving data publishing (PPDP) and privacy preserving data mining (PPDM) have been developed.

Researchers in PPDP and PPDM have disclosed their concerns of an attackers' negative use of such a helpful tool. For instance, Wang et al. [436] wrote:

> Recent development in privacy-preserving data mining has proposed many efficient and practical techniques for hiding sensitive patterns or information from been discovered by data mining algorithms.

Zhang and Zhao [456] also noted that although successful in many applications, data mining poses special concerns for private data. Other researchers [14, 161, 175, 258], have gone farther showing how easily an attacker could uncover an individual's private/confidential data using readily available data mining tools. So, in order to take advantage of the good that can result from data mining while protecting the privacy of individuals, researchers have come up with many privacy protection techniques in the areas of PPDP and PPDM.

PPDP covers methods and tools used to disguise raw data for publishing, while PPDM covers methods and tools used to limit the amount of extra information gained by an attacker after performing some data mining task on published data. In spite of their relatively short existence, there are a plethora of published privacy protecting techniques designed to address a number of different scenarios. Therefore, to narrow the scope of this chapter, we will focus on PPDP and the simple scenario of disguising one data set for publication.

In this chapter we answer the following questions:

- What is PPDP and why is it important?
- What is considered a breach of privacy?
- How do you avoid privacy breaches?
- How are privacy preserving algorithms evaluated?

Finally, we conclude this chapter with a case study of privacy in cross-company defect prediction (CCDP) (Section 16.6).

16.2 WHAT IS PPDP AND WHY IS IT IMPORTANT?

Similarly, researchers agree that PPDP involves the use of techniques to disguise the microdata records that contain information about specific individuals, while delivering a useful data set for analysis. This is indicated clearly by Fung et al. [138], who noted that PPDP is a collection of methods and tools for publishing data in a hostile environment so that the published data remains practically useful while individual privacy is preserved. Along the same lines, Domingo-Ferrer and Gonzalez-Nicolas [104] states:

> Statistical disclosure control (also known as privacy-preserving data mining) of micro-data is about releasing data-sets containing the answers of individual respondents protected in such a way that: (i) the respondents corresponding to the released records cannot be re-identified; (ii) the released data stay analytically useful.

Also, according to LeFevre et al. [247], protecting individual privacy is an important problem in microdata distribution and publishing. Anonymization (privacy) algorithms typically aim to satisfy certain privacy definitions with minimal impact on the quality of the resulting data.

The importance of PPDP can be answered with a question: *What is data mining without data?* However, privacy concerns can limit data sharing. For instance, when America on Line (AOL) released the query logs of its users for the purpose of research, Thelma Arnold was reidentified by the examination of query terms from the logs [22]. AOL removed the logs immediately.

Reidentification is *sensitive attribute disclosure*. This is where an individual in a data set can be associated with a sensitive attribute value. Consider the example in Figure 16.1. Here the shaded column represents the sensitive attribute values, while the other columns represent the quasi-identifiers (QIDs). QIDs are attributes that can potentially reidentify an individual record such as age, zip code, and birth date. (Please note that the names are only included for ease of explanation. Normally, these are removed before publication.)

So, let us consider Jenny. In order for an attacker (let's say Jenny's boss, Bill) to reidentify her in the data set, through casual investigation Bill can figure out that Jenny had a recent stay at the hospital. Furthermore, once he figures out Jenny's age, he will find Jenny's record with 100% certainty and realize that Jenny is HIV positive. Clearly, privacy breaches of this nature can lead, in Jenny's case, to being discriminated against. Other scenarios could involve identity theft, loans and health insurance coverage can be denied, and an individual can become a victim to financial fraud.

In this regard, the goal of privacy algorithms is to add uncertainty to the point where, if Bill only has access to the table in Figure 16.2, then he can only reidentify Jenny's record with 33% certainty; therefore, only know that there is a 33% chance that Jenny has HIV rather than being 100% sure (Figure 16.1).

Ever-increasing data collection has led to privacy concerns [429]. The examples above show justification for such concerns. In the remainder of this chapter we aim to show that given some trade-off between privacy and utility or the usefulness of data, we can limit the occurrences of the examples above.

Name	Job	Sex	Age	Disease
Dawn	Lawyer	Female	39	Hepatitis
Jenny	Teacher	Female	23	HIV
John	Nurse	Male	41	HIV
Stan	Mayor	Male	56	Hepatitis

FIGURE 16.1

Patient table before privatization.

Name	Job	Sex	Age	Disease
Dawn	Lawyer	Female	35-40	Hepatitis
Jenny	Teacher	Female	20-25	HIV
Mary	Teacher	Female	20-25	Hepatitis
Joan	Teacher	Female	20-25	None
John	Nurse	Male	41	HIV
Stan	Mayor	Male	56	Hepatitis

FIGURE 16.2

Patient table after privatization.

16.3 WHAT IS CONSIDERED A BREACH OF PRIVACY?

In order to discover privacy breaches, one needs to define what constitutes a privacy breach for a particular data set. There are different levels of privacy. Some levels are determined by individuals in the data set or by the creators of a privacy policy or laws. An optimal result of a privacy model is defined by Dalenius [89] where he states that access to published data should not enable the attacker to learn anything extra about any target victim, compared to no access to the database, even with the presence of any attacker's background knowledge obtained from other sources [138].

Fung et al. [138], considers two categories of privacy models:

1. A privacy threat occurs when an attacker is able to link a record owner to a sensitive attribute in a published data table. These are specified as record linkage, attribute linkage, and table linkage, respectively.

2. The published data should provide the attacker with little additional information beyond his or her background knowledge.

Brickell and Shmatikov [57], defines a privacy model called *sensitive attribute disclosure*, which occurs when the attacker or adversary learns information about an individual's sensitive attributes. In other words, it captures the gain in the attacker's knowledge due to his/her observations of the disguised data set. Also, "Microdata privacy can be understood as prevention of membership disclosure," where the attacker should not learn whether a particular individual is included in the database.

In 2007, Wang et al. [437] put forward other definitions of privacy. The article explains:

There have been two types of privacy concerning data mining. The first type of privacy, called output privacy, is that the data is minimally altered so that the mining result will not disclose certain privacy. The second type of privacy, called input privacy, is that the data is manipulated so that the mining result is not affected or minimally affected.

For the scenario used, we assume a privacy definition of *high*, where an attacker is unsuccessful at getting more information from the sanitized data set. The methods used to avoid privacy breaches are described in the following section.

16.4 HOW TO AVOID PRIVACY BREACHES?

The idea of disguising a data set is known as anonymization. This is performed on the original data set to "satisfy a specified privacy requirement" [138] resulting in a modified data set being published. There are five general categories for anonymization: (1) generalization, (2) suppression, (3) anatomization, (4) permutation, and (5) perturbation. Most methods and tools created for preserving privacy fall into one or more of these categories and have some drawbacks.

Before we expand on the above categories, we repeat some definitions from Fung et al. [138]:

- The *explicit identifier* is a set of attributes, such as name and Social Security number, containing information that explicitly identifies record owners.
- The *QID* is a set of attributes that could potentially identify record owners.
- The *sensitive attributes* consists of sensitive person-specific information such as disease, salary, and disability status.
- The *nonsensitive attributes* contains all attributes that do not fall into the previous three categories.

16.4.1 GENERALIZATION AND SUPPRESSION

Many researchers comment on how privatization algorithms can distort data. For example, consider privatization via generalization and suppression. Generalization can be done by replacing exact numeric values with intervals that cover a subrange of values; e.g., 17 might become 15...20 or by replacing symbols with more general terms; e.g., "date of birth" becomes "month of birth." Suppression can be done by replacing exact values with symbols such as a *star* or a phrase like "don't know" [433].

According to Fung et al. [138], generalization and suppression hide potentially important details in the QIDs that can confuse classification. Worse, these transforms may not guarantee privacy.

Widely used generalization and suppression approaches include k-anonymity, l-diversity, and t-closeness k-anonymity [412] makes each record in the table indistinguishable with $k - 1$ other records by suppression or generalization [353, 375, 412]. The limitations of k-anonymity, as listed by Brickell and Shmatikov [57], are many-fold. They state that k-anonymity does not hide whether a given individual is in the database. Also, in theory, k-anonymity hides uniqueness (and hence identity) in a data set, thus reducing the certainty that an attacker has uncovered sensitive information. However, in practice, k-anonymity does not ensure privacy if the attacker has background knowledge of the domain (see Figure 16.3). An example of k-anonymity in action and how background knowledge of an attacker can affect privacy is shown in Figure 16.3.

Machanavajjhala et al. [278] proposed l-diversity. The aim of l-diversity is to address the limitations of k-anonymity by requiring that for each QID group,[1] there are at least l distinct values for each sensitive attribute value. In this way an attacker is less likely to "guess" the sensitive attribute value of any member of a QID group.

Work by Li and Li [255] later showed that l-diversity was vulnerable to *skewness* and *similarity* attacks, making it insufficient to prevent attribute disclosure. Hence, Li and Li proposed t-closeness to address this problem. t-Closeness focuses on keeping the distance between the distributions of a sensitive attribute in a QID group and that of the whole table no more than a threshold t apart. The

---

[1] A QID group is a set of instances whose QID values are the same because of generalization or suppression.

Consider the abbreviated *ant-1.3* data shown in the following table from the PROMISE data repository [306]. We assume that we want to share this data.

ID	QIDs								
name	wmc	dit	noc	cbo	rfc	lcom	ca	ce	loc*
taskdefs.ExecuteOn	11	4	2	14	42	29	2	12	395
DefaultLogger	14	1	1	8	32	49	4	4	257
taskdefs.TaskOutputStream	3	2	0	1	9	0	0	1	58
taskdefs.Cvs	12	3	0	12	37	32	0	12	310
taskdefs.Copyfile	6	3	0	4	21	1	0	4	136
types.Enumerated-Attribute	5	1	5	12	11	8	11	1	59
NoBannerLogger	4	2	0	3	16	0	0	3	59

The ten attributes of this table divide into two categories: *identifier* (ID) *quasi-identifiers* (QIDs). Note that the sensitive QID is indicated by a superscript "*"; in this case it's lines of code (loc). An ID could be anything that specifically identifies an individual or thing such as a Social Security number, first and last names, or a filename. Unlike an ID, QIDs are not specific to a particular individual or thing. However, they can be used to reidentify an individual record in a database.

The first step in privatizing this data set is to deidentify the table, i.e., remove the identity attribute "name" (but note that for the ease of explanation, we leave the ID for the example). One might think that removing the ID column should be enough to protect individual privacy; however, research has shown that this is not the case [61, 143, 419, 469]. In fact, using external public databases and/or personal background knowledge, an attacker can reidentify an individual record and associate that record with a sensitive attribute. For example, suppose the attacker has the following background knowledge:

$$rfc = 11 \, or \, lcom = 0$$

On the data with deleted IDs, this attacker might use this knowledge to select the rows containing *type.EnumeratedAttribute*, *taskdefs.TaskOutputStream*, and *NoBannerLogger*, thereby learning with 100% certainty that there are 58 or 59 lines of code in the target file.

Even after applying a privacy algorithm, that background knowledge can still be used to violate privacy. Suppose this attacker studies the following *k=2*-anonymous version of the above data:

ID	QIDs								
name	wmc	dit	noc	cbo	rfc	lcom	ca	ce	loc*
taskdefs.ExecuteOn	11-14	<5	≤5	8-14	32-42	29-49	*	*	395
taskdefs.Cvs	11-14	<5	≤5	8-14	32-42	29-49	*	*	310
Default Logger	11-14	<5	≤5	8-14	32-42	29-49	*	*	257
taskdefs.TaskOutputStream	<7	<5	≤5	1-4	*	≤8	0	≤4	58
taskdefs. Copyfile	<7	<5	≤5	1-4	*	≤8	0	≤4	136
types. Enumerated Attribute	<7	<5	≤5	*	11-16	≤8	*	≤4	59
NoBanner Logger	<7	<5	≤5	*	11-16	≤8	*	≤4	59

"*" denotes that any value is possible

The background knowledge that $rfc = 11$ and $lcom = 0$ will result in 4 records being returned (the last four rows). With this result, because of the lack of diversity in the sensitive attribute of the result, an attacker will know with 75% certainty that the target has 58 or 59 lines of code.

FIGURE 16.3

Effects of background knowledge on privacy. (From [356].)

intuition is that even if an attacker can locate the QID group of the target record, as long as the distribution of the sensitive attribute is similar to the distribution in the whole table, any knowledge gained by the attacker cannot be considered as a privacy breach because the information is already public. However, with *t*-closeness, information about the correlation between QIDs and sensitive attributes is limited [255] and so causes degradation of data utility.

16.4.2 ANATOMIZATION AND PERMUTATION

Anatomization and permutation both accomplish a similar task; that is, the deassociation of the relationship between the QID and sensitive attributes. However, anatomization does it by releasing "the data on QID and the data on the sensitive attribute in two separate tables..." with "one common attribute, *GroupID*" [138]. On the other hand, permutation deassociates the relationship between a QID and a numerical sensitive attribute. This is done by partitioning a set of data records into groups and shuffling the sensitive values within each group [456].

16.4.3 PERTURBATION

A precise definition of perturbation is put forward by Fung et al. [138]:

> The general idea is to replace the original data values with some synthetic data values, so that the statistical information computed from the perturbed data does not differ significantly from the statistical information computed from the original data.

It is important to note that the perturbed data records do not correspond to real-world record owners. Also, methods used for perturbation include additive noise, data swapping, and synthetic data generation. The drawback of these transforms is that they may not guarantee privacy. For example, suppose an attacker has access to multiple independent samples from the same distribution from which the original data was drawn. In that case, a principal component analysis could reconstruct the transform from the original to privatized data [142]. Here, the attacker's goal is to estimate the matrix (M_T) used to transform the original data to its privatized version. M_T is then used to undo the data perturbation applied to the original data. According to Giannella et al. [142], $M_T = WD_0Z'$, where W is the eigenvector matrix of the covariance matrix of the privatized data. Z' is the transform of the eigenvector matrix of the covariance matrix of the independent samples. Finally, D_0 is an identity matrix.

16.4.4 OUTPUT PERTURBATION

Different than perturbation where the data is transformed to maintain its privacy, output perturbation maintains the original data in a database and instead adds noise to the output of a query [101]. Differential privacy falls into the category of *output perturbation*. Work by Dinur and Nissim [101] also falls into this category and forms the basis of Dwork's work on differential privacy [108, 109] (ϵ-differential).

According to Fung et al. [138], ϵ-differential privacy is based on the idea that the risk to the record owner's privacy should not substantially increase as a result of participating in a statistical database. So, instead of comparing the prior probability and the posterior probability before and after accessing the published data, Dwork [108, 109] proposed to compare the risk with and without the record owner's data in the published data.

Dwork [108, 109] defines ϵ-differential privacy as follows:

> We say databases D1 and D2 differ in at most one element if one is a proper subset of the other and the larger database contains just one additional row.

Although ϵ-differential privacy assures record owners that they may submit their personal information to the database securely, it does not prevent membership disclosure and sensitive attribute disclosure studied in this work. This is shown in an example from Chin and Klinefelter [76] in a Facebook advertiser case study. Through reverse engineering, Chin and Klinefelter [76] inferred that Facebook uses differential privacy for its targeted advertising system. To illustrate the problem of membership and sensitive attribute disclosure, the authors described Jane's curiosity about her neighbor John's HIV status when she learned that he was on the finisher's list for the 2011 Asheville AIDS Walk and 5K Run. So, armed with John's age and zip code, she went to Facebook's targeted advertising area and found that there was exactly one male Facebook user age 36 from zip code 27514 who listed the "2011 Asheville AIDS Walk and 5K Run" as an interest. At this point, Jane placed a targeted advertisement offering free information to HIV-positive patients about a new antiretroviral treatment. If charged by Facebook for having her ad clicked, Jane can assume with some level of certainty that John is HIV positive.

16.5 HOW ARE PRIVACY-PRESERVING ALGORITHMS EVALUATED?

Three privacy evaluation methods are outlined in work by Torra et al. [418]. These measures are (1) information loss measures, (2) disclosure risk measures, and (3) scores. Information loss measures are designed to establish to which extent published data is still valid for carrying out the experiments planned on the original data. They take into account the similarity between the original data set and the protected one, as well as the differences between the results that would be obtained with the original data set and the results that would be obtained from the disguised data set. Torra et al. [418] further explain that disclosure risk measures are used to evaluate the extent in which the protected data ensures privacy and that *scores* is a summary of both information loss and disclosure risk; that is, when these two measures are commensurate, it is possible just to combine them using the average.

In the following sections we explain some of the privacy metrics used and how the attacker's background knowledge is used in these metrics.

16.5.1 PRIVACY METRICS

Privacy metrics allows you to know how private the sanitized version of your data is. There are two categories of privacy metrics in the literature: syntactic and semantic [57]. The syntactic measures consider the distribution of attribute values in the privatized data set and are used by algorithms such as k-anonymity and l-diversity. In comparison, the semantic metrics measure what an attacker may learn or the incremental gain in knowledge caused by the privatized data set [57] and use distance measures such as the earth movers distance, KL divergence, and JS divergence to quantify this difference in the attackers knowledge. Other methods in the literature include increased privacy ratio (IPR) [355, 356], entropy [67, 79], and guessing anonymity [364, 413].

Previous privacy studies in software engineering (SE) [67, 79] have used entropy to measure privacy. Entropy (H) measures the level of uncertainty an attacker will have in trying to associate a target to a sensitive attribute. For example, if querying a data set produces two instances with the same sensitive attribute value then the attacker's uncertainty level or entropy is zero(0). However, if the sensitive attribute values are different, the attacker has a $\frac{1}{2}$ chance of associating the target with the correct sensitive attribute value. The entropy here is 1 bit, assuming that there are only two possible sensitive values. In general, the entropy of a data set is, $H = \sum_{i=1}^{|S|} p(s_i)| \log_2 p(s_i)|$ bits, which corresponds to the number of bits needed to describe the outcome. Here, s_i is the probability that $S = s_i$.

Guessing anonymity was introduced by Rachlin et al. [364] and it is described as a privacy definition for noise perturbation methods. Guessing anonymity of a privatized record in a data set is the number of guesses that the optimal guessing strategy of the attacker requires to correctly guess the record used to generate the privatized record [364, 413].

We introduced IPR in previous work [355]. It is based on the *adversarial accuracy gain*, A_{acc} from the work of Brickell and Shamtikov [57]. According to the authors' definition of A_{acc}, it quantifies an attacker's ability to predict the sensitive attribute value of a target t. A_{acc} measures the increase in the attacker's accuracy after he observes a privatized data set and compares it to the baseline from a trivially privatized data set that offers perfect privacy by removing either all sensitive attribute values or all the other QIDs.

For IPR, we assume the role of an attacker armed with some background knowledge from the original data set and also supplied with the private data set. When the attacker predicts the sensitive attribute value of a target we use the original data to see if the prediction is correct. If it is we consider this as a privacy breach; otherwise, it is not. The IPR is the percentage of the total number of predictions that are incorrect. More specific details about IPR are in the *Evaluating Privacy* section of the case study later in this chapter (Section 16.6.8).

16.5.2 MODELING THE BACKGROUND KNOWLEDGE OF AN ATTACKER

The attacker's background knowledge is an essential element of privacy metrics. Syntactic measures of privacy do not consider background knowledge; however, the semantic measures do. Incorporating the attacker's background knowledge is an active area of research [72, 106, 256, 257, 282]. These works measure the privacy risk when an attacker has a certain amount of knowledge. However, the major challenge facing you as the data owner, is that you're not a mind reader; you don't know the specific background knowledge of any attacker.

Martin et al. [282] provide one of the first methods for modeling an attacker's background knowledge. Their work does not assume that you know the attacker's background knowledge; instead, they assume bounds on the attacker's knowledge in terms of the number of basic units of knowledge of the attacker. In other words, the authors take the worst-case view where the attacker obtained the complete information about which individuals have records in the data set.

This work was then extended by Chen et al. [72]. They complained that the formal language developed by Martin et al. quantified background knowledge in a less than intuitive fashion. They also stated that because of this it would be difficult for you as the data owner to set an appropriate value for k which is the number of k, implications that an attacker may know. To improve on this, Chen et al. provide an intuitive, and therefore usable, quantification of an attacker's background knowledge. They consider three types of knowledge that arise naturally:

1. Knowledge about the target individual.
2. Knowledge about others.
3. Knowledge about same value families.

Li and Li [256] represented background knowledge as patterns or negative association rules that exist in the data. Unlike the work done by Martin et al. [282] and Chen et al. [72], this work lifts the burden from the user by not requiring the background knowledge as an input parameter. The authors believe that it should be possible to discover certain negative facts from the data such as, "male can never have ovarian cancer." Further, such knowledge is helpful when privatizing data via grouping. An anonymization technique will avoid including ovarian cancer in any group including males.

Privacy-MaxEnt is a generic and systematic method to integrate background knowledge in privacy quantification. According to Du et al. [106], it can deal with many different types of background knowledge such as it is rare for males to have breast cancer, a probability or inequality, and that "Frank has pneumonia," or "either Iris or Brian has lung cancer." Du et al.'s work focuses mainly on distributional knowledge and states that most of this type of knowledge can be expressed using conditional probability. For example $P(\text{Breast Cancer}|\text{Male}) = 0$. So they formulate background knowledge as constraints and use maximal entropy modeling to derive the conditional probabilities between the QIDs and the sensitive attribute values [257].

In a later work by Li et al. [257], titled "Modeling and integrating background knowledge in data anonymization," the authors presented a framework for modeling and computing background knowledge using kernel methods. The authors chose to use kernel regression method to approximate the probability distribution function; in other words, the attacker's prior knowledge or belief. Accordingly, this kernel estimation framework has three characteristics:

1. Focus on background knowledge that is consistent with the data.
2. Model background knowledge as probability distributions.
3. Use a kernel regression estimator to compute background knowledge.

All these studies about background knowledge have one thing in common: they acknowledge the difficulty in modeling an attacker's exact background knowledge. In addition, none can claim that they have addressed all types of background knowledge.

16.6 CASE STUDY: PRIVACY AND CROSS-COMPANY DEFECT PREDICTION

Software development produces many types of artifacts such as requirements, defect data, bug reports, and more. Privacy issues are dealt with differently for these different artifacts, and in this case study we focus on protecting the privacy of defect data used in CCDP.

Within-company defect prediction (WCDP) is the means by which organizations predict the number of defects in their software. CCDP looks at the feasibility of learning defect predictors using data from other companies. Recent studies show that defect and effort predictors built from *cross-company data* can be just as effective as predictors learned using *within-company data* [221, 427] (caveat: the cross-company data must be carefully filtered before being applied locally). This is potentially a very important result that implies the existence of general principles of SE (such generalities would lead us to general models of SE).

However, before we conduct widespread CCDP experiments, we must address the privacy concerns of data owners. Extracting data from organizations is often difficult due to the business sensitivity associated with the data. Because of this sensitivity, data owners who want to share limited amounts of useful data (say, to advance scientific research leading to improved software) need to do so without breaching any data privacy laws or company privacy policies.

For these reasons, many researchers doubt the practicality of data sharing for the purposes of research. In a personal communication, Barry Boehm reports he can release none of the data that his COCOMO team collected after 1981. Similarly, at a keynote address at ESEM'11, Elaine Weyuker doubted that she will ever be able to release the AT&T data she used to build defect predictors [440].

For companies with common concerns (e.g., subcontractors for a primary company), the benefits of sharing data can include improved software quality and reduced SE costs. Ideally, these organizations should be able to share data without revealing too much. Such organizations need to

1. Prevent the disclosure of specific sensitive metric values from their released data.
2. Ensure that the privatized data remain useful for research purposes, such as CCDP.

As shown below, standard methods such as k-anonymity do not protect against any background knowledge of an *attacker* (Table 16.1 defines this and other terms used in this study) and so may still reveal the sensitive attribute of a record. Moreover, two recent reports concluded that the *more* we privatize data, the *less* useful it becomes for certain utilities of certain tasks; for example, *classification*. Grechanik et al. [146] and Brickell and Shmatikov [57] reported that the application of standard privacy methods such as k-anonymity, l-diversity, and t-closeness damages inference power as privacy increases.

Table 16.1 Definitions of Terms Used in the Case Study (Section 16.6) of this Chapter	
Terms	**Definitions**
Classification	• For a data set containing independent attributes and one dependent attribute (class) • We find a model for the dependent attribute as a function of the independent attributes • The goal is to assign the right class value to an unseen instance • Defect prediction is an example of a classification task
Class boundary	The border between neighboring regions of different classes
EFB	Equal frequency binning. EFB divides the range of possible values into n bins or subranges, each of which holds the same number of attribute values. If duplicate values are placed into different bins, boundaries of every pair of neighboring bins are adjusted so that duplicate values belong to one bin only [240]
CLIFF	An instance selection method

Continued

Table 16.1 Definitions of Terms Used in the Case Study (Section 16.6) of this Chapter *Continued*

Terms	Definitions
Power subrange	Power of each attribute subrange; i.e., how much more frequently that subrange appears in one class more than any other
MORPH	Data transformation via perturbation to create synthetic data
t_i	A tuple of attribute values representing an individual record in a data set. Also referred to as a *target* in this work
T	Original data set containing targets
T'	Privatized data set
T^*	Represents either T or T'
A	Set of attributes
a_i	Attribute
$t[a_i]$	The value of attribute a_i for t
ID	Identifier—anything that specifically identifies an individual or thing such as a Social Security number
QIDs	Quasi-identifiers are attributes that can be used to reidentify an individual record in a data set. These attributes can also be sensitive
s_i	Sensitive attribute value
S	Set of possible sensitive attribute values that we do not want an attacker to associate with a target, t in a data set
q_i	A query is made up of attribute value pair(s). Example q_3 is "$a_1 = t[a_1]$ and $a_2 = t[a_2]$" It represents information an attacker has about a specific target in a data set
$|q_i|$	Query sizes in this work are 1, 2, and 4. Example, $|q_3| = 2$
Q	Set of *Queries* generated randomly from T In this work $|Q| \leq 1000$
G^*	Group of t's from either the original or privatized data set that matches a query, q_i. $G_i = t$'s from the original data set and $G'_i = t$'s from the privatized data set
$s_{max}(G_i)$	Most common sensitive attribute value in G_i
$s_{max}(G'_i)$	Most common sensitive attribute value in G'_i
$Breach(S, G_i^*)$	Privacy breach $$Breach(S, G_i^*) = \begin{cases} 1, & \text{if } s_{max}(G_i) = s_{max}(G'_i) \\ 0, & \text{otherwise} \end{cases}$$
$IPR(T^*)$	Increase privacy ratio $$IPR(T^*) = 1 - \frac{1}{|Q|} \sum_{i=0}^{|Q|} Breach(S, G_i^*)$$

Terms that are related to each other are grouped together.

This study proposes two privatization algorithms. The CLIFF instance pruner finds attribute subranges in the data that are more present in one class versus any other classes. These *power subranges* are those that drive instances farthest from the *class boundaries*. If an instance lacks these power subranges then their classification is more ambiguous. CLIFF deletes the instances with the fewest power subranges.

After CLIFF, the MORPH instance mutator perturbs all instance values by a random amount. This amount is selected to create a new instance that is different from the original instance and does not cross class boundaries.

Potentially, CLIFF&MORPH can increase privacy in three ways. First, CLIFF preserves the privacy of the individuals it deletes (these data are no longer available). Second, MORPH increases the privacy of all mutated individuals because their original data is now distorted. Last, to ensure that MORPHed instances are different from instances in the original data set, if a MORPHed instance matches an instance from the original data, it is either MORPHed again until it no longer matches the original or it is removed.

To assess the privacy and utility of CLIFF&MORPH we explore three research questions:

- RQ1: Does CLIFF&MORPH provide better balance between privacy and utility than other state-of-the-art privacy algorithms?
- RQ2: Do different classifiers affect the experimental results?
- RQ3: Does CLIFF&MORPH perform better than MORPH?

16.6.1 RESULTS AND CONTRIBUTIONS

The experiments of this study show that after applying CLIFF&MORPH, both the efficacy of classification and privacy are increased. Also, combining CLIFF&MORPH improves on prior results. Previously, Peters and Menzies [355] used MORPH and found that, sometimes, the privatized data exhibited worse performance than the original data. In this study, we combine CLIFF&MORPH and show that there is no significant reductions in the classification performance in any of the data sets we study. Note that these are *CCDP results* where data from many outside companies were combined to learn defect predictors for a local company.

Further, it is well known that pruning before classifying usually saves time [368]. For instance, *tomcat*, the largest data set used in the study is more than 163 times faster when CLIFF prunes away 90% of the data prior to MORPHing. That is, using this combination of CLIFF&MORPH, we achieve *more* privacy for effective CCDP in *less* time.

These results are novel and promising. To the best of our knowledge, this is the first report of a privacy algorithm that increases privacy while preserving inference power. Hence, we believe CLIFF&MORPH is a better option for preserving privacy in a scenario where data is shared for the purpose of CCDP.

16.6.2 PRIVACY AND CCDP

Data sharing across companies exposes the data provider to unwanted risks. Some of these concerns reflect the low quality of our current anonymization technologies. For example, recall when the state of Massachusetts released some health-care data anonymized according to HIPPA regulations [176]. This "anonymized" data was joined to other data (Massachusetts' list of registered voters) and it was possible to identify which health-care data corresponded to specific individuals (e.g., former Massachusetts governor William Weld [412]).

We mentioned earlier that *reidentification* occurs when an attacker with external information such as a voters' list, can identify an individual from a privatized data set. The data sets used in this study are aggregated at the project level and do not contain personnel or company information. Hence, reidentification of individuals is not explored further in this study.

On the other hand, *sensitive attribute disclosure* is of great concern with the data used in this study. This is where an individual in a data set can be associated with a sensitive attribute value; e.g., software development time. Such sensitive attribute disclosure can prove problematic. Some of the metrics contained in defect data can be considered as *sensitive* to the data owners. These can include lines of code (loc) or cyclomatic complexity (max-cc or avg-cc).[2] If these software measures are joined to development time, privacy policy may be breached by revealing (say) slow development times.

This section describes how we use CLIFF&MORPH to privatize data sets. As mentioned in Section 16.1, privatization with CLIFF&MORPH starts with removing a certain percentage of the original data. For our experiments we remove 90%, 80%, and 60% of the original data with CLIFF (Section 16.6.3). The remaining data is then MORPHed (Section 16.6.4). The result is a privatized data set with fewer instances, none of which could be found in the original data set. When we perform our CCDP experiments, we combine multiple CLIFFed + MORPHed data sets to create a defect predictor that is used to predict defects in nonprivatized data sets. An example of how CLIFF&MORPH work together is provided in Section 16.6.5.

16.6.3 CLIFF

CLIFF is an instance pruner that assumes tables of training data can be divided into *classes*. For example, for a table of defect data containing code metrics, different rows might be labeled accordingly (defective or not defective).

CLIFF executes as follows:

- For each column of data, find the *power* of each attribute subrange; in other words, how much more frequently that subrange appears in one class more than any other.
- In prior work [357], at this point we selected the subrange with the highest *power* and removed all instances without this subrange. From the remaining instances, those with subranges containing the second highest *power* were kept while the others were removed. This process continued until at least two instances were left or to the point before there were zero instances left.
- In this work, to control the amount of instances left by CLIFF, we find the product of the *powers* for each row, then remove the less *powerful* rows.

The result is a reduced data set with fewer rows. In theory, this reduced data set is less susceptible to privacy breaches.

Algorithm 1: *Power* is based on BORE [184]. First we assume that the target class is divided into one class as *first* and the other classes as *rest*. This makes it easy to find the attribute values that have a

---

[2] In future work, we will explore multiple sensitive attributes. For the current study, we scope this work to data with a single sensitive attribute.

high probability of belonging to the current *first* class using Bayes' theorem. The theorem uses evidence E and a prior probability $P(H)$ for hypothesis $H \in \{first, rest\}$, to calculate a likelihood (hereafter, *like*) of the evidence selecting for one class:

$$like(H|E) = P(E|H) \times P(H).$$

This calculation is then normalized to create probabilities:

$$P(first|E) = \frac{like(first|E)}{like(first|E) + like(rest|E)} \tag{16.1}$$

Jalali et al. [184] found that Equation (16.1) was a poor ranking heuristic for low-frequency evidence. To alleviate this problem, the support measure was introduced. Note that $like(first|E)$ is also a measure of support because it is maximal when a value occurs all the time in every example of one class. Hence, adding the support term is just

$$P(first|E) * support(first|E) = \frac{like(first|E)^2}{like(first|E) + like(rest|E)} \tag{16.2}$$

To compute the *power* of a subrange, we first apply equal frequency binning (EFB) to each attribute in the data set. EFB divides the range of possible values into n bins or subranges, each of which holds the same number of attribute values. However, to avoid duplicate values being placed into different bins, boundaries of every pair of neighboring bins are adjusted so that duplicate values should belong to one bin only [240]. For these experiments, we did not optimize the value for n for each data set. We simply used $n = 10$ bins. In future work we will dynamically set the value of n for a given data set.

ALGORITHM 1 FINDING SUBRANGE *POWER*

1: **Power**(D, E) {D is the data-set, and E is a set of sub-ranges for a given attribute}
2: **Partition**(D) ↦ C {Returns data partitioned according to the class label.}
3: PR ← Ø {Initialize sub-ranges with power for each sub-range in E}
4: **for** $j=0$ to # of class values in $|C|$ **do**
5:      first ← C_j
6:      rest ← $C_{\neq j}$
7:      $p_{first} \leftarrow \frac{|first|}{|D|}$ {Probability of first data}
8:      $p_{rest} \leftarrow \frac{|rest|}{|D|}$ {Probability of rest data}
9:      **for** $k=0$ to # of sub-ranges in $|E|$ **do**
10:         like(first$|E_k$) ← number of times E_k appears in first × p_{first}
11:         like(rest$|E_k$) ← number of times E_k appears in rest × p_{rest}
12:         $power_k \leftarrow \frac{like(first|E_k)^2}{like(first|E_k)+like(rest|E_k)}$
13:         PR ← $power_k$
14:      **end for**
15: **end for**
16: **return** PR

Next, *CLIFF* selects $p\%$ of the rows in a data set D containing the most powerful subranges. The matrix M holds the result of *Power* for each attribute, for each class in D. This is used to help select the rows from D to produce D' within *CliffSelection*.

The *for*-loop in lines 3-9 of Algorithm 2 iterates through attributes in D and *UniqueRanges* is called to find and return the unique subranges for each attribute. Inside that loop, at lines 5-8, a nested *for*-loop iterates through the unique subranges for a given attribute and *Power* is called to find the power of each subrange. Last, once the *powers* are found for each attribute subrange, *CliffSelection* is called to determine which rows in D will make up the final sample in D':

- Partition D by the class label.
- For each row in each partition, find the product of the *power* of the subranges in that row.
- For each partition, return the p percent of the partitioned data with the highest *power*.

An example of how CLIFF is applied to a data set is described in Section 16.6.5.

ALGORITHM 2 THE *CLIFF* ALGORITHM

1: **CLIFF**(D, p) {D is the original data-set, and p is the percentage of data to be returned}
2: M ← ∅ {Initialize sub-range *power* for each attribute}
3: **for** i=0 to # of attributes in D **do**
4:     **UniqueRanges**(D_i) ↦ R_i {Returns set of unique sub-ranges for a given attribute}
5:     **for** j=0 to # of sub-ranges in R_i **do**
6:         **Power**(D, R_i) ↦ PR_j {Returns the sub-ranges with their powers for each class}
7:             M ← PR_j
8:     **end for**
9: **end for**
10: **CliffSelection**(D, p, M) ↦ D' {Returns p of the original data}
11: **return** D'

16.6.4 MORPH

MORPH is an instance mutator used as a privacy algorithm [355]. It changes the numeric attribute values of each row by replacing these original values with *MORPHed* values.

The trick to MORPHing data is to keep the new values close enough to the original in order to maintain the utility of the data but far enough to keep the original data private. MORPHed instances are created by applying Equation (16.3) to each attribute value of the instance. MORPH takes care never to change an instance such that it moves across the boundary between the original instance and instances of another class. This boundary is determined by r in Equation (16.3). The smaller r is the closer the boundary is to the original row, and the larger r is the farther away the boundary is to the original row.

$$y_i = x_i \pm (x_i - z_i) * r \qquad (16.3)$$

Let $x \in data$ be the original instance to be changed, y the resulting MORPHed instance, and $z \in data$ the nearest unlike neighbor of x, whose class label is different from x's class label. Distance is calculated using the *Euclidean* distance. The random number r is calculated with the property

$$\alpha \leq r \leq \beta$$

where $\alpha = 0.15$ and $\beta = 0.35$. This range of values for r worked previously in our work on MORPH [355].

A simple hashing scheme lets us check if the new instance y is the same as an existing instance (and we keep MORPHing x until it does not hash to the same value as an existing instance). Hence, we can assert that none of the original instances are found in the final data set.

An example of how MORPH is applied to a data set is described in Section 16.6.5.

16.6.5 EXAMPLE OF CLIFF&MORPH

For this example we use the abbreviated version of the *ant-1.3* data set shown in Table 16.2a. This data set contains 10 attributes. One dependent attribute (class) and nine independent attributes. Each row is labeled as 1 (containing at least one defect) or 0 (having no defects). The first column holds the row number and each cell contains the original metric values.

The result of applying CLIFF&MORPH is shown in Table 16.2e. To get to that point, first the original data is binned using EFB. The result of this is shown in Table 16.2b. For example the attribute values of *wmc* are replaced by two subranges of values ([3-6] and (6-14]). Here all values from 3 to 6 inclusive are placed in the first subrange and all values between 6 and 14 (not including 6) are placed in the last subrange.

Following this, each subrange is the ranked according to Equation (16.2). To find the *power* of each subrange, we first divide the data into *first* and *rest*. For this example, let us say that all the rows with the 0 class label are *first* while the others are *rest*. Figure 16.4 shows an example of finding the *power* of (6-14] for attribute *wmc*, and Table 16.2c shows the *power* values for all the subranges of Table 16.2b.

Next, the *power* of each row is calculated by finding the product of the subrange *powers* of each row. In this example the row with the highest *power* for each class is selected. In this case that is row 3 for the 0 class label and row 8 for the 1 class label. This result is shown in Table 16.2d.

Finally, we MORPH this result according to Equation (16.3) to obtain the result in Table 16.2e.

16.6.6 EVALUATION METRICS

This section assesses the privacy and utility offered by CLIFF&MORPH.

16.6.7 EVALUATING UTILITY VIA CLASSIFICATION

We say that the classification performance of a privatized data set is *adequate* if it performs no worse than the *baseline* computed from the original data set defined as follows:

For data-sets in $T, T_1, \ldots, T_{|T|}$, performance data is collected when a defect model is learned from the $All - T_i$, then applied to T_i.

Table 16.3 defines performance measures used in this work to assess defect predictors. It also includes a new measure used in this work called the *g*-measure.

$$
\begin{aligned}
E &= (6\text{ - }14] \\
P(\textit{first}) &= {}^{6}/_{8} \\
P(\textit{rest}) &= {}^{2}/_{8} \\
\textit{freq}(E|\textit{first}) &= {}^{2}/_{6} \\
\textit{freq}(E|\textit{rest}) &= {}^{2}/_{2} \\
\textit{like}(\textit{first}|E) &= {}^{2}/_{6} \times {}^{6}/_{8} = 0.25 \\
\textit{like}(\textit{rest}|E) &= {}^{2}/_{2} \times {}^{2}/_{8} = 0.25 \\
P(\textit{first}|E) \times \textit{support}(\textit{first}|E) &= \frac{0.25^2}{0.25+0.25} = 0.13
\end{aligned}
$$

FIGURE 16.4

Finding the *power* of $(6 - 14]$.

Table 16.2 Example of CLIFF&MORPH

#	wmc	dit	noc	cbo	rfc	lcom	ca	ce	loc	class
(a) Partial ant-1.3 defect data										
1	11	4	2	14	42	29	2	12	395	0
2	14	1	1	8	32	49	4	4	297	1
3	3	2	0	1	9	0	0	1	58	0
4	12	3	0	12	37	32	0	12	310	0
5	6	3	0	4	21	1	0	4	136	0
6	5	1	5	12	11	8	11	1	59	0
7	4	2	0	3	16	0	0	3	59	0
8	14	1	0	24	63	63	20	20	822	1
(b) ant-1.3 after equal frequency binning										
1	(6-14]	[1-4]	[0-5]	(8-24]	(21-63]	(8-63]	(2-20]	(4-20]	(136-822]	0
2	(6-14]	[1-4]	[0-5]	[1-8]	(21-63]	(8-63]	(2-20]	[1-4]	(136-822]	1
3	[3-6]	[1-4]	[0-5]	[1-8]	[9-21]	[0-8]	0	[1-4]	[58-136]	0
4	(6-14]	[1-4]	[0-5]	(8-24]	(21-63]	(8-63]	0	(4-20]	(136-822]	0
5	[3-6]	[1-4]	[0-5]	[1-8]	[9-21]	[0-8]	0	[1-4]	[58-136]	0
6	[3-6]	[1-4]	[0-5]	(8-24]	[9-21]	[0-8]	(2-20]	[1-4]	[58-136]	0
7	[3-6]	[1-4]	[0-5]	[1-8]	[9-21]	[0-8]	0	[1-4]	[58-136]	0
8	(6-14]	[1-4]	[0-5]	(8-24]	(21-63]	(8-63]	(2-20]	(4-20]	(136-822]	1
(c) ant-1.3 power values										
1	0.13	0.56	0.60	0.28	0.13	0.13	0.28	0.17	0.28	0
2	0.13	0.06	0.06	0.03	0.13	0.13	0.03	0.03	0.03	1
3	**0.50**	**0.56**	**0.56**	**0.28**	**0.50**	**0.50**	**0.75**	**0.40**	**0.50**	**0**
4	0.13	0.56	0.56	0.28	0.13	0.13	0.75	0.17	0.28	0
5	0.50	0.56	0.56	0.28	0.50	0.50	0.75	0.40	0.50	0
6	0.50	0.56	0.56	0.28	0.50	0.50	0.28	0.40	0.50	0
7	0.50	0.56	0.56	0.28	0.50	0.50	0.75	0.40	0.50	0
8	**0.13**	**0.06**	**0.06**	**0.03**	**0.13**	**0.13**	**0.03**	**0.04**	**0.03**	**1**
(d) CLIFF result										
3	3	2	0	1	9	0	0	1	58	0
8	14	1	0	24	63	63	20	20	822	1
(e) MORPH result										
3	2	2	0	1	5	5	2	0	1	0
8	15	1	0	26	67	68	22	21	879	1

(a) Shows the original data and is an abbreviated version of ant-1.3. *(b) Data from a binned using EFB. (c) Power values for each subrange in b. (d) CLIFF result. (e) MORPH result.*
The bold rows show what rows have most power for predicting for class "1" or class "0".

Table 16.3 Some Popular Measures Used in Software Defect Prediction Work

		Actual	
		Yes	No
Predicted	Yes	TP	FP
	No	FN	TN
Recall (p_d)		$\frac{TP}{TP+FN}$	
p_f		$\frac{FP}{FP+TN}$	
g-Measure		$\frac{2*p_d*(1-p_f)}{p_d+(1-p_f)}$	

Table 16.4 Defect Data Set Characteristics

Data	Instances	Attributes	Class	Defect%
ant13	125	20	2	20
arc	234	20	2	12
camel10	339	20	2	4
poi15	237	20	2	41
redaktor	176	20	2	15
skarbonka	45	20	2	20
tomcat	858	20	2	9
velocity14	196	20	2	25
xalan24	723	20	2	15
xerces12	440	20	2	16

- Recall, or p_d, measures how many of the target (defective) instances are found. The higher the p_d, the fewer the false negative results;
- Probability of false alarm, or p_f, measures how many of the instances that triggered the detector actually did not contained the target (defective) concept. Like p_d, the highest p_f is 100% however its desired result is 0%;
- g-measure (harmonic mean of p_d and $1 - p_f$): In this work, we report on the g-measure. The $1 - p_f$ represents *specificity* (not predicting instances without defects as defective). *Specificity* $(1 - p_f)$ is used together with p_d to form the *G-mean$_2$* measure seen in Jiang et al. [186]. It is the geometric mean of the p_ds for both the majority and the minority class. In our case, we use these to form the g-measure which is the harmonic mean of p_d and $1 - p_f$.

Other measures such as *accuracy, precision*, and *f-measure* were not used as they are poor indicators of performance for data where the target class is rare (in our case, the *defective* instances). This is based on a study done by Menzies et al. [303] that shows that when data sets contain a low percentage of defects, precision can be unstable. If we look at the data sets in Table 16.4, we see that the percentage of defects are low in most cases.

16.6.8 EVALUATING PRIVATIZATION

In Section 16.5.1, we talked about the different privacy measures used in different studies. The existence of multiple privacy measures raises the question, "How do the different privacy measures compare with each other?" We will investigate this issue in future work. However, here we use IPR because it is based on work done by Brickell and Shmatikov [57].

Privacy is not a binary step function where something is either 100% private or 100% disclosed. Rather it is a probabilistic process where we strive to decrease the likelihood that an attacker can uncover something that they should not know. The rest of this section defines privacy using a probabilistic *increased privacy ratio*, or IPR, of privatized data sets.

16.6.8.1 Defining privacy

To investigate how well the original defect data is privatized, we assume the role of an attacker armed with some background knowledge from the original data set and also supplied with the private data set. In order to keep the privatized data set *truthful*, Brickell and Shmatikov [57] kept the sensitive attribute values as is and privatized only the QIDs. However in this work, in addition to privatizing the QIDs with CLIFF&MORPH, we apply EFB to the sensitive attribute to create 10 subranges of values to easily report on the privacy level of the privatized data set.

We propose the following privacy metric based on the *adversarial accuracy gain*, A_{acc} from the work of Brickell and Shamtikov [57]. According to the authors definition of A_{acc}, it quantifies an attacker's ability to predict the sensitive attribute value of a target t. The attacker accomplishes this by guessing the most common sensitive attribute value in $\langle t \rangle$, (a QID group).

Specifically, A_{acc} measures the increase in the attacker's accuracy after he observes a privatized data set and compares it to the baseline from a trivially privatized data set which offers perfect privacy by removing either all sensitive attribute values or all the other QIDs.

Recall that we assume that the attacker has access to a privatized version (T') of an original data set (T), and knowledge of nonsensitive QID values for a specific target in T. We refer to the latter as a *query*. For our experiments we randomly generate up to 1000 of these queries, $|Q| \leq 1000$ (Section 16.6.12 describes how queries are generated).

For each query, q in a set $Q = \{q_1, \ldots, q_{|Q|}\}$, G_i^* is a group of rows from any data set that matches q_i. Hence, let G_i be the group from the original data set and G_i' be the group from the privatized data set that matches q_i. Next, for every sensitive attribute subrange in the set $S = \{s_1, \ldots, s_{|S|}\}$, we denote the idea of the most common sensitive attribute value as $s_{max}(G_i^*)$.

Now, we define a breach of privacy as follows:

$$Breach(S, G_i^*) = \begin{cases} 1, & \text{if } s_{max}(G_i) = s_{max}(G_i'), \\ 0, & \text{otherwise.} \end{cases}$$

Therefore, the privacy level of the privatized data set is

$$100 \times IPR(T^*) = 1 - \frac{1}{|Q|} \sum_{i=0}^{|Q|} Breach(S, G_i^*).$$

$IPR(T^*)$ stands for *increased privacy ratio* and has some similarity to A_{acc} of Brickell and Shamtikov [57], where $IPR(T^*)$ measures the attacker's ability to cause privacy breaches after observing the privatized data set T' compared to a baseline of the original data set T. To be more precise, IPR(T^*) measures the percent of total queries that did not cause a privacy *Breach*.

We baseline our work against the original data set (our worst-case scenario) which offers no privacy and therefore its IPR$(T) = 0$. In our case, to have perfect privacy (our best-case scenario) we create a privatized data set by simply removing the sensitive attribute values. This will leave us with IPR$(T') = 1$.

16.6.9 EXPERIMENTS

16.6.9.1 Data

In order to assist replication, our data comes from the online PROMISE data repository [300]. Table 16.5 describes the attributes of these data sets and Table 16.4 shows other details.

16.6.10 DESIGN

From our experiments, the goal is to determine whether we can have effective defect prediction from shared data while preserving privacy. To test the shared data scenario, we do CCDP experiments for all the data sets of Table 16.4 in their original state and after they have been privatized. When experimenting with the original data, from the 10 data sets used, one is used as a test set while a defect predictor was made from *All* the data in the other nine data sets. This process is repeated for each data set. The same process is followed when the data sets are privatized. Each of the nine data sets used to create a defect predictor are first privatized, then combined into *All*. The test set is not privatized.

In a separate experiment to test how *private* the data sets are after the privatization algorithms are applied, we model an attacker's background knowledge with queries (see Section 16.6.12). These queries are applied to both the original and privatized data sets. The *IPR*s for each privatized data set are then calculated (see Section 16.6.8).

16.6.11 DEFECT PREDICTORS

To analyze the utility of CLIFF&MORPH, we perform CCDP experiments with three classification techniques implemented in WEKA [156]. These are Naive Bayes (NB) [252], support vector machines (SVMs) [360], and neural networks (NN) [33]. The default values for these classifiers in WEKA are used in our experiments.

These three classification techniques have been widely used for defect prediction [157, 249, 294]. Lewis [252] describes NB as a classifier based on Bayes' rule. It is a statistical-based learning scheme that assumes attributes are equally important and statistically independent. To classify an unknown instance, NB chooses the class with the maximum likelihood of containing the evidence in the test case. SVMs seek to minimize misclassification errors by selecting a boundary or hyperplane that leaves the maximum margin between the two classes, where the margin is defined as the sum of the distances of the hyperplane from the closest point of the two classes [350]. According to Lessmann et al. [249], NNs depict a network structure that defines a concatenation of weighting, aggregation, and thresholding functions that are applied to a software module's attributes to obtain an approximation of its posterior probability of being fault prone.

Table 16.5 The C-K Metrics of the Data Sets Used in this Work (see Table 16.4)

Attributes	Symbols	Description
Average method complexity	amc	For example, number of JAVA byte codes
Average McCabe	avg_cc	Average McCabe's cyclomatic complexity seen in class
Afferent couplings	ca	How many other classes use the specific class
Cohesion amongst classes	cam	Summation of number of different types of method parameters in every method divided by a multiplication of number of different method parameter types in whole class and number of methods
Coupling between methods	cbm	Total number of new/redefined methods to which all the inherited methods are coupled
Coupling between objects	cbo	Increased when the methods of one class access services of another
Efferent couplings	ce	How many other classes is used by the specific class
Data access	dam	Ratio of the number of private (protected) attributes to the total number of attributes
Depth of inheritance tree	dit	Provides the position of the class in the inheritance tree
Inheritance coupling	ic	Number of parent classes to which a given class is coupled (includes counts of methods and variables inherited)
Lack of cohesion in methods	lcom	Number of pairs of methods that do not share a reference to an instance variable
Another lack of cohesion measure	locm3	If m, a are the number of *methods*, *attributes* in a class number and $\mu(a)$ is the number of methods accessing an attribute, then $lcom3 = ((\frac{1}{a}\sum_j^a \mu(a_j)) - m)/(1 - m)$
Lines of code	loc	Measures the volume of code
Maximum McCabe	max_cc	Maximum McCabe's cyclomatic complexity seen in class
Functional abstraction	mfa	Number of methods inherited by a class plus number of methods accessible by member methods of the class
Aggregation	moa	Count of the number of data declarations (class fields) whose types are user-defined classes
Number of children	noc	Measures the number of immediate descendants of the class
Number of public methods	npm	Counts all the methods in a class that are declared as public. The metric is known also as class interface size (CIS)
Response for a class	rfc	Number of methods invoked in response to a message to the object
Weighted methods per class	wmc	The number of methods in the class (assuming unity weights for all methods)
Defects	defects	Number of defects per class, seen in postrelease bug-tracking systems

The last row is the dependent variable. Jureczko and Madeyski [198] provide more information on these metrics.

16.6.12 QUERY GENERATOR

A *query generator* is used to provide a sample of attacks on the data. Before discussing the query generator, a few details must be established. First, to maintain some "truthfulness" to the data, a selected sensitive attribute and the class attribute are not used as part of query generation. Here we are

Table 16.6 Example: Queries, Query Sizes and the Number of Rows that Match the Queries, $|G|$

Query	Size	$\|G\|$	Row#
cbo = (8-24]	1	4	1,4,6,8
cbo = (8-24] and wmc = (6-14]	2	3	1,4,8
cbo = (8-24] and wmc = (6-14] and noc = [0-5] and ca = 0	4	1	4

Table 16.2b is used for this example.

assuming that the only information an attacker could have is information about the nonsensitive QIDs in the data set. As a result these attribute values (sensitive and class) are unchanged in the privatized data set.

To illustrate the application of the query generator, we use Table 16.2a and b. First EFB is applied to the original data in Table 16.2a to create the subranges shown in Table 16.2b. Next, to create a query, we proceed as follows:

1. Given a query size (measured as the number of {attribute subrange} pairs; for this example we use a query size of 1);
2. Given the set of attributes $A = $ (wmc, dit, noc, cbo, rfc, lcom, ca, ce) and all their possible subranges;
3. Randomly select an attribute from A, e.g., *wmc* with two possible subranges (6-14] and [0-6];
4. Randomly select a subrange from all possible subranges of *wmc*, e.g., (6-14].

In the end the query we generate is, *wmc* = (6-14]. Table 16.6, shows more examples of queries, their sizes, and the number and rows they match from the data set.

For each query size, we generate up to 1000 queries because it is not practical to test every possible query. With these data sets the number of possible queries with arity 4 and no repeats is 38,760,000.[3]

Each query must also satisfy the following *sanity checks*:

- It must not include attribute value pairs from either the designated sensitive attribute or the class attribute.
- It must return at least two instances after a search of the original data set.
- It must not be the same as another query no matter the order of the individual {attribute subrange} pairs in the query.

16.6.13 BENCHMARK PRIVACY ALGORITHMS

In order to benchmark our approach, we compare it against data swapping and k-anonymity. Data swapping is a standard perturbation technique used for privacy [138, 413, 457]. This is a permutation approach that disassociates the relationship between a nonsensitive QID and a numerical sensitive

---

[3] $\frac{n!}{k!(n-k)!} = \binom{n}{k}$, where n is 19 (all attributes minus the class and sensitive attributes), and $k = 4$. This gives 3876 combinations. Four queries over a variable with 10 values (i.e., the 10 values generated by EFB) generates a space of 10^4 options. Therefore, the total number of possible queries of arity four is $10^4 * 3876 = 38,760,000$.

attribute. In our implementation of data swapping, for each QID a certain percent of the values are swapped with any other value in that QID. For our experiments, these percentages are 10%, 20%, and 40%.

An example of k-anonymity is shown in Figure 16.3. Our implementation follows the Datafly algorithm [411] for k-anonymity. The core Datafly algorithm starts with the input of a set of QIDs, k, and a generalization hierarchy. An example of a hierarchy is shown in the tree below using the values of *wmc* from Table 16.2a. Values at the leaves are generalized by replacing them with the subranges [3-6] or (6-14]. These in turn can be replaced by [3-14]. Or the leaf values can be suppressed by replacing them with a symbol such as the *stars* at the top of the tree.

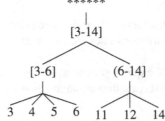

Datafly then replaces values in the QIDs according to the hierarchy. This generalization continues until there are k or fewer distinct instances. These instances are suppressed.

16.6.14 EXPERIMENTAL EVALUATION

This section presents the results of our experiments. Before going forward, Table 16.7 shows the notation and meaning of the algorithms used in this work.

RQ1: Does CLIFF&MORPH provide better balance between privacy and utility than other state-of-the-art privacy algorithms?

To see whether CLIFF&MORPH offers a better balance between privacy and utility, we privatized the original data sets shown in Table 16.4 with data swapping, k-anonymity, and CLIFF&MORPH. Then, the IPR and g-measures are calculated for each privatized data set. The experimental results are displayed in Figure 16.5. For each chart, we plot IPR on the x-axis and g-measures on the y-axis. The g-measures are based on the NB and the IPR based on queries of size 1. There is not enough space here to repeat Figure 16.5 for each query size and each classifier used in this work (a total of nine figures).

Table 16.7 Algorithm Characteristics		
Algorithms	**Symbol**	**Meaning**
MORPHed	m	Data privatized by MORPH only
MORPHedX	mX: m10, m20, m40	X represents the percentage of the original data that remains after CLIFF is applied and m indicates that the remaining data is then MORPHed. These are collectively referred to as CLIFF&MORPH algorithms
swappedX	sX: s10, s20, s40	X represents the percentage of the original data swapped
X-anonymity	kX: k2, k4	X represents the size of the QID group, where each member of the group is indistinguishable from $k - 1$ others in the group

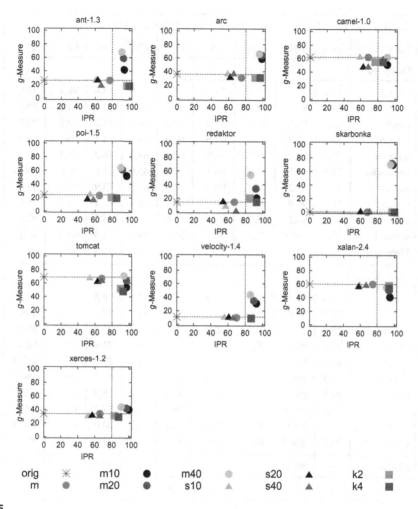

FIGURE 16.5

g-Measure vs. IPR with query size 1 for all 10 data sets. The *horizontal* and *vertical* lines show the CCDP
g-measures from the Naive Bayes defect model and IPR = 80% (respectively). Note that points above and to
the right of these lines are *private enough* (IPR over 80%) and *perform adequately* (as good as or better than
the original data). (From [356].)

Instead, we present IPR results for query sizes 2 and 4 in Table 16.8, and *g*-measures for NB, SVM,
and NN in Tables 16.9–16.11, respectively.

In Figure 16.5, the *horizontal* and *vertical* lines show the CCDP *g*-measures of the original data set
and IPR = 80%, respectively. To answer RQ1, we say that the privatized data sets appearing to the *right*
and *above* these lines, are *private enough* (IPR over 80%) and *perform adequately* (as good or better
than the nonprivatized data). In other words this region corresponds to data that provide the best balance
between privacy and utility.

Table 16.8 The IPR for Query Sizes 2 and 4 (From [356].)

Data	m	m10	m20	m40	s10	s20	s40	k2	k4
Query size = 2									
ant-1.3	77.1	**97.3**	95.9	91.9	60.2	67.6	**78.6**	98.4	**99.9**
arc	75.4	**99.4**	98.3	96.8	60.7	64.7	**79.0**	94.0	**99.2**
camel-1.0	80.3	**95.6**	94.1	93.9	62.3	68.2	**78.7**	89.9	**94.7**
poi-1.5	76.2	**97.9**	97.1	94.6	60.5	66.9	**74.1**	90.7	**95.3**
redaktor	75.3	**94.9**	93.7	90.8	61.3	64.2	**76.2**	89.3	**97.6**
skarbonka	77.5	**99.7**	97.9	96.1	57.5	65.0	**76.6**	98.8	**100.0**
tomcat	79.6	**98.2**	96.0	90.6	64.0	69.6	**73.9**	92.9	**96.6**
velocity-1.4	76.6	**96.0**	94.6	90.5	60.1	65.8	**75.7**	92.9	**95.4**
xalan-2.4	79.6	**96.5**	93.9	91.8	63.6	67.8	**76.3**	93.4	**97.0**
xerces-1.2	76.7	**100.0**	99.2	96.9	58.3	64.1	**72.6**	89.6	**95.1**
Median	76.9	**97.6**	96.0	92.9	60.6	66.4	**76.3**	92.9	**96.8**
Query size = 4									
ant-1.3	78.6	**97.5**	97.0	95.4	62.2	68.5	**78.3**	99.6	**99.6**
arc	78.0	**99.5**	98.6	98.2	59.3	69.2	**77.7**	99.2	**100.0**
camel-1.0	75.0	**81.1**	80.4	80.0	57.9	67.3	**72.8**	80.0	**80.8**
poi-1.5	78.0	**99.8**	99.5	98.9	60.8	70.6	**77.9**	97.5	**98.4**
redaktor	81.6	**98.8**	97.6	95.9	60.2	68.0	**77.5**	95.8	**100.0**
skarbonka	61.5	**100.0**	100.0	98.9	56.2	59.0	**64.2**	100.0	**100.0**
tomcat	84.3	**99.7**	99.5	98.8	61.3	72.3	**85.0**	99.1	**99.8**
velocity-1.4	77.8	**100.0**	98.7	98.1	59.8	67.8	**77.7**	99.1	**99.5**
xalan-2.4	81.1	**99.9**	99.1	98.2	60.4	69.7	**80.0**	99.2	**100.0**
xerces-1.2	78.3	**100.0**	100.0	100.0	59.8	65.5	**77.6**	99.0	**99.5**
Median	78.2	**99.8**	98.9	98.2	60.0	68.3	**77.7**	99.1	**99.7**

The numbers in bold are the highest for the different types of privacy algorithms.

Note that for most cases, $\frac{7}{10}$, the CLIFF&MORPH algorithms (m10, m20, and m40) fall to the *right* and *above* these lines. We expect this result for IPRs; however, one may question why the g-measures are higher than those of the original data set in those seven cases. This is due to instance selection done by CLIFF. Research has shown that instance selection can produce comparable or improved classification results [58, 357]. This makes CLIFF a perfect compliment to MORPH. Other studies on instance selection are included in the surveys [29, 30, 211, 346].

Of the three remaining data sets (camel-1.0, tomcat, and xalan-2.4), all offer IPRs above the 80% baseline; however, their g-measures are either as good as those of the original data set or worse. This is particularly true in the case of xalan-2.4. We see this as an issue concerning the structure of the data set rather than the CLIFF&MORPH algorithms themselves, considering that it performs well for most of the privatized data sets used in this study.

Table 16.9 The Cross-Company Experiment for 10 Data Sets with Naive Bayes: The p_ds, p_fs, and g-Measures are Shown with the g-Measures Shown in Bold (From [356].)

NB		orig	m	m10	m20	m40	s10	s20	s40	k2	k4
ant1.3	g	**26**	**26**	**42**	**59**	**68**	**26**	**26**	**18**	**18**	**18**
	p_d	15	15	95	85	90	15	15	10	10	10
	p_f	5	7	73	55	46	5	5	5	7	7
arc	g	**36**	**31**	**59**	**64**	**66**	**36**	**31**	**36**	**31**	**31**
	p_d	22	19	81	67	59	22	19	22	19	19
	p_f	5	5	54	38	26	5	5	5	5	5
camel1.0	g	**62**	**62**	**51**	**59**	**62**	**62**	**47**	**47**	**55**	**55**
	p_d	46	46	92	77	62	46	31	31	38	38
	p_f	5	5	64	52	38	3	4	4	4	4
poi1.5	g	**24**	**23**	**52**	**61**	**64**	**24**	**17**	**16**	**20**	**19**
	p_d	13	13	84	78	54	13	9	9	11	11
	p_f	4	4	63	50	22	4	3	3	4	4
redaktor	g	**14**	**14**	**20**	**34**	**54**	**7**	**14**	**0**	**20**	**14**
	p_d	7	7	96	89	78	4	7	0	11	7
	p_f	7	5	89	79	59	7	7	3	7	6
skarbonka	g	**0**	**0**	**70**	**72**	**70**	**0**	**0**	**0**	**0**	**0**
	p_d	0	0	89	89	78	0	0	0	0	0
	p_f	8	8	42	39	36	8	3	3	3	3
tomcat	g	**69**	**67**	**54**	**64**	**71**	**67**	**62**	**63**	**52**	**48**
	p_d	57	55	92	88	81	55	48	48	36	32
	p_f	12	12	62	50	36	12	11	10	9	8
velocity1.4	g	**11**	**10**	**31**	**35**	**44**	**10**	**10**	**9**	**9**	**9**
	p_d	6	5	64	41	35	5	5	5	5	5
	p_f	12	12	80	69	41	8	8	8	10	10
xalan2.4	g	**60**	**60**	**41**	**51**	**55**	**58**	**56**	**58**	**58**	**54**
	p_d	49	48	92	89	88	47	44	45	47	42
	p_f	24	22	74	64	60	23	22	20	24	23
xerces1.2	g	**34**	**34**	**40**	**42**	**44**	**30**	**31**	**30**	**31**	**29**
	p_d	21	21	51	42	34	18	18	18	18	17
	p_f	9	9	67	59	36	9	8	10	7	7
Median (g)		30	28	**47**	**59**	**63**	28	28	24	25	24

Equally important is the fact that, generally, the data swapping algorithms are *less* private than the CLIFF&MORPH algorithms and k-anonymity. This effect is seen clearly in Figure 16.5, where all 10 data sets show the best IPRs belonging to the CLIFF&MORPH algorithms and k-anonymity; while the utility of data swapping and k-anonymity are generally as good as or worse than the nonprivatized data set.

Table 16.10 The Cross-Company Experiment for 10 Data Sets with Support Vector Machines: The p_ds, p_fs, and g-Measures are Shown with the g-Measures Shown in Bold (From [356].)

SVM		orig	m	m10	m20	m40	s10	s20	s40	k2	k4
ant1.3	**g**	**0**	**0**	**62**	**75**	**75**	**0**	**0**	**0**	**0**	**0**
	p_d	0	0	90	70	70	0	0	0	0	0
	p_f	0	0	52	20	18	0	0	0	0	0
arc	**g**	**0**	**0**	**67**	**59**	**56**	**0**	**0**	**0**	**0**	**0**
	p_d	0	0	70	44	41	0	0	0	0	0
	p_f	0	0	36	14	9	0	0	0	0	0
camel1.0	**g**	**0**	**0**	**70**	**71**	**67**	**0**	**0**	**0**	**0**	**0**
	p_d	0	0	85	62	54	0	0	0	0	0
	p_f	0	0	41	16	13	0	0	0	0	0
poi1.5	**g**	**0**	**0**	**54**	**25**	**30**	**0**	**0**	**0**	**0**	**0**
	p_d	0	0	41	14	18	0	0	0	0	0
	p_f	0	0	20	2	4	0	0	0	0	0
redaktor	**g**	**0**	**0**	**40**	**50**	**55**	**0**	**0**	**0**	**0**	**0**
	p_d	0	0	63	59	56	0	0	0	0	0
	p_f	0	0	70	56	46	0	0	0	0	0
skarbonka	**g**	**0**	**0**	**68**	**48**	**35**	**0**	**0**	**0**	**0**	**0**
	p_d	0	0	67	33	22	0	0	0	0	0
	p_f	0	0	31	14	14	0	0	0	0	0
tomcat	**g**	**0**	**0**	**60**	**73**	**65**	**0**	**0**	**0**	**0**	**5**
	p_d	0	0	90	65	51	0	0	0	0	3
	p_f	0	0	54	16	9	0	0	0	0	0
velocity1.4	**g**	**0**	**0**	**43**	**27**	**18**	**0**	**0**	**0**	**0**	**0**
	p_d	0	0	44	16	10	0	0	0	0	0
	p_f	0	0	57	16	10	0	0	0	0	0
xalan2.4	**g**	**0**	**0**	**66**	**61**	**62**	**0**	**0**	**0**	**0**	**24**
	p_d	0	0	70	56	63	0	0	0	0	14
	p_f	0	0	37	34	38	0	0	0	0	2
xerces1.2	**g**	**0**	**0**	**46**	**48**	**42**	**0**	**0**	**0**	**0**	**0**
	p_d	0	0	45	39	28	0	0	0	0	0
	p_f	0	0	52	38	14	0	0	0	0	0
Median (g)		0	0	**61**	**54**	**55**	0	0	0	0	0

This summary of results also holds true when measuring IPRs for query sizes 2 and 4 (Table 16.8), and g-measures for SVM (Table 16.10) and NN (Table 16.11).

So, to answer RQ1, at least for the defect data sets used in this study and the baselines used, CLIFF&MORPH generally provides a better balance between privacy and utility than data swapping and k-anonymity.

Table 16.11 The Cross-Company Experiment for 10 Data Sets with Neural Networks: The p_ds, p_fs, and g-Measures are Shown with the g-Measures Shown in Bold

NN		orig	m	m10	m20	m40	s10	s20	s40	k2	k4
ant1.3	g	**38**	**32**	**59**	**56**	**62**	**38**	**51**	**44**	**32**	**0**
	p_d	25	20	70	65	65	25	35	30	20	0
	p_f	17	18	50	51	41	20	7	15	20	7
arc	g	**57**	**19**	**60**	**60**	**63**	**43**	**42**	**47**	**68**	**0**
	p_d	44	11	59	59	74	30	30	33	59	0
	p_f	22	22	40	40	45	20	26	20	20	7
camel1.0	g	**45**	**57**	**65**	**59**	**52**	**52**	**51**	**58**	**44**	**0**
	p_d	31	46	69	62	46	38	38	46	31	0
	p_f	19	25	38	43	41	22	24	21	24	6
poi1.5	g	**37**	**20**	**45**	**49**	**53**	**33**	**18**	**19**	**42**	**7**
	p_d	23	11	31	36	40	21	10	11	29	4
	p_f	16	16	20	25	25	10	9	8	23	6
redaktor	g	**43**	**39**	**56**	**63**	**51**	**29**	**48**	**20**	**67**	**14**
	p_d	30	26	74	78	70	19	33	11	59	7
	p_f	23	23	54	48	60	38	17	17	24	1
skarbonka	g	**20**	**33**	**46**	**47**	**63**	**0**	**20**	**20**	**20**	**0**
	p_d	11	22	44	44	56	0	11	11	11	0
	p_f	19	36	53	50	28	14	11	8	11	0
tomcat	g	**39**	**38**	**58**	**69**	**68**	**44**	**42**	**46**	**41**	**3**
	p_d	26	25	52	73	68	30	29	32	29	1
	p_f	20	20	34	34	31	20	18	19	25	8
velocity1.4	g	**14**	**15**	**35**	**35**	**37**	**9**	**13**	**15**	**19**	**5**
	p_d	7	8	34	37	29	5	7	8	11	3
	p_f	4	12	63	67	47	20	4	10	14	0
xalan2.4	g	**41**	**44**	**58**	**57**	**62**	**35**	**35**	**39**	**36**	**13**
	p_d	27	30	64	59	65	22	22	25	23	7
	p_f	17	20	46	46	41	13	13	17	18	11
xerces1.2	g	**18**	**28**	**52**	**47**	**45**	**13**	**26**	**13**	**18**	**16**
	p_d	10	17	56	35	32	7	15	7	10	8
	p_f	9	11	51	31	24	11	11	11	14	6
Median (g)		39	33	**57**	**56**	**57**	34	39	29	38	4

RQ2: Do different classifiers affect the experimental results?

Looking at the raw results from Tables 16.9–16.11, the SVM results shown in Table 16.10 stand out for CLIFF&MORPH and the other privacy algorithms. Here, in all cases CLIFF&MORPH has better g-measures, while in $\frac{8}{10}$ cases, only CLIFF&MORPH has g-measures above zero. The privacy algorithms for NB and the NN generally show better g-measure results than SVM.

For a substantial comparison between classifiers we use the Mann-Whitney U test [281] at 95% confidence for the g-measures over all data sets. The results show that there is no significant difference in the performance of NB and NN. However when g-measures from SVM are compared to those of NB and NN, it performs significantly worse. Therefore, to answer RQ2, although the results show that the NB and NN classifiers perform better than SVM, the g-measures show that the CLIFF&MORPH algorithms have the best performance for all three classifiers used in this study. Therefore, based on this result for these different types of classifiers we conclude that the performance of CLIFF&MORPH is not dependent on the type of classifier used.

RQ3: Does CLIFF&MORPH perform better than MORPH?
Previous work by Peters and Menzies [355], showed that a data set privatized by MORPH offered at least four times more privacy than the original data set and comparable utility results. In this work we enhance the performance of the MORPH algorithm by first applying the instance selector CLIFF to the original data set.

All results in this study indicate that CLIFF&MORPH performs better than just MORPH. This is because as CLIFF removes the instances with the fewest *power subranges*, it is getting rid of those instances that may cause ambiguous classification. This improves utility. An exceptional example of this can be seen in Figure 16.5 with *skarbonka*. When NB is use to create the defect predictor, we see much higher g-measures for the CLIFF&MORPH algorithms (between 60% and 80%), while the MORPH algorithm has a 0% g-measure. This general trend of the CLIFF&MORPH algorithms having better utility than the MORPH algorithm can also be seen in Figure 16.5 for *ant-1.3, arc, poi-1.5, redaktor, velocity-1.4*, and *xerces-1.2*. Additionally, Tables 16.10, 16.11 confirm these results with both SVM and NN having greater median g-measures for the CLIFF&MORPH algorithms than for the MORPH algorithm. The best performance is shown with SVM, where MORPH has a 0% median g-measure and *m10* has a median 61% g-measure.

Privacy is improved because we are first removing 90%, 80%, and 60% of the original data, then MORPHing the remaining instances. The removed instances are guaranteed 100% protection due to their absence. By then, applying MORPH to the remaining instances, we have (in all cases) IPRs for the CLIFF&MORPH algorithms that are *private enough* (>80%) and greater than those for MORPH, which in most cases are not >80%. These results are shown in Figure 16.5 and Table 16.8.

16.6.15 DISCUSSION
As with any empirical study, biases can affect the final results. Therefore any conclusions made from this work must be considered with the following issues in mind:

1. *Sampling bias* threatens any classification experiment; i.e., what matters there may not be true here. For example, the data sets used here come from the PROMISE repository and were supplied by one individual. The best we can do is define our methods and publicize our data so that other researchers can try to repeat our results and, perhaps, point out a previously unknown bias in our analysis. Hopefully, other researchers will emulate our methods in order to repeat, refute, or improve our results.
2. *Learner bias*: Another source of bias in this study are the learners used for the defect prediction studies. Classification is a large and active field and any single study can only use a small subset of

the known classification algorithms. In this work, only results for NB, SVMs, and NN are published.

3. *Evaluation bias*: This chapter has focused on background knowledge specific to the original data sets without regard for other types of background knowledge, which cannot be captured by the queries used in this study. For instance, correlation knowledge and knowledge about knowing information about related files. This is a subject for future work.

4. *Other evaluation bias*: The utility of a privatized data set can be measured semantically (where the workload is unknown) or empirically (known workload, e.g., classification or aggregate query answering). In this work, we measure utility empirically for defect prediction.

5. *Comparison bias*: There are many anonymization algorithms and it would be difficult to compare the performance of CLIFF&MORPH against them all. This paper compares our approach against privatization methods that are known *not* to damage classification; this is why we used the data swapping (also used by Taneja et al. [413]). We also used k-anonymity [411], a widely used privacy algorithm.

16.6.16 RELATED WORK: PRIVACY IN SE

Research on privacy in SE has focused on software testing and debugging [63, 67, 79, 413], and defect prediction [355, 356]. Work published by Castro et al. [67] sought to provide a solution to the problem of software vendors who need to include sensitive user information in error reports in order to reproduce a bug. To protect sensitive user information, Castro et al. [67] used symbolic execution along the path followed by a failed execution to compute path conditions. Their goal was to compute new input values unrelated to the original input. These new input values satisfied the path conditions required to make the software follow the same execution path until it failed.

As a follow-up to the Castro et al. [67] paper, Clause and Orso [79] presented an algorithm that anonymized input sent from users to developers for debugging. Like Castro et al. [67], the aim of Clause and Orso was to supply the developer with anonymized input that causes the same failure as the original input. To accomplish this, they first use a novel "path condition relaxation" technique to relax the constraints in path conditions thereby increasing the number of solutions for computed conditions.

In contrast to the work done by Castro et al. [67] and Clause and Orso [79], Taneja et al. [413] proposed PRIEST, a privacy framework. Unlike our work, which privatizes data randomly within the nearest unlike neighbor border constraints, the privacy algorithm in PRIEST is based on data swapping where each value in a data set is replaced by another distinct value of the same attribute. This is done according to some probability that the original value will remain unchanged. An additional difference is in the privacy metric used. They make use of a "guessing anonymity" technique that generates a similarity matrix between the original and privatized data. The values in this matrix are then used to calculate three privacy metrics: (1) mean guessing anonymity, (2) fraction of records with a guessing anonymity greater than $m = 1$, and (3) unique records that determine if any records from the original data remain after privatization.

Work by Taneja et al. [413] followed work done by Budi et al. [63]. Similarly, their work focused on providing privatized data for testing and debugging. They were able to accomplish this with a novel privacy algorithm called kb-anonymity. This algorithm combined k-anonymity with the concept of program behavior preservation, which guide the generation of new test cases based on known ones and make sure the new test cases satisfy certain properties [63]. The difference with the follow-up work by Taneja et al. [413], is that while Budi et al. [63] replaces the original data with new data, in Taneja's work [413], the data swapping algorithm maintains the original data and offers individual privacy by swapping values.

16.6.17 SUMMARY

Studies have shown that early detection and fixing of defects in software projects is less expensive than finding defects later on [39, 87]. Organizations with local data can take full advantage of this early detection benefit by doing WCDP. When an organization does not have enough local data to build defect predictors, they might try to access relevant data from other organizations in order to perform CCDP. That access will be denied unless the privacy concerns of the data owners can be addressed. Current research in privacy seeks to address one issue, i.e., providing adequate privacy for data while maintaining the efficacy of the data. However, reaching an adequate balance between privacy and efficacy has proven to be a challenge because intuitively, the more the data is privatized the less useful the data becomes.

To address this issue we present CLIFF&MORPH, a pair of privacy algorithms designed to privatize defect data sets for CCDP. The data is privatized in two steps: instance pruning with CLIFF, where CLIFF gets rid of irrelevant instances thereby increasing the distances between the remaining instances, and perturbation (synthetic data generation) with MORPH where MORPH is able to move the remaining instances further and create new synthetic instances that do not cross class boundaries.

Unlike previous studies, we show in Figure 16.5 that CLIFF&MORPH maintains increasing data privacy of data sets without damaging the usefulness of the data for defect prediction. Note that this is a significant result as prior work with the standard privatization technologies could not achieve those two goals.

We hope that this result encourages more data sharing, more cross-company experiments, and more work on building SE models that are general to large-scale systems.

Our results suggest the following future work:

- The experiments of this chapter should be repeated on additional data sets.
- The current nearest unlike neighbor algorithm used in MORPH is $O(N^2)$. We are exploring ways to optimize that with some clustering index method (e.g., k-means).
- While Figure 16.5 shows that we can increase privacy, it also shows that we cannot 100% guarantee it. At this time, we do not know the exact levels of privacy required in industry or if the results of Figure 16.5 meet those needs. This requires further investigation.
- Currently, we use the MORPH algorithm with set experimental parameter values (α and β). Further investigation is needed to determine the optimal values for these parameters.
- This work focused on showing how to prevent an attacker from associating a target t to a single sensitive attribute value. We are exploring ways to show how a data set with multiple sensitive attributes can be adequately privatized.
- In the study of data privacy, modeling the attacker's background knowledge is important to determine how private a data set is. In this chapter we only focused on background knowledge specific to the original data sets. Other types of background knowledge need to be considered.

COMPENSATING FOR MISSING DATA

Name:	POP1
Also known as:	Reverse nearest neighbor, instance selection.
Intent:	When some columns of data are unavailable, use other columns to "stand in" for the missing values.
Motivation:	In the early stages of a software project, we cannot accurately estimate the size of the final system. Hence, we would like some method to estimate effort *without* needing size variables.
Solution:	Use nearest-neighbor methods, ignoring the unknown columns (e.g., those relating to software size).
Constraints:	Ignoring some training data (e.g., columns relating to size data) damages our ability to make estimates *unless* we also ignore rows containing outlier values (numbers that are suspiciously distant from the usual values).
Implementation:	The *reverse nearest neighbor* (rNN) count measures how many times one row is the closest neighbor to another. Hence, to cull outliers, POP1 removes rows with *lowest* rNN scores (i.e., those that are most distant from everyone else).
Applicability:	While using the size columns generates better estimates, the results from applying the POP1 preprocessor are a good close second-best solution. Hence, where possible, try to find values for all columns shared by all rows. However, when some are missing, prune outlier rows prior to making estimates.
Related to:	The QUICK system of Chapter 18 extends POP1 to apply reverse nearest-neighbor pruning to rows *and* columns. For large data sets, the reverse nearest-neighbor calculation could be optimized with the CHUNK preprocessor of Chapter 12.

This chapter is an update to "Size doesn't matter?: on the value of software size features for effort estimation" by E. Kocaguneli, T. Menzies, Jairus Hihn, and Byeong Ho Kang, which is published in the PROMISE: Proceedings of the 2012 PROMISE conference. During the update and adaptation to the chapter, the text was rewritten to a large extent with practitioners in mind. Irrelevant parts were removed to make the text more focused. Particularly, recommendations, cautionary notes, and adaptation strategies have been added for a practitioner audience.

> Measuring software productivity by lines of code is like measuring progress on an airplane by how much it weighs.
>
> **Bill Gates**

The issue of feature and instance selection can be utilized in a variety of ways, particularly in the case of noisy and small data sets, e.g., software effort estimation (SEE) data sets. In this chapter and in

Chapter 18 we will utilize a *popularity-based*[1] instance and feature selection idea. We will utilize this idea to address two important contexts: the necessity of size attributes and addressing the lack of labels through an active learning solution (subject of Chapter 18). As we will see, the idea of *popularity* is based on the contexts of similarity and k-nearest neighbor (k-NN) algorithm. There are reasons why the presented popularity algorithm uses k-NN, but not, say, support vector machines: k-NN is simple enough and has a demonstrably good performance on SEE data sets. As you read the popularity idea, keep in mind that the presented algorithm based on k-NN may not be optimum for your data set, but the presented idea can be augmented in the favor of an algorithm that performs well on your particular data set.

For example, during a discussion with an industry practitioner working in the online advertisement area (where—unlike SEE—the data is huge and the problem is classification), the practitioner told me that k-NN would not perform well on his data sets, but decision trees would. As an initial suggestion, my reply was to augment the similarity idea in favor of decision trees; for example, the instances ending up in the same leaf node may be considered similar. The reason for quoting this discussion and the simple solution is to remind the reader that reading this chapter (as well as the next one) while asking: "How can my best performing algorithm be adapted to the popularity idea?" may be more helpful.

The use of size attributes,[2] such as lines of code (LOC), function points (FPs), and so on is essential for some of the predictive models built in software engineering. For example, size attributes play a fundamental role in some of the most widely used SEE techniques like COCOMO [38]. Unfortunately, as we quoted from Bill Gates above, there may be very little trust on the industry practitioners side to put in size features. So it is a reasonable question to ask whether there is a definite need of size attributes for prediction purposes or whether there is a way to compensate for their absence through the use of other nonsize features. In this chapter, we tackle this problem and advocate that it is possible to avoid the requirement of size attributes through the selective use of nonsize attributes.

SEE is a maturing field with decades of research effort behind it. One of the most widely used SEE methods by practitioners (e.g., in DOD and NASA [274]) are parametric effort models like COCOMO [34].Although the development of parametric effort models has made the estimation process repeatable, there are still concerns about their overall accuracy [127, 205, 308, 331]. Difficulty with accurately sizing software systems is a major cause of this observed inaccuracy.

Due to some *de facto* rules in the SE industry such as "the bigger the system is, the more effort it requires" or "more complex systems require more effort," it is somewhat difficult to get around the sizing problem as most of the effort models utilized in industry require size attributes as the primary input. There are two widely used software size measures: logical LOC [35] and FPs [4]. In addition, there are many other sizing metrics such as physical LOC, number of requirements, number of modules [172], number of Web pages [218], and so on. From now on we will refer to such size related metrics generally as "size features."

One of the main problems with size features is that in the early stages of a software project, there is not enough information regarding how big the project is going to be or how much code development

---

[1] Popularity will be used in the context of instances. An instance's popularity is the count of how many other instances mark it as their closest neighbor.

[2] A size attribute is a certain measurement of a piece of software with the purpose of identifying its size, e.g., how long it is in terms of lines of code.

and/or code reuse will be performed. Hence, this poses a significant handicap for the size-based SEE methods. So for accurate estimates that need to be made very early in the software life cycle what is very much needed is a simple global method that can work without size features. Unfortunately, standard SEE methods such as standard analogy-based estimation (ABE) methods like 1-nearest neighbor (1NN) as well as classification and regression trees (CART) cannot be this global method. Our results show that standard SEE methods perform poorly with the lack of size features.

The focus of this chapter is to propose an ABE method called POP1, which is short for "popularity-based instance selection using 1-nearest neighbor." POP1 is a simple method that only requires normalization of an array of numbers and Euclidean distance calculation. Our results show that POP1 (compared to 1NN) compensates for the lack of size features in 11 out of 13 data sets. A simple method like POP1 running on data sets without size features can attain the same performance as a more complex learner like CART running on data sets with size features. Therefore, for the cases where it is difficult to measure size features, POP1 can aid practitioners get around the problem of necessarily using size features.

17.1 BACKGROUND NOTES ON SEE AND INSTANCE SELECTION
17.1.1 SOFTWARE EFFORT ESTIMATION

SEE is fundamentally the process of estimating the total effort that will be necessary to complete a software project [208]. Jorgensen and Shepherd report in their review that more than half the SEE manuscripts published since 1980 tackle developing new estimation models [193].

This large corpus of SEE estimation methods are grouped w.r.t. different taxonomies, although Briand et al. report that there is no agreement on a certain best taxonomy [52]. For example, Menzies et al. divide SEE methods into two groups: model-based and expert-based [301]. According to this taxonomy model-based methods use some algorithm(s) to summarize old data and to make predictions for the new data. Expert-based methods make use of human expertise, which is possibly supported by process guidelines and/or checklists. Myrtveit et al. propose a data set dependent differentiation between methods [335]. According to that taxonomy, the methods are divided into:

- Sparse-data methods that require few or no historical data, e.g., expert-estimation [190].
- Many-data approaches where a certain amount of historical data is a must, e.g., functions and arbitrary function approximations (such as classification and regression trees).

Shepperd et al. propose a three-class taxonomy [394]: (1) expert-based estimation, (2) algorithmic models, and (3) analogy. Expert-based models target the consensus of human experts. Jorgensen et al. define expert-based methods as a human-intensive process of negotiating the estimate of a new project [190].

17.1.2 INSTANCE SELECTION IN SEE

The fundamental idea behind instance selection is that most of the instances in a data set are uninformative and can be removed. In Ref. [71], Chang finds prototypes for nearest-neighbor classifiers. Chang's prototype generators explore data sets *A*, *B*, *C* of size 514, 150, 66 instances, respectively. He converts A, B, C into new data sets A', B', C' containing 34, 14, 6 prototypes, respectively. Note that the new data sets contain only 7%, 9%, and 9% of the original data.

The methodology promoted in this chapter is a standard ABE method, which is augmented with a popularity-based instance selection mechanism. We will see in the experimental results section of this chapter that although standard ABE methods are incapable of dealing with the lack of size attributes, when the right instances are selected, the presented algorithm can compensate for the lack of size features.

Our hypothesis behind the success of instance selection in the condition of a missing feature (size attributes) is that when a dimension of the space disappears, it helps to select only the most informative instances to make the signal clearer. For example, in a prior study Kocaguneli et al. use a variance-based instance selection mechanism in an ABE context [229]. In this variance-based instance selection mechanism, instances of a data set are clustered according to their distances and only the clusters with low dependent variable variance are selected. The estimates made from the remaining clusters have a much lower error rate than standard ABE methods.

There are a number of other instance selection studies in SEE. Keung et al.'s Analogy-X method also works as an instance selection method in an ABE context [208]. Analogy-X selects the instances of a data set based on the assumed distribution model of that data set, i.e., only the instances that conform to the distribution model are selected. Another example is Li et al.'s study, where they use a genetic algorithm for instance selection to provide estimation accuracy improvements [259].

17.2 DATA SETS AND PERFORMANCE MEASURES

17.2.1 DATA SETS

So as to expose the proposed algorithm to a variety of different settings, we used data sets coming from multiple resources. The standard **COCOMO** data sets (cocomo*, nasa*) contain contractor projects developed in the United States and are collected with the COCOMO approach [34]. The **desharnais** data set and its subsets are collected with FP approach from software companies in Canada [98]. **sdr** contains data from projects of various software companies in Turkey and it is collected by SoftLab with a COCOMO approach [21].

Using the data sets of Table 17.1 we would like to define two terms that will be fundamental to our discussion: *full data set* and *reduced data set*. We will refer to a data set used with all the features (including the size feature(s)) as a "full data set." A data set whose size feature(s) are removed (for the experiments of this chapter) will be called a "reduced data set." The features of the full data sets are given in Table 17.2. Note in Table 17.2 that the full data sets are grouped under three categories (under the "Methodology" column) depending on their collection method: COCOMO [34], COCOMOII [35], and FP [13, 98]. These groupings mean that all the data sets in one group share the features listed under the "Features" column. The difference between COCOMO data sets (cocomo81* and nasa93*) and COCOMOII data sets (sdr) is the additional five cost drivers: *prec, flex, resl, team, pmat*. Hence, instead of repeating the COCOMO features for COCOMOII, we listed only the additional cost driver features for COCOMOII under the column "Features."

The bold font features in Table 17.2 are identified as size (or size-related) features. These features are removed in reduced data sets. In other words, the full data sets minus the highlighted features gives us the reduced data sets. For convenience, the features that remain after removing the size features are

Table 17.1 The 494 Projects Used in this Study Come from 13 Data Sets

Dataset	Features	Size	Description	Units
cocomo81	17	63	NASA projects	months
cocomo81e	17	28	Cocomo81 embedded projects	months
cocomo81o	17	24	Cocomo81 organic projects	months
cocomo81s	17	11	Cocomo81 semidetached projects	months
nasa93	17	93	NASA projects	months
nasa93c1	17	12	nasa93 projects from center 1	months
nasa93c2	17	37	nasa93 projects from center 2	months
nasa93c5	17	40	nasa93 projects from center 5	months
desharnais	10	81	Canadian software projects	hours
desharnaisL1	10	46	Projects developed with Language1	hours
desharnaisL2	10	25	Projects developed with Language2	hours
desharnaisL3	10	10	Projects developed with Language3	hours
sdr	22	24	Turkish software projects	months
		Total: 494		

Indentation in column one denotes a data set that is a subset of another data set.

Table 17.2 The Full Data Sets, Their Features, and Collection Methodology

Methodology	Dataset	Features
COCOMO	cocomo81	RELY, ACAP, SCED
	cocomo81o	DATA, AEXP, **KLOC**
	cocomo81s	CPLX, PCAP, EFFORT
	nasa93	TIME, VEXP
	nasa93c1	STOR, LEXP
	nasa93c2	VIRT, MODP
	nasa93c5	TURN, TOOL
COCOMOII	sdr	*Addition to COCOMO features*
		PREC
		FLEX
		RESL
		TEAM
		PMAT
FP	desharnais	TeamExp, Effort, **Adjustment**
	desharnaisL1	ManagerExp, **Transactions**, **PointsAjust**
	desharnaisL2	YearEnd, **Entities**, Language
	desharnaisL3	**PointsNonAdjust**

The boldface features are identified as size (or size-related) features.

Table 17.3 The Reduced Data Sets, Their Collection Methodology, and Their Nonsize Features

Methodology	Dataset	Features
COCOMO	cocomo81	RELY, ACAP, SCED
	cocomo81o	DATA, AEXP
	cocomo81s	CPLX, PCAP, EFFORT
	nasa93	TIME, VEXP
	nasa93c1	STOR, LEXP
	nasa93c2	VIRT, MODP
	nasa93c5	TURN, TOOL
COCOMOII	sdr	*Addition to COCOMO features*
		PREC
		FLEX
		RESL
		TEAM
		PMAT
FP	desharnais	TeamExp, Effort
	desharnaisL1	ManagerExp
	desharnaisL2	YearEnd, Language
	desharnaisL3	

Reduced data sets are defined to be the full data sets minus size-related features (boldface features of Table 17.2).

given in Table 17.3. Note that both in Table 17.2 and in Table 17.3, the acronyms of the features are used. These acronyms stand for various software product-related features. For example, COCOMO groups features under six categories:

- Product factors
    - RELY: Required Software Reliability
    - DATA: Database Size
    - CPLX: Product Complexity
    - RUSE: Required Reusability
    - DOCU: Documentation match to life cycle needs
- Platform factors
    - TIME: Execution Time Constraint
    - STOR: Main Storage Constraint
    - PVOL: Platform Volatility
- Personnel factors
    - ACAP: Analyst Capability
    - PCAP: Programmer Capability
    - PCON: Personnel Continuity
    - AEXP: Applications Experience

- PEXP: Platform Experience
- LTEX: Language and Tool Experience
- Project factors
  - TOOL: Use of Software Tools
  - SITE: Multisite Development
  - SCED: Development Schedule
- Input
  - LOC: Lines of Code
- Output
  - EFFORT: Effort spent for project in terms of man-months

In addition to the original COCOMO method, the improved COCOMOII version defines an additional new category called exponential cost drivers, under which the following features are defined:

- Exponential cost drivers
  - PREC: Precedentedness
  - FLEX: Development Flexibility
  - RESL: Arch/Risk Resolution
  - TEAM: Team Cohesion
  - PMAT: Process Maturity

For detailed information and an in depth discussion regarding the above-listed COCOMO and COCOMOII features, refer to Refs. [34, 35]. The FP approach adopts a different strategy than COCOMO. The definitions of the FP data sets (desharnais*) features are as follows:

- *TeamExp*: Team experience in years
- *ManagerExp*: Project management experience in years
- *YearEnd*: The year in which the project ended
- *Transactions*: The count of basic logical transactions
- *Entities*: The number of entities in the systems data model
- *PointsNonAdjust*: Equal to *Transactions* + *Entities*
- *Adjustment*: FP complexity adjustment factor
- *PointsAdjust*: The adjusted FPs
- *Language*: Categorical variable for programming language
- *Effort*: The actual effort measured in person-hours

For more details on these features refer to the work of Desharnais [98] or Li et al. [261]. Note that 4 projects out of 81 in the desharnais data set have missing feature values. Instead of removing these projects from the data set, we employed a missing value handling technique called simple mean imputation [7].

17.2.2 ERROR MEASURES

Error measures are used to assess the success of a prediction. In this chapter, we stick with the commonly used error measures in SEE.

The absolute residual (AR) is defined as the difference between the predicted and the actual:

$$AR_i = |x_i - \hat{x}_i| \tag{17.1}$$

where x_i and $\hat{x}_i$ are the actual and predicted value for test instance i. MAR is the mean of all the AR values.

The magnitude of relative error (MRE) measure is one of the *de facto* error measures [133, 390]. MRE measures the ratio between the effort estimation error and the actual effort:

$$MRE_i = \frac{|x_i - \hat{x}_i|}{x_i} = \frac{AR_i}{x_i} \tag{17.2}$$

A related measure is the magnitude of error relative (MER) to the estimate [133]):

$$MER_i = \frac{|x_i - \hat{x}_i|}{\hat{x}_i} = \frac{AR_i}{\hat{x}_i} \tag{17.3}$$

The overall average error of MRE can be derived as the mean or median of MRE, or MMRE and MdMRE, respectively:

$$MMRE = \text{mean}(\text{all MRE}_i) \tag{17.4}$$

$$MdMRE = \text{median}(\text{all MRE}_i) \tag{17.5}$$

A common alternative to MMRE is PRED(25), and it is defined as the percentage of successful predictions falling within 25% of the actual values, and can be expressed as follows, where N is the dataset size:

$$PRED(25) = \frac{100}{N} \sum_{i=1}^{N} \begin{cases} 1 & \text{if MRE}_i \leq \frac{25}{100} \\ 0 & \text{otherwise} \end{cases} \tag{17.6}$$

For example, PRED(25) = 50% implies that half of the estimates are failing within 25% of the actual values [390].

There are many other error measures including mean balanced relative error (MBRE) and the mean inverted balanced relative error (MIBRE) studied by Foss et al. [133]:

$$MBRE_i = \frac{|\hat{x}_i - x_i|}{\min(\hat{x}_i, x_i)} \tag{17.7}$$

$$MIBRE_i = \frac{|\hat{x}_i - x_i|}{\max(\hat{x}_i, x_i)} \tag{17.8}$$

We test the numerical comparison of performance measures via a statistical test called the Mann-Whitney rank-sum test (95% confidence). We use Mann-Whitney instead of Student's t-test, as it compares the sums of ranks, unlike Student's t-test, which may introduce spurious findings as a result of outliers in the given data sets.

We use Mann-Whitney to generate *win, tie, loss* statistics. The procedure used for that purpose is defined in Figure 17.1: First, two distributions i, j (e.g., arrays of MREs or ARs) are compared to see if they are statistically different (Mann-Whitney rank-sum test, 95% confidence); if not, then the related *tie* values (tie_i and tie_j) are incremented. If the distributions are different, we update win_i, win_j and $loss_i, loss_j$ after error measure comparison.

When comparing the performance of a method (*method_i*) run on reduced data sets to a method *method_j* run on full data sets, we will specifically focus on *loss* values. Note that to make the case for

if Mann-Whitney(Err_i, Err_j, 95) says there is no statistical difference. **then**
    $tie_i = tie_i + 1;$
    $tie_j = tie_j + 1;$
else
  if better(Err_i, Err_j) **then**
    $win_i = win_i + 1$
    $loss_j = loss_j + 1$
  else
    $win_j = win_j + 1$
    $loss_i = loss_i + 1$
  end if
end if

FIGURE 17.1

Comparing error measures of method (i,j) (Err_i,Err_j). For MRE and PRED(25) "better" means lower, higher values (respectively).

$method_i$, we do not need to show that its performance is "better" than $method_j$. We can recommend $method_i$ over $method_j$ as long as its performance is no worse than $method_j$, i.e., as long as it does not "lose" against $method_j$.

17.3 EXPERIMENTAL CONDITIONS
17.3.1 THE ALGORITHMS ADOPTED

In this chapter we use two algorithms due their success reported in prior SEE work: a baseline analogy-based estimation method called ABE0 [229] and a decision tree learner called CART [48]. Several papers conclude that CART and nearest-neighbor methods are useful comparison algorithms for SEE. For example, Walkerden and Jeffrey [434] endorse CART as a state-of-the-art SEE method. Dejaeger et al. also claim that, in terms of assessing new SEE methods, methods like CART may prove to be more adequate. The previous work published by the authors is also in the same direction of the conclusions of Walkerden, Jeffrey, Dejaeger et al. Our 2011 study reports an extensive comparison of 90 SEE methods (generated using all combinations of 10 preprocessors and 9 learners) [223]. In this study the most successful SEE methods turn out to be ABE0 with 1-nearest neighbor (which will be referred to as 1NN from now on) and CART.

ABE methods generate an estimate for a future project by retrieving similar instances among past projects. Then the effort values of the retrieved past projects are adapted into an estimate. There are various design options associated with ABE methods, yet a basic ABE method can be defined as follows:

- Input a database of past projects.
- For each test instance, retrieve k similar projects (analogies) according to a similarity function.
- Adapt the effort values of the k nearest analogies to come up with the effort estimate.

ABE0 uses the Euclidean distance as a similarity measure, whose formula is given in Equation (17.9), where w_i corresponds to feature weights applied on independent features fA_i and fB_i of instances A and B, respectively. t is the total number of independent features. ABE0 framework equally favors all instances, i.e., $w_i = 1$. For adaptation, ABE0 takes the median of retrieved k projects. The ABE0 adopted in this research uses a 1-nearest neighbor (i.e., $k = 1$); hence, the name 1NN.

$$\text{Distance} = \sqrt{\sum_{i=1}^{t} w_i (fA_i - fB_i)^2} \qquad (17.9)$$

Iterative dichotomizers like CART find the feature that most divides the data such that the variance of each division is minimized [48]. The algorithm then recurses into each division. Once the tree is generated, the cost data of the instances in the leaf nodes are averaged to generate an estimate for the test case. For more details on CART, refer to Breiman et al. [48].

17.3.2 PROPOSED METHOD: POP1

The 1NN variant proposed in this chapter utilizes the popularity of the instances in a training set. We define the "popularity" of an instance as the number of times it happens to be the nearest neighbor of other instances. The proposed method is called POP1 (short for popularity-based-1NN). The basic steps of POP1 can be defined as follows:

Step 1: Calculate distances between every instance tuple in the training set.
Step 2: Convert distances of step 1 into ordering of neighbors.
Step 3: Mark closest neighbors and calculate popularity.
Step 4: Order training instances in decreasing popularity.
Step 5: Decide which instances to select.
Step 6: Return estimates for the test instances.

The following paragraphs describe the details of each step:

Step 1: Calculate distances between every instance tuple in the training set. This step uses the Euclidean distance function (as in 1NN) to calculate the distances between every pair of instances within the training set. The distance calculation is kept in a matrix called D, where ith row keeps the distance of the ith instance to other instances. Note that this calculation requires only the independent features. Furthermore, because POP1 runs on reduced data sets, size features are not used in this step.

Step 2: Convert distances of Step 1 into ordering of neighbors. This step requires us to merely replace the distance values with their corresponding rank from the closest to the farthest. We work one row at a time on matrix D: Start from row #1, rank distance values in ascending order, then replace distance values with their corresponding ranks, which gives us the matrix D'. The ith row of D' keeps the ranks of the neighbors of the ith instance.

Step 3: Mark closest neighbors and calculate popularity. Because POP1 uses only the closest neighbors, we leave the cells of D' that contain 1 (i.e., that contain a closest neighbor) untouched and replace the contents of all the other cells with zeros. The remaining matrix D'' marks only the instances that appeared as the closest neighbor to another instance.

Step 4: Order training instances in decreasing popularity. This step starts summing up the "columns" of D''. The sum of, say, ith column shows how many times the ith instance was marked as the closest neighbor to another instance. The sum of the ith column equals the popularity of the ith instance. Finally, in this step we rank the instances in decreasing popularity, i.e., the most popular instance is ranked #1, the second is ranked #2, and so on.

Step 5: Decide which instances to select. This step tries to find how many of the most popular instances will be selected. For that purpose we perform a 10-way cross-validation on the train set. For each cross-validation (i.e., 10 times), we do the following:

- Perform steps 1-4 for the popularity order.
- Build a set S, into which instances are added one at a time from the most popular to the least popular.
- After each addition to S make predictions for the hold-out set, i.e., find the closest neighbor from S of each instance in the hold-out set and use the effort value of that closest instance as the estimate.
- Calculate the error measure of the hold-out set for each size of S. As the size of S increases (i.e., as we place more and more popular instances into S) the error measure is expected to decrease.
- Traverse the error measures of S with only one instance of S with t instances (where t is the size of the training set minus the hold-out set). Mark the size of S (represented by s') when the error measure has not decreased more than Δ for *n-many* consecutive times.

Note that because we use a 10-way cross-validation, at the end of the above steps we will have 10 s' values (1 s' value from each cross-validation). We take the median of these values as the final s' value. This means that POP1 only selects the most popular s'-many instances from the training set. For convenience, we refer to the new training set of selected s'-many instances as *Train'*.

Step 6: Return estimates for the test instances. This step is fairly straightforward. The estimate for a test instance is the effort value of its nearest neighbor in *Train'* (Figure 17.2).

For the error measure in Step 5, we used MRE, which is only one of the many possible error measures. As shown in Section 17.4, even though we guide the search using only MRE, the resulting estimations score very well across a wide range of error measures. In the following experiments, we used $n = 3$ and $\Delta < 0.1$. The selection of (n, Δ) values is based on our engineering judgment. The sensitivity analysis of (n, Δ) values can be a promising future work.

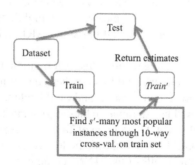

FIGURE 17.2

A simple illustration of the POP1 method. Note that the test and train sets are generated through a 10-way cross-validation as well. From Ref. [230].

17.3.3 EXPERIMENTS

So as to observe the performance of the proposed POP1 method in terms of compensating for the lack of size attributes, we designed a two-stage experimentation: (1) 1NN and CART performances on reduced data sets compared to their performance on full data sets; (2) POP1 performance on reduced data sets compared to 1NN and CART performance on full data sets.

In the first stage we question whether standard SEE methods can compensate for mere removal of the size features. For that purpose, we run 1NN as well as CART on reduced and full data sets separately through 10-way cross-validation. Then each method's results on reduced data sets are compared to its results on full data sets. The outcome of this stage tells us whether there is a need for POP1-like methods or not. If the performance of CART and 1NN on reduced data sets are statistically the same as their performances on the full data sets, then this would mean that standard successful estimation methods are able to compensate for the lack of size features. However, as we see in Section 17.4, that is not the case. The removal of size features has a negative effect on 1NN and CART.

The second stage tries to answer whether simple SEE methods like 1NN can be augmented with a preprocessing step, so that the removal of size features can be tolerated. For that purpose we run POP1 on the reduced data sets and compare its performance to 1NN and CART (run on full data sets) through 10-way cross-validation. The performance is measured in 7 error measures.

17.4 RESULTS

17.4.1 RESULTS WITHOUT INSTANCE SELECTION

Table 17.4 shows the CART results for the first stage of our experimentation, i.e., whether or not standard estimation methods, in that case CART, can compensate for the lack of size. In Table 17.4 we compare CART run on reduced data sets to CART run on full data sets and report the loss values. The loss value in each cell is associated with an error measure and a data set. Each loss value shows whether CART on reduced data lost against CART on full data. Note that it is acceptable for CART-on-reduced-data, as long as it does not lose against CART-on-full-data, Because we want the former to perform just as well as (not necessarily better than) the latter. The last column of Table 17.4 is the sum of the loss values over 7 error measures. The rows in which CART on reduced data loses for most of the error measures (4 or more out of 7 error measures) are highlighted. See in Table 17.4 that 7 out of 13 data sets are highlighted; i.e., more than half the time CART cannot compensate the lack of size features.

Although Table 17.4 is good to see the detailed loss information, the fundamental information we are after is summarized in the last column: total loss number. Repeating Table 17.4 for all the methods in both stages of the experimentation is cumbersome and would redundantly take too much space in this chapter. Hence, from now on we will use summary tables as given in Table 17.5, which shows only the total number of losses. Note that the "CART" column of Table 17.5 is just the last column of Table 17.4. Aside from the CART results, Table 17.5 also shows the loss results for 1NN run on reduced data vs. 1NN run on full data. The highlighted cells of the "1NN" column show the cases where 1NN lost most of the time, i.e., 4 or more out of 7 error measures. Similar to the results of CART, 1NN-on-reduced-data loses against 1NN-on-full-data for 7 out of 13 data sets. In other words, for more than half the data sets mere use of 1NN cannot compensate for the lack of size features.

Table 17.4 The Loss Values of CART Run on Reduced Data Set vs. CART Run on Full Data Set, Measured Per Error Measure

	MMRE	MAR	Pred(25)	MdMRE	MBRE	MIBRE	MMER	Total
cocomo81	1	0	1	1	1	1	0	5
cocomo81e	0	0	0	0	0	0	0	0
cocomo81o	0	0	0	0	0	0	0	0
cocomo81s	0	0	0	0	0	0	0	0
desharnais	1	0	1	1	1	1	0	5
desharnaisL1	1	1	1	1	1	1	1	7
desharnaisL2	0	0	0	0	0	0	0	0
desharnaisL3	0	0	0	0	0	0	0	0
nasa93	1	1	1	1	1	1	1	7
nasa93c1	1	0	1	1	1	1	0	5
nasa93c2	1	1	1	1	1	1	1	7
nasa93c5	0	0	0	0	0	0	0	0
sdr	1	0	1	1	0	0	1	4

The last column shows the loss values in the total of 7 error measures. The data sets where CART is running on reduced data sets lose more than half the time (i.e., 4 or more out of 7 error measures) against CART running on full data sets are highlighted. From Ref. [230].

Table 17.5 The Loss Values of Estimation Methods Run on Reduced Data Sets vs. Run on Full Data Sets

	Methods	
	CART	1NN
Data sets		
cocomo81	5	5
cocomo81e	0	0
cocomo81o	0	0
cocomo81s	0	0
desharnais	5	7
desharnaisL1	7	7
desharnaisL2	0	2
desharnaisL3	0	0
nasa93	7	7
nasa93c1	5	6
nasa93c2	7	7
nasa93c5	0	6
sdr	4	0

The cases where reduced data set results lose more than half the time (i.e., 4 or more out of 7 error measures) are highlighted.

The summary of the first stage of experimentation is that standard SEE methods are unable to compensate for the size features for most of the data sets experimented in this chapter. In the next section we show the interesting result that it is possible to augment a very simple ABE method like 1NN so that it can compensate for size features in a great majority of the data sets.

17.4.2 RESULTS WITH INSTANCE SELECTION

The comparison of POP1 (which runs on reduced data sets) to 1NN and CART (which run on full data sets) is given in Table 17.6. Table 17.6 shows the total loss values of POP1 over 7 error measures, so the highest number of times POP1 can lose against 1NN or CART is 7. The cases where POP1 loses more than half the time (i.e., 4 or more out of 7 error measures) are highlighted.

The comparison of POP1 against 1NN shows whether the proposed POP1 method helps standard ABE methods to compensate for the lack of size features. Note that in the second column of Table 17.6 there are only two highlighted cells. For 11 out of 13 data sets, the performance of POP1 is statistically the same as that of 1NN. The only two data sets, where POP1 cannot compensate for size are *cocomo81e* and *desharnais*.

The fact that POP1 compensates for size in cocomo81e's superset (cocomo81) and in desharnis' subsets (desharnaisL1, desharnaisL2, and desharnaisL3) but not in these two data sets may at first seem puzzling, because the expectation is that subsets share similar properties as their supersets. However, a recent work by Posnett et al. has shown that this is not necessarily the case [361]. The focus of Posnet et al.'s work is the "ecological inference"; i.e., the delta between the conclusions drawn from subsets

Table 17.6 The Loss Values of POP1 vs. 1NN and CART Over 7 Error Measures		
	POP1 vs. 1NN	**POP1 vs. CART**
cocomo81	0	3
cocomo81e	7	3
cocomo81o	0	7
cocomo81s	0	0
desharnais	7	5
desharnaisL1	0	0
desharnaisL2	0	7
desharnaisL3	0	0
nasa93	3	0
nasa93c1	0	7
nasa93c2	0	3
nasa93c5	0	0
sdr	0	0

The data sets where POP1 (running on reduced data sets) lose more than half the time (i.e., 4 or more out of 7 error measures) against 1NN or CART (running on full data sets) are highlighted.

vs. the conclusions from the supersets. They document the interesting finding that conclusions from the subsets may be significantly different than the conclusions drawn from the supersets. Our results support their claim that supersets and subsets may have different characteristics.

The last column of Table 17.6 shows the number of times POP1 lost against CART. Again, the cases where POP1 loses for more than 4 error measures are highlighted. The purpose of POP1's comparison to CART is to evaluate a simple ABE method like POP1 against a state-of-the-art learner like CART. As can be seen in Table 17.6, there are four highlighted cells under the last column, i.e., for $13 - 4 = 9$ data sets, the performance of POP1 is statistically identical to that of CART. This is an important result for two reasons: (1) a simple ABE method like POP1 can attain performance values as good as CART for most of the data sets and (2) the performance of POP1 comes from data sets without any size features.

17.5 SUMMARY

The implication of the POP1 algorithm presented in this chapter should not be taken as a proposition to deprecate the use of size attributes. There are still a many parametric methods that are in practical use such as COCOMO and FP. On the other hand, in the case of SEE, it is possible to tolerate the lack of size features, given that an instance selection mechanism selects only the relevant instances. We evaluate 1NN and CART, which are reported as the best methods out of 90 methods in a prior SEE study [223]. Our results show that the performance of 1NN and CART on reduced data sets is worse than their performance on full data sets. Hence, mere use of these methods without size features is not recommended.

Then we augmented 1NN with a popularity-based preprocessor to come up with POP1. We run POP1 on reduced data sets and compare its performance to 1NN and CART, which are both run on full data sets. The results of this comparison show that for most of the cases (11 out of 13 data sets), POP1 running on reduced data sets attains the same performance as its counterpart 1NN running on full data sets.

Size features are essential for standard learners such as 1NN and CART. SEE practitioners with enough resources to collect accurate size features should do so. On the other hand, when standard learners (in this research it is 1NN) are augmented with preprocessing options (in this research it is a popularity-based preprocessor), it is possible to remove the necessity of size features. Hence, SEE practitioners without sufficient resources to measure accurate size features should consider alternatives like POP1. Note that the proposed method was built on a successful learner on SEE data sets. Hence, if ABE methods are poor performers for the data sets of your domain, it may be a disappointing trial to stick with 1NN on such a domain. The recommendation for such a case would be to

- Identify high-performing learners on the data sets of your domain.
- Identify biases of these learners and how they can be utilized in the context of instance selection.
- Augment and utilize the identified biases to propose an ordering of the training instances (e.g., the similarity idea and the decision trees we discussed in the introduction).

ACTIVE LEARNING: LEARNING MORE WITH LESS

18

Name:	QUICK
Also known as:	Active learning, reverse nearest neighbor.
Intent:	When data collection is expensive or slow, it is useful to reflect on the currently available information to define the next, most informative, questions.
Motivation:	When collecting software effort data, some data points are more expensive to collect than others. For example, on US government projects, it is easier to get (i) descriptions of the delivered software than to get (ii) detailed costing information about the development of that software from subcontractors (as those subcontractors may want to hide their *actual* development costs).
Solution:	Active learning focuses software effort data collection on what might be the most informative next data items to collect. Specifically, to reduce the cost of data collection, (1) collect an *initial sample* of whatever you can; (2) reflect over that data to find what most distinguishes that data; and (3) focus your subsequent data collection on just the most "distinguishing" data.
Constraints:	When working with effort estimation data, the *initial sample* may be very small indeed (just a few rows and columns). Hence, apply outlier pruning to sort that initial sample into *central* and *peripheral* information (and then focus on the former and ignore the latter).
Implementation:	QUICK applies the POP1 measure from the last chapter (the *reverse nearest neighbor* counts, a.k.a. popularity) to columns and rows. Peripheral rows are those with lowest popularity (fewest near neighbors) while the most central and most important columns are the ones with least nearest neighbors (as that means they are least correlated to other columns). The QUICK algorithm hence sorts rows and columns using POP1, then keeps the *most* popular rows and the *least* popular columns.
Applicability:	QUICK found that for 18 effort estimation data sets, estimates could be generated using just 10% (median value) of the cells in that data. Those estimates were very nearly as good as estimates generated by state-of-the-art tools using all the data. That is, with tools like QUICK, it is *not* required to collect all data points on all projects. Rather, active learners like QUICK can quickly find what data matters and what other data points can be ignored.
Related to:	QUICK extends the POP1 system of the previous chapter.

This chapter is an extension to "Active learning and effort estimation: Finding the essential content of software effort estimation data" by E. Kocaguneli, T. Menzies, J. Keung, D. Cok, and R. Madachy, which is published in *IEEE Transactions on Software Engineering*, Volume 39, Number 9, pages 1040 to 1053, 2013. In this chapter we extend that prior paper with new preliminary results on defect prediction, additional related work from recent publications, as well as an extensive rewrite with a strong practitioner focus.

So far in this book we have dealt with a number of different learners for a variety of different problems such as the issues of privacy, software defect prediction, as well as software effort estimation (SEE). Some of these learners (e.g., k-NN) are simpler in comparison to more complex alternatives (e.g., neural nets, support vector machines). The discussion of why a more complex learner is preferred over a less complex one is an important, yet often overlooked issue. In this chapter, we will argue that the complexity of the learner should match the essential content of the data set. In other words, if a data set can be summarized with only a handful of instances and features, then there may be no need for a complex learner. We will call the summary of a data set its "essential content." More formally, the essential content can be defined as follows: Given a matrix of N instances and F features, the essential content is $N' * F'$ where N' and F' are subsets of the instances and features, respectively. The models learned from N' and F' perform as well as the models learned from N and F.

The mere fact that it is possible to find an essential content of a data set—an essential subset of instances and features—is quite exciting because relatively large data sets that are not appropriate for manual investigation become available for discussion by the experts. For example, imagine a data set with hundreds of instances and tens of features, which is not easy to be discussed in a meeting. However, the essential content of this data set summarized by tens of instances and a couple of features (we will see examples of such cases in the results of this chapter) is much more feasible to be tackled by domain experts.

The fact that an essential subset of a data set can be much smaller than the original data set also opens another possibility for a practitioner collecting data. One of the problems of predictive analytics is that the labels are difficult to collect and they come with a cost. In the case of SEE, the cost may be the domain experts that are employed to collect accurate information about the time spent by the software engineers. In the case of defect prediction, it may be the cost of matching the reported bugs to the related software modules. We argue in this chapter that it is possible to reduce the cost associated with collecting labels. Another term that we will frequently use throughout this chapter is "active learning," which is a variant of semisupervised learning. In active learning, the learner is allowed to query a human expert (or another source of information) for the labels of instances. Some heuristic is used to sort instances from the most informative to the least informative and the instances are queried in this order. The fundamental idea is that each instance label comes with a cost (e.g., time or effort of human experts) and ideally we want the learner to ask for as few labels as possible, yet have a good estimation performance.

In this chapter we introduce an active learner called QUICK, which discovers the essential content of a data set and asks labels of only a few instances, which belong to the essential content. We will show our results in the context of SEE data sets. Here is a quick description of how simply the QUICK algorithm works (more formal description to follow in later sections): QUICK computes the Euclidean distance between the rows (instances) of SEE data sets. That distance calculation is also performed between matrix columns (features) using a transposed copy of the matrix. QUICK then removes features that are very close to other features (we will refer to such features as *synonyms*) and rows that are very distant to the other rows (we will refer to such rows as *outliers*). QUICK then reuses the distance calculations a final time to find estimates for test cases, using their nearest neighbor in the reduced space.

Although seemingly simple, we demonstrate in this chapter that QUICK's estimates from the reduced space are as good as those of state-of-the-art supervised learners that require all the labels in a data set. The essential content used by QUICK for its performance is 10% (or less) of the original data (see Table 18.1).

It is important to justify the success of a simple method like QUICK that learns from a very limited subset of the data. From our experimentation, the explanation we derived is that the essential content

Table 18.1 Last Column Shows Fraction of Data $\frac{N'*F'}{N*F}$ Selected by QUICK

Data Set	Used By	% Selected Cells
nasa93	[3, 16, 238]	4%
cocomo81	[3, 34, 238]	7%
cocomo81o	[12, 188, 275]	7%
maxwell	[3, 260, 384]	8%
kemerer	[3, 130, 390]	9%
desharnais	[213, 253, 260]	9%
miyazaki94	[329]	10%
desharnaisL1	[259]	10%
nasa93_center_5	[275, 344, 371]	11%
nasa93_center_2	[275, 344, 371]	11%
cocomo81e	[12, 21, 344]	14%
desharnaisL2	[227]	14%
sdr	[3, 243, 423]	16%
desharnaisL3	[227]	18%
nasa93_center_1	[275, 344, 371]	19%
cocomo81s	[12, 275]	20%
finnish	[55, 390]	26%
albrecht	[259, 260, 390]	31%

of data sets (in this context the effort and defect data sets) may be summarized by just a few rows and columns. The implication of this observation for a practitioner is that for data sets with small essential content, elaborate estimation methods may be creating very limited added value. In such cases, simpler methods should be preferred, which saves time invested in creating an elaborate estimation method.

18.1 HOW DOES THE QUICK ALGORITHM WORK?

In this section we will describe how QUICK works. Basically QUICK has two passes on the data set to find the essential content: pruning synonyms (synonyms are similar features) and pruning outliers. At the end of these two passes, the estimate is generated using a 1 nearest-neighbor (1NN) predictor (Table 18.2).

18.1.1 GETTING RID OF SIMILAR FEATURES: SYNONYM PRUNING

Throughout the rest of the chapter we will use the term *synonyms*, which is nothing but features that are similar to one another according to a certain measure (e.g., Euclidean distance in this chapter). QUICK discovers such features and removes them from the data set as follows:

(1) Take an unlabeled data set (i.e., no effort value) and transpose it, so that the independent features become the instances (rows) in a space whose dimensions (columns) are defined by the original instances.

Table 18.2 Explanation of the Symbols that will be Used in the Rest of this Chapter	
Symbol	**Meaning**
D	Denotes a specific data set
D'	Denotes the reduced version of D by QUICK
D^T	Transposed version of D
N	Number of instances in D
N'	Number of *selected* instances by QUICK from D
F	Number of independent features in D
F'	Number of independent features by QUICK from D
P	Represents a project in D
$Feat$	Represents a feature in D
i, j	Subscripts used for enumeration
P_i, P_j	ith and jth projects of D, respectively
DM	An $N \times N$ distance matrix that keeps distances between all projects of D
$DM(i, j)$	The distance value between P_i and P_j
k	Number of analogies used for estimation
E_{NN}	Everyone's nearest-neighbor matrix, which shows the order of P's neighbors w.r.t. a distance measure
$E(k)$	$E(k)[i,j]$ is 1 for $i \neq j$ and $E_{NN} \leq k$, 0 otherwise
$E(1)$	Specific case of $E(k)$, where $E(1)[i,j]$ is 1 if j is i's closest neighbor, 0 otherwise
$E(1)[i,j]$	The cell of $E(1)$ that corresponds to ith row and jth column
$Pop(j)$	Popularity of j: $Pop(j) = \sum_{i=1}^{n} E(1)[i,j]$
n	Number of projects consecutively added to active pool, i.e., a subset of D, i.e., $n \leq N$
Δ	The difference between the best and the worst error of the last n instances
$x_i, \hat{x}_i$	Actual and predicted effort values of P_i, respectively
$Perf_i, Perf_j$	ith and jth performance measures
M_i, M_j	ith and jth estimation methods

(2) Let E_{NN} be a matrix ranking the neighbors of a feature: closest feature is #1, the next is #2, and so on.

(3) $E(k)$ marks k-closest features (e.g., $E(1)$ marks #1s).

(4) Calculate the *popularity* of a feature by summing up how many times it was marked as #1.

(5) Leave only the unmarked features, i.e., the ones with a popularity of zero.

The features with a popularity of zero are the unique features, which are not similar to any other feature. In our data set, we want to have features that are different from one another so that they convey different information. That is why we are picking only the features that have a popularity of zero.

18.1.2 GETTING RID OF DISSIMILAR INSTANCES: OUTLIER PRUNING

The concept of outlier pruning is very similar to the concept of synonym pruning, they both remove cells in a multidimensional space. A good explanation is given by Lipowezky [262], who says that the two tasks (feature and outlier pruning) are quite similar: They both remove cells in the hypercube of all instances times all features. According to the viewpoint of Lipowezky, it should be possible to convert a case selection mechanism into a feature selector and vice versa. Here we will see that the feature selector mechanism we used above is used almost in an as-is manner as an instance selector, with some minor, yet important, differences:

- With synonym pruning, we *transpose* the data set, so that the features are defined as rows, which are what we want to work on. Then we find the distances between "rows" (which, in the transposed data are the features). We count the *popularity* of each feature and delete the *popular* ones (note that these are the synonyms, the features that needlessly repeat the information found in other features).
- With outlier pruning, we *do not transpose* the data before finding the distances between rows (as rows are already what we want to work on, i.e., instances). Then we count the *popularity* of each instance and delete the *unpopular* ones (these are the instances that are most distant, hence most dissimilar to the other instances).

A quick note of caution here is that the data set on which we prune outliers contains only the selected features of the previous phase. Also note that the terms feature and variable will be used interchangeably from now on. To summarize, the outlier pruning phase works as follows:

(1) Let E_{NN} be a matrix ranking the neighbors of a project, i.e., closest project is #1, the next is #2, etc.

(2) $E(k)$ marks only the k-closest projects, e.g., $E(1)$ marks only #1s.

(3) Calculate the *popularity* of a project by summing up how many times it was marked as #1.

(4) Collect the costing data, one project at a time in decreasing *popularity*, then place it in the "active pool."

(5) Before a project's, say project A, costing data is placed into the active pool, generate an estimate for A. The estimate is the costing data of A's closest neighbor in the active pool. Note the difference between the estimate and the actual cost of A.

(6) Stop collecting costing data if the active pool's error rate does not decrease in three consecutive project additions.

(7) Once the stopping point is found, a future project—say project B—can be estimated. QUICK's estimate is the costing data of B's closest neighbor in the active pool.

18.2 NOTES ON ACTIVE LEARNING

In the introduction of this chapter, we talked about active learning and how it can be used to reduce the labeling costs of a data set for a practitioner. However, QUICK's possible use as an active learner may have been somewhat implicit until this point. That is why in the remainder of this section, we will provide some notes and pointers regarding the active learning literature as well as how QUICK can be used as an active learner.

Active learning is a version of semisupervised learning, where we usually start with an unlabeled data set. A certain heuristic is then used to sort instances from the most interesting to the least interesting. Here, interesting means the highest value of a certain metric that is used to measure the possible information gain from each instance. In the case of this chapter, the heuristic we use is each row's *popularity* value. Hence, the most interesting instances to be investigated would be the ones with the highest popularity metric values. After sorting, the instances are investigated in accordance with the sort order for their labels. Ideally we should terminate the investigation for labels, before we investigate all the instances. Learning can terminate early if the results from all the N instances are not better than the results from a subset of M instances, where $M < N$.

There is a wealth of active learning studies in machine learning literature for a practitioner willing to gain in-depth information about the subject. For example, Dasgupta [90] use a greedy active learning heuristic and show that it is able to deliver performance values as good as any other heuristic, in terms of reducing the number of required labels [90]. In Ref. [435], Wallace et al. used active learning for a deployed practical application example. They propose a citation screening model based on active learning augmented with *a priori* expert knowledge.

In software engineering, the practical applications of active learning can be found in software testing [44, 449]. In Bowring et al.'s study[44], active learning is used to augment learners for automatic classification of program behavior. Xie and Notkin [449] use human inspection as an active learning strategy for effective test generation and specification inference. In their experiments, the number of tests selected for human inspection were feasible; the direct implication is that labeling required significantly less effort than screening all single test cases. Hassan and Xie listed active learning as part of the future of software engineering data mining [166] and the recent work has proven it to be true. For example, Li et al. use a sample-based active semisupervised learning method called ACoForest [254]. Their use of ACoForest shares the same purpose as QUICK: finding a small percentage of the data that can practically deliver a similar performance as using all the data. In a similar fashion, Lu and Cukic use active learning in defect prediction and target the cases, where there are not previous releases of a software (hence, not defect labels) [272]. They propose an adaptive approach that combines active learning with supervised learning by introducing more and more labels into the training set. At each iteration of introducing more labels, Lu and Cukic compare the performance of the adaptive method to that of a purely supervised method (that uses all the labels) and report that the adaptive approach outperforms the supervised one. The possibility of identifying which instances to label first can also pave the way to the use of cross-company data (the data coming from another organization is called cross-company data) in the context of active learning. Kocaguneli et al. explore this direction [226], where they propose a hybrid of active learning and cross-company learning. Firstly, they use QUICK so as to discover the essential content of an unlabeled within-company data (an organization's own data). Then they use TEAK (as introduced previously in this book) to filter labeled cross-company data. The filtered cross-company data is employed to label the essential content of the within-data, so that the domain experts have initial labels to start the discussion on their essential set.

18.3 THE APPLICATION AND IMPLEMENTATION DETAILS OF QUICK

We have discussed an overview of QUICK so far, but for a practitioner looking for a pseudocode or some equations to follow, the overview may not be enough. This section provides the extra details for such a practitioner. Recall that QUICK has two main phases: synonym pruning and outlier removal. In the following subsections, we use this separation to provide the details.

18.3.1 PHASE 1: SYNONYM PRUNING

The first phase (synonym pruning) is composed of four steps:

1. Transpose data set matrix.
2. Generate distance-matrices.

3. Generate $E(k)$ matrices using E_{NN}.

4. Calculate the popularity index based on $E(1)$ and select nonpopular features.

1. *Transpose data set matrix.* It is assumed that the instances of your data set are stored as the rows prior to transposition. Hence, this step is not necessary if the rows of your data set in fact represent the dependent variables. However, rows of SEE as well as software defect data sets almost always represent the past project instances, whereas the columns represent the features defining these projects. When such a matrix is transposed the project instances are represented by columns and project features are represented by rows. Note that columns are normalized to 0-1 interval before transposing to remove the superfluous effect of large numbers in the next step. To make things clear for readers, who are not familiar with distance calculation: The main reason of dealing with the transposition of a data set is to prepare it for step #2, where we generate the distance matrices. At the end of step #1 we aim the rows to represent whatever objects (in synonym pruning they are the features) between which we want to calculate the distances.

2. *Generate distance-matrices.* For the transposed dataset D^T of size F, the associated distance-matrix (DM) is an $F \times F$ matrix keeping the distances between every feature-pair according to Euclidean distance function. For example, a cell located at ith row and jth column ($DM(i,j)$) keeps the distance between ith and jth features (diagonal cells ($DM(i,i)$) are ignored as we are not interested in the distance of a feature to itself, which is 0).

3. *Generate E_{NN} and $E(1)$ matrices.* $E_{NN}[i,j]$ shows the neighbor rank of "j" with regard to "i," e.g., if "j" is "i's" third nearest neighbor, then $E_{NN}[i,j] = 3$. The trivial case where $i = j$ is ignored, because an instance cannot be its own neighbor. The $E(k)$ matrix is defined as follows: if $i \neq j$ and $E_{NN}[i,j] \leq k$, then $E(k)[i,j] = 1$; otherwise $E(k)[i,j] = 0$. In synonym pruning, we want to select the unique features without any nearest neighbors, as these are dimensions of our space that are most unique and different from other dimensions. For that purpose we start with $k = 1$; hence, $E(1)$ identifies the features that have at least another nearest neighbor and the ones without any nearest neighbor. The features that appear as one of the k-closest neighbors of another feature are said to be popular. The "popularity index" (or simply "popularity") of feature "j," $Pop(Feat_j)$, is defined to be $Pop(Feat_j) = \sum_{i=1}^{n} E(1)[i,j]$, i.e., how often "$j$th" feature is some other feature's nearest neighbor.

4. *Calculate the popularity index based on $E(1)$ and select nonpopular features. Nonpopular* features are the ones that have a popularity of zero, i.e., $Pop(Feat_i) = 0$.

18.3.2 PHASE 2: OUTLIER REMOVAL AND ESTIMATION

Outlier removal is almost identical to synonym pruning in terms of implementation, with a few important distinctions. However, most of your code implemented for synonym pruning can be reused in the outlier removal. Below are the four steps of forming the outlier removal:

1. Generate distance-matrices.

2. Generate $E(k)$ matrices using E_{NN}.

3. Calculate a "popularity" index.

4. After sorting by popularity, find the stopping point.

1. *Generate distance-matrices.* Similar to the case of synonym pruning, a data set D of size N would have an associated distance-matrix (DM), which is an $N \times N$ matrix whose cell located at row i

and column j ($DM(i,j)$) keeps the distance between the ith and jth instances of D. The cells on the diagonal ($DM(i, i)$) are ignored. Note that D in this phase comes from the prior phase of synonym pruning; hence, it only has the selected features. Remember to retranspose (or revert the previous transpose) your matrix, so that in this phase the rows correspond to the instances of your data set (e.g., the projects for SEE data sets or the software modules for software defect data sets would correspond to rows).

2. *Generate E_{NN} and $E(1)$ matrices.* This step is identical to that of synonym pruning in terms of how we calculate the E_{NN} and $E(1)$ matrices. To reiterate the process: $E_{NN}[i,j]$ shows the neighbor rank of "j" with regard to "i." Similar to the step of synonym pruning, if "j" is "i's" third nearest neighbor, then $E_{NN}[i,j] = 3$. Again, the trivial case of $i = j$ is ignored (nearest neighbor does not include itself). The $E(k)$ matrix has exactly the same definition as the one in the synonym pruning phase: if $i \neq j$ and $E_{NN}[i,j] \le k$, then $E(k)[i,j] = 1$; otherwise $E(k)[i,j] = 0$. In this study the nearest-neighbor-based Analogy-based estimation (ABE) is considered, i.e., we use $k = 1$; hence, $E(1)$ describes just the single nearest neighbor. All instances that appear as one of the k-closest neighbors of another instance are defined to be popular. The "popularity index" (or simply "popularity") of instance "j", $Pop(j)$, is defined to be $Pop(j) = \sum_{i=1}^{n} E(1)[i,j]$, i.e., how often "$j$" is someone else's nearest neighbor.

3. *Calculate the popularity index based on $E(1)$ and determine the sort order for labeling.* Table 18.3 shows the popular instances (instances that are the closest neighbor of another instance) among the SEE projects experimented with in this chapter. As shown in Table 18.3, the popular instances j with $Pop(j) \ge 1$ (equivalently, $E(1)[i,j]$ is 1 for some i) have a median percentage of 63% among all data sets; i.e., more than one-third of the data is unpopular with $Pop(j) = 0$. The meaning of this observation is that if we were to use a k-NN algorithm with $k = 1$, then one-third of the labels that we have would never be used for the estimation of a test instance.

4. *Find the stopping point and halt.* Remember that, ideally, active learning should finish asking for labels before all the unlabeled instances are labeled, so that there would be some sense in going into all the trouble of forming an active learner. This step finds that stopping point before asking for all the labels. QUICK labels instances from the most popular to the least popular and adds each instance to the so-called active pool. QUICK stops asking for labels if one of the following rules fire:

   1. All instances with $Pop(j) \ge 1$ are exhausted (i.e., QUICK never labels unpopular instances).
   2. Or if there is no estimation accuracy improvement in the active pool for n consecutive times.
   3. Or if the Δ between the best and the worst error of the last n instances in the active pool is very small.

   For the error measure in point #3, we used MRE; in other words, the magnitude of relative error ($abs(actual - predicted)/actual$). MRE is only one of many possible error measures. As shown below, even though we guide the search using only MRE, the resulting estimations score very well across a wide range of error measures. During the implementation of the algorithm, a practitioner should feel free to opt for the most appropriate learner for his domain. In the experiments that we will report in this chapter, we used $n = 3$ and $\Delta < 0.1$. The selection of (n, Δ) values is based on our engineering judgment, so refrain from seeing these values as absolute. The sensitivity analysis of trying different values of (n, Δ) can reveal the best values for a different domain.

Table 18.3 The Percentage of the Popular Instances (to Data Set Size) Useful for Prediction in a Closest-Neighbor Setting

Data Set	% Popular Instances
kemerer	80
telecom1	78
nasa93_center_1	75
cocomo81s	73
finnish	71
cocomo81e	68
cocomo81	65
nasa93_center_2	65
nasa93_center_5	64
nasa93	63
cocomo81o	63
sdr	63
desharnaisL1	61
desharnaisL2	60
desharnaisL3	60
miyazaki94	58
desharnais	57
albrecht	54
maxwell	13

Only the instances that are closest neighbors of another instance are said to be popular. The median percentage value is 63%, or one-third of the instances are not the closest neighbors and will never be used by, say, a nearest-neighbor system.

18.3.3 SEEING QUICK IN ACTION WITH A TOY EXAMPLE

The above pseudocode and formulation probably makes things clearer for the reader; however, personally we find it very helpful to view an algorithm in action with a small example. This subsection provides such an example. Assume that the training set of the example consists of three instances/projects: P_1, P_2, and P_3. Also assume that these projects have one dependent and three independent features. Our data set would look like Figure 18.1.

Project	$Feat_1$	$Feat_2$	$Feat_3$	Effort
P_1	1	2	20	3
P_2	2	3	10	4
P_3	3	6	40	7

FIGURE 18.1

Three projects defined by three independent features/variables and a dependent variable (staff-months).

18.3.3.1 Phase 1: Synonym pruning

Step 1: *Transpose data set matrix.* After normalization to 0-1 interval, then transposing our data set, the resulting matrix would look like Figure 18.2.

Step 2: *Generate distance-matrices.* The distance matrix *DM* keeps the Euclidean distance between features. The matrix of Figure 18.2 is used to calculate the *DM* of Figure 18.3.

Step 3: *Generate E_{NN} and $E(1)$ matrices.* According to the distance matrix of Figure 18.3, the resulting $E_{NN}[i,j]$ of Figure 18.4 shows the neighbor ranks of features. Using E_{NN} we calculate the $E(1)$ matrix that identifies the features that have at least another nearest neighbor. $E(1)$ matrix is given in Figure 18.5.

Step 4: *Calculate the popularity index based on $E(1)$ and select nonpopular features.* Popularity of a feature is the total of $E(1)$'s columns (see the summation in Figure 18.5). *Nonpopular* features are

	P_1	P_2	P_3
$Feat_1$	0.0	0.5	1
$Feat_2$	0.0	0.5	1
$Feat_3$	0.3	0.0	1

FIGURE 18.2

Resulting matrix after normalizing and transposing *D*.

	$Feat_1$	$Feat_2$	$Feat_3$
$Feat_1$	na	0.0	0.6
$Feat_2$	0.0	na	0.6
$Feat_3$	0.6	0.6	na

FIGURE 18.3

DM for features.

	$Feat_1$	$Feat_2$	$Feat_3$
$Feat_1$	na	1	2
$Feat_2$	1	na	2
$Feat_3$	1	1	na

FIGURE 18.4

The E_{NN} matrix for features, resulting from the distance matrix of Figure 18.3. Diagonal cells are ignored.

	$Feat_1$	$Feat_2$	$Feat_3$
$Feat_1$	0	1	0
$Feat_2$	1	0	0
+ $Feat_3$	1	1	0
Popularity :	2	1	0

FIGURE 18.5

Popularity of the features. Popularity is the sum of the $E(1)$ matrix columns.

the ones with zero popularity. In this toy example, we only select $Feat_3$, as it is the only column with zero popularity.

18.3.3.2 Phase 2: Outlier removal and estimation

In this phase, QUICK continues execution with only the selected features. After the first phase, our data set now looks like Figure 18.6.

Since our data now has only one independent variable, we can visualize it on a linear scale as in Figure 18.7.

Step 1: The first step of QUICK in this phase is to *build the distance matrix*. Because projects are described by a single attribute $Feat_3$ (say KLOC), the Euclidean distance between two projects will be the difference between the normalized KLOC values. The resulting *distance-matrix* is given in Figure 18.8.

Step 2: *Creating the E_{NN} matrix* based on the distance matrix is the second step. As we are creating the E_{NN} matrix we traverse the distance matrix row-by-row and label the instances depending on their distance order: closest neighbor is labeled 1, the second closest neighbor is labeled 2, and so on. Note that diagonal entries with the distance values of 0 are ignored, as they represent the distance of the instance to itself, not to a neighbor. After this traversal, the resulting E_{NN} is given in Figure 18.9.

Step 3: *Calculating the popularity index based on E_{NN} and determining the labeling order* is the final step of the algorithm. Remember from the previous section that $E(1)$ is generated from E_{NN}: $E(1)[i,j] = 1$ if $E_{NN}[i,j] = 1$; otherwise, $E(1)[i,j] = 0$. The popularity index associated with

Project	$Feat_3$	Effort
P_1	20	3
P_2	10	4
P_3	40	7

FIGURE 18.6

Three projects defined by $Feat_3$ (say KLOC) and effort (say, in staff-months).

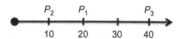

FIGURE 18.7

Visualization of projects on a linear KLOC scale. From Ref. [231].

	P_1	P_2	P_3
P_1	0	0.3	0.7
P_2	0.3	0	1
P_3	0.7	1	0

FIGURE 18.8

The distance matrix of the projects P_1, P_2, and P_3.

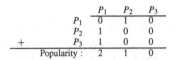

	P_1	P_2	P_3
P_1	na	1	2
P_2	1	na	2
P_3	1	2	na

FIGURE 18.9

The E_{NN} matrix resulting from the distance matrix of Figure 18.8. Diagonal cells are ignored.

	P_1	P_2	P_3
P_1	0	1	0
P_2	1	0	0
P_3	1	0	0
Popularity :	2	1	0

FIGURE 18.10

Popularity is the sum of the $E(1)$'s columns.

each instance is then calculated by summing the values in every column (i.e., the sum of the first column is the popularity index of the first instance, the sum of the second column is the popularity index of the second instance, and so forth). The $E(1)$ matrix and the popularity indices of our example is given in Figure 18.10. Note that $E(k)$ matrices are not necessarily symmetric; see that $E(1)$ of Figure 18.10 is not symmetric.

In our data set example, Figure 18.10 produces the labeling order of the instances $\{P_1, P_2, P_3\}$. In other words, in the first round we will ask our expert to label P_1 and place that label in the active pool. In that round, because the active pool contains only 1 *labeled instance* it will be the closest labeled neighbor of every test instance and the estimates for all the test instances will be the same (the label of P_1).

In the second round, P_2 will be labeled by the expert and placed into a pool of "active" (i.e., labeled) examples. This time the test instances will have two alternatives to choose their closest-neighbor from; hence, the estimates will be either the label of P_1 or the label of P_2. Finally, the expert will label P_3 and place it into the active pool. The change of the active pool is shown in Figure 18.11. Note that we only move from $Round_i$ to $Round_{i+1}$ if the stopping rules (described above) do not fire.

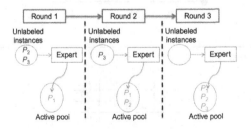

FIGURE 18.11

The change of active pool for the toy example. Note that in an actual setting transition between $Round_i$ to $Round_{i+1}$ is governed by the stopping rules. From Ref. [231].

18.4 **HOW THE EXPERIMENTS ARE DESIGNED**

Our experiments start with forming a baseline of the successful supervised learners. These are the learners that we choose based on the previous literature. Then we run QUICK and find its performance on SEE data sets. Finally, we compare QUICK's performance to the baseline to see how good or bad it performs. In other words, our experiments are composed of three main parts:

1. Generate *baseline* results. Apply CART and passiveNN (passiveNN is the standard ABE0 algorithm, i.e., k-NN with $k = 1$) on the entire training set (we select CART and passiveNN due to their previous high performance on SEE data sets; a practitioner may change these learners with other successful candidates in his/her domain).
2. Generate the *active learning* results. Run QUICK on the same data sets as CART and passiveNN.
3. Compare the baseline results against the results of QUICK.

1. *Generate baseline results* by applying CART and passiveNN on the entire training set. The algorithms are run on the entire training set and their estimations are stored using a 10-way cross-validation, which works as follows:
   - Randomize the order of instances in the data set.
   - Divide data set into 10 bins.
   - Choose 1 bin at a time as the test set and use the remaining bins as the training set.
   - Repeat the previous step using each one of the 10 bins in turn as the test set.
2. *Generate the active learning results* by running QUICK. At each iteration, first the features are selected and the active pool is populated with training instances in the order of their popularity. Training instances outside the active pool are considered unlabeled and QUICK is only allowed to use instances in the pool. Train and test sets are generated by 10-way-cross-validation.

   Before a training instance is placed in the active pool, an expert labels that instance, i.e., the costing data is collected. When the active pool only contains 1 instance, the estimates will all be the same. As the active pool is populated, QUICK has more labeled training instances to estimate from.
3. *Compare baseline to active learning.* Once the execution of the algorithms is complete, the performance of QUICK, passiveNN, and CART are compared under different performance measures.

For our experiments, we use seven different error measures that are commonly employed in the SEE domain: MAR, MMRE, MdMRE, MMER, PRED(25), MBRE, and MIBRE. Below is the derivation and explanation of these error measures: The absolute residual (AR) is the absolute difference between the predicted and the actual values of a test instance

$$AR_i = |x_i - \hat{x}_i| \qquad (18.1)$$

where x_i and $\hat{x}_i$ are the actual and predicted value for test instance i, respectively. The summary of AR is taken through the mean of AR, which is known as mean AR (MAR).

The magnitude of relative error measure, a.k.a. MRE, is quite widely used in SEE (and other domains). It is the error ratio between the actual effort and its delta with the predicted effort

$$MRE_i = \frac{|x_i - \hat{x}_i|}{x_i} = \frac{AR_i}{x_i} \qquad (18.2)$$

A related measure is MER (magnitude of error relative to the estimate [133]):

$$\text{MER}_i = \frac{|x_i - \hat{x}_i|}{\hat{x}_i} = \frac{\text{AR}_i}{\hat{x}_i} \tag{18.3}$$

The overall average error of MRE can be derived as the mean or median magnitude of relative error measure (MMRE and MdMRE, respectively):

$$\text{MMRE} = \text{mean(all MRE}_i) \tag{18.4}$$

$$\text{MdMRE} = \text{median(all MRE}_i) \tag{18.5}$$

A common alternative is PRED(25), which is defined as the percentage of successful predictions falling within 25% of the actual values:

$$\text{PRED}(25) = \frac{100}{N} \sum_{i=1}^{N} \begin{cases} 1 & \text{if MRE}_i \leq \frac{25}{100} \\ 0 & \text{otherwise} \end{cases}, \tag{18.6}$$

where N is the dataset size. For example, PRED(25) = 50% implies that half of the estimates fall within 25% of the actual values (Figure 18.12).

Mean balanced relative error (MBRE) and the mean inverted balanced relative error (MIBRE) are two other performance measures, which are both suggested by Foss et al. [133]:

$$\text{MBRE}_i = \frac{|\hat{x}_i - x_i|}{\min(\hat{x}_i, x_i)} \tag{18.7}$$

$$\text{MIBRE}_i = \frac{|\hat{x}_i - x_i|}{\max(\hat{x}_i, x_i)} \tag{18.8}$$

There are a number different alternatives to summarize each error measure; however, we will use a simple—yet effective—technique called the win-tie-loss calculation. In this procedure, one method is compared to another one using the procedure of Figure 18.13. In this chapter, among *win, loss, loss*

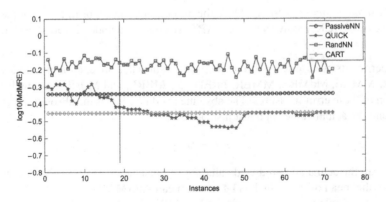

FIGURE 18.12

Sample plot of a representative (in that case desharnais) data set showing the stopping point (the line parallel to the *y*-axis at *x* = 19) and MdMRE values (logged with base 10 for easier visualization). Note that QUICK uses only the selected 4 features of the desharnis data set, whereas other methods use all of the 10 features. From Ref. [231].

$$\textbf{if } \text{NonParametricTest}(E_i, E_j, 95) \text{ says they are the same } \textbf{then}$$
$$tie_i = tie_i + 1;$$
$$tie_j = tie_j + 1;$$
$$\textbf{else}$$
$$\quad \textbf{if } \text{better}(E_i, E_j) \textbf{ then}$$
$$\quad\quad win_i = win_i + 1$$
$$\quad\quad loss_j = loss_j + 1$$
$$\quad \textbf{else}$$
$$\quad\quad win_j = win_j + 1$$
$$\quad\quad loss_i = loss_i + 1$$
$$\quad \textbf{end if}$$
$$\textbf{end if}$$

FIGURE 18.13

Comparing methods (i,j).

Dataset	Features	Size	Description	Units
cocomo81	17	63	NASA projects	months
cocomo81e	17	28	Cocomo81 embedded projects	months
cocomo81o	17	24	Cocomo81 organic projects	months
cocomo81s	17	11	Cocomo81 semidetached projects	months
nasa93	17	93	NASA projects	months
nasa93_center_1	17	12	Nasa93 projects from center 1	months
nasa93_center_2	17	37	Nasa93 projects from center 2	months
nasa93_center_5	17	40	Nasa93 projects from center 5	months
desharnais	12	81	Canadian software projects	hours
desharnaisL1	11	46	Projects in Desharnais that are developed with Language1	hours
desharnaisL2	11	25	Projects in Desharnais that are developed with Language2	hours
desharnaisL3	11	10	Projects in Desharnais that are developed with Language3	hours
sdr	22	24	Turkish software projects	months
albrecht	7	24	Projects from IBM	months
finnish	8	38	Software projects developed in Finland	hours
kemerer	7	15	Large business applications	months
maxwell	27	62	Projects from commercial banks in Finland	hours
miyazaki94	8	48	Japanese software projects developed in COBOL	months

FIGURE 18.14

The 18 public data sets used in this chapter. Indentation in column one denotes a data set that is a subset of another data set.

values we will make use of the loss values, because we want QUICK to perform just as well as the other methods, not better. QUICK's main contribution is not better performance, but statistically significantly the same performance with much less instances and features. The calculation of the *win, loss, loss* values is as follows:

We use a total of 18 public SEE data sets to test QUICK in this chapter. We already talked about these data sets in a prior chapter, so it will suffice to provide a summary with Figure 18.14 in this chapter.

18.5 RESULTS

In this section we will take a look at the performance of QUICK with regard to the baseline that is formed by the supervised learners of CART and passiveNN. QUICK is an active learner working on the essential content of the data set, so we will also investigate how many instances QUICK asks to be labeled as well as the size of the essential content.

18.5.1 PERFORMANCE

Before we start looking at the plots of performance vs. number of labeled training instances, we will walk through a sample plot step-by-step to explain how to interpret these plots. Figure 18.12 is a sample plot that is derived from an actual representative data set (shown is the **desharnais** data set). Figure 18.12 is the result of QUICK's synonym pruning (four features are selected for the sample desharnais data set) followed by labeling N' instances in decreasing popularity. Here is how we can read Figure 18.12:

- Y-axis is the logged MdMRE error measures: The smaller the value the better the performance. In case MdMRE is not the ideal error measure for a practitioner's problem domain, he/she should feel free to switch it with an appropriate error measure.
- The line with star-dots shows the error seen when i^{th} instance was estimated using the labels $1, \ldots, (i-1)$, i.e., each instance can only use the $i-1$ labeled instances in the active pool.
- The horizontal lines show the errors seen when estimates were generated using all the data (either from CART or passiveNN).
- The vertical line shows the point where QUICK advised that labeling can stop (i.e., N'). Recall that QUICK stops asking for labels if one of the predefined rules fire.
- The square-dotted line shows *randNN*, which is the result of picking any random instance from the training set and using its effort value as the estimate.

Figure 18.12 shows that QUICK uses a considerably smaller number of labeled instances with fewer features. But of course the reduction in the labels and features would not have much meaning unless QUICK can also show a high performance. However, to observe the possible scenarios we cannot make use of Figure 18.12 any more for two reasons: Repeating Figure 18.12 for *7 error measures × 17 data sets* would consume too much space without conveying any new information and more importantly, Figure 18.12 does not tell whether or not differences are significant; e.g., see Tables 18.5, 18.6 showing that performance differences among QUICK, passiveNN, and CART are not significant for the desharnais data set. Therefore, we will continue our performance analysis with summary tables in the following subsections.

18.5.2 REDUCTION VIA SYNONYM AND OUTLIER PRUNING

Table 18.4 shows reduction results from all 18 data sets used in this study. The N column shows the size of the data and the N' column shows how much of that data was labeled by QUICK. The $\frac{N'}{N}$ column expresses the percentage ratio of these two numbers. In a similar fashion, F shows the number of *independent features* for each data set, whereas F' shows the number of selected features by QUICK. The $\frac{F'}{F}$ ratio expresses the percentage of selected features to the total number of the features. The important observation of Table 18.4 is that, given N projects and F features, it is neither necessary to collect detailed costing details on 100% of N nor is it necessary to use all the features. For nearly half the data sets studied here, labeling around one-third of N would suffice (median of $\frac{N'}{N}$ for 18 data sets is 32.5%). There is a similar scenario for the amount of features required. QUICK selects around one-third of F for half the data sets. The median value of $\frac{F'}{F}$ for 18 data sets is 38%.

The combined effect of synonym and outlier pruning becomes clearer when we look at the last column of Table 18.4. Assuming that a data set D of N instances and F independent features is defined as an N-by-F matrix, the reduced data set D' is a matrix of size N'-by-F'. The last column shows the

Table 18.4 The Essential Content of the SEE Data Sets Used in Our Experimentation (From Ref. [231].)

Data Set	N	N'	$\frac{N'}{N}$	F	F'	$\frac{F'}{F}$	$\frac{N'*F'}{N*F}$
nasa93	93	21	23%	16	3	19%	4%
cocomo81	63	11	17%	16	6	38%	7%
cocomo81o	24	13	54%	16	2	13%	7%
maxwell	62	10	16%	26	13	50%	8%
kemerer	15	4	27%	6	2	33%	9%
desharnais	81	19	23%	10	4	40%	9%
miyazaki94	48	17	35%	7	2	29%	10%
desharnaisL1	46	12	26%	10	4	40%	10%
nasa93_center_5	39	11	28%	16	6	38%	11%
nasa93_center_2	37	16	43%	16	4	25%	11%
cocomo81e	28	9	32%	16	7	44%	14%
desharnaisL2	25	6	24%	10	6	60%	14%
sdr	24	10	42%	21	8	38%	16%
desharnaisL3	10	6	60%	10	3	30%	18%
nasa93_center_1	12	4	33%	16	9	56%	19%
cocomo81s	11	7	64%	16	5	31%	20%
finnish	38	17	45%	7	4	57%	26%
albrecht	24	9	38%	6	5	83%	31%

The essential content of a data set D with N instances and F independent features would be the ratio of its actual features and instances to the selected features (F') and selected instances (N'), i.e., $\frac{N'*F'}{N*F}$.

total reduction provided by QUICK in the form of a ratio: $\frac{N'*F'}{N*F}$. The rows of Table 18.4 are sorted according to this ratio. Note that the maximum size requirement (albrecht data set) is only 32% of the original data set and with QUICK we can go as low as only 4% of the actual data set size (nasa93).

18.5.3 COMPARISON OF QUICK VS. CART

Figure 18.15 shows the PRED(25) difference between CART (using all the data) and QUICK (using just a subset of the data). The difference is calculated as *PRED(25) of CART minus PRED(25) of QUICK*. Hence, a *negative* value indicates that QUICK offers better PRED(25) estimates than CART. The left-hand side (starting from the value of −35) shows QUICK is better than CART, whereas in other cases CART outperformed QUICK (see the right-hand side until the value of +35).

From Figure 18.15 we see that 50th percentile corresponds around the PRED(25) value of 2, which means that at the median point the performance of CART and QUICK are very close. Also note that 75th percentile corresponds to less than 15, meaning that for the cases when CART is better than QUICK the difference is not dramatic.

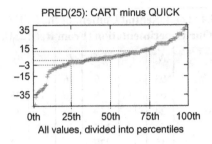

FIGURE 18.15

CART minus QUICK values for PRED(25) in 18 data sets. Negative values mean that QUICK outperformed CART. The median is only 2% with a small interquartile range (75th-25th percentile) of 15%.

18.5.4 DETAILED LOOK AT THE STATISTICAL ANALYSIS

Tables 18.5, 18.6 compare QUICK to passiveNN and CART using 7 error measures. *Smaller* values are *better* in these tables, as they show the number of losses: A method loses against another method if its performance is worse than the other method and if the two methods are statistically significantly different from one another. When calculating "loss" for six of the measures, "loss" means higher error values. On the other hand, for PRED(25), "loss" means lower values. The last column of each table sums the losses associated with the method in the related row.

By sorting the values in the last column of Table 18.5, we can show that the number of losses is very similar to the nearest neighbor results:

QUICK :   0, 0, 0, 0, 0, 0, 0, 0, 0, 0, 0, 0, 0, 0, 0, 0, 3, 6
passiveNN : 0, 0, 0, 0, 0, 0, 0, 0, 0, 0, 0, 0, 0, 0, 2, 3, 6, 6, 7

The gray rows of Table 18.5 show the datasets where QUICK loses over most of the error measures (4 times out of 7 error measures, or more). The key observation here is that, when using nearest-neighbor methods, a QUICK analysis loses infrequently (only 1 gray row) compared to a full analysis of all projects.

As noted in Figure 18.15, QUICK has a close performance to CART. This can also be seen in the number of losses summed in the last column of Table 18.6. The 4 gray rows of Table 18.6 show the data sets where QUICK loses most of the time (4 or more out of 7) to CART. In just $4/18 = 22\%$ of the data sets is a full CART analysis better than a QUICK partial analysis of a small subset of the data. The sorted last column of Table 18.6:

QUICK : 0, 0, 0, 0, 0, 0, 0, 0, 0, 0, 0, 0, 0, 1, 3, 6, 7, 7, 7
CART :   0, 0, 0, 0, 0, 0, 0, 0, 0, 0, 0, 0, 0, 0, 0, 0, 0, 0, 0

18.5.5 EARLY RESULTS ON DEFECT DATA SETS

To question the robustness of QUICK, we also adapted it to defect prediction (which is a classification problem unlike SEE). The data set and the statistical comparison of QUICK to other methods is provided in Table 18.8. We compared QUICK to successful learners in defect prediction domain such as CART,

Table 18.5 QUICK (on the Reduced Data Set) vs. passiveNN (on the Whole Data Set) with Regard to the Number of Losses, i.e., *Lower* Values are *Better*

Data Set	Method	MMRE	MAR	Pred(25)	MdMRE	MBRE	MIBRE	MMER	Sum of Losses
cocomo81	passiveNN	0	0	0	0	0	0	0	0
	QUICK	0	0	0	0	0	0	0	0
cocomo81e	passiveNN	0	0	0	0	0	0	0	0
	QUICK	0	0	0	0	0	0	0	0
cocomo81o	passiveNN	0	0	0	0	0	0	0	0
	QUICK	0	0	0	0	0	0	0	0
cocomo81s	passiveNN	0	0	0	0	0	0	0	0
	QUICK	0	0	0	0	0	0	0	0
desharnais	passiveNN	0	0	0	0	0	0	0	0
	QUICK	0	0	0	0	0	0	0	0
desharnaisL1	passiveNN	0	0	0	0	0	0	0	0
	QUICK	0	0	0	0	0	0	0	0
desharnaisL2	passiveNN	0	0	0	0	0	0	0	0
	QUICK	0	0	0	0	0	0	0	0
desharnaisL3	passiveNN	0	0	0	0	0	0	0	0
	QUICK	1	0	1	1	1	1	1	6
nasa93	passiveNN	0	0	0	0	1	1	0	2
	QUICK	0	0	0	0	0	0	0	0
nasa93_center_1	passiveNN	1	0	1	1	1	1	1	6
	QUICK	0	0	0	0	0	0	0	0
nasa93_center_2	passiveNN	1	1	1	1	1	1	1	7
	QUICK	0	0	0	0	0	0	0	0
nasa93_center_5	passiveNN	0	0	0	0	0	0	0	0
	QUICK	0	0	0	0	0	0	0	0
sdr	passiveNN	0	0	0	0	0	0	0	0
	QUICK	0	0	0	0	0	0	0	0
albrecht	passiveNN	1	1	1	1	1	1	0	6
	QUICK	0	0	0	0	0	0	0	0
finnish	passiveNN	0	0	0	0	0	0	0	0
	QUICK	0	0	0	0	0	0	0	0
kemerer	passiveNN	0	0	0	0	0	0	0	0
	QUICK	0	0	0	0	0	0	0	0
maxwell	passiveNN	0	0	0	0	0	0	0	0
	QUICK	0	0	0	0	1	1	1	3
miyazaki94	passiveNN	0	0	0	0	0	0	0	0
	QUICK	0	0	0	0	0	0	0	0

The right-hand column sums the number of losses. Rows highlighted in gray show data sets where QUICK performs worse than passiveNN in the majority case (4 times out of 7, or more). Note that only 1 row is highlighted.

Table 18.6 QUICK (on the Reduced Data Set) vs. CART (on the Whole Data Set) with Regard to the Number of Losses, i.e., *Lower* Values are *Better*

Data Set	Method	MMRE	MAR	Pred(25)	MdMRE	MBRE	MIBRE	MMER	Sum of Losses
cocomo81	CART	0	0	0	0	0	0	0	0
	QUICK	1	1	1	1	1	1	1	7
cocomo81e	CART	0	0	0	0	0	0	0	0
	QUICK	0	0	0	0	0	0	0	0
cocomo81o	CART	0	0	0	0	0	0	0	0
	QUICK	0	0	0	0	0	0	0	0
cocomo81s	CART	0	0	0	0	0	0	0	0
	QUICK	0	0	0	0	0	0	0	0
desharnais	CART	0	0	0	0	0	0	0	0
	QUICK	0	0	0	0	0	0	0	0
desharnaisL1	CART	0	0	0	0	0	0	0	0
	QUICK	0	0	0	0	0	0	0	0
desharnaisL2	CART	0	0	0	0	0	0	0	0
	QUICK	0	0	0	0	0	0	0	0
desharnaisL3	CART	0	0	0	0	0	0	0	0
	QUICK	0	0	0	0	1	1	1	3
nasa93	CART	0	0	0	0	0	0	0	0
	QUICK	0	1	0	0	0	0	0	1
nasa93_center_1	CART	0	0	0	0	0	0	0	0
	QUICK	0	0	0	0	0	0	0	0
nasa93_center_2	CART	0	0	0	0	0	0	0	0
	QUICK	0	0	0	0	0	0	0	0
nasa93_center_5	CART	0	0	0	0	0	0	0	0
	QUICK	0	0	0	0	0	0	0	0
sdr	CART	0	0	0	0	0	0	0	0
	QUICK	0	0	0	0	0	0	0	0
albrecht	CART	0	0	0	0	0	0	0	0
	QUICK	0	0	0	0	0	0	0	0
finnish	CART	0	0	0	0	0	0	0	0
	QUICK	1	1	1	1	1	1	1	7
kemerer	CART	0	0	0	0	0	0	0	0
	QUICK	0	0	0	0	0	0	0	0
maxwell	CART	0	0	0	0	0	0	0	0
	QUICK	1	1	1	1	1	1	1	7
miyazaki94	CART	0	0	0	0	0	0	0	0
	QUICK	1	0	1	1	1	1	1	6

The right-hand column sums the number of losses. Gray rows are the data sets where QUICK performs worse than CART in the majority case (4 times out of 7, or more).

k-NN (i.e., passiveNN), as well as Naive Bayes. Because defect prediction is a classification problem, we used different evaluation criteria: Let A, B, C, D denote the true negatives, false negatives, false positives, and true positives, respectively. Then $p_d = (D/(B + D))$ and $p_f = (C/(A + C))$, where p_d stands for probability of detection and p_f stands for probability of false alarm rate. We combined the p_d and p_f into a single measure called the G-value, which is the harmonic mean of the p_d and $(1 - p_f)$ values (Table 18.7).

Table 18.8 shows whether QUICK is statistically significantly better than the compared method (according to the Cohen significance test). As can be seen, in 18 out of 32 comparisons, QUICK (that uses only a small fraction of the labels) is comparable or better than the supervised methods (that use all the labeled data). This is a good indicator that the performance of QUICK-like active learning solutions are transferable. The results of Table 18.8 is part of an ongoing study; hence, we will not go deep into other aspects of the results of QUICK's performance on defect data sets.

Table 18.7 QUICK's Sanity Check on 8 Company Data Sets (Company Codes are C1, C2, ..., C8) from Tukutuku

Data Set	Method	MMRE	MAR	Pred(25)	MdMRE	MBRE	MIBRE	MMER	Sum of Losses
C1	CART	0	0	0	0	0	0	0	0
	QUICK	1	1	1	1	1	1	1	7
C2	CART	0	0	0	0	0	0	0	0
	QUICK	1	1	1	1	1	1	1	7
C3	CART	0	0	0	0	0	0	0	0
	QUICK	0	0	0	0	0	0	0	0
C4	CART	0	0	0	0	0	0	0	0
	QUICK	0	0	0	0	0	0	0	0
C5	CART	1	0	1	1	0	0	0	3
	QUICK	0	0	0	0	0	0	0	0
C6	CART	0	0	0	0	0	0	0	0
	QUICK	0	0	0	0	0	0	0	0
C7	CART	0	0	0	0	0	0	0	0
	QUICK	1	1	1	1	1	1	1	7
C8	CART	0	0	0	0	0	0	0	0
	QUICK	0	0	0	0	0	0	0	0
C1	passiveNN	0	0	1	0	0	0	0	1
	QUICK	1	1	0	1	1	1	0	5
C2	passiveNN	0	0	1	0	0	0	0	1
	QUICK	1	1	0	1	1	1	0	5
C3	passiveNN	0	0	0	0	0	0	0	0
	QUICK	0	0	0	0	0	0	0	0
C4	passiveNN	0	0	0	0	0	0	0	0
	QUICK	0	0	0	0	0	0	0	0

Continued

Table 18.7 QUICK's Sanity Check on 8 Company Data Sets (Company Codes are C1, C2, ..., C8) from Tukutuku *Continued*

Data Set	Method	MMRE	MAR	Pred(25)	MdMRE	MBRE	MIBRE	MMER	Sum of Losses
C5	passiveNN	0	0	0	0	0	0	0	0
	QUICK	0	0	0	0	0	0	0	0
C6	passiveNN	0	0	0	0	0	0	0	0
	QUICK	0	0	0	0	0	0	0	0
C7	passiveNN	0	0	0	0	0	0	0	0
	QUICK	1	1	1	1	1	1	1	7
C8	passiveNN	0	0	0	0	0	0	0	0
	QUICK	0	0	0	0	0	0	0	0

Cases where QUICK loses for the majority of the error measures (4 or more) are highlighted. QUICK is statistically significantly the same as CART for 5 out of 8 company data sets for the majority of the error measures (4 or more). Similarly, QUICK is significantly the same as passiveNN for 5 out of 8 company data sets.

Table 18.8 Statistical Significance of the *G*-Value Comparison

Dataset	G-QUICK	G-passiveNN	G-CART	G-Bayes	G-Forest	Total
lucene2dot2	0.59	√	√	√	√	18 of 32
lucene2dot4	0.63	√	√	√		
velocity1dot5	0.51			√		
xerces1dot4	0.73			√		
synapse1dot2	0.59					
velocity1dot6	0.67	√	√	√	√	
xalan2dot5	0.57			√		
xalan2dot6	0.74	√	√	√	√	

18.6 SUMMARY

In this chapter, we have tried to find the essential content of data sets and use the instances of the essential content as part of an active learner called QUICK. Our results on SEE data sets showed that essential content of SEE data sets is surprisingly small. This may not be the case for all the data sets of all the domains; hence, a practitioner experimenting with other data sets may observe different percentages of his/her data sets being the essential content. However, the fact that essential content is considerably smaller than the original data set is likely to hold.

Also, as we noted from time to time throughout the chapter, there are particular choices in the implementation of QUICK that are domain specific. For example, to check whether QUICK should stop asking for labels, we used MRE as an error measure. The error measure could be different for other domains. Another design decision that could be altered by the experts is the firing of stopping rules. The stopping rules that QUICK uses come from expert judgment; hence, a practitioner should be open to experimentation and flexible to come up with different stopping criteria.

SHARING
MODELS

IV

SHARING MODELS

SHARING MODELS: CHALLENGES AND METHODS

19

So far, we have been concerned with sharing data from one project to another. Now we turn to a more complex issue—how to share models from one project to another.

The key concepts in this part of the book are *ensembles* and *multiobjective optimization*. Ensembles are committees of artificially generated experts where each expert is trained on slightly different sections of the data.

- Chapter 20 offers an introduction to *ensemble-based learning* and presents experiments with ensemble learning and effort estimation.
- Chapter 21 extends ensembles with online learning. Specifically, it discusses how to incrementally modify a model as new data arrives. It proposed a novel dynamic method whereby a "toolbox" of different models is built by adapting multiple models. When new data arrive, this method asks each item in the toolbox how much it is the right tool for the job of making that next prediction. The resulting prediction is the weighted sum of each model's prediction times its confidence in that prediction.
- Chapter 22 offers a very large experiment in ensemble-based learning. After studying 90 different learners, it proposes a selection rule for adding learners to an ensemble. The resulting ensemble is shown to perform much better than any of the 90 individual learners.

After that, this part of the book turns to multiobjective optimization. The motto of multiobjective optimization is *know your goals*. In terms of sharing models, the lesson of this kind of optimization is that model sharing between projects works best when those projects understand and share their goals:

- Chapter 23 shows that the same data can generate radically different models, depending on the goals of the learning. This means that unless two projects share the same goals, then it is pointless trying to share models between them.
- Given that models are goal-dependent, it is important to reason explicitly about those goals. Chapter 24 shows that multigoal optimizers can significantly improve effort estimation results.

ENSEMBLES OF LEARNING MACHINES

In summary, this chapter proposes the following data analysis pattern:

Name:	Bootstrap aggregating regression trees (bagging + RTs).
Also known as:	Ensemble of learning machines; local learning method, when using local learning machines as base learners.
Intent:	Bagging + RTs is a general method that can be used for several different prediction tasks. Here, we particularly recommend it as an easily accessible method for generating software effort estimates, when companies do not have resources to run their own experiments for determining what the best software effort estimation method is in their context.
Motivation:	Learning machines can be combined into ensembles with the aim of improving predictive performance [46, 73, 264, 444]. Local learning methods are potentially beneficial for SEE due to their ability to deal with small training sets [321, 326].
Solution:	In order to benefit from both ensembles and locality for improving SEE, we use bagging ensembles of RTs, which are local learning machines.
Applicability:	Bagging + RTs were highly ranked in terms of performance across multiple SEE data sets, were frequently among the best approaches for each data set, and rarely performed considerably worse than the best approach for any data set [326].
Related to:	This chapter presents not only bagging + RTs, but also an introduction to ensembles in general. Chapters 21, 22 and 24 present other ensembles of learning machines further tailored to SEE. This chapter is also related to Chapter 14 in terms of locality.

This chapter is partially based on Minku and Yao [326]. Additionally, the following new material has been added: (1) the intuition and the theory behind the importance of diversity in ensemble learning (Section 20.1); (2) a didactic description of bagging (Section 20.2); (3) a didactic description of RTs; and (4) an introduction to why RTs are useful base learners for bagging in SEE (Section 20.3). Note that, for pedagogical reasons, we have moved (3) to the earlier tutorial section of this book (see Section 10.10).

So far in the book we have come across several machine learning (ML) methods that can be applied to software estimation data. In this chapter, we will show that it is possible to combine learning machines trained to perform the same task into an ensemble, with the aim of improving predictive performance [73]. The learning machines composing an ensemble are often referred to as *base learners*, whereas the models resulting from the training of these learning machines are referred to as *base models*.

Ensembles of learning machines have been attracting the attention of the software engineering community due to their promising results. For example, Azhar et al. [15] employed ensemble learning on Web project effort estimation. They showed that, even though no single best learning machine exists, combining a set of superior learning machines into an ensemble can yield very robust results. Another example of the use of ensemble methods is automated text classification. Noll et al. [341] employed ensemble methods to analyze unstructured software content data and compared their performance to that of human experts. They reported that ensembles can be used to discover common categories in unstructured software project data so that the work for human experts is reduced to discovering more complex categories of the data. We will also show in this chapter and Chapters 21, 22 and 24 that ensembles can yield to very robust results in the context of software effort estimation (SEE).

This chapter will first provide the intuition and theory behind the success of ensembles in improving performance with respect to their base models (Section 20.1). Then, it will present a tutorial on an accessible ensemble method (bootstrap aggregating [46], Section 20.2) and notes on a suitable base learner in the context of SEE (RTs, Section 20.3). Several other ensemble methods exist, but we will concentrate on this one not only because it is one of the most widely known ensemble methods, but also because it has shown to perform well in the context of SEE [326]. So, this chapter will provide the readers with a good base knowledge to understand other types of ensembles later on, and explain an accessible ensemble method that can be used off-the-shelf for SEE. Several ready implementations of bootstrap aggregating regression trees (bagging + RTs) can be found on the Web, facilitating its use. In particular, the Waikato environment for knowledge analysis (WEKA) [156] contains an open-source implementation under the GNU general public license.

A comprehensive evaluation of bagging + RTs in the context of SEE will be presented in Sections 20.4, 20.5, showing that bagging + RTs are able to achieve very competitive results in comparison to several other SEE methods. Bagging + RTs were highly ranked in terms of performance across different data sets. When they were not the best method for a given data set, they rarely performed considerably worse than the best method for that data set. So, bagging + RTs are recommended over other methods should an organization have no resources to perform their own detailed experiments for deciding which ML approach to use for SEE. This may reduce the cost and level of expertise necessary to perform SEE.

Section 20.6 will further analyze why bagging + RTs obtained competitive performance in SEE and give an insight into how to improve SEE further. Section 20.7 will provide a summary of the main contributions of this chapter. Other ensemble methods specifically developed for the context of SEE will be presented in Chapters 21, 22 and 24.

20.1 WHEN AND WHY ENSEMBLES WORK

This section provides a better understanding of why and under what conditions ensembles work for improving predictive performance. One of the key ideas behind ensembles in general is the fact that their success depends not only on the accuracy of their base models, but also on the *diversity* among their base models [62]. Diversity here refers to the errors/predictions made by the models. Two models are said to be diverse if they make different errors on the same data points [69], i.e., if they disagree on their predictions.

It is commonly agreed that ensembles should be composed of base models that behave diversely. Otherwise, the overall ensemble prediction will be no better than the individual predictions [61, 62, 244]. Different ensemble learning methods can thus be seen as different ways to generate diversity among base models. For instance, they can be roughly separated into methods that generate diversity by using different types of base learners and methods that generate diversity when using the same type of base learner to create all base models. The former methods are concerned with how to choose different types of base learners to produce accurate ensembles (e.g., Azhar et al. [15]'s). The latter methods are concerned with how to generate a good level of diversity for creating accurate ensembles, considering that the same base learner is used for all base models (e.g., bootstrap aggregating [46], boosting [136], negative correlation learning (NCL) [263, 264] and randomizer [156, 444]).

Section 20.1.1 explains the intuition and Section 20.1.2 explains the theoretical foundation of the importance of accuracy and diversity in ensemble learning.

20.1.1 INTUITION

It is very intuitive to think that the base models of an ensemble should be accurate so that the ensemble is also accurate. The importance of diversity among the base models usually requires extra thought, but it also matches intuition. After all, if the base models of an ensemble make the same mistakes, then the ensemble will make the same mistakes as the individual base models and its error will be no better than the individual errors. On the other hand, ensembles composed of diverse models can compensate for the mistakes of certain models through the correct predictions given by the other models.

Table 20.1 shows an illustrative example of how diversity can help in reducing the error of prediction systems. For simplicity, this example considers a classification problem where the predictions made by the models can be either correct (dark gray) or incorrect (white). Table 20.1a Table 20.1b show the prediction error of two ensembles and their base models on ten hypothetical data points. The ensemble shown in Table 20.1a is composed of three nondiverse base models, whereas the ensemble shown in Table 20.1b is composed of three diverse base models. All base models have fairly good accuracy, obtaining the same classification error of 30%, i.e., they gave incorrect predictions in 30% of the cases.

The predictions given by the ensembles in this example are the majority vote among the predictions of their base models. So, as long as the majority of the base models gives a correct prediction, the ensemble also gives a correct prediction. As the base models from Table 20.1a make the same mistakes, the ensemble also makes the same mistakes and has the same classification error of 30% as its base models. On the other hand, the diverse ensemble shown in Table 20.1b achieves a better classification error of 10%, because the mistakes made by each base model were frequently compensated by the correct predictions given by the other base models.

20.1.2 THEORETICAL FOUNDATION

Many studies in the literature show that the accuracy of ensembles is influenced not only by the accuracy of its base models, but also by their diversity [100, 244, 414]. For classification problems, there is still no generally accepted measure to quantify diversity, making the development of a theoretically well-grounded framework to explain the relationship between diversity and accuracy of classification

Table 20.1 An Illustrative Example of the Importance of Ensemble Diversity

Prediction System	Predictions: Correct (Dark gray) or Incorrect (White)	Percentage of Incorrect Predictions
(a) Ensemble of nondiverse models		
Base model 1		30%
Base model 2		30%
Base model 3		30%
Ensemble		30%
(b) Ensemble of diverse models		
Base model 1		30%
Base model 2		30%
Base model 3		30%
Ensemble		10%

Each ensemble is composed of the three base models shown in its corresponding table, and its prediction is the majority vote among the predictions of these base models.

ensembles difficult. Nevertheless, there are very clear theoretical frameworks explaining the role of base models' accuracy and diversity in regression ensembles. The *ambiguity decomposition* [241] and the *bias-variance-covariance decomposition* [336] provide a solid quantification of diversity and formally explain the role of diversity in ensemble learning. This section will concentrate on the ambiguity decomposition, because we believe it to be easier to understand. In fact, basic knowledge of algebra is enough to understand the general idea of the framework. So, even though this section can be skipped should the reader wish to, we encourage the reader to read it through to gain a deeper understanding on why ensembles can be useful and why their base models should be diverse.

Assume the regression task of learning a function based on examples of the format $(\mathbf{x}, y)$ where $\mathbf{x} = [x_1, \cdots, x_k]$ are the input features and y is the target real valued output, which is a function of $\mathbf{x}$. The examples are drawn randomly from the distribution $p(\mathbf{x})$. Consider an ensemble whose output is the weighted average of the outputs of its base models

$$f_{ens}(\mathbf{x}) = \sum_{i=1}^{N} w_i f_i(\mathbf{x}),$$

where N is the number of base models, $f_i(\mathbf{x})$ is the output of the base model i for the input features $\mathbf{x}$, w_i is the weight associated to the base model i, and the weights are positive and sum to one. The weights can be seen as our belief on the respective base models. For example, in bagging (Section 20.2), all weights are equal to $1/N$.

The quadratic error of the ensemble on the example $(\mathbf{x}, y)$ is given by

$$e_{ens}(\mathbf{x}) = (f_{ens}(\mathbf{x}) - y)^2.$$

Based on some algebra manipulation using the fact that the weights of the base models sum to one, Krogh and Vedelsby have shown that [241]

$$e_{ens}(\mathbf{x}) = \underbrace{\frac{\sum_i w_i (f_i(x) - y)^2}{}}_{\text{weighted error}} - \underbrace{\frac{\sum_i w_i (f_i(x) - f_{ens}(x))^2}{}}_{\text{ambiguity term}}.$$

This equation is over a single example, but can be generalized for the whole distribution by integrating over $p(\mathbf{x})$. This equation shows that the quadratic error of the ensemble can be decomposed into two terms. The first term is the weighted average error of the base models. The second term is called the ambiguity term. It measures the amount of disagreement among the base models. This can be seen as the amount of diversity in the ensemble. This equation shows that the error of an ensemble depends not only on the error/accuracy of its base models, but also on the diversity among its base models.

Note that the ambiguity term is never negative. As it is subtracted from the first term, the ensemble is guaranteed to have error equal to or lower than the average error of *its own base models*. The larger the ambiguity term, the larger the ensemble error reduction. However, as the ambiguity term increases, so does the first term. Therefore, diversity on its own is not enough—the right balance between diversity (ambiguity term) and individual base model's accuracy (average error term) needs to be used in order to achieve the lowest overall ensemble error [61].

20.2 BOOTSTRAP AGGREGATING (BAGGING)
20.2.1 HOW BAGGING WORKS

Bootstrap aggregating (bagging) [46] is an ensemble method that uses a single type of base learner to produce different base models. Figure 20.1 illustrates how it works. Consider a training data set D of size $|D|$. In the case of SEE, each of the $|D|$ training examples that composes D could be a completed project with known required effort. The input features of this project could be, for example, its functional size, development type, language type, team expertise, etc. The target output would be the true required

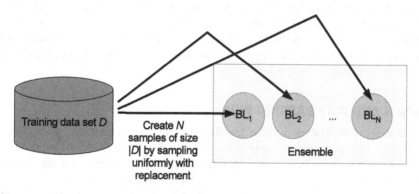

FIGURE 20.1

Bagging scheme. BL stands for base learner.

Table 20.2 An Illustrative Software Effort Estimation Training Set

	Input Feature			Target Output
Project ID	Functional Size	Development Type	Language Type	True Effort
1	100	New	3GL	520
2	102	Enhancement	3GL	530
3	111	New	4GL	300
4	130	Enhancement	4GL	310
5	203	Enhancement	3GL	900
6	210	New	3GL	910
7	215	New	4GL	700
8	300	Enhancement	3GL	1500
9	295	New	4GL	2000
10	300	Enhancement	4GL	1340

The project IDs are usually not used for learning.

effort of this project. An example of illustrative training set is given in Table 20.2. Consider also that one would like to create an ensemble with N base models, where N is a predefined value, by using a certain base learning algorithm. The procedure to create the ensemble's base models is as follows. Generate N bootstrap samples S_i ($1 \leq i \leq N$) of size $|D|$ by sampling training examples uniformly[1] with replacement from D. For example, let's say that D is the training set shown in Table 20.2 and $N = 15$. An example of fifteen bootstrap samples is given in Table 20.3. The procedure then uses the base learning algorithm to create each base model i using sample S_i as the training set.

After the ensemble is created, then it can start being used to make predictions for future instances based on their input features. In the case of SEE, future instances are new projects to which we do not know the true required effort and wish to estimate it. In the case of regression tasks, where the value to be estimated is numeric, the predictions given by the ensemble are the simple average of the predictions given by its base models. This would be the case for SEE. However, bagging can also be used for classification tasks, where the value to be predicted is a class. An example of classification task would be to predict whether a certain module of a software is faulty or nonfaulty. In the case of classification tasks, the prediction given by the ensemble is the majority vote, i.e., the class most often predicted by its base models.

20.2.2 WHEN AND WHY BAGGING WORKS

The success of bagging depends on its base learning algorithm being *unstable*, where unstable means that a small change in the training sample can result in a large change in the predictions given by the resulting base model. It has been shown that bagging is able to improve the performance of good but unstable base learning algorithms. On the other hand, bagging could even slightly degrade the performance of stable base learning algorithms [46]. It has been pointed out that classification and

---

[1] Uniform sampling assigns the same probability to select any of the elements of a set.

Table 20.3 Example of Fifteen Bootstrap Samples from the Training Set Shown in Table 20.2

Bootstrap Sample	Project IDs									
S_1	7	6	3	3	2	6	2	6	6	3
S_2	10	5	3	5	3	8	8	4	5	9
S_3	4	9	9	4	5	7	10	5	5	1
S_4	5	7	5	2	1	1	10	1	7	7
S_5	10	10	9	2	3	3	10	3	8	2
S_6	7	5	9	6	1	5	5	3	10	3
S_7	5	4	7	7	5	5	2	8	7	3
S_8	5	1	9	8	7	6	1	7	8	7
S_9	10	6	7	10	7	10	9	9	7	5
S_{10}	1	9	8	5	5	8	8	7	3	2
S_{11}	7	8	8	2	3	4	9	2	4	5
S_{12}	7	7	9	10	7	7	8	7	5	9
S_{13}	7	6	4	2	2	5	7	8	10	5
S_{14}	10	8	5	2	10	2	5	5	9	2
S_{15}	10	10	1	1	6	9	10	7	5	8

Only the project IDs are shown for simplicity.

RTs, neural networks, and subset selection in linear regression are typically unstable, whereas k-nearest neighbor is stable [46, 47].

The reason why bagging needs good but unstable base learning algorithms is related to accuracy and diversity (Section 20.1). If a stable base learning algorithm is used, then the predictions given by different base models created with different bootstrap samples of the training set will be very similar. A good but unstable base learning algorithm will create accurate but diverse base models, making bagging successful. In terms of the ambiguity decomposition explained in Section 20.1.2, good but unstable base learning algorithms would increase the ambiguity term, helping to reduce the error of the ensemble. Even if each of the base models is slightly less accurate than a single model trained on the whole training set, the reduction of the error caused by the ambiguity term would compensate for that. On the other hand, bagging using a stable base learning algorithm would not get its error reduced because the ambiguity term would be very small—in the extreme case, zero. At the same time, its base models may be slightly less accurate than single models trained on the whole data set would be. So, the error of the bagging ensemble could be slightly worse than single models trained on the *whole* training set if its base learners are stable.

20.2.3 POTENTIAL ADVANTAGES OF BAGGING FOR SEE

Bagging is a simple and well-known ensemble learning approach that has three main features that make it potentially beneficial for SEE: (1) several ready implementations of bagging can be easily found on the Web, (2) it does not require extensive human participation in the process of building ensembles, and (3) it has theoretically and empirically shown to improve performance in comparison to the base learning algorithm provided that its base learning algorithm is unstable enough [46].

20.3 REGRESSION TREES (RTs) FOR BAGGING

RTs were introduced earlier in this book (see Section 10.10). Such learners generate a tree of decisions whose leaves are a prediction for some numeric class (for example, see Figure 20.2).

In turns out that these kinds of tree learning are very useful for bagging. To see this, consider the following. As explained in Section 20.2, bagging uses a single type of base learning algorithm, which should allow for diversity to be produced, besides being accurate. Examples of learners that are typically unstable are RTs, neural networks, and subset selection in linear regression [46, 47]. In terms of accuracy, RTs have several potential advantages for SEE in comparison to other single learners, as explained in Section 10.10.5. Sections 20.5, 20.6 will confirm that RTs present relatively good performance and that their locality structure, which takes into account the difference in importance among input features, is key for their performance in SEE. The fact that RTs are typically unstable and accurate for SEE makes them good base learners for bagging in SEE. Our experimental study in Section 20.5 shows that bagging + RTs indeed present very competitive accuracy in SEE.

20.4 EVALUATION FRAMEWORK

This chapter will present an experimental study with the aims of (1) evaluating bagging + RTs in comparison to several other fully automated ML approaches for SEE, and (2) providing further understanding on why bagging + RTs manage to obtain competitive performance in SEE. We refer to an approach as fully automated when, given the project data, it does not require human intervention and decision making in order to be used. This is an algorithmic feature that reduces the complexity and cost of using the SEE tool, as a person operating it would just need to provide the project data and push a button to obtain a SEE. It is worth noting that parameter choice can usually be automated as well. For instance, bagging + RT is an approach that can be fully automated.

Current work on frameworks for evaluation of SEE approaches considers issues such as explicit preprocessing [292], evaluation measures [133, 389], and the importance of the magnitude of the

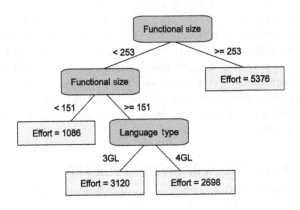

FIGURE 20.2

An example of RT for software effort estimation, where efforts are measured in person-hours.

differences in performance [389]. There has also been work on statistical approaches for evaluating models across multiple data sets in the general ML literature [96]. In this section, we build upon existing work and present a framework that explicitly considers four important points: (1) choice of data sets and preprocessing techniques, (2) choice of learning machines, (3) choice of evaluation methods, and (4) choice of parameters. All these points should be considered carefully based on the aims of the experiments. The design chosen in this section concentrates mainly on the aim of evaluating (and choosing) ML models for SEE. Further design choices for providing additional understanding about why bagging + RTs obtain competitive performance are provided in Section 20.6.

20.4.1 CHOICE OF DATA SETS AND PREPROCESSING TECHNIQUES

The first point in our framework is the choice of data sets and preprocessing techniques to be used in the study. Considering the aim of providing a general evaluation of a certain SEE approach in comparison to others, the data sets should cover a wide range of problem features, such as number of projects, types of features, countries, and companies. In this work, this is achieved by using five data sets from the PRedictOr Models In Software Engineering Software (PROMISE) Repository [300] and eight data sets based on the International Software Benchmarking Standards Group (ISBSG) Repository [271] Release 10. Sections 20.4.1.1, 20.4.1.2 provide their description and preprocessing.

20.4.1.1 PROMISE data

The PROMISE data sets used in this study are cocomo81, nasa93, nasa, sdr, and desharnais. Cocomo81 consists of the projects analyzed by Boehm to introduce COCOMO [34]. Nasa93 and nasa are two data sets containing Nasa projects from the 1970s to the 1980s and from the 1980s to the 1990s, respectively. Sdr contains projects implemented in the 2000s and was collected at Bogazici University Software Engineering Research Laboratory from software development organizations in Turkey. Desharnais' projects are dated from late 1980s. Table 20.4 provides additional details and the next paragraphs explain their features, missing values, and outliers.

Features

Cocomo81, nasa93, and nasa are based on the COCOMO [34] format, containing as input features 15 cost, drivers, the number of lines of code (LOC) and the development type (except for nasa, which does

Table 20.4 PROMISE Data Sets						
Data Set	# Projs	# Feats	Min Eff	Max Eff	Avg Eff	Std Dev Eff
Cocomo81	63	17	5.9	11,400	683.53	1821.51
Nasa93	93	17	8.4	8211	624.41	1135.93
Nasa	60	16	8.4	3240	406.41	656.95
Sdr	12	23	1	22	5.73	6.84
Desharnais	81	9	546	23,940	5046.31	4418.77

The effort is measured in person-months for all data sets but desharnais, where it is measured in person-hours. # Projs stands for number of projects, # Feats for number of features, and Eff for true required effort. Adapted from [326].

not contain the latter feature). The actual effort in person-months is the dependent variable. Sdr is based on COCOMO II [37], containing as input features 22 cost drivers and the number of LOC. The actual effort in person-months is the dependent variable. The data sets were processed to use the COCOMO numeric values for the cost drivers. The development type was transformed into dummy variables.

Desharnais follows an independent format, containing as input features the team experience in years, the manager experience in years, the year the project ended, the number of basic logical transactions in function points, the number of entities in the system's data model in function points, the total number of nonadjusted function points, the number of adjusted function points, the adjustment factor, and the programming language. Actual effort in person-hours is the dependent variable.

Missing Values

The only data set with missing values is desharnais. In total, it contains only 4 in 81 projects with missing values. So, these projects were eliminated.

Outliers

The literature shows that SEE data sets frequently have a few outliers, which may hinder the SEEs for future projects [385]. In the current work, outliers were detected using k-means. This method was chosen because it has shown to improve performance in the SEE context [385]. K-means is used to divide the projects into clusters. The silhouette value for each project represents the similarity of the project to the other projects of its cluster in comparison to projects of the other clusters, ranging from -1 (more dissimilar) to 1 (more similar). So, the average silhouette value can be used to determine the number of clusters k. After applying k-means to the data, clusters with less than a certain number n of projects or projects with negative silhouette values are considered outliers.

We used $n = 3$, as in [385]'s work. The number of clusters k was chosen among $k = \{2, 3, 4, 5\}$, according to the average silhouette values. As shown in Table 20.5, the highest average silhouette values were always for $k = 2$ and were very high for all data sets (between 0.8367 and 0.9778), indicating that the clusters are generally homogeneous. The number of outliers was also small (from none to 3), representing less than 5% of the total number of projects, except for sdr. The projects considered as outliers were eliminated from the data sets, apart from the outlier identified for sdr. As this data set is very small (only 11 projects), there is not enough evidence to consider the identified project as an outlier.

Table 20.5 PROMISE Data Sets—Outliers Detection

Data Set	K	Avg Silhouette	Outliers	# Outliers/# Projs
Cocomo81	2	0.9778	None	0.00%
Nasa93	2	0.9103	42, 46, 62	3.23%
Nasa	2	0.9070	2, 3	3.33%
Sdr	2	0.9585	9	8.33%
Desharnais	2	0.8367	9, 39, 54	3.70%

The numbers identifying the outlier projects represent the order in which they appear in the original data set, starting from one. # Outliers stands for number of outliers and # Projs for the total number of projects in the data set. Adapted from [327].

20.4.1.2 ISBSG data

The ISBSG repository contains a large body of data about completed software projects. Release 10 contains 5052 projects, covering many different companies, several countries, organization types, application types, etc. The data can be used for several different purposes, such as evaluating the benefits of changing a software or hardware development environment; improving practices and performance; and estimation.

In order to produce reasonable SEE using ISBSG data, a set of relevant comparison projects needs to be selected. We preprocessed the data set to use projects that are compatible and do not present strong issues affecting their effort or sizes, as these are the most important variables for SEE. With that in mind, we maintained only projects with

- Data quality and function points quality A (assessed as being sound with nothing being identified that might affect their integrity) or B (appears sound but there are some factors that could affect their integrity; integrity cannot be assured).
- Recorded effort that considers only the development team.
- Normalized effort equal to total recorded effort, meaning that the reported effort is the actual effort across the whole life cycle.
- Functional sizing method IFPUG version 4+ or NESMA.
- No missing organization-type field. Projects with missing organization-type field were eliminated because we use this field to create different subsets, as explained in the next paragraph.

The preprocessing resulted in 621 projects.

After that, with the objective of creating different subsets, the projects were grouped according to organization type. Only the groups with at least 20 projects were maintained, following ISBSG's data set size guidelines. The resulting organization types are shown in Table 20.6. In addition, a data set containing the union of all the ISBSG subsets will also be used in our analysis, in order to create a data set likely to be more heterogeneous than the other ones.

Table 20.6 ISBSG Data—Organization Types Used in the Study

Organization Type	ID	# Projs
Financial, Property, & Business Services	Org1	76
Banking	Org2	32
Communications	Org3	162
Government	Org4	122
Manufacturing, Transport, & Storage	Org5	21
Ordering	Org6	22
Billing	Org7	21

 # Projs stands for number of projects in the organization-type subset. From [326].

Table 20.7 ISBSG Subsets				
ID	Min	Max	Avg	Std Dev
(a) Unadjusted function points				
Org1	43	2906	215.32	383.72
Org2	53	499	225.44	135.12
Org3	3	893	133.24	154.42
Org4	32	3088	371.41	394.10
Org5	17	13,580	1112.19	2994.62
Org6	50	1278	163.41	255.07
Org7	51	615	160.10	142.88
(b) Effort				
Org1	91	134,211	4081.64	15,951.03
Org2	737	14,040	3218.50	3114.34
Org3	4	20,164	2007.10	2665.93
Org4	360	60,826	5970.32	8141.26
Org5	762	54,620	8842.62	11,715.39
Org6	361	28,441	4855.41	6093.45
Org7	867	19,888	6960.19	5932.72
(c) Productivity				
Org1	1.2	75.2	12.71	12.58
Org2	4.5	55.1	15.05	9.94
Org3	0.3	43.5	17.37	9.98
Org4	1.4	97.9	18.75	16.69
Org5	2.2	52.5	23.38	14.17
Org6	5.6	60.4	30.52	17.70
Org7	14.4	203.8	58.10	61.63
Adapted from [326].				

Table 20.7 contains additional information about the subsets. As we can see, the productivity rate of different companies varies. A 7-way 1-factor analysis of variance (ANOVA) [332] was used to determine whether the mean productivity rate for all different subsets are equal or not. The factor considered was organization type, with seven different levels representing each of the organization types, and each level containing its corresponding projects as the observations. ANOVA indicates that there is statistically significant difference at the 95% confidence interval (p-value $< 2.2e-16$).

The next paragraphs explain how the features were selected and how to deal with the missing values and outliers.

Features
The ISBSG suggests that the most important criteria for estimation purposes are the functional size; the development type (new development, enhancement, or redevelopment); the primary programming

language or the language type (e.g., 3GL, 4GL); and the development platform (mainframe, midrange, or PC). As the development platform has more than 40% missing feature values for two organization types, the following criteria were used as features:

- Functional size.
- Development type.
- Language type.

The normalized work effort in hours is the dependent variable. Due to the preprocessing, this is the actual development effort across the whole life cycle.

Missing Values
The features "functional size" and "development type" have no missing values. The feature "language type" is missing in several subsets, even though it is never missing in more than 40% of the projects of any subset.

So, an imputation method based on k-nearest neighbors (k-NN) was used so that this feature can be kept without having to discard the projects in which it is missing. K-NN imputation has been shown to be able to improve SEEs [66]. It is particularly beneficial for this area because it is simple and does not require large data sets. Another method, based on the sample mean, also presents these features, but k-NN has been shown to outperform it in two SEE case studies [66].

According to [66], "k-NN works by finding the k most similar complete cases to the target case to be imputed where similarity is measured by Euclidean distance." When $k > 1$, several different methods can be used to determine the value to be imputed; for example, simple average. For categorical values, vote counting is adopted. Typically, $k = 1$ or 2. As language type is a categorical feature, using $k = 2$ could cause draws. So, we chose $k = 1$. The Euclidean distance considered normalized data sets.

Outliers
Similarly to the PROMISE data sets (Section 20.4.1.1), outliers were detected through k-means [165] and eliminated. K was chosen among $k = \{2,3,4,5\}$ based on the average silhouette values. The best silhouette values, their corresponding ks, and the projects considered as outliers are shown in Table 20.8.

As with the PROMISE data sets, the silhouette values were high (between 0.8821 and 0.9961), showing that the clusters are homogeneous. The number of outliers varied from none to 5, representing always less than 5% of the total number of projects. None of the data sets were reduced to less than 20 projects after outliers elimination.

20.4.2 CHOICE OF LEARNING MACHINES
The second point to be considered when designing a ML experiment is the approaches that will be included in the analysis. As explained in the beginning of Section 20.4, our design will concentrate on the aim of evaluating bagging + RTs against several other fully automated ML approaches. With that aim, three ensemble and three single fully automated learning machines were chosen to be used:

- Single learning machines:
  - REPTree RTs [156, 444];
  - Radial Basis Function (RBFs) networks [32]; and
  - MultiLayer Perceptrons (MLPs) [32].

Table 20.8 ISBSG Subsets—Outliers Detection

ID	K	Avg Silhouette	Outliers	# Outliers/# Projs
Org1	2	0.9961	38	1.32%
Org2	2	0.9074	None	0.00%
Org3	2	0.8911	80, 91, 103, 160	2.47%
Org4	2	0.8956	4, 10, 75, 89, 104	4.10%
Org5	2	0.9734	20	4.76%
Org6	3	0.8821	4	4.55%
Org7	3	0.8898	None	0.00%

The numbers identifying the outlier projects represent the order in which they appear in the original data set, starting from one. # Outliers stands for number of outliers and # Projs stands for number of projects in the organization type subset. Adapted from [327].

- Ensembles of learning machines:
  - Bagging [46] with MLPs (bagging + MLPs), with RBFs (bagging + RBFs) and with RTs (bagging + RTs);
  - Ensembles based on randomization [156, 444] of MLPs (randomizer + MLPs); and
  - NCL [263, 264] with MLPs (NCL + MLPs).

RTs were chosen because they present several potential advantages for SEE, including their specific type of locality, as explained in Section 20.3. A study comparing different locality approaches, including the traditional SEE by analogy approach k-NN [390], and three clustering approaches, has shown that even though RTs obtained similar average ranking across data sets to the other locality approaches, when they were not the best, they rarely performed considerably worse than the best [326], being generally more adequate for SEE than the others.

RBFs were included because they are also learners based on locality, due to the RBFs (typically Gaussians) used in their hidden nodes. When the inputs are fed into the hidden layer, their distances (e.g., Euclidean distances) to the center of each neuron are calculated. After that, each node applies a RBF to the distance, which will produce lower/higher values for larger/shorter distances. Each hidden neuron i is connected to each output neuron j with weight w_{ji}, and output neurons usually compute a linear function of their inputs when working with regression problems. Due to the use of a RBF, changes in the weights connecting a given hidden neuron to the output neurons do not affect input values that are far from the center of this neuron.

Even though the choice of RTs and RBFs was based on their relation to locality, MLPs are not local learning machines and were included as an example of a nonlocal approach. They were chosen for being popular learning machines that can approximate any continuous function [32]. They have also been investigated in the SEE context [25, 45, 171, 242, 403, 422, 445]. For instance, Tronto et al. [422] showed that they can outperform linear regression because they are able to model observations that lie far from the best straight line. MLPs can be easily combined using several different ensemble approaches, such as bagging, random ensembles, and NCL. Other nonlocal approaches that are not restricted to certain function shapes were not chosen because they do not perform well for regression tasks (e.g., NaiveBayes [135]) or have not been so much used for SEE (e.g., support vector machines).

Bagging + RBFs and bagging + MLPs were also included to check whether other types of base learners could achieve similar performance to bagging + RTs.

Even though bagging is a well-known and accessible ensemble approach, each of its base learning machines is trained with only about 63.2% of the unique examples from the available original training set [26]. As the training data sets used for SEE are typically small, it is important to check whether using samples of the training set would not affect bagging badly in comparison to ensemble methods that train each of their base models with 100% of the training examples. So, our evaluation also included ensembles based on randomization of MLPs. They are based on the fact that different initial conditions may cause different neural networks to converge into different local minima of the cost function. They turn an apparent disadvantage, local minima in training neural networks, into something useful by averaging (in the case of regression) the predictions of base learning machines trained using different random seeds. Despite its simplicity, this procedure works surprisingly well in many, but not all, cases [92, 467, 468]. Their weakness is that a good level of diversity is not always achieved just by using different random seeds [264]. Note also that this approach can only be used with base learners that rely on random seeds, and are typically used with neural networks [421]. So, we used MLPs as their base learners in this study.

NCL [263, 264] is an ensemble approach that has strong theoretical foundations for regression problems, explicitly controlling diversity through the error function of the base learning machines [62]. So, it was also chosen to be included in the analysis. Its disadvantage is that its base models usually have to be very strong. Also, it can only be used with neural networks. Other learning machines such as RTs cannot be currently used. So, we used it with MLPs as the base learners in this study.

All the learning machines but NCL were based on the WEKA implementation [156, 444]. The RTs were based on the REPTree implementation available from Weka. We recommend the software WEKA [156, 444] should the reader wish to get more details about the implementation and parameters. The software used for NCL is available upon request.

20.4.3 CHOICE OF EVALUATION METHODS

The third point in the experimental framework is the choice of evaluation methods. The evaluation was based on 30 runs for each data set. In each run, for each data set, 10 examples were randomly picked for testing and the remaining were used for the training of all the approaches being compared. Holdout of size 10 was suggested by Menzies et al. [292] and allows the largest possible number of projects to be used for training without hindering the testing. For sdr, half of the examples were used for testing and half for training, due to the small size of this data set.

The approaches are compared against each other based on their performance on the test set. Foss et al. [133] show that performance measures based on magnitude of the relative error (MRE) are potentially problematic due to their asymmetry, biasing toward prediction models that underestimate. That includes a performance measure very popular in the SEE literature: mean MRE (MMRE). Another measure, mean absolute error (MAE), does not present asymmetry problems and is not biased. However, it is difficult to interpret, as the residuals are not standardized. So, measures such as MMRE have continued to be widely used by most researchers in the area. However, Shepperd and Mc Donell [389] very recently proposed a new measure called standardized accuracy (SA), defined as follows:

$$SA = 1 - \frac{MAE_{P_i}}{MAE_{P_0}},$$

where MAE_{P_i} is the MAE of the prediction model P_i and $\overline{MAE_{P_0}}$ is the mean value of a large number, typically 1000, runs of random guessing. This is defined as predicting $\hat{y}$ for the example t by randomly sampling over the remaining $n - 1$ examples and taking $\hat{y}_t = y_r$, where r is drawn randomly with equal probability from $1 \ldots n \wedge r \neq t$. Even though this measure is a ratio, such as MMRE, this is not problematic because we are interested in a single direction—better than random [389]. SA can be interpreted as the ratio of how much better P_i is than random guessing, giving a very good idea of how well the approach does.

The following measures of performance were used in this work [242, 292, 389]: MMRE, percentage of estimates within 25% of the actual values (PRED(25)), MAE, and SA. MMRE and PRED(25) were included for reference purposes, as they were reported in previous work evaluating ensembles [321]. In addition, verifying whether different results are achieved when using different performance measures can also provide interesting insights into the behavior of the approaches, as will be discussed in Section 20.5.4.

However, we will consider MAE and SA as more reliable performance measures. Unless stated otherwise, the analysis will always refer to the measures calculated on the test set.

As warned by Shepperd and Mc Donell [389], some papers in the SEE literature have been comparing approaches that do not perform better than random guess. To judge the effect size of the differences in performance against random guess, the following measure has been suggested:

$$\Delta = \frac{\overline{MAE_{P_0}} - MAE_{P_i}}{s_{P_0}},$$

where s_{P_0} is the sample standard deviation of the random guessing strategy. The values of Δ can be interpreted in terms of the categories proposed by Cohen [80] of small (≈ 0.2), medium (≈ 0.5), and large (≈ 0.8). We use this measure to show how big the effect of the difference in MAE between each approach and random guess is likely to be in practice, validating our comparisons.

In order to determine whether the performance of the learning machines in terms of MAE is statistically significantly different from each other considering multiple data sets, we use the Friedman statistical test. Friedman was recommended by Demšar [96] as an adequate test for comparing multiple learning machines across multiple data sets. This statistical test also provides a ranking of algorithms as follows. Let r_i^j be the rank of the jth of k algorithms on the ith of N data sets. The average rank of algorithm j is calculated as $R_j = \frac{1}{N} \sum_i r_i^j$. The rounded average ranks can provide a fair comparison of the algorithms given rejection of the null hypothesis that all the approaches are equivalent. Nevertheless, Wilcoxon sign-rank tests [442] are typically used to compare a particular model to other models across multiple data sets after rejection of the Friedman null hypothesis, where necessary. Holm-Bonferroni corrections can be used to avoid high Type-I error due to the multiple tests performed.

As data sets are very heterogeneous in SEE and the performance of the approaches may vary greatly depending on the data set, it is also important to check what approaches are usually among the best and, when they are among the worst, whether the magnitude of the performance is much worse than the best approach for that data set or not. This type of analysis also helps to identify for what type of data sets certain approaches behave better. It is worth noting that statistical tests such as Friedman and Wilcoxon are based on the relative ranking of approaches, thus not considering the real magnitude of the differences in performance when used for comparison across multiple data sets. So, even if a Friedman test accepts the null hypothesis that all approaches perform similarly across multiple data sets, it is still valid to check what approaches are most often among the best, on what type of data sets, and the magnitude of the differences in performance. In this work, we check the magnitude of the differences in performance between an approach and the best approach for a given data set by determining whether this approach has SA worse than the best in more than 0.1 units.

So, building upon previous work [96, 321, 389], an evaluation framework based on the following three steps is proposed by Minku and Yao (2012) [326]:

1. Friedman statistical test and ranking across multiple data sets to determine whether approaches behave statistically significantly differently considering several data sets.
2. Determine which approaches are usually among the first and second highest ranked approaches and, possibly, identify to which type of data sets approaches tend to perform better.
3. Check how much worse each approach is from the best approach for each data set.

A good approach would be highly ranked by Friedman and statistically significantly different from lower ranked approaches, would be more frequently among the best, and would not perform too bad in terms of SA when it is not among the best.

20.4.4 CHOICE OF PARAMETERS

The fourth point considered in our framework is the choice of parameters for the approaches used in the experiments. The choice of parameters is a critical step in ML experiments, as results can vary greatly depending on it. For instance, a learning machine that would have better performance under certain choices could have worse performance under other choices. It is important that the method used for choosing the parameters is made clear in papers using ML, so that differences in the results obtained can be better understood.

In order to choose the parameters, we performed five preliminary runs using all combinations of the parameters shown in Table 20.9 for each data set and learning approach. The parameters providing the lowest MMRE for each data set were chosen to perform the thirty runs used in the comparison analysis. In this way, each approach enters the comparison using the parameters that are most likely to provide the best results for each particular data set. These parameters were omitted due to the large number of combinations of approaches and data sets used. The performance measure MMRE was chosen for being used in all previous work evaluating existing automated ensembles.

20.5 EVALUATION OF BAGGING + RTs IN SEE

This section mainly aims at evaluating bagging + RTs in comparison to other automated ML approaches in SEE. As a preanalysis, we can observe that very different performances were obtained by the approaches for different data sets as follows. The MMRE obtained by the best performing approach for each particular data set varied from 0.37 to 2.00. The PRED(25) varied from 0.17 to 0.55. The correlation between estimated and real effort varied from 0.05 to 0.91. The SA varied from 0.26 to 0.64. Table 20.10 shows the SA and effect size Δ in comparison to random guess obtained by the approach with the highest, second highest, and lowest SA for each data set.

Table 20.9 Parameter Values for Preliminary Executions	
Approach	**Parameters**
MLP	Learning rate = $\{0.1, 0.2, 0.3, 0.4, 0.5\}$ Momentum = $\{0.1, 0.2, 0.3, 0.4, 0.5\}$ # epochs = $\{100, 500, 1000\}$ # hidden nodes = $\{3, 5, 9\}$
RBF	# clusters = $\{2, 3, 4, 5, 6\}$ Minimum std. deviation for the clusters $\quad = \{0.01, 0.1, 0.2, 0.3, 0.4\}$
REPTree	Minimum total weight for instances in a leaf $\quad = \{1, 2, 3, 4, 5\}$ Minimum proportion of the data variance at $\quad$ a node for splitting to be performed $\quad = \{0.0001, 0.001, 0.01, 0.1\}$
Ensembles	# base learning machines = $\{10, 25, 50\}$ All the possible parameters of the adopted $\quad$ base learning machines, as shown above
NCL	Penalty strength = $\{0.3, 0.4, 0.5\}$
K-NN	Number of neighbors = $\{1, 2, 4, 8, 16\}$
From [326].	

20.5.1 FRIEDMAN RANKING

As a first step of the evaluation, the Friedman ranking of the ensembles, single learning machines, and random guess in terms of MAE was determined and the Friedman statistical test was used to check whether these approaches have statistically significantly different MAE. The ranking generated by the test is shown in Table 20.11. The Friedman test rejects the null hypothesis that all approaches perform similarly (statistic $F_f = 12.124 > F(8, 96) = 2.036$). As we can see from the table, random guess was always ranked last. An additional test was performed without including random guess and the null hypothesis was also rejected (statistic $F_f = 4.887 > F(7, 84) = 2.121$).

All bagging approaches performed comparatively well, being on average ranked third. RTs were ranked on average just below, as fourth. As the null hypothesis that all approaches perform similarly was rejected, Wilcoxon sign-rank tests with Holm-Bonferroni corrections were performed to determine whether the RT's MAE is similar or different from bagging + RT's, bagging + MLP's, and bagging + RBF's across multiple data sets. Table 20.12 shows the p-values. The tests reveal that ensembles in general do not necessarily perform better than an adequate locality approach such as RTs. Bagging + MLP and bagging + RBF obtained statistically similar performance to RTs. However, bagging + RT, which is an ensemble of locality learning machines, obtained higher and statistically significantly different Friedman ranking in terms of MAE from single RTs. The number of win/tie/loss

Table 20.10 SA and Effect Size Δ for Approaches Ranked as First, Second, and Last in Terms of SA for Each Data Set

	Approach	SA	Δ
Cocomo81	Bagging + MLP	0.5968	0.9679
	RT	0.5902	0.9572
	RBF	0.3024	0.4904
Nasa93	RT	0.6205	1.2647
	Bagging + RT	0.6167	1.2569
	NCL	0.1207	0.2460
Nasa	Bagging + RT	0.6423	1.5401
	RT	0.6409	1.5367
	RBF	0.2618	0.6277
Sdr	RT	0.2626	0.7508
	Bagging + RT	0.2066	0.5907
	Randomizer + MLP	$-2.9981 \cdot 10^8$	$-1.3140 \cdot 10^8$
Desharnais	Bagging + MLP	0.5248	1.7132
	Bagging + RT	0.5049	1.6484
	RBF	0.3724	1.2157
Org1	MLP	0.4573	0.6670
	Bagging + MLP	0.4441	0.6478
	RT	0.2245	0.3275
Org2	Bagging + RBF	0.2719	0.9941
	Bagging + MLP	0.2716	0.9930
	NCL	0.0280	0.1025
Org3	Bagging + RT	0.5511	1.3237
	RT	0.5347	1.2843
	NCL	0.4331	1.0402
Org4	MLP	0.3276	0.6995
	RBF	0.3175	0.6779
	NCL	0.0248	0.0530
Org5	Bagging + RT	0.4259	1.9993
	Bagging + MLP	0.4038	1.8957
	NCL	0.2117	0.9939
Org6	Bagging + RBF	0.4930	2.2358
	MLP	0.4680	2.1224
	NCL	0.3617	1.6405
Org7	Bagging + RBF	0.3017	1.3739
	Bagging + MLP	0.2948	1.3425
	RBF	0.0285	0.1300
OrgAll	Bagging + RT	0.4416	1.0523
	RT	0.4318	1.0288
	Bagging + MLP	0.3319	0.7907

Adapted from [326].

Table 20.11 Friedman Ranking of Approaches in Terms of MAE

Rounded Avg. Rank	Avg. Rank	Std. Dev. Rank	Approach
3	2.77	1.69	Bagging + RT
	3.38	2.18	Bagging + MLP
	3.46	1.98	Bagging + RBF
4	4.15	2.58	RT
5	4.54	2.22	MLP
	5.23	1.54	Randomizer + MLP
6	5.92	2.02	RBF
7	6.54	1.66	NCL + MLP
9	9.00	0.00	Random Guess

Adapted from [326].

Table 20.12 Wilcoxon Sign-Rank Tests for Comparison of RT's MAE to Bagging + RT's, Bagging + MLP's, and Bagging + RBF's Across Multiple Data Sets

Approaches Compared	p-value
RT vs Bagging + RT	0.0134
RT vs Bagging + MLP	0.4143
RT vs Bagging + RBF	0.4143

The p-value in light grey background represents statistically significant difference with Holm-Bonferroni corrections at the overall level of significance of 0.05. Adapted from [326].

of bagging + RT versus RT is 10/1/2, further confirming the good performance of bagging + RTs, and demonstrating that RTs do not provide enough instability to allow bagging to improve upon its base learning algorithm only very rarely.

Even though single RBFs use locality, they did not perform so well. A possible reason for that is that, even though locality is used in the hidden nodes, the output nodes are based on linear functions.

20.5.2 APPROACHES MOST OFTEN RANKED FIRST OR SECOND IN TERMS OF MAE, MMRE AND PRED(25)

As a second step of the evaluation, the learning machines most often ranked as first or second in terms of MAE, MMRE, and PRED(25) were determined. Some results in terms of SA are also presented in order to provide more easily interpretable results.

In order to check how valid this analysis is, we first compare the SA and effect size Δ of the approach ranked as first, second, and last in terms of MAE for each data set. Table 20.10 shows these values. As we can see, the approaches ranked first or second frequently achieved SA at least 0.20 higher (better) than the worst approaches. That is reflected in the overall average SA considering all data sets, which improves from 0.2251 (approaches ranked last) to 0.4599 and 0.4712 (approaches ranked first and second). The effect size Δ in relation to random guess was frequently changed from small/medium to large, emphasizing the importance of using higher ranked approaches. Wilcoxon rank-sum statistical tests using Holm-Bonferroni corrections at the overall level of significance of 0.05 for comparing the approaches ranked first and second against random guess detected statistically significant difference for all cases. The p-values were very low, ranging from $1.6492 \cdot 10^{-4}$ to $5.6823 \cdot 10^{-19}$, confirming that the performance of these approaches is indeed better than random guessing.

Table 20.13a shows the learning machines ranked most often as first or second in terms of MAE. The results show that bagging + RTs, bagging + MLPs, and RTs are singled out, appearing among the first two ranked approaches in 27%, 23%, and 23% of the cases, whereas all other approaches together sum up to 27% of the cases. It is worth noting that bagging + RBF, which achieved high Friedman rank, does not appear so often among the best two approaches. One might think that bagging + RBFs rank for each data set could be more median, but more stable. However, the standard deviation of the ranks (Table 20.11) is similar to bagging + RTs and bagging + MLPs. So, the latter approaches are preferable over bagging + RBFs.

The table also shows that RTs are comparatively higher ranked for PROMISE than for ISBSG, achieving similar ranking to bagging approaches for PROMISE, but lower ranking for ISBSG. Even though RTs perform statistically similarly to bagging + MLPs and bagging + RBFs (Section 20.5.1), the difference in performance is statistically significant in comparison to bagging + RTs. Further, Wilcoxon sign-rank tests to compare RTs and bagging + RTs considering separately PROMISE and ISBSG data show that there is no statistically significant difference considering PROMISE on its own (p-value 1), but there is considering ISBSG (p-value 0.0078). So, approaches joining the power of bagging ensembles to the locality of RTs may be particularly helpful for more heterogeneous data.

Table 20.13b shows the two learning machines most often ranked as first and second in terms of MMRE. Both RTs and bagging + MLPs are very often among the first two ranked learning machines according to MMRE. The trend can be observed both in the PROMISE and ISBSG data sets. For PROMISE, RTs, or bagging + MLPs appear among the first two ranked approaches in 70% of the cases, whereas all other learning machines together sum up to 30%. For ISBSG, RTs, or bagging + MLPs appear among the first two ranked in 62.5% of the cases, whereas all other learning machines together sum up to 37.5%. Wilcoxon sign-rank tests show that these two approaches perform similarly in terms of MMRE (p-value of 0.2439).

The analysis considering PRED(25) shows that both RTs and bagging + MLPs are again frequently among the first two ranked (Table 20.13c), but randomizer + MLP becomes more competitive. If we consider PROMISE data by itself, ensembles such as bagging + MLPs are more frequently ranked higher than single learning machines, even though that is not the case for ISBSG. However, a Wilcoxon sign-rank test across multiple data sets shows that bagging + MLPs and RTs are statistically similar in terms of PRED(25) (p-value of 0.7483). Tests considering PROMISE and ISBSG data separately do not find statistically significant difference either (p-value of 0.8125 and 0.3828, respectively).

As we can see, RTs and bagging + MLPs are singled out as more frequently among the best both in terms of MMRE, PRED(25) and MAE and they perform statistically similarly independent of the

Table 20.13 Number of Data Sets in Which Each Learning Machine was Ranked First or Second According to MAE, MMRE, and PRED(25)

PROMISE Data	ISBSG Data	All Data
(a) According to MAE		
RT: 4 Bagging + RT: 4 Bagging + MLP: 2	Bagging + MLP: 4 Bagging + RT: 3 Bagging + RBF: 3 MLP: 3 RT: 2 RBF: 1	Bagging + RT: 7 RT: 6 Bagging + MLP: 6 MLP: 3 Bagging + RBF: 3 RBF: 1
(b) According to MMRE		
RT: 4 Bagging + MLP: 3 Bagging + RT: 2 MLP: 1	RT: 5 Bagging + MLP 5 Bagging + RBF: 3 MLP: 1 Rand + MLP: 1 NCL + MLP: 1	RT: 9 Bagging + MLP: 8 Bagging + RBF: 3 MLP: 2 Bagging + RT: 2 Rand + MLP: 1 NCL + MLP: 1
(c) According to PRED(25)		
Bagging + MLP: 3 Rand + MLP: 3 Bagging + RT: 2 RT: 1 MLP: 1	RT: 5 Rand + MLP: 3 Bagging + MLP: 2 MLP: 2 RBF: 2 Bagging + RBF: 1 Bagging + RT: 1	RT: 6 Rand + MLP: 6 Bagging + MLP: 5 Bagging + RT: 3 MLP: 3 RBF: 2 Bagging + RBF: 1

Learning machines never among the first or second are omitted. Adapted from [326].

performance measure. Other approaches such as randomizer + MLP and bagging + RTs become more or less competitive depending on the performance measure considered. Bagging + RBFs, differently from the Friedman ranking, is not singled out, i.e., it is not frequently among the best. Our study also shows that bagging + RTs outperform RTs in terms of MAE mainly for ISBSG data sets, which are likely to be more heterogeneous.

20.5.3 MAGNITUDE OF PERFORMANCE AGAINST THE BEST

In this section, we analyze how frequently an approach is worse than the best MAE approach in more than 0.1 units of SA. There are 34 cases in which approaches are worse than the best MAE approach

Table 20.14 Number of Times That an Approach is Worse than the Best MAE Approach of the Data Set in More than 0.1 Units of SA	
Approaches	**Number of Times**
RT, Bagging + RT	1
Bagging + MLP, Bagging + RBF, MLP	3
Randomizer + MLP	5
RBF	8
NCL + MLP	10
Adapted from [326].	

of the data set in more than 0.1 units of SA. *p*-values of Wilcoxon tests to compare these approaches to the best MAE are below 0.05 in 28 cases. If we apply Holm-Bonferroni corrections considering all the 34 comparisons, the difference is statistically significant in 20 out of 34 cases (59%). So, it is reasonable to consider the number of times that each approach is worse than the best in order to evaluate its performance.

Table 20.14 shows how many times each approach is worse than the best MAE approach in more than 0.1 units of SA. As we can see, RTs and bagging + RTs are rarely worse than the best MAE approach in more than 0.1 SA. They are worse in only 1 in 13 data sets. Bagging + MLPs, bagging + RBFs, and MLPs behave slightly worse, with the difference in SA higher than 0.1 SA in 3 data sets.

20.5.4 DISCUSSION

The analyzes presented in Sections 20.5.1, 20.5.2, and 20.5.3 show that bagging + RTs present a very good behavior for SEE. They have higher average (Friedman) rank, are more frequently among the best in terms of MAE, and are rarely worse than the best MAE approach for each data set in more than 0.1 units of SA. This is an example of how joining the power of bagging ensembles to a good locality approach can help improving SEE. Bagging + RTs were particularly helpful to improve performance in terms of MAE for ISBSG data sets, which are likely to be more heterogeneous. Future research on improving SEE using automated learning machines may benefit from further exploiting the advantages of ensembles and locality together.

As no approach is always the best independent of the data set, ideally, an organization should perform experiments following a principled framework in order to choose a model for their particular data set. Nevertheless, if an organization has no resources to perform such experiments, bagging + RTs are more likely to perform comparatively well across different data sets and are rarely worse than the best approach for a particular data set in more than 0.1 SA. Even though single RTs may perform slightly worse than bagging + RTs, they perform comparatively well in comparison to other approaches and may be used if the practitioners would like to understand the rules used by the learning machine to perform estimations.

The conclusions above are mainly drawn based on MAE and SA, which are considered to be more adequate and reliable performance measures than MMRE and PRED(N). In terms of behavior independent of the performance measure used, RTs and bagging + MLPs are always singled out as being frequently first or second ranked, whereas bagging + RT is less frequently among the best in terms of MMRE and PRED(25). Such a difference in the evaluation based on MAE and MRE-based measures gives us an interesting insight. It suggests that the slightly worse performance of RTs and bagging + MLPs in comparison to bagging + RTs in terms of MAE may be related to the fact that RTs and bagging + MLPs suffer more from underestimations. This issue should be further analyzed as future work and could be helpful for improving the performance of these approaches for SEE.

It is also worth making a note on the preprocessing of the data sets. As explained in Section 20.4.1, data sets were preprocessed using k-means for outliers removal. Outliers are examples different from usual and that cannot be well estimated by the models generated. Experiments done using RTs and bagging + MLPs reveal that the error obtained when attempting to use the models to estimate solely outlier projects is worse than the average obtained using nonoutlier examples, both in terms of MAE and PRED(25). Interestingly, the error in terms of MMRE is not much affected. As MMRE tends to bias models toward underestimations [389], these outliers are likely to be projects underestimated by the models.

We have also repeated the experiments using bagging + RTs, bagging + MLPs, and RTs, but without performing this part of the preprocessing, i.e., allowing the train/test sets to contain outliers. The experiments reveal that the SAs obtained are considerably reduced. So, in practice, the use of a clustering approach such as k-means is recommendable to remove outliers from the training sets and to identify whether a test example is an outlier.

20.6 FURTHER UNDERSTANDING OF BAGGING + RTs IN SEE

Section 20.2 provides a clear explanation on why ensembles such as bagging using unstable base learners can perform well. Section 20.5 then shows that bagging + RTs only very rarely do not manage to outperform RTs. So, the amount of instability provided by RTs is enough for most SEE data sets investigated in this study. This explains part of the reason why bagging + RTs were successful. The other feature that makes an ensemble such as bagging successful is the accuracy of its base models. We will consider here MAE as the most appropriate measure for the analysis. As shown in Section 20.5, even though RTs did not perform as well as bagging + RTs, they obtained comparatively good performance in comparison to several other approaches and rarely performed worse than the best approach for a given data set in more than 0.1 units of SA. They have also allowed bagging + RTs to obtain in general better results in terms of MAE than bagging + MLPs and bagging + RBFs. So, we can consider RTs as accurate base learners for SEE. In order to provide a further understanding on why bagging + RTs performed well, we thus need to provide a further understanding on why RTs performed well.

As explained in Section 20.3, one of the key potential advantages of RTs over other approaches is that they perform not only feature selection, but also naturally consider and use the relative importance of input features. In order to confirm that the relative importance is one of the keys to RT's performance, we analyze in this section whether the separation of features provided by RTs provides better performance than using solely feature selection.

A correlation-based feature selection (CFS) method [154] with greedy stepwise search [156] was used in the analysis. This method was chosen because it uses a similar idea to RTs to check what features are more significant. It additionally checks the correlation among features themselves. Greedy stepwise search was used because it allows ranking features. The main reason for using this CFS is its similarity

Table 20.15 CFS Ranking and RT Features Relative Importance for cocomo81: Features Ranking, First Tree Level in Which the Feature Appeared in More than 50% of the Trees, and Percentage of the Trees in Which it Appears in That Level

Features Ranking	Tree Level	% of Trees
LOC	Level 0	100.00%
Development mode		
Required software reliability	Level 1	90.00%
Modern programming practices		
Time constraint for cpu	Level 2	73.33%
Database size	Level 2	83.34%
Main memory constraint		
Turnaround time		
Programmers' capability		
Analysts' capability		
Language experience		
Virtual machine experience		
Schedule constraint		
Application experience	Level 2	66.67%
Use of software tools		
Machine volatility		
Process complexity		

Features below the horizontal line are not selected by CFS. From [326].

to the working of RTs, with the key difference that simply using its selected features as inputs for a learning machine does not provide it with a hierarchy of relative importance of the features. So, CFS is particularly helpful for understanding the behavior of RTs and how beneficial its use of the relative importance of features is to SEE. This filter method was also used instead of a wrapper method so that the same set of features can be used for different models, as explained below.

As a first step, we ran all the experiments using the design presented in Section 20.4, but after performing feature selection. This study showed that feature selection by itself did not change the fact that RTs and bagging + MLPs were usually among the best in terms of MMRE, PRED(25), and MAE. The approaches that obtained most improvements in performance were bagging + RBF, RBF, and NCL. However, the improvements were not large even for these approaches. Bagging + RBF's SA average considering all data sets was 0.0522 higher, RBF's was 0.0533, and NCL's was 0.0484 higher than when not using features selection.

As a second step for this analysis, we compared the ranking of features given by feature selection against the features appearing in more than 50% of the RTs until their third level, for each data set. An example is shown in Table 20.15. The results show that (1) the RTs do not use all the features selected by CFS, even though they usually use at least one of these; (2) the RTs use some features not

Table 20.16 CPU Time Constraint Information				
Data Set	Minimum	Maximum	Avg	Std. Dev
Nasa93	1.00	1.66	1.133	0.203
Nasa	1.00	1.66	1.076	0.138
From [326].				

selected by CFS; and (3) the RTs put higher ranked features according to CFS in higher levels of the tree, confirming the use of the relative importance of features.

So, feature selection by itself was not able to change the relative performance of different learning approaches. However, instead of simply using a subset with the most important features, RTs gave more importance to more important features as shown by the feature ranking, being able to achieve comparatively good performance and showing that hierarchy of features is important when working with ML for SEE. Future approaches tailored to SEE may be able to improve performance further by combining the power of ensembles to good locality features such as the hierarchy of features used by RTs.

It is also interesting to verify which features are usually at the top level of the hierarchy produced by the RTs, as these are considered to be the most influential features for the SEE. The number of LOC and the functional size are the features that most frequently appear at the top level. Table 20.15 shows an example for cocomo81, for which 100% of the RTs used LOC at the top level (level 0). It is reasonable that this feature appears at the top of the hierarchy, as larger programs require involvement of many programmers, increasing the communication complexity and effort.

Nasa93 was the only data set where a feature other than LOC or functional size appeared at the top level in more than 50% of the RTs. For this data set, 100% of the RTs used the feature CPU time constraint at the top level. Interestingly, even though nasa and nasa93 are two data sets from the same organization, the RTs did not use the same feature at the top level for these two data sets. For nasa, 96.67% of the RTs used LOC at the top level. In order to better understand why this happened, we analyzed the values of the feature CPU time constraint for these two data sets. As shown in Table 20.16, the standard deviation of this feature for nasa93 is much higher than that for nasa. A Levene test [250] shows that the difference in variance is statistically significant (p-value of 0.0036). This indicates that CPU time constraint varies more for nasa93 than for nasa. Very different CPU time constraints are likely to directly affect the difficulty of the software development, thus considerably influencing its required effort. For example, extra high CPU time constraint should require much more effort than low CPU time constraint. So, it is reasonable that this is considered as an important feature for nasa93.

It is also worth noting that the nonfunctional system features that are becoming more important in the modern systems could also affect the hierarchy provided by the RTs. For example, as writing secure code becomes more important for some companies, security-related features may raise in the hierarchy.

20.7 SUMMARY

This chapter presents a didactic explanation of ensembles, in particular bagging; a principled and comprehensive evaluation of bagging + RTs for SEE; and an explanation of why bagging + RTs perform well in SEE. An additional contribution of this chapter is a principled framework for evaluating SEE approaches, which considers explicitly the choice of data sets and preprocessing techniques, learning approaches, evaluation methods, and parameters.

Bagging + RTs are shown to perform well in terms of MAE (and SA): they were highly ranked in terms of performance across multiple data sets, they were frequently among the best approaches for each data set, and rarely performed considerably worse than the best approach for any data set. Overall, they performed better than several other approaches. This is an encouraging result, specially considering that bagging + RTs are accessible and fully automated approaches. If an organization has no resources to perform experiments to choose the SEE approach that is most suitable to their own data, bagging + RTs are recommended for the reasons above. Even though RTs performed slightly worse than bagging + RTs, they could still be used should the software manager wish to easily understand the rules underlying the model's behavior.

The good results provided by bagging + RTs are obtained thanks to the successful combination of bagging, which can improve performance of diverse and accurate base models, to the success of RTs in SEE, which can create accurate base models through its locality based on hierarchy of features. Other approaches further exploiting ensembles and locality, in particular the use of a hierarchy of input features, may be able to improve SEE further.

HOW TO ADAPT MODELS IN A DYNAMIC WORLD

In summary, this chapter proposes the following data analysis pattern:

Name:	Dynamic cross-company learning (DCL).
Also known as:	Online/dynamic adaptive ensemble of learning machines; cross-company (CC)/transfer learning approach; local learning method, when using local learning machines as base learners.
Intent:	Software effort estimation, when one wishes to (1) adapt to changes that a company may suffer throughout time, and (2) combine models from different companies.
Motivation:	Software prediction tasks are unlikely to be stationary [269, 322], as software development companies and their employees evolve/change with time. Changes may also cause a company to behave more or less similarly to other companies throughout time [322]. Software effort estimation models for a given company should be able to dynamically adapt to changes and identify if and when models from other companies are useful.
Solution:	A model continuously updated with single-company data is combined with CC models into an ensemble. Models are associated with weights representing how useful they currently are to the single company. Effort estimations for the single company are based on the weighted average of the models' estimations.
Applicability:	DCL was generally successful in identifying when CC models were useful and using them to improve performance by adapting to changes [322]. DCL is the first CC learning approach able to improve performance with respect to single-company learning in software effort estimation.
Related to:	Chapter 20 in terms of ensemble learning; Chapters 13, 14 in terms of transfer learning; and Chapters 14, 20 in terms of locality.

This chapter is based on Minku and Yao [322]. Additionally, the following new material has been added: (1) a more detailed explanation of related work (Section 21.2); and (2) a replicated study modifying two databases (Sections 21.5, 21.7).

So far, we have shown how to create models for tasks such as software effort estimation (SEE) and software defect prediction in an offline way. In offline learning, a set of completed software projects is used as training examples for building models to predict another set of projects without considering their chronology. Most SEE research treats both the construction and the evaluation of SEE models as an offline learning problem. However, software prediction tasks are online learning tasks, where new completed projects can arrive with time. These tasks are unlikely to be stationary, as software development companies and their employees evolve/change with time. For example, employees can be hired (or fired!), training can be provided, employees can become more experienced, new types of software projects can be accepted, management strategies can change, new programming languages can be introduced, etc. Therefore, models developed at a certain point in time may become obsolete. In a similar way, models that were good in the past and poor at present may become useful again in the future, as a company may start behaving similarly to a previous situation. Considering the chronology of the projects is thus important when developing and evaluating software prediction models. Models should ideally dynamically (i.e., whenever necessary) adapt to changes that may affect software predictions. This chapter presents a dynamic adaptive automated approach for SEE.

This chapter is further organized as follows. Section 21.1 presents the motivation to use CC data in dynamic adaptive approaches, and formulates the questions answered by this chapter. Section 21.2 presents related work. Section 21.3 presents our formulation of SEE as an online changing environment problem. Section 21.4 describes the databases used in the study. Section 21.5 presents an analysis to identify whether and when CC data are beneficial for SEE. Section 21.6 presents a dynamic adaptive approach for SEE. Section 21.7 presents an evaluation of this approach. Section 21.8 discusses the study and its implications to practice. Section 21.9 presents a summary and discussion.

21.1 CROSS-COMPANY DATA AND QUESTIONS TACKLED

One of the big challenges in SEE is that the number of completed projects available for being used as training examples is typically small. When companies suffer changes, some of the existing completed projects may not reflect the current situation of the company well. So, the number of training examples available for building predictive models can be reduced further, and it may be difficult to build accurate models based on such small training sets. In order to create a dynamic adaptive approach for SEE, we thus examine the possibility of using CC data in addition to within-company (WC) data in an online learning scenario.

There has been a long debate in the software engineering literature concerning how useful CC data are for SEE in comparison to WC data. Most studies so far did not consider the possibility of changes in the companies' environments, and indicated that CC models obtained either similar or worse performance than WC models [216, 266–268, 288]. The first work to perform a detailed analysis of the *potential* benefit of CC data in comparison to WC data was the work by Minku and Yao [322]. It investigated whether CC data are potentially beneficial for improving SEE, and revealed that CC data can be beneficial or detrimental *depending on the moment in time*. So, a dynamic adaptive approach able to identify when CC data are beneficial was proposed [322]. The main questions answered by Minku and Yao [322] and this chapter are:

- *RQ1.* Under what conditions are CC data potentially beneficial for improving SEE?
- *RQ2.* How can this potential benefit be used?

RQ1 is answered by showing that CC data can be beneficial or detrimental depending on the moment in time, as SEE tasks operate under concept drifting conditions (Section 21.5). Such concept drifts are very particular to SEE environments, having each concept active for a relatively short number of projects. The analysis reveals that CC data are potentially particularly helpful for this sort of concept drift. RQ2 is answered by presenting and evaluating a new approach called DCL to make use of CC data's potential for SEE (Sections 21.6, 21.7). The evaluation across multiple databases shows that DCL successfully uses CC data to improve performance in comparison to the sole use of WC data.

The study presented in this chapter is a replication of the study published by Minku and Yao [322]. It makes two alterations to the original study. The first one is the order of the projects from one of the data sets (Cocomo 81) used in the study. In the original work, the order of the projects was set to the order in which they appear in the data set at the PROMISE repository [300]. However, Boehm [34] provides the real chronological order of the projects in his book. So, the real chronological order has been adopted in the replicated study. In the original work, one of the CC data sets (Nasa 93) had an overlap of projects with the corresponding WC data set (Cocomo Nasa). This can be observed by a manual comparison of the projects belonging to these data sets. In terms of the evaluation of the proposed dynamic adaptive automated SEE approach, this overlap does not matter. This is because the evaluation is concerned with determining whether or not the approach is able to identify when certain subsets are useful. A successful approach should be able to identify the usefulness of Nasa 93 for predicting projects from Cocomo Nasa. However, the overlapping data sets cannot be used to reveal how much improvement in performance can be obtained by using CC data in SEE. So, in the replicated work, we have replaced the corresponding database by another one with no overlaps (KitchenMax).

The following contributions to SEE are provided:

- SEE changing features are examined and their particularities in comparison to usual changing environments tackled by the machine learning literature are identified.
- CC data are revealed to be potentially beneficial for improving the performance of SEEs over WC models when considering the online and changing nature of these tasks. Changes can cause CC models to become more or less beneficial/detrimental.
- Interesting features of SEE data sets commonly used in the literature are revealed, showing that different partitions of CC projects present different usefulness and are better used separately than as a single set. Separating CC projects according to their productivity increases their potential benefit for estimating projects of a single company.
- A new approach able to successfully use CC to improve performance over WC models is described. This approach is carefully evaluated not only to analyze its success in finding out when CC models are useful, but also to show how much improvement it can provide in comparison to WC models.
- We show that the online changing nature of software prediction tasks should be further exploited, being an important issue to be considered in the next research frontier on software project estimation.

21.2 RELATED WORK

21.2.1 SEE LITERATURE ON CHRONOLOGY AND CHANGING ENVIRONMENTS

The previous chapters of this book provide a thorough literature review of SEE approaches. This section concentrates on works considering the chronology of the projects used to create SEE models and the changing environments where software companies are embedded.

21.2.1.1 Chronology

Most work in the SEE literature did not consider the chronology of projects and concluded that CC models obtain either similar or worse performance than WC models [216]. A few studies considered chronology. For instance, Lokan and Mendes considered two types of SEE problem formulation based on chronology: project-by-project splitting [266] and date-based splitting [268].

In project-by-project splitting [266], a project p in the single-company data set is chosen as the project to have its effort estimated. Only the projects with completion date before p's starting date are used for building a SEE model. Cook's distance is used to determine whether highly influential projects should be eliminated from the training set, and then a new SEE model is built based on the reduced set. This model is used for estimating p. This process is repeated for each project p in the single-company data set, so that each project is estimated based on the most up-to-date model that can be built by its starting date. The difference between WC and CC learning is that, in WC learning, the projects used to build the SEE model are WC projects, whereas in CC learning they are CC projects.

In date-based splitting [268], a set of projects completed until date d is used to build a SEE model. In CC learning, the set of completed projects contains CC projects, whereas in WC learning it contains WC projects. Cook's distance is also used to filter out highly influential completed projects. The reduced set of completed projects is then used to build a SEE model for estimating a set of WC projects starting after d.

These studies indicate that it is important to consider chronology, as this can influence the results obtained. Nevertheless, CC models still obtained either similar or worse performance than WC models in terms of mean absolute error (MAE) [266, 268]. The results in terms of Z-measure further suggest that the CC models were more likely to underestimate effort. Even though these studies considered chronology, they did not consider the possibility of companies suffering changes, which could result in projects from different periods becoming more or less useful with time.

21.2.1.2 Changing environments

Previous work on locality [229, 326, 390] did not analyze the chronology of projects, but can implicitly deal with some specific types of changes that may happen in the environment of a given company over time. These are changes in the distribution of the input features describing the projects developed by the company. Locality approaches implicitly consider these types of changes because they make predictions about a given project based on the other projects that are most similar to it in terms of their input features. Therefore, if a given company suffers changes that affect the input features describing its projects, such approaches can try and identify whether there were any past WC or CC projects described by input features similar to the ones after the change. The prediction given to a new project will then be based on these most similar projects.

However, such approaches did not consider the fact that changes may affect not only the distribution of input features, but also the relationship between input features and target outputs of the data collected.

This issue can affect not only WC predictions made for a company that are evolving with time, but also the usefulness of CC data for estimating effort in a given company. For example, different companies may give different interpretations to data collection guidelines, causing similar projects to be described by different attributes. This can result in projects described by similar attributes having different efforts in different companies, breaking the principle upon which locality approaches are based. Therefore, locality approaches should still be combined with other mechanisms for considering changing environments fully.

21.2.1.3 Chronology and changing environments

A posterior work [269] that considers chronology shows that using a window of the most recent projects can provide better performance than using all the previous projects available. This is to our knowledge the first work to fully consider the possibility of changes in SEE. Nevertheless, it does not consider the issue of CC versus WC. It does not consider that older projects may become useful again in the future either, e.g., an experienced employee could leave the company, causing its productivity to become similar to the time before this employee was hired.

21.2.2 MACHINE LEARNING LITERATURE ON ONLINE LEARNING IN CHANGING ENVIRONMENTS

In machine learning (ML), changes to environments are called *concept drifts*. Formally, concept drifts are changes in the underlying distribution of the problem [320]. A certain joint problem distribution can be called a concept. Approaches for dealing with online learning and concept drift in the ML literature typically assume the availability of large amounts of data, forming a data stream [334] unlikely to exist in SEE. Even though SEE concept drifts can be very particular (Section 21.5.2.1), ML approaches for dealing with drifts may be helpful and could be used to inspire the proposal of new SEE approaches. This section thus explains online learning algorithms for dealing with concept drifts.

Dynamic weight majority (DWM) [237] (Algorithm 3) is a widely known ensemble approach for dealing with concept drifts in online learning classification tasks. This approach maintains a set of base learners that are updated with new training examples whenever they are made available (line 24). Each base learner is associated with weight, which represents how much the base learner should contribute to predictions. DWM's predictions are based on the weighted majority vote among the base learners' predictions. Weights start with value one and are multiplied by a predefined parameter β, $0 \leq \beta < 1$, when their associated learner gives a wrong prediction to a training example received on a time step multiple of p (line 9). So, base learners that currently perform poorly are associated with lower weights, whereas more accurate base learners are associated with higher weights. The algorithm normalizes the weights by uniformly scaling them such that the highest weight will be equal to one (line 15). The parameter p controls how often the weights are allowed to change. Smaller p leads to faster adaptation to changes, but makes the approach more sensitive to noise. Larger p makes the approach more robust to noise, but leads to slower adaptation.

DWM also allows removal and addition of base learners at every p time step (lines 16 and 19). Base learners that currently perform very poorly are removed so that they will not risk hindering the predictions. The removal of learners is controlled by a predefined weight threshold parameter θ. New base learners can be created to learn potentially new concepts from scratch. This is because base learners

ALGORITHM 3 DWM [237]

Parameters:
p: period between learner removal, creation and weight update
β: factor for decreasing weights $0 \leq \beta < 1$
θ: threshold for deleting learners

```
 1:  m = 1 {Number of learners.}
 2:  Create learner Lm
 3:  wm = 1 {Learner's weight.}
 4:  t = 1
 5:  for each new incoming data example d = (x⃗, y) do
 6:      σ⃗ = 0 {Sum of weighted predictions for each class.}
 7:      for each learner Li, 1 ≤ i ≤ m do
 8:          if the estimation ŷ = Li(x⃗) is wrong and
                 t mod p == 0 then
 9:              wi = βwj
10:          end if
11:          σŷ = σŷ + wj
12:      end for
13:      ŷ = argmaxjσj
14:      if t mod p == 0 then
15:          Normalize all weights
16:          Remove learners Li, 1 ≤ i ≤ m, wi < θ
17:          if the estimation ŷ is wrong then
18:              m = m + 1
19:              Create new learner Lm
20:              wm = 1
21:          end if
22:      end if
23:      for each learner Li, 1 ≤ i ≤ m do
24:          Use Lm to learn d
25:      end for
26:      t = t + 1
27:  end for
```

trained well with examples from old concepts frequently struggle to adapt to new concepts in a timely fashion [320]. In order to decide whether to add a new base learner, DWM makes use of a heuristic. Consider that the current time step is a multiple of p. If the ensemble misclassified the current training example, then it is more likely not to contain base learners that represent the current concept well. So, a new base learner is added. If the ensemble classifies the current training example correctly, then it is more likely to contain base learners that represent the current concept well. So, no new base learner is added.

Additive expert ensemble (AddExp) [236] is an approach similar to DWM that works for both classification and regression tasks, even though regression is restricted to predictions in the interval $[0, 1]$. For classification, the AddExp model's weights are multiplied by β, $0 \leq \beta < 1$, whenever the base model gives a wrong prediction. This is similar to DWM using $p = 1$. The problem with this strategy is that several new base learners will be added to the ensemble depending on its performance and on how noisy the incoming training examples are, even when there is no concept drift. For example, if the ensemble has an accuracy of 70% and there is no concept drift, it is likely that three new base learners will be added to the ensemble at every 10 time steps. As these new base learners have to start learning the current concept from scratch, they will be less accurate than the previously existing base learners, unnecessarily hindering the performance of the ensemble as a whole during periods of stability and making AddExp sensitive to noise. DWM is able to reduce this problem by allowing $p > 1$. For regression, whenever a new training example becomes available, weights are multiplied by $\beta^{|\hat{y}-y|}$, where $0 \leq \beta < 1$, $\hat{y}$ is the prediction given by the corresponding base model and y is the actual value. New models are inserted in the ensemble whenever its absolute error on the current training example is higher than a certain threshold τ.

Another approach is diversity for dealing with drifts (DDD) [323]. DDD is an ensemble learning approach for dealing with concept drift in online classification tasks based on drift detection methods, e.g., [18]. During stable periods of time, DDD maintains two ensembles: an ensemble with low diversity and an ensemble with a very high level of diversity. Please refer to Section 20.1 for an explanation of ensemble diversity. During stable periods, the low-diversity ensemble is likely to be more accurate, because too much diversity hinders performance. So, only the low-diversity ensemble is used for predictions, even though the two ensembles perform learning. When a drift is detected, DDD reacts to adapt to the new concept by combining different strategies that are likely to be beneficial for different types of concept drift. When the concept drift causes very quick and drastic changes, then the best strategy is to reset the system and start learning the new concept from scratch. When the concept drift causes slow changes or changes that are not very drastic, then the best strategy is to use ensembles trained on the old concept with very high diversity. These ensembles are able to adapt faster to the new concept as long as low diversity is enforced after the drift commences. When there are false positive drift detections, then the best strategy is to keep using the low-diversity ensemble trained on the current concept. DDD is able to emphasize the best strategy by associating weights to their corresponding ensembles. These weights are proportional to the accuracy of the ensembles calculated based on the training examples received since the drift detection. The prediction given by DDD after a drift detection is the weighted majority vote of the predictions given by each ensemble.

21.3 FORMULATION OF THE PROBLEM

We formulate SEE as an online learning problem in which a new project implemented *by a single company* is received as a training example at each time step, forming a WC data stream. Differently from typical online data stream problems [334], even though new projects arrive with time, the volume of incoming data is small. So, there are no tight space or time constraints. For instance, it is acceptable for a new model to be created from scratch whenever a new training project becomes available. Considering SEE's nature, it is likely that concept drifts occur. This assumption is shown to be correct in Section 21.5.2.1.

We consider that there is a preexisting set (or sets) of CC data. So, time steps are only counted for the WC data stream, not for the CC data. The use of fixed CC data sets does not make our study unrealistic. As we will show in Section 21.5.2, fixed CC data sets do not become less and less useful with time. In fact, even after some periods of time when they are not useful, they can still become very useful later. This shows that CC data sets can be useful for extended periods of time. Moreover, a certain company may not actually have access to ever-growing numbers of CC projects, or may have access to CC data that grow very slowly. For instance, several CC data sets used in SEE studies (e.g., Cocomo 81 [300]) have had their size unchanged for many years. Having access to a continuously growing CC data set could imply the company having contracts with other companies to be able to access such data. These contracts may not be so easy to set up. Our approach can be extended to incoming CC data and we leave the investigation of incoming CC data as future work.

We assume that companies other than the single company being estimated may represent different concepts. This is a reasonable assumption, as it is widely accepted that different companies are heterogeneous. The experiments shown in Section 21.5.2.2 indicate that they indeed represent different concepts.

At each time step, after the model is updated with the new training project, the next 10 projects of the WC data stream are estimated. The number of WC projects for which up-to-date estimations should be provided at each time step depends on the needs of the company being estimated. Investigation of values different than 10 is left as future work.

21.4 DATABASES

Five different databases were used: ISBSG2000, ISBSG2001, ISBSG, CocNasaCoc81, and Kitchen-Max. These include both databases derived from the International Software Benchmarking Standards Group (ISBSG) Repository [271] and the PRedictOr Models In Software Engineering Software (PROMISE) Repository [300]. Each database uses projects from a particular company as the WC data stream, and projects from other companies to comprise CC data sets. The term CC is used from this point onward to identify only projects from other companies, excluding projects from the single company.

21.4.1 ISBSG DATABASES

Three SEE databases were derived from ISBSG Release 10, which contains software project information from several companies. The data were preprocessed, maintaining only projects with

- Data and function points quality A (assessed as being sound with nothing being identified that might affect their integrity) or B (appears sound but there are some factors that could affect their integrity).
- Recorded effort that considers only development team.
- Normalized effort equal to total recorded effort, meaning that the reported effort is the actual effort across the whole life cycle.
- Functional sizing method IFPUG version 4+ or identified as with addendum to existing standards.

The preprocessing resulted in 187 projects from a single company (WC) and 826 projects from other companies (CC). Three different databases were then created:

- ISBSG2000—119 WC projects implemented after the year 2000 and 168 CC projects implemented up to the end of year 2000.

- ISBSG2001—69 WC projects implemented after the year 2001 and 224 CC projects implemented up to the end of year 2001.
- ISBSG—no date restriction to the 187 WC and 826 CC projects, meaning that CC projects with an implementation date more recent than WC projects are allowed. This database can be used to simulate the case in which it is known that other companies can be more evolved than the single company analyzed.

Four input features (development type, language type, development platform and functional size) and one target output (software effort in person-hours) were used. The 1-nearest neighbors imputation method [66] was used for dealing with missing features for WC and CC data separately.

The approach DCL proposed in this paper further uses a separation of CC projects into subsets. This was done according to their normalized level 1 productivity rate provided by the repository. The separation was based on the distribution of productivity. A representative example of productivity and its skewness is shown in Figure 21.1. The ranges used for creating the subsets are shown in Table 21.1 and were chosen to provide similar size partitions. This process could be easily automated in practice.

21.4.2 CocNasaCoc81

Cocomo Nasa and Cocomo 81 are two software effort estimation data sets available from the PROMISE Repository. Cocomo Nasa contains 60 Nasa projects from the 1980s to the 1990s, and Cocomo 81 consists of the 63 projects analyzed by Boehm to develop the software cost estimation model COCOMO [34] first published in 1981. Both data sets contain 16 input features (15 cost drivers [34] and number of lines of code) and one target output (software effort in person-months). Cocomo 81 contains an additional input feature (development type) not present in Cocomo Nasa, which was thus removed. These data sets contain no feature values missing.

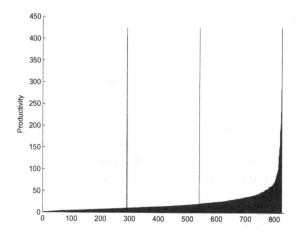

FIGURE 21.1

Sorted productivity for ISBSG CC projects. The vertical black lines represent the ranges used to separate the projects into subsets. From [322].

Table 21.1 Productivity Ranges for CC Data Sets

CC Data	Productivity Band	# Examples
ISBSG2000	High: [0.00, 5.00]	56
	Medium: (5.00, 13.00]	57
	Low: (13.0, 155.70]	55
ISBSG2001	High: [0.00, 6.00]	72
	Medium: (6.00, 14.00]	79
	Low: (14.00, 155.70]	73
ISBSG	High: [0.00, 10.00]	291
	Medium: (10.00, 20.00]	250
	Low: (20.00, 424.90]	285
Cocomo 81	High: [0.7, 2.85]	19
	Medium: (2.85, 6.60]	20
	Low: (6.60, 49.00]	24
Maxwell	High: [3.85, 7.40]	17
	Medium: (7.40, 15.30]	24
	Low: (15.30, 38.00]	21

Cocomo Nasa's projects were considered as the WC data and Cocomo 81's projects were considered as the CC data. The data sets provide no information on whether the projects were sorted in chronological order. The original order of the Cocomo Nasa projects was preserved in order to simulate the WC data stream. Even though this may not be the true chronological order, it is still useful to evaluate whether approaches are able to make use of CC data when/if they are beneficial. In order to create different CC data sets for DCL, Cocomo 81's projects were split based on the productivity in terms of effort divided by the number of lines of code using the ranges in Table 21.1. The productivity values are skewed, similarly to ISBSG's.

21.4.3 KITCHENMAX

The database KitchenMax is composed of Kitchenham and Maxwell, which are two SEE data sets available from the PROMISE Repository. Kitchenham's detailed description can be found in [214]. It comprises 145 maintenance and development projects undertaken between 1994 and 1998 by a single software development company. Maxwell's detailed description can be found in [384]. It contains 62 projects from one of the biggest commercial banks in Finland, covering the years 1985 to 1993 and both in-house and outsourced development. In order to make these data sets compatible, a single input feature (functional size) was used. Still, Maxwell uses functional size, whereas Kitchenham uses adjusted functional size. An appropriate dynamic adaptive approach should be able to identify if one of these data sets would still be useful for predicting projects of the other despite this problem. There were no functional size feature values missing. The target is the effort in person-hours.

Kitchenham was considered as the WC data, and was sorted according to the actual start date plus the duration. This sorting corresponds to the exact completion order of the projects. Maxwell was

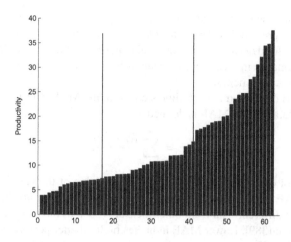

FIGURE 21.2

Sorted productivity for Maxwell CC projects. The vertical black lines represent the ranges used to separate the projects into subsets.

considered as the CC data and was split into three CC sets according to their productivity in terms of effort divided by functional size. The ranges used for the different CC sets are shown in Table 21.1 and were chosen to provide similar size partitions. Maxwell's productivity values are not as skewed as ISBSG's (see Figure 21.2).

21.5 POTENTIAL BENEFIT OF CC DATA

This section presents an analysis that reveals the potential benefit of CC data and answers RQ1. The analysis performed with ISBSG2000, ISBSG2001, ISBSG and CocNasaCoc81 has been presented in [322], whereas the analysis using KitchenMax is new to this book. Sections 21.5.1, 21.5.2 present the experimental setup and analysis.

21.5.1 EXPERIMENTAL SETUP

Regression trees (RTs) were used as the data models in the experiments. They were chosen because they are local approaches where estimations are based on the projects most similar to the project being predicted. This can help dealing with the heterogeneity within each data set, as explained in Chapter 20. They also achieve good performance for SEE in comparison to several other approaches [321]. The REPTree implementation from Weka [156] was used in two ways:

- A CC-RT was trained offline on each CC data set. After that, at each time step, each RT was used to predict the next 10 projects of the WC data stream.
- WC-RTs were created to reflect online learning. At each time step, the current RT was discarded and a new RT was trained on all projects so far (including the one received at the current time step). This RT was then used to predict the next 10 projects of the WC data stream.

The CC-RTs were not used for learning projects of the single company because, as explained in Section 21.3, they may represent different concepts. Moreover, this allows us to use the performance obtained by each CC-RT for determining its potential benefit over the current WC-RT. If a certain CC-RT obtains better performance in a certain time step, it is potentially beneficial at this time step. If its performance is worse, it is detrimental.

The performance was calculated at each time step using the MAE over the predictions on the next 10 projects of the WC data stream. MAE is defined as

$$MAE = \sum_{1}^{n} \frac{|y_i - \hat{y}_i|}{n},$$

where n is the number of cases considered, y_i is the actual value of the variable being predicted, and $\hat{y}_i$ is its estimation. MAE was chosen for being a symmetric measure not biased toward under- or overestimates, making it different than from other measures such as the magnitude of the relative error (MRE) and the Z-measure [389]. Lower MAE indicates higher/better performance.

The parameters for the RTs were minimum total weight of 1 for the instances in a leaf, and minimum proportion of the variance on all the data that need to be present at a node in order for splitting to be performed 0.0001. These parameters were the most likely to produce good results in [321]. A single execution was performed for each database, as we used deterministic RTs. The databases used in the study were the ones presented in Section 21.4.

21.5.2 ANALYSIS

Figure 21.3 shows the MAE for each RT at each time step. Sections 21.5.2.1 and 21.5.2.3 present interesting findings that reveal the potential benefit of CC data sets in SEE.

21.5.2.1 Concept drift in SEE

The first point to be analyzed regard the existence of concept drift in SEE. The databases ISBSG2000, ISBSG2001, ISBSG, and KitchenMax (Figure 21.3a, b, c and e) use the WC data stream in true chronological order, being the most relevant databases for this part of the analysis. We can see from the graphs that the WC-RT does not present a general trend of always reducing its MAE. There are frequently periods in which the MAE increases before starting to decrease again. This is a strong indication of concept drift. CocNasaCoc81 uses the original order of the Cocomo Nasa data set to simulate chronological order. The sudden changes in MAE (both increasing and decreasing MAE) suggest that Cocomo Nasa is likely to contain approximately one drift at every fourth of the projects.

We can also observe that concept drifts in SEE have a key difference in comparison to the concept drifts usually tackled by the ML literature. Those approaches are designed to deal with data streams where input data arrive at very high rates, enough to cause storage and processing issues [18, 334]. In SEE, the incoming rate is typically very low. For instance, ISBSG2000 shows that in a period of around two and a half years, only 119 projects were made available for the single company analyzed. As a consequence, each different concept associated with the single company is likely to be active for very few projects. For example, the concept likely to be active from time steps 1-15 in ISBSG2001 is associated with only 15 WC projects. A new model trained using solely these projects would be likely to perform poorly. So, certain existing concept drift approaches to learn the WC data may be somewhat helpful, but unlikely to provide very good results, especially if they reset the system to deal with certain types of concept drift.

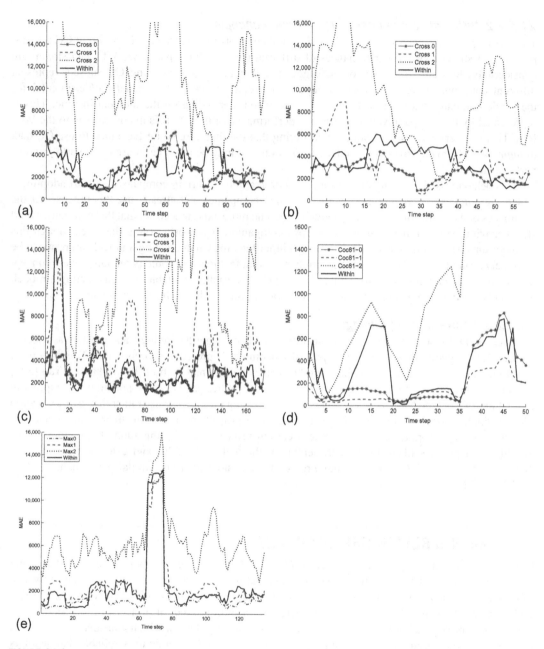

FIGURE 21.3

Performance of offline CC and online WC-RTs for each database in terms of MAE. Some RTs obtain very high MAE, but the limit of the y-axis was not increased to avoid hindering visualization of the better performing RTs. (a) ISBSG2000, from [322]; (b) ISBSG2001, from [322]; (c) ISBSG, from [322]; (d) CocNasaCoc81, adapted from [322]; (e) KitchenMax.

21.5.2.2 Different sets representing different concepts

The second point to be analyzed regard the different concepts represented by the different CC subsets. Figure 21.3 shows that the performances of different CC-RTs for a particular WC data stream are considerably different from each other, suggesting that their corresponding CC subsets represent different concepts. Moreover, these concepts can become more or less beneficial/detrimental for the single company whose projects are being estimated, depending on the moment in time. This is represented by the comparatively better/worse performance of the CC-RTs in comparison to the WC-RTs. This is a very interesting finding, considering that the literature so far has failed to use CC data to *improve* performance over WC models. It shows that it may be possible to use CC data to *improve* performance.

This behavior is also intuitively reasonable. For example, a certain company may start adopting a new design process, becoming more similar to other companies that already use this process. Or the employees of a certain company may gradually become more experienced, so that this company would start behaving more similar to more productive companies. It is worth noting that even though this behavior matches intuition, capturing it through input features when creating a model can prove to be extremely difficult. The reason is that the number of input features that could potentially reveal concept drift is too large in comparison to the number of projects usually available for constructing a model. So, simply adding more features to the model is not a feasible solution for this problem.

21.5.2.3 CocNasaCoc81 findings

The last point to be observed in this section's analysis regards findings about CocNasaCoc81. Figure 21.3d suggests that even though part of Cocomo 81's projects (subsets 1 and 2) is beneficial for estimating Cocomo Nasa's projects, another part is detrimental (subset 0). Minku and Yao [322] further reveal that the set of all Cocomo 81's projects together has very low potential for improving estimations of Cocomo Nasa's projects. This is an interesting finding because rather than using Cocomo 81 as a single data set, it may be worthier to separate projects according to their features and use only the most appropriate ones to estimate a certain project. This finding supports previous works that filter out projects likely to be detrimental for the SEE [129, 220] and extends them to show that using the "correct" CC projects may provide better, rather than just similar performance to WC models in SEE.

21.6 MAKING BETTER USE OF CC DATA

Considering the analysis presented in Section 21.5.2, a dynamic adaptive approach able to detect and successfully use CC data when they become beneficial is desirable and would provide an answer to RQ2. This approach should consider the fact that CC data may belong to different concepts, and that each concept of the WC data stream may be active for a short number of projects. In this section, we present an approach called Dynamic Cross-company Learning (DCL), which considers these issues. DCL is based on a preliminary general purpose algorithm called dynamic un + reliable data learners (DUR) [324], but it uses a filtering mechanism and a new dynamic weighting scheme which makes it more suitable for SEE and allows it to obtain better results than DUR in this domain [322].

DCL is inspired by the fact that models performing poorly at a certain moment may become beneficial in the event of concept drift [320, 323]. So, it uses a fixed size memory of m models trained on preexisting available CC data and one model specifically for WC data stream learning. The CC models are never trained with projects from the single company. Each model is associated with a weight representing how useful it currently is, similar to [236, 237]. These weights are dynamically updated and allow DCL to emphasize estimations given by CC data models when they are useful.

DCL's estimations are based on the weighted average of the base models' estimations. However, the use of CC models is restricted/filtered. If the project to be estimated is "too different" from the projects used to build a CC model, this model is filtered out, i.e., is not allowed to contribute to the weighted average for estimating this project. Filtering out CC data for localization has shown to be useful for SEE [220].

The method to filter CC models out in DCL is as follows. The input feature project size is used to define whether a certain project is "too different" from the projects used to build a CC model. This feature was chosen for being likely to have the highest impact on the estimations and can be, for example, the functional size or the number of lines of code. In the absence of project size, another feature likely to be highly influential could be used. A CC model is then used for estimating a certain project only if the size of this project is lower than the quantile Q of the size of the training projects used to build this model, where Q is a predefined parameter. CC models that do not satisfy this requirement are filtered out of the estimation of this project, but are kept in the system so that they can possibly contribute to the estimation of other projects in the future. As the WC model is likely to be poor and unstable in the beginning of its life due to the small number of WC training projects, CC models only start being filtered out after a considerable number of WC projects have been presented (time step $> T_{start}$).

The separation of preexisting CC data into m different sets is based on some a priori knowledge. For example, a set can be created for each different company, or different sets can be created based on different ranges of a certain input feature or target output. Separation based on ranges can be particularly useful and easily automated. An example of ranges separation is the productivity-based separation shown in Section 21.5.2. The reason for the usefulness of productivity-based separation is that different productivity ranges simulate different possible concepts. When a concept drift happens, an organization may become more or less productive, and CC models built using different productivity ranges could become more or less beneficial. Note that productivity is based on the effort. So, we cannot use the productivity of the project being estimated to decide what CC models are likely to be more beneficial for this project. Instead, DCL uses weights updated through its learning algorithm whenever a new WC project is completed in order to determine what base models are likely to be more or less beneficial at each time step.

Algorithm 4 presents the learning algorithm. Learning is divided into two stages: offline learning based on preexisting CC training data and online learning based on WC training data stream. In the first stage, one base model is created to learn each CC data set in an offline way (line 3). As future work, the case in which CC data are also incoming will be investigated. Weights associated with CC models are initialized to $1/m$ (line 4). Weights associated with WC models are initialized to zero (line 6), so that DCL can be used for predictions before WC training projects become available.

The second stage of the learning is lifelong and one WC training project from the stream is received at each iteration, which corresponds to one time step. Each WC project is used for (1) weight update and (2) training the WC model. The WC model's training is done at the end of the iteration (line 17). It consists of using the incoming training project to train the WC model using its own learning algorithm, which may or may not need retraining on the previous projects.

ALGORITHM 4 DCL [322]

Parameters:

$D_c, 1 \leq c \leq m$: CC data sets.

β_c, β_w: factors for decreasing model weights $0 \leq \beta_c, \beta_w < 1$

1: {CC data learning:}
2: **for** each CC data set $D_c, 1 \leq c \leq m$ **do**
3:     Create CC model L_c using D_c
4:     $w_c = 1/m$ {Initialize weight.}
5: **end for**
6: $w_{m+1} = 0$ {WC model weight.}
7: {WC data learning:}
8: **for** each new WC training project $p = (\vec{x}, y)$ **do**
9:     $winner = \text{argmin}_{i,1 \leq i \leq m+1} |L_i(\vec{x}) - y|$
10:    **for** $loser, 1 \leq loser \leq m + 1 \wedge loser \neq winner$ **do**
11:        $w_{loser} = \beta w_{loser}$, where $\beta = \beta_c$ if $loser <= m$ and $\beta = \beta_w$ otherwise.
12:    **end for**
13:    **if** p is the first WC training project **then**
14:        $w_{m+1} = \frac{1}{m+1}$
15:    **end if**
16:    Divide each weight by the sum of all weights
17:    Use WC model L_{m+1} to learn p
18: **end for**

The weight update rule is shown in lines 9-16. Each base model is used to perform an estimation for the incoming training project. The model with the lowest absolute error estimate is considered to be the winner (line 9). This can be either the WC or a CC model. The weight associated to all the loser models is multiplied by β, $0 \leq \beta < 1$, where $\beta = \beta_c$ for the CC models and $\beta = \beta_w$ for the WC model. Lower/higher β values cause the system to quickly/slowly reduce its emphasis on models that are providing wrong estimations. The ideal values for β depend on the problem, but the median value of $\beta_c = \beta_w = 0.5$ can be used as a default value. The initial weight for the WC model is $1/(m + 1)$ (line 14). After all weights are updated, they are divided by the sum of all weights (line 16).

21.7 EXPERIMENTAL ANALYSIS

This section completes the answer to RQ2, presenting the experiments and analysis done to validate DCL. We also present an analysis on whether an existing approach prepared for dealing with concept drifts is able to improve performance for SEE in comparison to an approach not prepared for dealing with drifts. Sections 21.7.1, 21.7.2 explain the experimental setup and analysis, respectively. The experiments performed with ISBSG2000, ISBSG2001, and ISBSG have been used in [322]. The experiments involving the chronological order of Cocomo 81 in CocNasaCoc81 are new to this book, as well as the experiments with KitchenMax. All statistical tests and analyzes involving these data sets have been redone. Sections 21.5.1, 21.5.2 present the experimental setup and analysis.

21.7.1 EXPERIMENTAL SETUP

DCL and the following approaches were compared:

*   RT trained on the WC data stream as in Section 21.5.1. RT was used as a baseline approach to represent WC models not prepared for concept drift. As explained in Section 21.7.1, RTs have shown to produce comparatively good performance for SEE [321].
*   DWM trained on WC data stream (WC-DWM). WC-DWM was used to represent a concept drift handling approach from the ML literature [237]. It is included in the analysis to check whether it would be able to improve SEE performance in comparison to an approach not prepared for concept drift (RT).
*   DWM first trained using the CC data as a stream and then trained on the WC data stream (CC-DWM). CC-DWM was used to verify whether using an existing concept drift approach to learn CC data would be enough to improve performance over WC models.

The base models used by DCL, WC-DWM, and CC-DWM were RTs using Weka's [156] REPTree implementation. The weight update rule used in WC-DWM and CC-DWM was the same as the one used in DCL, to provide a fair comparison and allow for regression tasks. A new base model is added to the DWM ensemble if its estimation on the current training project has absolute error higher than τ in a time step multiple of p. Existing base models with weight $< \theta$ are deleted also in time steps multiple of p.

The performance was measured in terms of MAE over the predictions on the next 10 projects of the WC data stream. Additionally, the overall MAE across time steps was used to provide interpretable results in terms of the magnitude of the performance based on standardized accuracy (SA) and effect size Δ [389]. SA is defined as

$$SA = \left(1 - \frac{MAE_L}{\overline{MAE_R}} \right) \times 100,$$

where L is the approach being evaluated, MAE_L is the MAE of this approach, and $\overline{MAE_R}$ is the MAE of a large number, typically 1000, of runs of random guessing. Here, we used 1000 runs of random guessing (rguess), defined as follows. The estimated effort for a certain WC project predicted in a time step t is the effort of a WC project p_i, $1 \leq i < t$ sampled uniformly at random. SA is viewed as the ratio of how much better L is than random guessing.

The effect size Δ_C of an approach against the control approach C in terms of MAE is defined as

$$\Delta_C = \frac{MAE_C - MAE_L}{S_C},$$

where MAE_C and S_C are the MAE and the sample standard deviation of the control approach. As suggested by Shepperd and McDonell [389], we interpret the absolute value of the effect size, which is standardized (i.e., scale-free), in terms of the categories proposed by Cohen [80]: small (≈ 0.2), medium (≈ 0.5), and large (≈ 0.8). So, the effect size can be used to explain how large the difference in MAE between an approach and a control approach is, and thus give insight into how large the impact of this difference is likely to be in practice.

The parameters used for DCL were the default values of $\beta_r = \beta_u = 0.5$, $T_{start} = 15$ and $Q = 0.9$. The parameters of the RTs for all approaches were the same as in Section 21.5. Seven different combinations of parameters were used for WC-DWM and CC-DWM: the default values of $\beta = 0.5$,

$p = 1$ and $\theta = 0.01$, and all the combinations obtained by fixing two parameters to their default values and varying the remaining parameter using: $\beta \in \{0.3, 0.7\}$; $p \in \{10, 50\}$ for the larger databases ISBSG2000 and ISBSG, and $p \in \{10, 15\}$ for the other databases; and $\theta \in \{0.001, 0.1\}$. The best performing parameters combination for each database was used in the analysis, representing the best possible behavior achievable by WC-DWM and CC-DWM considering these combinations. The parameter τ was set to $0.25y$, where y is the actual effort of the training project. We chose this value because effort estimations are frequently considered acceptable when they are within 25% of the actual effort [81, 94], and choosing a value independent of the magnitude would be very difficult in practice. The need for setting τ is a disadvantage of applying this approach for regression.

The analysis presented in Section 21.7.2 is based on a single run for each database and approach, as these approaches are deterministic when using the deterministic RTs from this study and the projects should be presented in a specific order to them.

21.7.2 ANALYSIS

21.7.2.1 Performance in comparison to random guess

As it is irrelevant to compare approaches that perform worse than random guess against each other, we initially analyze the approaches against random guess. Table 21.2 presents the overall performance across time steps in terms of MAE and SA, as well as the effect size Δ_{rguess}.

We first determine the statistical significance of each approach's overall MAE across time steps in comparison to random guess. Wilcoxon rank sum tests using Holm-Bonferroni corrections considering all databases and approaches at the overall level of significance of 0.05 were used for this purpose. The tests show that the overall MAE of all approaches is statistically significantly different from random guess.

Then, we verify the effect size Δ_{rguess} of this difference in performance. RT and WC-DWM have effect size varying from medium to large. DCL's and CC-DWM's effect sizes are always higher than RT's and WC-DWM's, demonstrating a better behavior. In particular, for all databases but KitchenMax, DCL's and CC-DWM's effect sizes were very high.

Finally, we check the SAs. We can see from Table 21.2 that the statistical tests and effect sizes are reflected on this performance measure. The SAs show considerably better performance than random guess in most cases, considering the SEE context and the difficultly of this task. RT and WC-DWM presented low SA for ISBSG2001, representing a clear need for improvement in this case.

The conclusions of this replicated analysis are the same as the ones obtained by Minku and Yao [322].

21.7.2.2 Overall performance across time steps

Section 21.5.2 showed that CC data can be beneficial to SEE. The current section checks whether DCL is successful in improving overall SEE performance when using CC models that can be useful for some periods of time. As recommended by Demšar [96], the Friedman statistical test was used for comparison of multiple models over multiple data sets. The measure compared was the overall MAE across time steps. The test detected statistically significant difference among the overall MAE of the approaches at the level of significance of 0.05 ($F_F = 27.25 > F(3, 12) = 3.49$, p-value < 0.0001). The ranking of

Table 21.2 Overall Performance Average Across Time Steps

Data Set	RT	WC-DWM	CC-DWM	DCL
MAE ± Std Dev.				
ISBSG2000	2753.40 ± 1257.50	2862.50 ± 1256.80	2566.00 ± 1045.20	2352.60 ± 925.84
ISBSG2001	3622.00 ± 1368.00	3279.80 ± 1025.90	2934.10 ± 890.39	2873.10 ± 1235.90
ISBSG	3253.90 ± 2476.10	3160.90 ± 2508.50	3037.10 ± 2105.20	2805.60 ± 1468.20
CocNasaCoc81	319.46 ± 250.23	300.24 ± 278.23	179.77 ± 115.71	205.83 ± 214.70
KitchenMax	2441.02 ± 2838.24	2190.70 ± 2918.90	2105.54 ± 2673.11	1992.45 ± 2861.40
SA				
ISBSG2000	37.05	34.55	41.33	46.21
ISBSG2001	11.93	20.25	28.65	30.14
ISBSG	46.29	47.82	49.87	53.69
CocNasaCoc81	33.14	37.16	62.37	56.92
KitchenMax	30.19	37.34	39.77	43.01
Δ_{rguess}				
ISBSG2000	2.57	2.40	2.87	3.21
ISBSG2001	0.96	1.63	2.31	2.43
ISBSG	1.34	1.38	1.44	1.55
CocNasaCoc81	0.57	0.63	1.07	0.97
KitchenMax	0.36	0.45	0.48	0.52

Notes: *Cells in light gray represent the best values. All approaches' MAEs are statistically significantly different from random guess according to Wilcoxon tests using Holm-Bonferroni corrections at the overall level of significance of 0.05. Part of the results are from [322], as explained in the beginning of the chapter.*

approaches obtained from the test is shown in Table 21.3. DCL was ranked first (lowest/best MAE) and CC-DWM was ranked second for all data sets but CocNasaCoc81. WC-DWM was ranked third and RT was ranked fourth for all data sets but ISBSG2000.

The only data set for which the ranking of another approach (CC-DWM) was better than DCL's was CocNasaCoc81. It is worth noting that CC-DWM's parameters were fine tuned in these experiments, whereas DCL is using its default parameters. When DCL's parameters are tuned, it is able to successfully achieve better ranking for this data set too. For instance, a single parameter change to cause DCL not to use filtering leads DCL to obtain MAE of 142.31 for CocNasaCoc81.

Average ranks by themselves provide a fair comparison of the approaches [96]. However, it is worth performing post hoc tests to compare all approaches against our control approach RT. The z- and p-values of the post hoc tests [96] are shown in Table 21.3. The tests over multiple data sets reveal that DCL's and CC-DWM's overall MAE are statistically significantly different from RT's,

Table 21.3 Ranking Average and Standard Deviation of Approaches Across Data Sets Based on the Overall MAE; and z- and p-Values of the Post Hoc Tests for Comparison of Each Approach Against RT

Approach	Rank Avg.	Rank Std	z	p-Value
DCL	$1.2 \approx 1$	0.45	3.1843	0.0015
CC-DWM	$1.8 \approx 2$	0.45	2.4495	0.0143
WC-DWM	$3.2 \approx 3$	0.45	0.7348	0.4624
RT	$3.8 \approx 4$	0.45	–	–

Notes: *The p-value in light gray represents statistically significant difference in the overall MAE using Holm-Bonferroni corrections at the overall level of significance of 0.05. For each data set, smaller ranking represents better overall MAE.*

but WC-DWM's is not. A further comparison between DCL and CC-DWM on each data set using Wilcoxon with Holm-Bonferroni corrections considering the five data sets shows that DCL was better in two data sets (ISBSG2000 and KitchenMax) and similar in three data sets (ISBSG, ISBSG2001 and CocNasaCoc81). These results suggest that the concept drift handling WC-DWM decreases the overall MAE slightly, CC-DWM is able to use the CC data to decrease it a bit further, and DCL can decrease it even further in some cases. Moreover, using DCL with tuned parameters could provide even better results. So, it is worth investigating DCL further.

Table 21.4 shows the effect size of each approach against RT. WC-DWM's Δ_{RT} was always small. CC-DWM's was always larger than WC-DWM's, being medium for two data sets. DCL's was larger than CC-DWM's in most cases, also being medium for two data sets. It is worth noting that this is the effect size across time steps. When considering different time periods separately, the effect sizes can be

Table 21.4 Effect Sizes Δ_{RT} for Each Approach

Data Set	WC-DWM	CC-DWM	DCL
ISBSG2000	−0.09	0.15	0.32
ISBSG2001	0.25	0.50	0.55
ISBSG	0.04	0.09	0.18
CocNasaCoc81	0.08	0.56	0.45
KitchenMax	0.09	0.12	0.16

Notes: *Effect sizes that could be considered as medium are in light gray. Part of the results are from [322], as explained in the beginning of the chapter.*

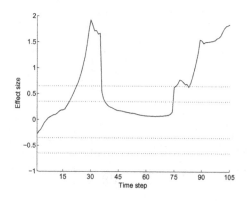

FIGURE 21.4

KitchenMax's effect size based on sliding windows of size 30. The horizontal dotted black lines represent the borders between what is considered a positive or negative small/medium/large effect size.

large. An example of representative behavior of that is shown in Figure 21.4, where KitchenMax's effect sizes are calculated over a sliding window of 30 time steps throughout time. We can see that sometimes the effect size is very small or even small and negative. However, for some prolonged periods of time, the effect size can be very high. Other databases obtained similar behavior, showing that it is worth to use DCL.

In general, the conclusions of this replicated analysis are similar to the ones obtained by Minku and Yao [322], i.e., DCL was able to improve performance in comparison to a corresponding WC model. CC-DWM became a bit more competitive when using the true chronological order of Cocomo 81, winning against DCL in terms of overall MAE on CocNasaCoc81. However, DCL can still win against CC-DWM if its parameters are tuned. In terms of effect size against RT, DCL can obtain from small to large effect size depending on the time period observed.

21.7.2.3 Performance at each time step
As a certain approach can be better at some time steps, but worse at others, it is important to verify the performance at each time step when working with online learning, in addition to the overall performance. This also allows us to verify how much of CC data's potential benefit (Section 21.5) is used by DCL.

Figure 21.5 shows the MAE at each time step for DCL and our control approach RT. There are several periods of around 20 time steps in which DCL outperforms RT. This number of time steps possibly involves several months (or even years) of worse RT estimations, which could have harmful consequences for a company. So, the improvements provided by DCL are considerable in terms of number of time steps.

By comparing Figure 21.5 to Figure 21.3, we can see that DCL managed to use the potential benefit from CC data in several cases. However, even though DCL rarely obtained worse performance than RT throughout the time steps, it still has room for improvement. For example, its MAE was a bit worse during the first 15 time steps for ISBSG2001. The reason for that may be related to the fact that two base models achieved similar performance during this period, but only one of them could be considered the

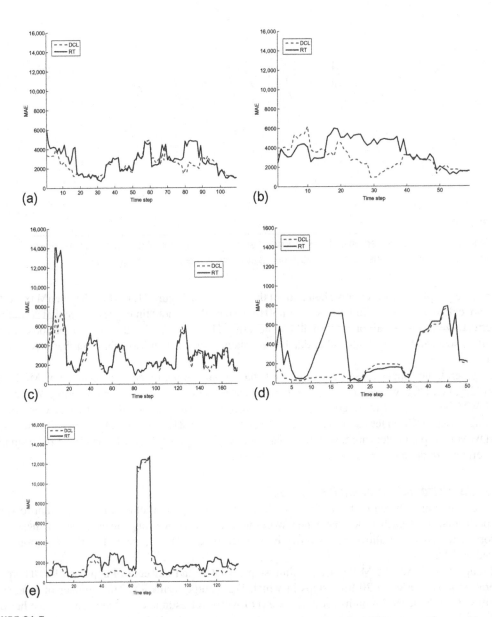

FIGURE 21.5

Performance of RT and DCL for each database in terms of MAE. The number of years represents the period covered by the time steps considering the implementation date of the single-company projects. (a) ISBSG 2000 (≈ 2.5 years), from [322]; (b) ISBSG 2001 (≈ 1.5 year), from [322]; (c) ISBSG (≈ 6.5 years), from [322]; (d) CocNasaCoc81 (≈ 17 years), from [322]; (e) KitchenMax (≈ 4 years).

winner. Allowing more than one winner might improve the results in this case. There were also some periods of time when DCL did not use the full potential of some of its CC subsets. For example, the full potential benefit from the CC subset Coc81 2 was not used in the last 15 time steps for CocNasaCoc81. The reason for that in this particular case was the filtering of CC models, which prevented using them in some cases where they were helpful.

The conclusions of this replicated analysis are the same as the ones obtained by Minku and Yao [322].

21.8 DISCUSSION AND IMPLICATIONS

In order to ensure internal validity [328], this study used several parameter values for WC-DWM and CC-DWM, showing that their worse behavior was not due to a bad parameters choice. RT's parameters were the most likely to produce good results in [321]. The construct validity was first dealt with by using MAE in Section 21.5. This measure is not biased toward under- or overestimations, being adequate for revealing the potential benefit of CC data. DCL was then compared against other approaches based on MAE, SA, and Δ. So, we considered not only the performance, but also the magnitude of the differences in performance and their effect size. Friedman and post hoc tests [96] were also used to show the significance of the differences in MAE. Besides never using a WC project for training before using it for testing, we considered five databases to handle external validity. Four databases with known WC chronological order were used both for revealing concept drift features in SEE and for evaluating approaches. Even though the chronological order is not known for the other database, it can still be used to evaluate whether the approaches are able to make use of CC data when/if they are beneficial, contributing to the generalization of our results.

Our results show that organizations can use CC data to improve SEEs provided by models that use solely WC data. They can acquire CC projects from different sources, e.g., ISBSG. Organizations willing to use an online learning tool based on DCL would need to collect a few features for each of their completed projects (e.g., development type, language type, development platform, and functional size). These must be features that are also provided by the CC database(s) and that can be used as input for DCL's CC models. After the completion of each project, these features together with the effort should be provided as a new training project to DCL, so that it can provide up-to-date estimations. It is worth emphasizing that DCL's potential may go well beyond SEE. Its use to other applications such as software defect prediction should be investigated.

21.9 SUMMARY

This chapter reveals the potential of CC data in comparison to WC data and presents an approach to make use of this potential to improve SEE. It provides answers to the research questions as follows:

RQ1: Under what conditions are CC data potentially beneficial for improving SEE? CC models based on different subsets of CC data can become more or less beneficial/detrimental in comparison to WC models under concept drifting conditions. The particular features of concept drifts induced by SEE tasks were analyzed. Concepts were found to be usually active for a short number of projects, making CC data potentially helpful. Moreover, separating CC data into subsets based on productivity was shown to be potentially more useful than a single set of CC projects.

RQ2: How can this potential benefit be used? A dynamic adaptive approach called DCL was presented to use the potential benefit of CC data for improving SEE. It uses weights to automatically determine when CC models are more or less helpful than a WC model. Each CC model is trained on a subset of CC data, representing different concepts and helping to deal with concept drifts in SEE. DCL was successful in using CC data to improve SEE performance and is able to improve SEE over an existing ML approach for handling drifts and a WC model not prepared for drifts.

The conclusions from the replicated study using the chronological order of Cocomo 81 and replacing the database CocNasaCoc81Nasa93 with KitchenMax are similar to the ones obtained by Minku and Yao [322]. They show that CC data can potentially benefit SEE when considering the online changing nature of this task. DCL was usually successful in recognizing the moments when CC data could lead to improvements in performance over WC models. DCL managed to obtain improvements that varied from small to large effect size in comparison to a WC RT, depending on the time period being observed.

This study shows that the online changing nature of software prediction tasks should be exploited, being an important issue to be considered in the next research frontier on software project estimation. For instance, DCL should be extrapolated and investigated in other software engineering applications, such as software defect prediction. One of the limitations of DCL is that it can only benefit from CC data during the moments in time when they directly match the WC context. Very recently, a study using functions to transform CC models into the WC context has been done, so that CC models can also be useful even when the CC and WC contexts do not match directly [318].

COMPLEXITY: USING ASSEMBLIES OF MULTIPLE MODELS

22

In summary, this chapter proposes the following data analysis pattern:

Name:	COMBA
Also known as:	Ensemble learning.
Intent:	Given access to many effort estimation methods, find the subset that is best suited to use in an ensemble.
Motivation:	Despite decades of work, there is still no consensus on what is the "best" effort estimation method. One reason for this is *ranking instability*; i.e., the same learners studied in different experimental settings are ranked in different ways.
Solution:	Rank and sort N learners. Repeat for multiple experimental conditions. Record the ranking, and the change in ranking, of each learner under different conditions.
Implementation:	When selecting learners, reflect not just on their ranking but the *change* in that ranking across different experimental conditions. Select the learners with the *highest* rank and *lowest* ranking delta.
Applicability:	When applied to 90 effort estimation methods, an ensemble built from the 16 top-ranked learners outperformed nearly all the individual effort estimation methods.
Related to:	Apart from its contribution to ensemble-based learning (on how to select learners for an ensemble), the other main message of COMBA is that there is no "best" single effort estimation method. Rather, there may be many "worst" learners that, once ignored, let us form useful *combinations* of learners.

This chapter is an update and extension to "On the Value of Ensemble Effort Estimation" by E. Kocaguneli, T. Menzies, and Jacky W. Keung, which was published in the *Journal of IEEE Transactions on Software Engineering* in 2012. This chapter is an extended rewrite of the original paper with a strong practitioner focus. Additional paragraphs and notes have been added throughout the chapter in the rewrite. Also, the parts that are not directly relevant to a practitioner audience have been removed during the rewrite. Extensive additional discussions and recommendations to practitioners regarding how to employ the proposed technology in an industry environment are also presented in the current version. Finally, the chapter provides more related work from the recent literature.

Usually we chase silver-bullet solutions, like a learner that would handle all the learning problems we have. Throughout this book, we have observed time and time again that such a silver-bullet learner does not exist. In fact, we have observed quite the opposite: The performance of a learner (hence its rank compared to other learners) change under different circumstances. However, we have also observed that some methods are used more frequently than the others for benchmarking a new learner, e.g., note that k-nearest neighbor (k-NN) as well as classification and regression tree (CART) algorithms are often used for comparing the success of a newly proposed algorithm. In this chapter, we will make use of these facts: No learner performs the best all the time, yet some learners are frequently used due to their relative success in different scenarios. Then, we will propose an interesting use of these facts: Although no single learner is a silverbullet solution, the ensemble of single learners through the right mechanism may come close to a silver-bullet. In the rest of this chapter, we will describe the details of a procedure to form such an ensemble.

Before we continue with the rest of this chapter, let us define some concepts that will help clarify our discussion in the previous paragraph. The rank of a method (r) is bound to change when we change the data set that it is applied to or the error measure under which it is evaluated. We represent the rank change of a method with δr. Also for the rest of the chapter, we refer to two different types of methods: solo methods and multimethods. Solo methods are simply learners augmented with a pre- or postprocessing option. Multimethods are the ensembles, i.e., combination of two or more solo methods.

The fundamental idea of this chapter is the following: Every solo method goes through a certain δr, i.e., the ranking of a method changes when a data set or error measure changes; however, for certain methods (so called *superior* solo methods) the rank change (δr value) is much less than the others and we exploit this fact to combine superior solo methods into multimethods. When the performance of the multimethods are compared to those of the solo methods (as we will see in the results of this chapter), we are able to observe that multimethods are consistently more successful than the solo methods. On the other hand, note that we are promoting the particular combination of solo methods or the solo methods themselves. What a practitioner should take away from this chapter is the process that is followed to come up with the superior multimethods.

The idea of superior multimethods is not completely foreign. Many researchers argue that, in theory, best estimates come from combinations of multiple predictions. For example, Jorgensen advises that, for expert-based estimation, it is best to generate estimates from multiple methods [190]. The machine learning community also shares this optimism regarding multimethods. For example, Seni et al. report that taking the average of the estimates coming from multiple solo methods yield better results than the individual solo methods [383]. Similar conclusions are offered by other researchers in the field of statistics [167] and machine learning [50, 233].

Although there is a considerable support for multimethods, the earlier practical applications in software effort estimation (SEE) has not always been very optimistic [19, 210, 228]. For example, Kocaguneli et al. failed to improve estimation through averaging the predictions of 14 estimators [228]. Similarly, Baker could not improve estimation accuracy through boosting [19]. The natural follow-up question to ask is why the results presented in this chapter of the book differ from prior SEE results. The difference between the prior work and the one presented in this chapter is that the prior work was based on the assumption that all the solo methods were good candidates that should all be included in multimethods. However, as we will see in the results section, only a small subset of all the solo methods are good candidates to be included in a multimethod. Therefore, we recommend the following steps to practitioners willing to make use of ensembles of solo methods:

1. Try a large number of methods among which there are at least some good methods (shown to have a good performance by previous work or by your own previous experiments).
2. Sort the methods using appropriate evaluation methods (e.g., the appropriate methods for SEE are discussed later in this chapter).
3. Discard all but the best solo methods (i.e., discard solo methods with high δr values).
4. Build the ensembles using the remaining solo methods, i.e., use solo methods with low δr values to form multimethods.

22.1 ENSEMBLE OF METHODS

In this section, we will provide a brief overview of what ensemble of methods (solo methods) means and take a look at the related literature. Although the related literature may not be immediately helpful from a practitioner's point of view, this section is a good starting point in terms of the right pointers for digging deeper into the subject of ensembles.

So far in the book we have seen that it is a standard machine learning practice to try multiple methods on the data and pick the best performing one [6]. A considerable number of papers proposing a new estimation technique apply this practice to demonstrate that (say) their preferred new method is superior to those proposed in prior work. *Ensemble learning* builds on the idea that we do not have to pick only one estimation method. Instead, we can build ensembles consisting of multiple predictors, where estimates coming from different learners are combined through particular mechanisms, e.g., voting of individual learner estimates on the final prediction [100].

The main usefulness of ensembles come from the fact that each learner (a stand-alone machine learning algorithm without any pre- or postprocessing step) has its own assumptions, biases, and—hence—restrictions [6]. These assumptions and biases may be best suited to different parts of the training data [6, 100, 219]. In ensembles, solo methods may be arranged in such a way that their biases act complementary to one another, i.e., a method patches errors made by another method.

Ensemble methods are also attracting attention in the SE community. For example, Azhar et al. follow a similar strategy to the one proposed in this chapter of the book [15]. However, they employ the ensemble learning on web project effort estimation (i.e., a different type of data set with different biases). Their results are encouraging in the sense that their findings were also along the findings of the results presented in this chapter: There is no single best solo method, but using superior solo methods can yield to very robust multimethods. The meaning of the results of Azhar et al.'s study is that the technique that is presented in this chapter is repeatable in different scenarios. Another example of the use of ensemble methods is the automated text classification [341]. Noll et al. employed the ensemble methods to analyze unstructured software content data and compared their performance of to that of the human experts. They report that ensembles can be used to discover common categories in unstructured software project data so that the work for human experts is reduced to discovering more complex categories of the data.

In our ensemble setup we want to have solo methods that can complement one another in an ensemble. It is a recommended practice to combine solo methods that have different characteristics [5, 6, 219]. Then the question becomes: "How can we introduce solo methods with different characteristics?" The first way is through different representation of the data. The multimethod structure may be based on unirepresentation (all learners use the same representation of data) or multirepresentation (different learners use different representations) [6]. Examples to such strategies are the use of different feature sets [149, 178] or different training sets [177].

The second way is through architectural methodologies. Bagging (bootstrap aggregating) and boosting are among the most common examples of that approach [6, 458]. In bagging n-many solo methods are independently applied on n-many different training samples, where each training sample is selected via bootstrap sampling [6] with replacement. Boosting, on the other hand, arranges solo methods in a sequential manner: Each solo method pays more attention to the instances on which a previous method was unsuccessful. Among the reported results, boosting is mostly reported to be considerably better than bagging [26, 444, 458], but has trouble in handling noisy data sets [26, 458].

22.2 SOLO METHODS AND MULTIMETHODS

The estimation methods that will be used in this chapter have been applied to software effort data sets. However, they are standard estimation methods that can also be applied to other data sets that present a regression or a classification problem. The estimation methods studied in this chapter fall into two groups: *solo* methods and *multi*methods. *Solo* methods are some combination of a *preprocessing option* and a *learner*. For example, Boehm's preferred effort estimation method uses a log transform (e.g., take the natural logarithm of a feature) as the preprocessing option, then linear regression as the learner [34]. *Multi*methods are combinations of at least two solo methods.

22.2.1 MULTIMETHODS

When combining solo methods into multimethods, the term "combining" refers to bringing together the estimations of the involved solo methods. As one might guess, there are a variety of schemes that were produced to bring together the estimates of solo methods from simple to more complex [5, 6, 219, 290]. Complex combination schemes include bagging [46], boosting [137] or random forests [51, 187]. Simpler methods include computing the mean, median, or inverse-ranked weighted mean (IRWM [290], see Figure 22.1) of estimates coming from n-many solo methods.

In this chapter we aim to observe how multimethods (that are built with only superior solo methods) perform compared to solo methods on effort data sets rather than investigating complex schemes. Therefore, we adopt simple schemes of mean, median, and IRWM. As we will see in the results section of this chapter, the use of only the superior solo methods in the multimethods prove to be a high-performing technique even with simple combination schemes. On the other hand, investigation of more complex combination schemes and their implications may be a good future direction to follow.

22.2.2 NINETY SOLO METHODS

In our experiments, we used 10 different preprocessing options and 9 learners. The combination of 10 preprocessing options and 9 learners results in 10*9=90 solo methods. Below are some details about the learners and preprocessing options used to form the solo methods.

In IRWM, the final estimates from M methods $e_1, e_2, ..., e_m$ that have been ranked $r_1, r_2, ..r_m$ is a weighted sum by the ranks of all methods in the ensemble. The top- and bottom-ranked methods of m methods get a weight of m and 1 (respectively). More generally, a method with rank r_i gets a weight of $m + 1 - r_i$. The final estimate in IRWM is, hence, $\left(\sum_i (m + 1 - r_i) \cdot e_i \right) / \left(\sum_i i \right)$.

FIGURE 22.1

IRWM. Generalized from [290].

22.2.2.1 Preprocessors

The 10 preprocessors used for investigation are

- 3 *simple preprocessors*: **none, norm, and log**;
- 1 *feature synthesis* methods called **PCA**;
- 2 *feature selection* methods: **SFS** (sequential forward selection) and **SWR**;
- 4 *discretization* methods: divided on 3 and 5-bins based on equal frequency and width.

None is just the simplest *option* of avoiding a preprocessor, i.e., all data values are unadjusted.

With the **norm** (max-min) preprocessor, numeric values are normalized to a 0-1 interval using Equation (22.1). Normalization means that no variable has a greater influence than any other. Otherwise, for particular learners (e.g., k-NN, which uses distance calculation) the variables with high numeric values (e.g., lines of code) would dominate over the ones with low numeric values (e.g., cyclomatic complexity).

$$normalizedValue = \frac{(actualValue - min(allValues))}{(max(allValues) - min(allValues))} \qquad (22.1)$$

With the **log** preprocessor, all numerics are replaced with their logarithm (oftentimes natural logarithm is used here). This **logging** procedure minimizes the effects of the occasional very large numeric values.

Principal component analysis [7], or **PCA**, is a *feature synthesis* preprocessor that converts a number of possibly correlated variables into a smaller number of uncorrelated variables called components. The first component accounts for as much of the variability in the data as possible, and each succeeding component accounts for as much of the remaining variability as possible.

Some of the preprocessors aim at finding a subset of all features according to certain criteria such as **SFS** (sequential forward selection) and **SWR** (stepwise regression). **SFS** adds features into an initially empty set until no estimation performance improvement is possible with the addition of another feature. Whenever the selected feature set is enlarged, some oracle is called to assess the value of that set of features. In this study, we used the MATLAB, *objective* function (which reports the mean squared error of a simple linear regression on the training set). One caution to be made here is that exhaustive search algorithms over all features can be very time-consuming (2^n combinations in an n-feature data set); therefore, SFS was designed to work only in the forward direction (no backtracking).

SWR adds and removes features from a multi-linear model. Addition and removal are controlled by the p-value in an F-statistic. At each step, the F-statistics for two models (models with/out one feature) are calculated. Provided that the feature was not in the model, the null hypothesis is: "Feature would have a zero coefficient in the model, when it is added." Having a zero coefficient for a feature means that its addition would have no impact. So, if the null hypothesis can be rejected (i.e., the feature has a certain impact), then the feature is added to the model.

Discretizers are preprocessors that map every numeric value in a column of data into a small number of discrete values (e.g., 1, 2, and 3 in a discretizer with 3 bins):

- **width3bin:** This procedure clumps the data features into 3 bins, depending on equal width of all bins (see Equation (22.2)).

$$binWidth = ceiling\left(\frac{max(allValues) - min(allValues)}{n}\right) \qquad (22.2)$$

- **width5bin:** Same as **width3bin**, but 5 bins instead.

- **freq3bin:** Generates 3 bins of equal population size out of sorted elements.
- **freq5bin:** Same as **freq3bin**, but *5* bins instead.

22.2.2.2 Predictors (learners)

Based on the effort estimation literature, we identified 9 commonly used learners:

- 2 *instance-based* learners: **ABE0-1NN, ABE0-5NN**.
- 2 *iterative dichotomizers*: **CART(yes),CART(no)**.
- 1 *neural net*: **NNet**.
- 4 *regression methods*: **LReg, PCR, PLSR, SWR**.

Instance-based learning can be used for analogy-based estimation (ABE). ABE0 is our name for a very basic type of ABE that we derived from various ABE studies [199, 259, 290]. In **ABE0-*k*NN**, features are first normalized to the 0-1 interval (recall the 0-1 normalization from the previous subsection), then the distance between test and train instances is measured according to Euclidean distance function, *k*-nearest neighbors are chosen from training set, and finally for finding estimated value (a.k.a adaptation procedure) the median of *k*-nearest neighbors is calculated. We explore two different *k*NN:

- **ABE0-1NN:** Only the closest analogy (hence 1NN) is used. Because the median of a single value is itself, the estimated value in **ABE0-1NN** is the actual effort value of the closest analogy.
- **ABE0-5NN:** The 5 closest analogies (hence 5NN) are used for adaptation.

Iterative dichotomizers seek the best attribute value *splitter* that most simplifies the data that fall into the different splits. Each such splitter becomes a root of a subtree. Subtrees are generated by calling iterative dichotomization recursively on each of the splits. The **C**lassification **A**nd **R**egression **T**rees (CART) iterative dichotomizer [48] is defined for continuous target concepts and its *splitters* strive to reduce the GINI index of the data that falls into each split. We use two variants of CART as learners:

- **CART (yes):** This version prunes (gets rid of a subtree) the generated tree using cross-validation. For each cross-validation, an internal node is made into a leaf (thus pruning its subnodes). The subtree that resulted in the lowest error rate is returned.
- **CART (no):** Uses the full tree (no pruning).

In *neural nets*, or **NNet**, an input layer of project details is connected to zero or more "hidden" layers, which then connect to an output node (which yields the final prediction). The connections are weighted be a certain value, so-called weights. If the signal arriving to a node sums to more than some threshold, the node "fires" and a weight is propagated across the network. Learning in a neural net compares the output value to the expected value, then applies some correction method to improve the edge weights (e.g., back propagation). The **NNet** used in this chapter is composed of four layers: input layer, two hidden layers, and an output layer.

We also use 4 *regression methods*. **LReg** is a simple linear regression algorithm. Given the dependent variables, this learner calculates the coefficient estimates of the independent variables. **SWR** is the stepwise regression discussed above. Whereas above, **SWR** was used to select features for other learners, here we use **SWR** as a learner (that is, the predicted value is a regression result using the features selected by the last step of **SWR**). Partial least squares regression (**PLSR**) as well as principal components regression (**PCR**) are algorithms that are used to model independent variables. While modeling, they both construct new independent variables as linear combinations of original ones. However, the ways they construct the new independent variables are different. **PCR** generates new independent variables to explain the observed variability in the actual ones. While generating new variables, the dependent variable is not considered at all. In that respect, **PCR** is similar to selection of *n-many* components via **PCA** (the default value of components to select is 2, so we used it that way) and applying linear regression. **PLSR**, on the other hand, considers the independent variable and picks up the *n-many* of the new components (again with a default value of 2) that yield the lowest error rate. Due to this particular property of **PLSR**, it usually results in a better fitting.

A practitioner should be careful at this point in the chapter so as not to take the presented learners and preprocessing options as absolute. Although the learners and the preprocessing options used here cover a wide range, new methods are being constantly invented (e.g., see [82, 243, 259]). So we make no claim that the 90 methods explored here cover the space of all possible estimators. Hence, we take care *not* to conclude that some particular combination of solo methods is the best. Rather, our conclusions will be that, given a set of models, it is best to rank them and generate multimodel estimators from the top-ranked models.

22.2.3 EXPERIMENTAL CONDITIONS

We are after superior solo methods (the solo methods that have relatively higher and more stable ranking), so we want to set up the experimental conditions in such a way that we cover a wide range of data sets and error measures; hence, more conditions. This point is also highlighted by Shepperd et al. [392] and Menzies et al. [307], who mention the importance of different conditions to evaluate the methods so that the change in experimental conditions is likely to change the ordering of methods. Below are the experimental conditions that are reported to be particularly important for SEE [307, 392]:

1. *Performance measures* that measure a method's performance.
2. *Summary* over multiple data sets and performance measures.
3. *Data sets*.

Although the above methods are considered important for SEE, note that they are fundamentally important for the success of any learner in any domain; i.e., we would want a learner to be successful under different error measures and over multiple relevant data sets. For our experiments, we use seven different error measures that are commonly employed in the SEE domain: MAR, MMRE, MdMRE, MMER, PRED(25), MBRE, and MIBRE. Below is the derivation and explanation of these error measures. The absolute residual (AR) is the absolute difference between the predicted and the actual values of a test instance:

$$AR_i = |x_i - \hat{x}_i| \tag{22.3}$$

where $x_i, \hat{x}_i$ are the actual and predicted value for test instance i, respectively. The summary of AR is taken through the mean of AR, which is known as mean AR (MAR).

The magnitude of relative error measure, a.k.a. MRE, is quite widely used in SEE (and other domains). It is the error ratio between the actual effort and its delta with the predicted effort:

$$MRE_i = \frac{|x_i - \hat{x}_i|}{x_i} = \frac{AR_i}{x_i} \tag{22.4}$$

A related measure is MER (magnitude of error relative to the estimate [133]):

$$MER_i = \frac{|x_i - \hat{x}_i|}{\hat{x}_i} = \frac{AR_i}{\hat{x}_i} \tag{22.5}$$

The overall average error of MRE can be derived as the mean or median magnitude of relative error measure (MMRE and MdMRE, respectively):

$$MMRE = mean(allMRE_i) \tag{22.6}$$

$$MdMRE = median(allMRE_i) \tag{22.7}$$

A common alternative is PRED(25), which is defined as the percentage of successful predictions falling within 25% of the actual values:

$$PRED(25) = \frac{100}{N} \sum_{i=1}^{N} \begin{cases} 1 \text{ if } MRE_i \leq \frac{25}{100}, \\ 0 \text{ otherwise} \end{cases} \tag{22.8}$$

where N is the data set size. For example, PRED(25)=50% implies that half of the estimates fall within 25% of the actual values.

Mean balanced relative error (MBRE) and the mean inverted balanced relative error (MIBRE) are two other performance measures, which are both suggested by Foss et al. [133]:

$$MBRE_i = \frac{|\hat{x}_i - x_i|}{min(\hat{x}_i, x_i)} \tag{22.9}$$

$$MIBRE_i = \frac{|\hat{x}_i - x_i|}{max(\hat{x}_i, x_i)} \tag{22.10}$$

As you can see the, issue of getting a summary out of a number of error measures and a number of data sets can be quite complicated. There are different alternatives for this purpose; however, we will use a simple—yet effective—technique called the win-tie-loss calculation. In this procedure, each of our 90 methods are compared to 89 others using the procedure in Figure 22.2. According to this procedure, we sum the *win, loss, win − loss* values coming from different error measures and data sets. The calculation of the *win, loss, loss* values is as follows:

```
if NonParametricTest(Eᵢ, Eⱼ, 95) says they are the same then
    tieᵢ = tieᵢ + 1;
    tieⱼ = tieⱼ + 1;
else
    if better(Eᵢ, Eⱼ) then
        winᵢ = winᵢ + 1
        lossⱼ = lossⱼ + 1
    else
        winⱼ = winⱼ + 1
        lossᵢ = lossᵢ + 1
    end if
end if
```

FIGURE 22.2

Comparing methods (i,j).

Data Set	Features	Size	Description	Units
cocomo81	17	63	NASA projects	months
cocomo81e	17	28	Cocomo81 embedded projects	months
cocomo81o	17	24	Cocomo81 organic projects	months
cocomo81s	17	11	Cocomo81 semi-detached projects	months
nasa93	17	93	NASA projects	months
nasa93_center_1	17	12	Nasa93 projects from center 1	months
nasa93_center_2	17	37	Nasa93 projects from center 2	months
nasa93_center_5	17	40	Nasa93 projects from center 5	months
desharnais	12	81	Canadian software projects	hours
desharnaisL1	11	46	Projects in Desharnais that are developed with Language1	hours
desharnaisL2	11	25	Projects in Desharnais that are developed with Language2	hours
desharnaisL3	11	10	Projects in Desharnais that are developed with Language3	hours
sdr	22	24	Turkish software projects	months
albrecht	7	24	Projects from IBM	months
finnish	8	38	Software projects developed in Finland	hours
kemerer	7	15	Large business applications	months
maxwell	27	62	Projects from commercial banks in Finland	hours
miyazaki94	8	48	Japanese software projects developed in COBOL	months
telecom	3	18	Maintenance projects for telecom companies	months
china	18	499	Projects from Chinese software companies	hours
		Total: 1198		

FIGURE 22.3

The 1198 projects coming from 20 public data sets. Indentation in column one denotes a data set that is a subset of another data set.

These comparisons can be summarized through:

1. Sum of the number of losses.
2. Sum of the number of wins.
3. Sum of the number of wins−losses (wins minus losses).

The summary through the above three sums means that for a solo method to be highly ranked, it must win a high number of times, it must not lose much against other solo methods, and its win values should be more than its losses. Eventually, we run this analysis over 20 public data sets in Figure 22.3. Note that the results of this chapter are an extensive analysis of different conditions for effort estimation experiments. Given 89 comparisons among solo methods, 7 error measures, and 20 data sets, then each method appears in $89 \times 7 \times 20 = 12,460$ comparisons.

22.3 METHODOLOGY
22.3.1 FOCUS ON SUPERIOR METHODS

Figure 22.4 shows the success of the solo methods through ranking (x-axis) and the variability in that ranking (y-axis). The x-axis of Figure 22.4 shows the ranking of the 90 solo methods, according to number of losses over all 7 error measures and 20 data sets. The most successful methods have the lowest number of total losses, whereas the least successful ones have the highest number of total losses.

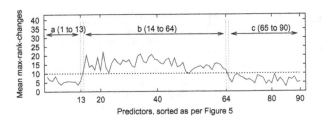

FIGURE 22.4

Methods and the associated rank changes, i.e., δr values. Note the sudden increase in δr values, after $X = 13$. We call methods in the region $1 \leq X \leq 13$ *superior*. From [225].

Then solo methods are ranked on the *x*-axis starting from the best one. Therefore, better methods appear on the left-hand side of that figure (so the top-ranked method appears at position $x = 1$).

The ranking of methods is identified by the *x*-axis of Figure 22.4, whereas the variability in that ranking is given by the *y*-axis. The *y*-axis of Figure 22.4 shows the maximum *changes*, δr, seen for each method as we compare the ranks across number of losses, number of wins, and number of wins-losses.

An inspection of Figure 22.4 shows that the region of maximal δr occurs after $X = 13$. This is an interesting division as the region $1 \leq X \leq 13$ contains methods with high rank and low δr. We call these methods *superior* and the rest *inferior*. The list of top 13 methods are shown in Table 22.1.

The names of the top 13 *superior* solo methods of Figure 22.4 are listed in Table 22.1. When we look at Table 22.1, we see that none of the superior solo methods try to fit one model to all the data:

- The CART regression tree learner appears at ranks 1 through 10 of Table 22.1. Each branch of a regression tree defines one context in which an estimate may be different.
- Analogy-based estimation (ABE) appears at ranks 11,12,13. ABE builds a different model for each test instance (using the test instance's *k*th nearest neighbors).

22.3.2 BRINGING SUPERIOR SOLO METHODS INTO ENSEMBLES

Note that in the previous section, we have identified the top 13 superior solo methods. In this section of the chapter we will bring the estimates of these solo methods together in the form of multimethods. We will use the top *M* solo methods in the sort order of Table 22.1, where $M \in \{2, 4, 8, 13\}$.

The estimate of a multimethod is the combination of the estimates of the solo methods via three ways: mean, median, and inverse-ranked weighted mean (IRWM). With this scheme, we have *4 groups of solo methods (group of top 2 methods, another group of top 4 methods, then a group of top 8 methods and finally the group of top 13 methods) times 3 (mean, median, IRWM) = 12 multimethods*. These multimethods are then ranked alongside the solo methods in the same manner as Figure 22.4. This gives us the comparison of *90 solo methods + 12 multimethods = 102 methods*. Every method is compared to 101 others with respect to 7 error measures and over 20 data sets. Therefore, the maximum number of comparisons for any method now becomes $101 \times 7 \times 20 = 14,140$.

Table 22.1 Ranking of Top 13 *superior* Solo Methods and Related δr Values

Rank	δr	Preprocessing Option	Learner
1	8	norm	CART (yes)
2	6	norm	CART (no)
3	6	none	CART (yes)
4	9	none	CART (no)
5	5	log	CART (yes)
6	4	log	CART (no)
7	5	SWR	CART (yes)
8	6	SWR	CART (no)
9	6	SFS	CART (yes)
10	5	SFS	CART (no)
11	5	SWR	ABE0-1NN
12	4	log	ABE0-1NN
13	5	SWR	ABE0-5NN

These solo methods are combined in various ways to form 12 multimethods.

22.4 RESULTS

Figure 22.5 shows the rank of solo methods as well as multimethods (i.e., a total of 102 methods). Similar to the previous rank versus δr plot (which we used to find the superior solo methods), the *x*-axis of Figure 22.5 ranks the methods according to number of losses and the *y*-axis shows the δr of each method.

Table 22.2 names all the methods, and shows their ranking. We can use that table to interpret Figure 22.5. The first aspect that is worth mentioning is the success of the multimethods, which are built

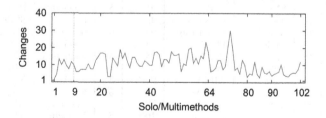

FIGURE 22.5

Rank changes of solo and multimethods together. Note that the region $1 \leq X \leq 9$ contains 9 out of 12 multimethods. Also note that **Top13/lrwm** at $X = 1$ has a δr of 1, which means that it outperforms all other methods with regard to all the error measures and data sets we used in the experimentation. From [225].

Table 22.2 Detailed Preprocessing Option and Learner Combinations with Their Related δr Values

Rank	δr	Pre-proc.	Learner	Rank	δr	Pre-proc.	Learner
1	1	Top13	Irwm	52	17	norm	SWReg
2	4	Top13	Mean	53	6	none	SWReg
3	13	Top13	Median	54	11	freq3bin	ABE0
4	10	Top2	Mean	55	10	width3bin	CART (yes)
5	13	Top4	Mean	56	19	width3bin	CART (no)
6	10	Top2	Median	57	20	PCA	ABE0
7	8	Top4	Median	58	11	PCA	NNet
8	12	Top8	Median	59	14	none	NNet
9	10	Top2	Irwm	60	11	width5bin	SWReg
10	6	Top4	Irwm	61	15	width3bin	ABE0
11	6	norm	CART (yes)	62	14	SWReg	NNet
12	7	norm	CART (no)	63	23	SFS	NNet
13	7	none	CART (yes)	64	18	width5bin	1NN
14	7	none	CART (no)	65	6	SWReg	SLReg
15	11	Top8	Irwm	66	7	none	SLReg
16	8	log	CART (yes)	67	8	norm	PLSR
17	8	log	CART (no)	68	13	width5bin	ABE0
18	12	Top8	Mean	69	13	norm	SLReg
19	15	SWReg	CART (yes)	70	7	freq5bin	1NN
20	17	SWReg	CART (no)	71	9	freq3bin	CART (yes)
21	17	SWReg	1NN	72	20	freq3bin	CART (no)
22	16	SFS	CART (yes)	73	30	PCA	1NN
23	3	SFS	CART (no)	74	20	freq3bin	1NN
24	3	log	1NN	75	7	width3bin	SWReg
25	14	SWReg	ABE0	76	9	log	SWReg
26	12	PCA	PLSR	77	5	width5bin	PLSR
27	9	none	PLSR	78	13	log	PCR
28	19	SWReg	PCR	79	10	log	PLSR
29	14	PCA	PCR	80	3	width3bin	1NN
30	17	none	PCR	81	5	width3bin	PLSR
31	12	SFS	1NN	82	4	width5bin	PCR
32	8	PCA	CART (yes)	83	12	norm	PCR
33	15	PCA	CART (no)	84	5	width3bin	SLReg
34	15	SFS	ABE0	85	3	width3bin	PCR
35	11	norm	1NN	86	9	freq5bin	PCR
36	9	none	1NN	87	6	freq5bin	SWReg
37	9	freq5bin	CART (yes)	88	5	width5bin	SLReg
38	12	freq5bin	CART (no)	89	6	freq3bin	PCR
39	11	freq5bin	ABE0	90	4	freq3bin	PLSR
40	10	SFS	SLReg	91	5	freq5bin	PLSR
41	10	width5bin	CART (yes)	92	5	log	SLReg
42	17	width5bin	CART (no)	93	6	freq3bin	SWReg
43	18	SWReg	PLSR	94	10	freq5bin	SLReg
44	16	SFS	PLSR	95	5	width5bin	NNet
45	9	SFS	PCR	96	4	norm	NNet
46	13	norm	ABE0	97	3	width3bin	NNet
47	13	PCA	SWReg	98	5	log	NNet
48	11	none	ABE0	99	6	freq3bin	NNet
49	18	SWReg	SWReg	100	5	freq5bin	NNet
50	16	log	ABE0	101	7	freq3bin	SLReg
51	16	SFS	SWReg	102	12	PCA	SLReg

*Methods are sorted from the least losing to the most losing. The method with fewest losses is ranked #1, which is **Top13/Mean**. From [225].*

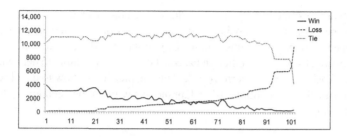

FIGURE 22.6

The sum of win, tie, and loss values for all methods of Figure 22.5. One method is compared to 101 other methods, over 7 error measures, and 20 data sets; hence, the total number of comparisons for a method is $101 \times 7 \times 20 = 14,140$. From [225].

with superior solo methods: The top $X = 9$ methods (marked by a dashed line) are all multimethods. The remaining multiple methods appear at ranks 14,15,18. That is, in the majority case ($\frac{9}{12} = 75\%$), combinations of methods perform better that any solo method. Further, in all cases ($\frac{12}{12} = 100\%$), they are ranked higher than the majority of other methods. The second aspect is the best performing multimethod at $X = 1$, which also has the lowest δr. This method generated estimates using the mean value of 13 top-ranked methods.

Figure 22.6 summarizes the sum of *win*, *tie*, and *loss* values for the multimethods as well as the solo methods. Each method (out of a total of 102 methods) is compared to 101 other methods, over 7 error measures, and 20 data sets. Hence, the maximum value of either of the *win*, *tie*, *loss* statistics can be at most $101 \times 7 \times 20 = 14,140$. Note in Figure 22.6 that except the low-performing methods on the right-hand side, the *tie* values are in the 10,000-12,000 band. Therefore, they would not be so informative as to differentiate the methods, so we consult the *win* and *loss* statistics. There is a considerable difference between the best and the worst methods in terms of *win* and *loss* values (in the extreme case, it is close to 4000).

22.5 SUMMARY

We have seen in this chapter that the result of a solo method will change when experimental conditions such as data set or error measures change. On the other hand, we also saw that some solo methods will be less affected by the change (i.e., the superior solo methods). The fact that some solo methods have less δr values under changing conditions can be utilized for ensembling multimethods. In this chapter, we provided evidence over SEE data sets and error measures that ensembles of superior solo methods can outperform all the solo methods that were utilized to build them. In summary, there are a number of benefits that a practitioner can get by building multimethods in his/her domain in the same manner as we did in this chapter:

- The multimethods outperform the solo methods that were used to form them.
- Multimethods provide higher and more stable ranking in comparison to solo methods.

Software companies operate in a dynamic world, where changes can affect the software prediction tasks. For example, new employees may be hired, training may be provided, new types of projects may start being developed, new programming languages may be introduced, etc. The number of changes that may potentially affect software prediction tasks is large and intractable to deal with explicitly, both in terms of cost and feasibility of the learning task. This chapter shows how to use chronological data in such a way to automatically and continuously adapt models without the need for explicitly or manually informing them of changes.

THE IMPORTANCE OF GOALS IN MODEL-BASED REASONING

23

In summary, this chapter proposes the following data analysis pattern:

Name:	SEESAW
Also known as:	Optimizer, constraint solver.
Intent:	Reasoning about a software process model.
Motivation:	The managers of software projects can make a very large number of decisions about those projects.
Solution:	Exploring all those options is a task better done by automatic methods, if only to whittle down thousands of options to just a few.
Constraints:	Different kinds of projects have different definitions of what is "best."
Implementation:	Rather than hardwire a rigid definition of "best" into our search algorithms, make "best" a domain-specific predicate that can be altered for different contexts.
Applicability:	SEESAW can produce recommendations about how to change a project that are tuned to the particulars of the goals of different projects. Those recommendations are radically different for different goals. Hence, rather than offer some trite "one-size-fits-all" solution for all projects, it is better to reason about the specifics of the local project.
Related to:	SEESAW uses an *aggregation* function to combine N goals into a single optimization goal. The optimizers of Chapter 24 can generate solutions across the *frontier* of best solutions over the space of all aggregation functions.

This chapter is an extension of a paper "Understanding the Value of Software Engineering Technologies" by Phillip Green, Tim Menzies, Steven Williams, and Oussama El-Rawas presented at the 2009 IEEE/ACM International Conference on Automated Software Engineering. This chapter adds extensive notes on the business implications and context of this work.

23.1 INTRODUCTION

This book is about sharing data and sharing models. A premise of share is that sharing is useful; i.e., if I give something to you, then you can look at it and say "yes, I understand." The message of this chapter is that unless we share the same *values*, then it is hard for you to see the value in what is shared. So this chapter is all about *values* and how different values can contort what is considered or useful.

This chapter presents a case study where a software process is explored using different *values*. Prior to work, we had a preexperimental intuition that concepts of *value* might change the organization of a project. However, we suspected that some things would remain constant, such as

- Condoning the use of execution testing tools.
- Encouraging increasing software process maturity.

This turned out *not* to be the case. In the case study for this chapter, for the value functions explored here, if one function approves of X then the other usually approves of *not X*.

This result, that *value can change everything*, should motivate the reader to spend more time on understanding and recording their own values, as well as the values of anyone with which they want to share data or models. This is important as sharing is unlikely between teams that have very different value systems.

23.2 VALUE-BASED MODELING
23.2.1 BIASES AND MODELS

To understand the flow of this chapter, the reader might want to first reread Chapter 3. That chapter remarked that any inductive process is fundamentally *biased*. That is, human reasoning and data mining algorithms search for models in their own particular biased way. This is unavoidable as the space of models that can be generated from any data set is very large. If we understand and apply user goals, then we can quickly focus a data mining project on the small set of most crucial issues. Hence, it is vital to talk to users in order to lever age their *biases* to better guide the data mining. The lesson of this chapter is that *bias* is a first-class modeling construct. It is important to search out, record, and implement biases because, as shown below, different biases lead to radically different results.

23.2.2 THE PROBLEM WITH EXPLORING VALUES

In software engineering, biases are expressed as the *values* business users espouse for a system. Barry Boehm [41] advocated assessing software development technologies by the *value* they give to particular stakeholders. Note that this is very different from the standard practice (which assesses technologies via their functionality).

In his description of value-based SE, Boehm favors continuous optimization methods to conduct cost/benefit trade-off studies. Translated into the terminology of this book, he is advocating data mining methods that are tuned to different value propositions.

A problem with this kind of trade-off is that it must explore some underlying space of options. In a conventional approach, some business process model could be developed, then exercised many times. Such a *data farming* approach

1. *Plants a seed.* Build a model from domain information. All uncertainties or missing parts of the domain information are modeled as a space of possibilities.
2. *Grows the data.* Execute the model and, when the model moves into the space of possibilities, output is created by selecting at random from the possibilities.
3. *Harvests.* Summarize the grown data via data mining.
4. Optionally, use the harvested summaries to improve the model; then, go to 1.

There are two problems with the above approach:

- Tuning instability (that complicates the above step 2);
- Value variability (that complicates the above step 3).

Tuning instability refers to the problem of tuning a model to some local domain. Ideally, there is enough local data to clearly define what outputs are expected from a model. In practice, this may not be the case so the second step of data farming, *grow the data*, results in very large variances in model performance.

Value variability is the point of this chapter. *After* doing everything we can to tame tuning instability, we still need to search the resulting space of options in order to make a recommendation that is useful for the user. If, during the third step (*harvest*), we change the *value* proposition used to guide that search then we get startlingly different recommendations.

The next two sections offer more details on tuning instability and value variability. While these two terms have many differences, they relate to a similar concept:

- Tuning instability refers to uncertainties inside a model;
- Value variability refers to uncertainty on how to assess the outputs of a model.

23.2.2.1 Tuning instability

In theory, software process models can be used to model the trade-offs associated with different technologies. However, such models can suffer from *tuning instability*. Large instabilities make it hard to recognize important influences on a project. For example, consider the following simplified COCOMO [42] model,

$$effort = a \cdot LOC^{b+pmat} \cdot acap. \tag{23.1}$$

While simplified, the equation presents the core assumption of COCOMO; i.e., that software development effort is exponential on the size of the program. In this equation, (a, b) control the linear and exponential effects (respectively) on model estimates; while *pmat* (process maturity) and *acap* (analyst capability) are project choices adjusted by managers. Equation (23.1) contains two features (*acap, pmat*) and a full COCOMO-II model contains 22 [42].

Baker [19] reports a study that learned values of (a, b) for a full COCOMO model using Boehm's local calibration method [34] from 30 randomly selected samples of 90% of the available project data. The ranges varied widely:

$$(2.2 \leq a \leq 9.18) \wedge (0.88 \leq b \leq 1.09) \tag{23.2}$$

Such large variations make it possible to misunderstand the effects of project options. Suppose some proposed technology doubles productivity, but *a* moves from 9 to 4.5. The improvement resulting from that change would be obscured by the tuning variance.

(For more on the issue of tuning instability in effort estimation, the reader could refer back to Figure 1.2.)

23.2.2.2 Value variability

Another source of variability in a model are the goals (a.k.a. *values*) used to generate that model. There are a surprisingly large number of ways to assess the outputs of models of software systems. For example, consider something as seemingly simple as a defect predictor. Such detectors read code and point to regions with larger odds of having bugs. What could be simpler than that?

As it turns out, defect predictors can be assessed on many criteria such as those listed in Figure 23.1. In that figure, *support* comments on how much training data was used to build this detector. Also, *effort* looks at how many lines of code are selected by the detector. Finally, *reward* comments on the ease of finding bugs. If *reward* is high, then an analyst can find many bugs after reading a small part of the code.

Figure 23.2 lists other performance measures that we have seen at client sites or in the literature. There are two important features of this figure:

1. This list is very long.
2. This list keeps growing.

As to this second point, often when we work with new clients, they surprise us with yet another domain-specific criteria that is important for the business. That is, neither Figure 23.1 nor Figure 23.2 is a complete list of all possible assessment criteria.

Our reading of the software engineering literature is that most papers only explore a small subset of Figure 23.1 or Figure 23.2. We think this is a mistake, and researchers should do more to create a more general framework where they explore a wide and changing set of evaluation criteria. The next section describes one such framework.

Let $\{A, B, C, D\}$ denote the true negatives, false negatives, false positives, and true positives (respectively) found by a software defect detector. Also, let L_a, L_b, L_c, L_d be the lines of code seen in the parts of system that fall into A, B, C, D. Then

$$pd = recall = D/(B + D)$$
$$pf = C/(A + C)$$
$$prec = precision = D/(D + C)$$
$$acc = accuracy = (A + D)/(A + B + C + D)$$
$$support = (C + D)/(A + B + C + D)$$
$$effort = (L_c + L_d)/(L_a + L_b + L_c + L_d)$$
$$reward = pd/effort$$

FIGURE 23.1

Some assessment criteria for defect predictors.

Some goals relate to aspects of defect prediction:

1. Mission-critical systems are risk averse and may accept very high false alarm rates, just as long as they catch any life-threatening possibility. That is, such projects do not care about effort—they want to *maximize recall* regardless of any impact that might have on the false alarm rate.
2. Cost averse managers may accept lower probabilities of detection (the recall measure), just as long as they *do not waste budgets on false alarms*. This community seeks to *minimize false alarms* while maintaining *some level of adequate recall.*
3. Suppose a new hire wants to impress his or her manager. That new hire might want to ensure that no result presented to management contains a true negative; i.e., he or she wants to *maximize precision.*
4. Some communities do not care about low precision, just as long as a small fraction of the data is returned. Hayes, Dekhytar, & Sundaram call this fraction *selectivity* and offer an extensive discussion of the merits of this measure [169].

Beyond defect prediction are other goals that combine defect prediction with other economic factors:

5. Arisholm and Briand [9], Ostrand and Weyeuker [348], and Rahman et al. [366] say that a defect predictor should maximize *reward*; i.e., find the fewest lines of code that contain the most bugs.
6. In other work, Lumpe et al. are concerned about *amateur bug fixes*; i.e., those that are made by programmers to regions of the code that are unfamiliar to them [276]. Such amateur fixes are highly correlated to errors and, hence, to avoid such incorrect bug fixes, we have to optimize for finding the most number of bugs in regions that *the most programmers have worked with before.*
7. In *better-faster-cheaper*, we seek project changes that lead to fewer defects and faster development times using less resources [115, 293, 304, 312].
8. *Rush-to-market* is another economic-based optimization measure. A learner that tries to maximize "rush-to-market" is trying to release the product as soon as possible, without too many bugs. Note that "rush-to-market" is an appropriate strategy for a company competing in a volatile and crowded marketplace where being first-to-market enables a revenue stream (that can be used to subsequently fix any issues with version 1.0) [183].
9. With Sayyad [378, 379], we have explored models of software product lines whose value propositions are fivefold: (1) offer feature rich products (i.e., that use as *many features* as possible); (2) selecting from features with the *fewest past defects*; favoring those that we have (3) *used before*; and that (4) *cost least* to adopt; all the while (5) avoiding *any violations* of required properties of these products.

All the above measures relate to the tendency of a predictor to find something. Another style of measure would be to check the *variability* of that predictor.

9. In their study on reproducibility of SE results, Anda, Sjoberg, and Mockus advocate using the coefficient of variation ($CV = \frac{stddev}{mean}$). Using this measure, they defined *reproducibility* as $\frac{1}{CV}$ [330].

FIGURE 23.2

Different users value different things. Note that some of these goals are defined in terms of Figure 23.1.

23.2.2.3 Exploring instability and variability

To address the above problems, we adopt two strategies:

- To address value variability we
    - Use tools that allow for the customization of the value proposition used to guide the search.
    - Then run the models using different value propositions.
- To address tuning instability we
    - Determine the space of known tunings for a model.
    - Allow models to range over that space.
    - Extensively simulate the models.
    - Look for stable conclusions over the entire space of tunings.

The rest of this chapter offers an example of this kind of analysis.

23.3 SETTING UP

To apply the above exploration rules, we first need to

- Represent multiple value propositions.
- Represent the space of options.

This *setting up* section discusses one way to implement those representations.

23.3.1 REPRESENTING VALUE PROPOSITIONS

A *value* function should model the goals of the business users who are making project decisions about some software development. We will explore two:

- BFC = Better, faster, cheaper.
- XPOS = Risk exposure.

Value proposition #1- Better, faster, cheaper (BFC). Ideally, software is built with fewer defects D, using less effort E, and in shorter time T. A value function for this goal can be modeled as the Euclidean distance to minimum effort, time, defects:

$$bfc = \sqrt{f\overline{T}^2 + c\overline{E}^2 + \left(b\overline{D}\left(1 + 1.8^{rely-3}\right)\right)^2} \qquad (23.3)$$

$$value_{bfc} = \frac{1}{bfc} \qquad (23.4)$$

In the above, *value* is highest when defects and effort and development time are lowest. Also, $0 \le (b,f,c) \le 1$ represents the business importance of (better, faster, cheaper). For this study, we use $b = f = c = 1$. In other work, we have explored the effects of using other b, f, and c values [304].

In Equation (23.3), $\overline{T}$, $\overline{E}$, and $\overline{D}$ are the time, effort, and defect scores normalized zero to one. Equation (23.3) models the business intuition that defects in high-reliability systems are exponentially more troublesome than in low-reliability systems:

- In the COCOMO model, variables have the range $1 \leq x \leq 6$ and at $x = 3$, the variable's influence on the output is *nominal*; in other words, its impact on effort is to multiply it by one (which is to say, it leaves it unchanged).
- In the COCOMO model, if reliability moves from very low to very high (1 to 6), the term 1.8^{rely-3} models a function that (a) is ten times larger for very high than very low reliability systems; and (b) passes through 1 at $rely = 3$ (so systems with nominal reliability do not change the importance of defects).

Value proposition #2- Risk exposure (XPOS). The BFC value function is somewhat idealistic in that it seeks to remove *all* defects by spending *less* money on *faster* developments. An alternate value function comes from Huang and Boehm [183]. This alternate value function, which we call XPOS, models the situation where a software company must rush a product to market, without compromising too much on software quality. Based on Huang's PhD dissertation [182], we operationalize XPOS as follows.

Huang defines business risk exposure (RE) as a combination of *software quality investment risk exposure* (RE_q) and *market share erosion risk exposure* (RE_m). We invert that expression to yield $value_{XPOS}$ (so an exposed project has low value):

$$RE = RE_q + RE_m \tag{23.5}$$

$$value_{XPOS} = \frac{1}{RE} \tag{23.6}$$

RE_q values high-quality software and therefore prioritizes quality over time. RE_q is composed of two primary components: probability of loss due to unacceptable quality $P_q(L)$ and size of loss due to unacceptable quality $S_q(L)$. $P_q(L)$ is calculated based on defects. $S_q(L)$ is calculated based on complexity (the COCOMO *cplx* feature), reliability (*rely*), and a cost function. S_c is a value from a Pareto-valued table based on *rely*. We choose the project months estimate as the basis of this cost function.

$$RE_q = P_q(L) * S_q(L) \tag{23.7}$$

$$P_q(L) = \frac{defects}{defects_{vl}} \tag{23.8}$$

$$S_q(L) = 3^{\frac{cplx-3}{2}} \cdot PM \cdot S_c \tag{23.9}$$

In Equation (23.8), $defects_{vl}$ is the lower bound on defects for that project.

In Equation (23.9), the $\frac{cplx-3}{2}$ term is similar to the $\overline{D}$ coefficient inside Equation (23.3): if complexity changes below or above 3, then it reduces or adds (respectively) to the unacceptable quality risk. However, at $cplx = 3$, the multiplier is one (i.e., no effect).

RE_m values a fast time-to-market and therefore prioritizes time over quality. RE_m is calculated from PM and reliability (*rely*). M_c is a value from a exponential-valued table based on *rely*.

$$RE_m = PM \cdot M_c \tag{23.10}$$

23.3.1.1 *Representing the space of options*

How do we allow models to range over the space of known tunings? To answer that question, we need to understand something about models. The predictions of a model about a software engineering project are altered by project variables P and tuning variables T:

$$prediction = model(P, T) \tag{23.11}$$

For example:

- In Equation (23.1), the tuning options T are the range of (a, b) and the project options P are the range of *pmat* (process maturity) and *acap* (analyst capability).
- Given what we know about the COCOMO model, we can say that the ranges of the project variables are $P = 1 \leq (pmat, acap) \leq 5$.
- Given the cone of uncertainty associated with a particular project p, we can identify the subset of the project options $p \subseteq P$ relevant to a particular project. For example, a project manager may be unsure of the exact skill level of team members. However, if she were to assert "my analysts are better than most," then p would include $\{acap = 4, acap = 5\}$.

Next, we make the following assumption:

The dominant influences on the prediction are the project options p (and not the tuning options T).

Under this assumption, the predictions can be controlled by

- Constraining p (using some AI tool);
- While leaving T unconstrained (and sampling $t \in T$ using Monte Carlo methods).

Specifically, we seek a treatment $r_x \subseteq p$ that maximizes the *value* of a model's predictions where *value* is a domain-specific function that scores model outputs according to user goals:

$$\arg\max_x \left(\overbrace{r_x \subseteq p}^{AI\ search}, \underbrace{t \subseteq T, value(model(r_x, t))}_{Monte\ Carlo} \right) \tag{23.12}$$

23.4 DETAILS

The last section offered, in broad strokes, an outline of how to handle tuning instability and value variability. To operationalize that high-level picture, we must now move into the inner details of a specific model.

The rest of this chapter is based on an example taken from the USC COCOMO suite of project management tools [36]:

- The COCOMO model offers effort and time predictions.
- The COQUALMO offers defect predictions.

Using the models, we can represent the project options P and tuning options T of Equation (23.11) as follows.

23.4.1 PROJECT OPTIONS: *P*

COCOMO and COQUALMO's features are shown in Figure 23.3 and Figure 23.4. The features have a range taken from {very low, low, nominal, high, very high, extremely high} or

$$\{vl = 1, l = 2, n = 3, h = 4, vh = 5, xh = 6\}$$

These features include manual methods for defect removal. High values for peer reviews (or *pr*, see Figure 23.4) denote formal peer group review activities (participants have well-defined and separate roles, the reviews are guided by extensive review checklists/root cause analysis, and reviews are a continuous process guided by statistical control theory [397]).

COQUALMO also models automatic methods for defect removal. Chulani [99] defines the top half of *automated analysis* as

Scale factors (exponentially decrease effort&cost)	prec: have we done this before? flex: development flexibility resl: any risk resolution activities? team: team cohesion pmat: process maturity
Upper (linearly decrease effort&cost)	acap: analyst capability pcap: programmer capability pcon: programmer continuity aexp: analyst experience pexp: programmer experience ltex: language and tool experience tool: tool use site: multiple site development sced: length of schedule
Lower (linearly increase effort&cost)	rely: required reliability data: secondary memory storage requirements cplx: program complexity ruse: software reuse docu: documentation requirements time: runtime pressure stor: main memory requirements pvol: platform volatility

FIGURE 23.3

The COCOMO "scale factors" and "effort multipliers" change effort and cost by an exponential and linear amount (respectively). Increasing these values has the effect described in column one.

aa: automated analysis etat: execution-based testing and tools pr: peer reviews

FIGURE 23.4

The COQUALMO defect removal methods. Increasing these values decreases delivered defects.

4 (high): intermediate-level module and intermodule code syntax and semantic analysis. Simple requirements/design view consistency checking.

5 (very high): More elaborate requirements/design view consistency checking. Basic distributed processing and temporal analysis, model checking, symbolic execution.

6 (extremely high): Formalized[1] specification and verification. Temporal analysis, model checking, symbolic execution.

The top half of *execution-based testing and tools* is

4 (high): Well-defined test sequence tailored to organization (acceptance / alpha / beta / flight / etc.) test. Basic test coverage tools, test support system.

5 (very high): More advanced tools, test data preparation, basic test oracle support, distributed monitoring and analysis, assertion checking. Metrics-based test process management.

6 (extremely high): Highly advanced tools: oracles, distributed monitoring and analysis, assertion checking. Integration of automated analysis and test tools. Model-based test process management.

In the sequel, the following observation will become important: Figure 23.3 is much longer than Figure 23.4. This reflects a modeling intuition of COCOMO/COQUALMO: it is better to prevent the introduction of defects (using changes to Figure 23.3) than to try and find them once they have been introduced (using Figure 23.4).

23.4.2 TUNING OPTIONS: *T*

For COCOMO effort multipliers (the features that that affect effort/cost in a linear manner), the off-nominal ranges {vl=1, l=2, h=4, vh=5, xh=6} change the prediction by some ratio. The nominal range {n=3}, however, corresponds to an effort multiplier of 1, causing no change to the prediction. Hence, these ranges can be modeled as straight lines $y = mx + b$ passing through the point $(x, y)=(3, 1)$. Such a line has a y-intercept of $b = 1 - 3m$. Substituting this value of b into $y = mx + b$ yields:

$$\forall x \in \{1..6\} \; EM_i = m_\alpha (x - 3) + 1 \tag{23.13}$$

where m_α is the effect of α on effort/cost.

We can also derive a general equation for the features that influence cost/effort in an exponential manner. These features do not "hinge" around (3,1) but take the following form:

$$\forall x \in \{1..6\} \; SF_i = m_\beta (x - 6) \tag{23.14}$$

where m_β is the effect of factor i on effort/cost.

COQUALMO contains equations of the same syntactic form as Equation (23.13) and Equation (23.14), but with different coefficients. Using experience for 161 projects [42], we can find the maximum and minimum values ever assigned to m for COQUALMO and COCOMO. Hence, to explore tuning variance (the $t \in T$ term in Equation (23.12)), all we need to do is select m values at random from the min/max m values ever seen.

---

[1] Consistency checkable preconditions and postconditions, but not necessarily mathematical theorems.

23.5 **AN EXPERIMENT**

This section describes an experiment where the value propositions of Section 23.3.1 are applied to the model described in Section 23.3.1.1 and Section 23.6.

23.5.1 **CASE STUDIES:** $p \subseteq P$

We use p to denote the subset of the project options $p_i \subseteq P$ relevant to particular projects. The four particular projects p_1, p_2, p_3, p_4 used as the case studies of this chapter are shown in Figure 23.5:

- OSP is the GNC (guidance, navigation, and control) component of NASA's *Orbital Space Plane*.
- OSP2 is a later version of OSP.
- Flight and ground systems reflect typical ranges seen at NASA's Jet Propulsion Laboratory.

Some of the features in Figure 23.5 are known precisely (see all the features with single *fixed settings*). But many of the features in Figure 23.5 do not have precise settings (see all the features that *range* from some *low* to *high* value). Sometimes the ranges are very narrow (e.g., the process maturity of JPL ground software is between 2 and 3), and sometimes the ranges are very broad.

Figure 23.5 does not mention all the features listed in Figure 23.3 inputs. For example, our defect predictor has inputs for use of *automated analysis*, *peer reviews*, and *execution-based testing tools*. For all inputs not mentioned in Figure 23.5, ranges are picked at random from (usually) $\{1, 2, 3, 4, 5\}$.

23.5.1.1 *Searching for* r_x

Our search runs two phases: a *forward select* and a *back select* phase. The *forward select* grows r_x, starting with the empty set. At each round i in the forward select one or more ranges (e.g., $acap = 3$) are added to r_x. The resulting r_x set found at round i is denoted r_x^i.

The forward select ends when the search engine cannot find more ranges to usefully add to r_x^i. Before termination, we say that the *open* features at round i are the features in Figure 23.3 and Figure 23.4 not mentioned by any range in r_x^i. The value of r_x^i is assessed by running the model N times with

1. All of r_x^i.
2. Any $t \in T$, selected at random.
3. Any range at random for *open* features.

In order to ensure minimality, a *back select* checks if the final r_x set can be pruned. If the forward select caches the simulation results seen at each round i, the back select can perform statistical tests to see if the results of round $i - 1$ are significantly different from round i. If the difference is *not* statistically significant, then the ranges added at round i are *pruned* away and the back select recurses for $i - 1$. We call the unpruned ranges the *selected* ranges and the point where pruning stops the *policy point*.

For example, in Figure 23.6, the policy point is round 13 and the decisions made at subsequent rounds are pruned by the back select. That is, the treatments returned by our search engines are all the ranges r_x^i for $1 \leq i \leq 13$. The *selected* ranges are shown in a table at the bottom of the figure and the effects of applying the conjunction of ranges in r_x^{13} can be seen by comparing the values at round=0 to round=13:

- Defects/KLOC reduced: 350 to 75;
- Time reduced: 16 to 10 months;
- Effort reduced: 170 to 80 staff months.

Project p_i	Ranges			Fixed settings	
	Feature	Low	High	Feature	Setting
p_1=OSP: Orbital space plane	prec	1	2	data	3
	flex	2	5	pvol	2
	resl	1	3	rely	5
	team	2	3	pcap	3
	pmat	1	4	plex	3
	stor	3	5	site	3
	ruse	2	4		
	docu	2	4		
	acap	2	3		
	pcon	2	3		
	apex	2	3		
	ltex	2	4		
	tool	2	3		
	sced	1	3		
	cplx	5	6		
	KSLOC	75	125		
p_2=OSP2	prec	3	5	flex	3
	pmat	4	5	resl	4
	docu	3	4	team	3
	ltex	2	5	time	3
	sced	2	4	stor	3
	KSLOC	75	125	data	4
				pvol	3
				ruse	4
				rely	5
				acap	4
				pcap	3
				pcon	3
				apex	4
				plex	4
				tool	5
				cplx	4
				site	6
p_3=JPL flight software	rely	3	5	tool	2
	data	2	3	sced	3
	cplx	3	6		
	time	3	4		
	stor	3	4		
	acap	3	5		
	apex	2	5		
	pcap	3	5		
	plex	1	4		
	ltex	1	4		
	pmat	2	3		
	KSLOC	7	418		
p_4=JPL ground software	rely	1	4	tool	2
	data	2	3	sced	3
	cplx	1	4		
	time	3	4		
	stor	3	4		
	acap	3	5		
	apex	2	5		
	pcap	3	5		
	plex	1	4		
	ltex	1	4		
	pmat	2	3		
	KSLOC	11	392		

FIGURE 23.5

Four case studies. Numeric values {1, 2, 3, 4, 5, 6} map to *very low, low, nominal, high, very high, extra high*. This data comes from experienced NASA managers summarizing over real-world projects.

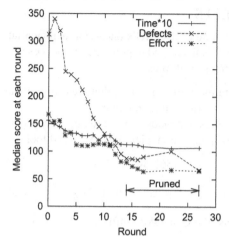

Decisions made from round=1 to round=13:

round0: $r_x = \emptyset$	round7: added {rely=3}
round1 added {pmat=3}	round8: added {stor = 3}
round2: added {resl=4}	round9: added {time = 3}
round3: added {team=5}	round10: added {tool = 4}
round4: added {aexp=4}	round11: added {sced = 2}
round5: added {docu=3}	round12: added {site = 4}
round6: added {plex=4}	round13: added {acap = 5}

FIGURE 23.6

Example forward and back select results. From [147].

23.5.2 SEARCH METHODS

Elsewhere, we have proposed and studied various methods for implementing the forward select using

- Simulated annealing: a classic nonlinear optimizer.
- MaxWalkSat: a local search algorithm from the 1990s [382].
- Various standard AI methods such as Beam search, ISSAMP, and A-Star [84].

Of all these, our own variant of MaxWalkSat called SEESAW performed best [304]. Hence, this rest of this chapter will discuss SEESAW.

While searching the ranges of a feature, this algorithm exploits the monotonic nature of Equation (23.13) and Equation (23.14). SEESAW ignores all ranges except the minimum and maximum values for a feature in p. Like MaxWalkSat, the feature chosen on each iteration is made randomly. However, SEESAW has the ability to delay bad decisions until the end of the algorithm (i.e., decisions where constraining the feature to *either* the minimum or maximum value results in a worse solution). These treatments are then guaranteed to be pruned during the back select.

23.6 INSIDE THE MODELS

In the following, m_α and m_β denote COCOMO's linear and exponential influences on effort/cost, and m_γ and m_δ denote COQUALMO's linear and exponential influences on number of defects.

There are two sets of effort/cost multipliers:

1. The *positive effort EM* features, with slopes m_α^+, that are proportional to effort/cost. These features are cplx, data, docu, pvol, rely, ruse, stor, and time.
2. The *negative effort EM* features, with slopes m_α^-, are inversely proportional to effort/cost. These features are acap, apex, ltex, pcap, pcon, plex, sced, site, and tool.

Their m ranges, as seen in 161 projects [36], are

$$(0.073 \le m_\alpha^+ \le 0.21) \wedge (-0.178 \le m_\alpha^- \le -0.078) \tag{23.15}$$

In the same sample of projects, the COCOMO effort/cost scale factors (prec, flex, resl, team, pmat) have the range

$$-1.56 \le m_\beta \le -1.014 \tag{23.16}$$

Similarly, there are two sets of defect multipliers and scale factors:

1. The *positive defect* features have slopes m_γ^+ and are proportional to estimated defects. These features are flex, DATA, ruse, cplx, time, stor, and pvol.
2. The *negative defect* features, with slopes m_γ^-, that are inversely proportional to the estimated defects. These features are acap, pcap, pcon, apex, plex, ltex, tool, site, sced, prec, resl, team, pmat, rely, and docu.

COQUALMO divides into three models describing how defects change in requirements, design, and coding. These tunings options have the range

$$requirements \begin{cases} 0 \le m_\gamma^+ \le 0.112 \\ -0.183 \le m_\gamma^- \le -0.035 \end{cases}$$

$$design \begin{cases} 0 \le m_\gamma^+ \le 0.14 \\ -0.208 \le m_\gamma^- \le -0.048 \end{cases} \tag{23.17}$$

$$coding \begin{cases} 0 \le m_\gamma^+ \le 0.14 \\ -0.19 \le m_\gamma^- \le -0.053 \end{cases}$$

The tuning options for the defect removal features are

$$\begin{aligned} \forall x \in \{1..6\} \quad SF_i &= m_\delta(x-1) \\ requirements : \quad 0.08 &\le m_\delta \le 0.14 \\ design : \quad 0.1 &\le m_\delta \le 0.156 \\ coding : \quad 0.11 &\le m_\delta \le 0.176 \end{aligned} \tag{23.18}$$

where m_δ denotes the effect of i on defect removal.

23.7 RESULTS

When SEESAW was used to explore the ranges of the above equations in the context of Figure 23.5, two sets of results were obtained. First, the SEESAW search engine was a *competent* method for exploring these models. Figure 23.7 shows the means reductions in defects, time, and effort found by SEESAW. Note that very large reductions are possible with this technique.

Second, as promised at the start of this chapter, *value changes everything*. When SEESAW generated results for the two different value functions, then very different recommendations were generated. Figure 23.8 shows the ranges seen in SEESAW's treatment (after a back select). The BFC and XPOS columns show the percent frequency of a range appearing when SEESAW used our different *value* functions. These experiments were repeated 20 times and only the ranges found in the majority (more than 50%) of the trials are reported. The results are divided into our four case studies: ground, flight, OSP, and OSP2. Within each case study, the results are sorted by the fraction $\frac{BFC}{BFC+XPOS}$. This fraction ranges 0 to 100 and

- If close to 100, then a range is selected by BFC more than XPOS.
- If close to 0, then a range is selected by XPOS more than BFC.

The right-hand columns of Figure 23.8 flag the presence of manual defect remove methods (*pr*=peer reviews) or automatic defect removal methods (*aa*=automated analysis; *etat*=execution testing tools). Note that high levels of automatic defect removal methods are only frequently required in ground systems, and only when valuing BFC. More usually, defect removal techniques are *not* recommended. In ground systems, $etat = 1$, $pr = 1$, and $aa = 1$ are all examples of SEESAW *discouraging* rather than endorsing the use of defect removal methods. That is, in three of our four case studies, it is more important to prevent defect introduction than to use after-the-fact defect removal methods. In ground, OSP, and OSP2 defect removal methods are very rare (only $pr = 1$ in flight systems).

Another important aspect of Figure 23.8 is that there is no example of both value functions frequently endorsing the same range. If a range is commonly selected by BFC, then it is usually *not* commonly accepted by XPOS. The most dramatic example of this is the OSP2 results of Figure 23.8: BFC always selects (at 100%) the low end of a feature (*sced*=2) while XPOS nearly always selects (at 80% frequency) the opposite high end of that feature.

Data Set	Defects	Time	Effort
flight	80%	39%	72%
ground	85%	38%	73%
osp	65%	4%	42%
ops2	26%	22%	5%
Median	73%	30%	57%

FIGURE 23.7

Percent reductions (1 − *final/initial*) achieved by SEESAW on the Figure 23.5 case studies. The *initial* values come from round 0 of the forward select. The *final* values come from the policy point. Note that all the initial and final values are statistically different (Mann-Whitney, 95% confidence). From [147].

Data	Range	value B=BFC	value X=XPOS	$\frac{B}{B+X}$	Defect removal Manual	Defect removal Automatic
ground	rely = 4	70	20	77		
	aa = 6	70	25	73		hi in B
	resl = 6	65	40	61		
	etat = 1	35	65	35		lo in X
	aexp = 5	45	85	34		
	pr = 1	35	80	30	lo in X	lo in X
	aa = 1	25	60	29		
	data = 2	25	70	26		
	rely = 1	15	70	17		
flight	rely = 5	65	25	72		
	flex = 6	80	50	61		
	docu = 1	55	85	39		
	site = 6	55	85	39		
	resl = 6	45	70	39		
	pr = 1	45	70	39	lo in X	
	pvol = 2	45	75	37		
	data = 2	35	60	36		
	cplx = 3	45	90	33		
	rely = 3	15	60	20		
OSP	pmat = 4	85	45	65		
	resl = 3	45	70	39		
	ruse = 2	40	65	38		
	docu = 2	25	90	21		
OSP2	sced = 2	100	0	100		
	sced = 4	0	80	0		

FIGURE 23.8

Frequency (in percents) of feature ranges seen in 20 repeats of SEESAW, using two different goal functions: BFC and XPOS. The last two columns comment on any defect reduction feature. Not shown in this figure are any feature ranges that occur less than 50% of the time. From [147].

23.8 DISCUSSION

One characterization of the Figure 23.8 results is that, for some projects, it is preferable to prevent defects before they arrive (by reorganizing the project) rather than try to remove them afterwards using (say) peer review, automated analysis, or execution test tools.

The other finding from this work is that *value* can change everything. Techniques that seem useful to one kind of project/value function may be counterindicated for another. This finding has significant implications for SE researchers and practitioners. It is no longer enough to just propose (say) some automated defect reduction tool. Rather, the value of some new tools for a software project needs to be carefully assessed with respect to the core *value*s of that project.

More generally, models that work on one project may be irrelevant on another, if the second project has a different value structure. Hence, the conclusion of this chapter is that if two teams want to share models, then before they do so they must first document and reflect on their different value structures.

USING GOALS IN MODEL-BASED REASONING

24

In summary, this chapter proposes the following data analysis pattern:

Name:	Multiobjective learning.
Also known as:	Pareto ensemble; multiobjective ensemble of learning machines.
Intent:	Software effort estimation (SEE), when one wishes to perform well in terms of different goals/objectives/performance measures.
Motivation:	Several performance measures can be used for evaluating the performance of SEE models. These measures can behave differently from each other [133, 389]. What is the relationship among different measures? Can we use this relationship in order to create models able to improve estimations in terms of different measures? Can we emphasize a particular measure if we wish to?
Solution:	SEE is formulated as a multiobjective learning problem, where different performance measures are seen as goals/objectives to be optimized. A multiobjective evolutionary algorithm (MOEA) is used to optimize on all these measures at the same time, allowing us to create an ensemble of models that provides a good trade-off among different measures (Pareto ensemble), or to emphasize particular measures.
Applicability:	Plots of models created by the multiobjective algorithm can be used to obtain a better understanding of the relationship among different measures. In particular, it was revealed that different measures can present even opposite behaviors. The Pareto ensemble was successful in obtaining similar or better performance than a traditional corresponding single-objective approach. Competitive performance was also obtained in comparison to several other approaches, in particular on more heterogeneous data sets [327].
Related to:	Chapter 20 in terms of ensemble learning; Chapter 23 in terms of the importance of objectives/goals.

This chapter is based on Minku and Yao [327]. Additionally, the following new material has been added: (1) a didactic explanation of multilayer perceptrons (MLPs) (Section 24.1); (2) an introduction to MOEAs and its components (Section 24.2); and (3) a didactic explanation of harmonic-distance MOEA (Section 24.3).

Much of the software prediction work involves empirical evaluation of models. Several different performance measures can be used for that. For instance, in SEE, one can use the mean magnitude of the relative error (MMRE), the percentage of estimations within $N\%$ of the actual value (PRED(N)), the logarithmic standard deviation (LSD) [133], the mean absolute error (MAE) [389], etc. Different performance measures can behave differently and it is highly unlikely that there is a "single, simple-to-use, universal goodness-of-fit kind of metric" [133], i.e., none of these measures is totally free of problems! Section 24.4.1 will explain some of these measures in more detail.

You may then be thinking: "If they are all measures of performance, why can not we just improve in all of them?" However, things are not so simple, because some of these measures may have conflicting behavior, i.e., as models are improved in one of them, they may be degraded in others. In this chapter, we show that improving on different performance measures that we are interested in can be seen as different goals/objectives when learning software prediction models. Ideally, we would indeed like to achieve all these goals. If the performance measures behave quite differently from each other on a given software prediction task, it may be possible to improve on different measures by using them as a natural way to generate diversity in ensembles.

As explained in Chapters 20, 22, ensembles have been showing relatively good performance for SEE, and diversity is a key component for their performance (Section 20.1). However, the ensemble presented in Chapter 22 requires a manual procedure for building the ensemble that focuses on improving accuracy of the base models. As there is a trade-off between accuracy and diversity of base models [69], focusing only on improving base models' accuracy may lead to lack of diversity, reducing the performance of the ensemble as a whole. The ensemble presented in Chapter 20 is automated and based on an ensemble method known to encourage diversity. However, despite the fact that it is somewhat tailored to SEE by joining the power of ensembles and locality, it is still based on general-purpose techniques. Additional improvements may be obtained by further tailoring ensembles for the task at hand [326]. Encouraging diversity based on a set of objectives specifically designed for a certain software prediction task may provide further improvements in this task. With that in mind, this chapter attempts to answer the following research questions:

- *RQ1.* What is the relationship among different performance measures for SEE? Despite existing studies on different performance measures [133, 215], it is still not well understood to what extend different performance measures behave differently in SEE. This is necessary in order to decide on how to use them for evaluation and model-building purposes.

- *RQ2.* Can we use different performance measures as a source of diversity to create SEE ensembles? In particular, can that improve the performance in comparison to models created without considering these measures explicitly? Existing models do not necessarily consider the performance measures in which we are interested explicitly. For example, MLPs are usually trained using backpropagation, which is based on the mean squared error (MSE). So, they can only improve on other performance measures indirectly. We will check whether creating an ensemble considering MMRE, PRED, and LSD explicitly leads to more improvements in the SEE context.

- *RQ3.* Is it possible to create SEE models that emphasize particular performance measures should we wish to do so? For example, if there is a certain measure that we believe to be more appropriate than the others, can we create a model that particularly improves performance considering this measure? This is useful not only for the case where the software manager has sufficient domain knowledge to chose a certain measure, but also (and mainly) if there are future developments of the SEE research showing that a certain measure is better than others for a certain purpose.

In order to answer these questions, we formulate the problem of creating SEE models as a multiobjective learning problem that considers different performance measures explicitly as objectives to be optimized. This formulation is key to answer the research questions because it allows us to use a MOEA [438] to generate SEE models that are generally good considering all the predefined performance measures. This feature allows us to use plots of the performances of these models in order to understand the relationship among the performance measures and how differently they behave. Once these models are obtained, the models that perform best for each different performance measure can be determined. These models behave differently from each other and can be used to form a diverse ensemble that provides an ideal trade-off among these measures. Therefore, this approach creates ensembles in such a way to encourage both accuracy and diversity, which is known to be beneficial for ensembles [61, 244]. Choosing a single performance measure is not an easy task. By using our ensemble, the software manager does not need to chose a single performance measure, as an ideal trade-off among different measures is provided. As an additional benefit of this approach, each of the models that compose the ensemble can also be used separately to emphasize a specific performance measure if desired.

The approach presented in this chapter is fully automated and tailored for SEE. Once developed, a tool using this approach can be easily run to learn models and create ensembles. It is worth noting that the parameters choice can also be automated for this approach, as long as the developer of the tool embeds on it several different parameter values to be tested on a certain percentage of the completed projects of the company being estimated.

Our analysis shows that the different performance measures MMRE, PRED, and LSD behave very differently when analyzed at their individual best level, and sometimes present even opposite behaviors (RQ1). For example, when considering nondominated (Section 24.2) solutions, as MMRE is improved, LSD tends to get worse. This is an indicator that these measures can be used to create diverse ensembles for SEE. We then show that MOEA is successful in generating SEE ensemble models by optimizing different performance measures explicitly at the same time (RQ2). The ensembles are composed of nondominated solutions selected from the last generation of the MOEA, as explained in Section 24.4. These ensembles present performance similar or better than a model that does not optimize the three measures concurrently. Furthermore, the similar or better performance is achieved considering all the measures used to create the ensemble, showing that these ensembles not only provide a better trade-off among different measures, but also improve the performance considering these measures. We also show that MOEA is flexible, allowing us to chose solutions that emphasize certain measures, if desired (RQ3).

The base models generated by the MOEA in this work are MLPs [32], which have been showing success for not being restricted to linear project data [422]. Even though we generate MLPs in this work, MOEAs could also be used to generate other types of base learners, such as radial basis function networks (RBFs), regression trees (RTs), and linear regression equations. An additional comparison of MOEA to evolve MLPs was performed against nine other approaches, involving other types of models. The comparison shows that the MOEA ensembles of MLPs were ranked first more often in terms of five different performance measures, but performed less well in terms of LSD. They were also ranked first more often for the data sets likely to be more heterogeneous. It is important to note, though, that this additional comparison is not only evaluating the MOEA and the multiobjective formulation of the problem, but also the type of model being evolved (MLP). Other types of models could also be evolved by the MOEA and could possibly provide better results in terms of LSD. As the key point of this work is to analyze the multiobjective formulation of the creation of SEE models, and not the comparison among different types of models, experimentation with different types of MOEA and different types of base models is left as future work.

This chapter is organized as follows. Section 24.1 explains MLPs. Section 24.2 explains MOEAs in general. Section 24.3 explains a particular type of MOEA. Section 24.4 explains our approach for creating SEE models (including ensembles) through MOEAs. In particular, Section 24.4.1 explains the multiobjective formulation of the problem of creating SEE models. Section 24.5 explains the experimental design for answering the research questions and evaluating our approach. Section 24.6 provides an analysis of the relationship among different performance measures (RQ1). Section 24.7 provides an evaluation of the MOEA's ability to create ensembles by optimizing several different measures at the same time (RQ2). Section 24.8 shows that MOEAs are flexible, allowing us to create models that emphasize particular performance measures, if desired (RQ3). Section 24.9 shows that there is still room for improvement in the choice of MOEA models to be used for SEE. Section 24.10 complements the evaluation by checking how well the Pareto ensemble of MLPs performs in comparison to other types of models. Section 24.11 presents a summary of the chapter.

24.1 MULTILAYER PERCEPTRONS

MLPs are neural network models that work as universal approximators, i.e., they can approximate any continuous function [180]. For instance, they can be used as SEE models. MLPs are composed of neurons called *perceptrons*. So, before explaining the general structure of MLPs, the general structure of a perceptron [372] will be explained. As shown in Figure 24.1, a perceptron receives n features as input ($\mathbf{x} = x_1, x_2, \ldots, x_n$), and each of these features is associated to a weight. Input features must be numeric. So, nonnumeric input features have to be converted to numeric ones in order to use a perceptron. For instance, a categorical feature with p possible values can be converted into p input features representing the presence/absence of these values. These are called *dummy variables*. For example, if the input feature "development type" can take the values "new development," "enhancement," or "re-development," it could be replaced by three dummy variables "new development," "enhancement," and "redevelopment," which take value 1 if the corresponding value is present and 0 if it is absent.

The input features are passed on to an input function u, which computes the weighted sum of the input features:

$$u(\mathbf{x}) = \sum_{i=1}^{n} w_i x_i .$$

The result of this computation is then passed onto an activation function f, which will produce the output of the perceptron. In the original perceptron, the activation function is a step function:

$$y = f(u(\mathbf{x})) = \begin{cases} 1, & \text{if } u(\mathbf{x}) > \theta \\ 0, & \text{otherwise,} \end{cases}$$

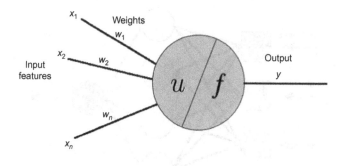

FIGURE 24.1

Scheme of a perceptron with n input features.

where θ is a threshold parameter. An example of step function with $\theta = 0$ is shown in Figure 24.2a. Thus, we can see that the perceptron determines whether $w_1x_1 + w_2x_2 + \cdots + w_nx_n - \theta > 0$ is true or false. The equation $w_1x_1 + w_2x_2 + \cdots + w_nx_n - \theta = 0$ is the equation of a hyperplane. The perceptron outputs 1 for any input point above the hyperplane, and outputs 0 for any input on or below the hyperplane. For this reason, the perceptron is called a *linear classifier*, i.e., it works well for data that are linearly separable. Perceptron learning consists of adjusting the weights so that a hyperplane that separates the training data well is determined. We refer the reader to Gurney [151] for more information on the perceptron's learning algorithm.

MLPs are able to approximate any continuous function, rather than only linear functions. They do so by combining several neurons, which are organized in at least three layers:

- One input layer, which simply distributes the input features to the first hidden layer.
- One or more hidden layers of perceptrons. The first hidden layer receives as inputs the features distributed by the input layer. The other hidden layers receive as inputs the output of each perceptron from the previous layer.
- One output layer of perceptrons, which receive as inputs the output of each perceptron of the last hidden layer.

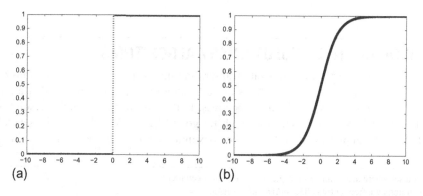

FIGURE 24.2

Examples of activation functions. (a) Example of step function and (b) Example of sigmoid function.

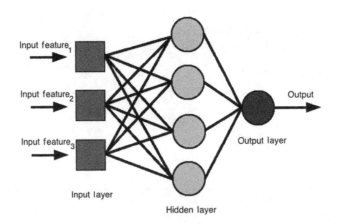

FIGURE 24.3

Scheme of a three-layer MLP with three input features, four hidden neurons and one output.

Figure 24.3 shows a scheme of an MLP with three layers. The perceptrons used by MLPs frequently use other types of activation functions than the step function. For the hidden layer neurons, sigmoid functions are frequently used. An example of a sigmoid function is shown in Figure 24.2b. Sigmoid functions will lead to smooth transitions instead of hardlined decision boundaries as when using step functions. The activation function of the output layer neurons is typically sigmoid for classification problems and the identity function for regression problems.

Learning in MLPs also consists in adjusting its perceptrons' weights so as to provide low error on the training data. This is traditionally done using the backpropagation algorithm [151], which attempts to minimize the MSE. However, other algorithms can also be used. In this chapter, we will show how to use MOEAs for training MLPs based on several different performance measures. Strategies can also be used to avoid overfitting the training data, i.e., to avoid creating models that have poor predictive performance due to modeling random error or noise present in the training data. Avoiding overfitting frequently involves allowing a higher error on the training data than the one that could be achieved by the model.

24.2 MULTIOBJECTIVE EVOLUTIONARY ALGORITHMS

Evolutionary algorithms (EAs) are optimization algorithms that search for optimal solutions by evolving a multiset [1] of candidate solutions.[2] MOEAs are EAs able to look for solutions that are optimal in terms of two or more possibly conflicting objectives. In the case of SEE, candidate solutions can be SEE models. So, MOEAs can be used to search for good SEE models. There exist several different types of MOEAs. Examples of MOEAs are the conventional and well-known nondominated sorting

---

[1] A multiset is a set where there can be multiple repetitions of an element.
[2] Candidate solutions are frequently called *individuals* in EAs.

genetic algorithm II (NSGA-II) [93]; the improved strength Pareto evolutionary algorithm (SPEA2) [465]; the two-archive algorithm [362]; the indicator-based evolutionary algorithm (IBEA) [464]; and the harmonic distance MOEA (HaD-MOEA) [438].

MOEAs typically operate by following the general scheme of EAs shown in Figure 24.4. Different MOEAs differ in the way they implement the steps shown in this figure. The scheme works as follows. EAs first generate a multiset of candidate solutions randomly. This multiset of candidate solutions are then evaluated to determine their quality. A certain number of candidate solutions are selected as *parents*. These are candidate solutions that will be used to generate new candidate solutions. The next steps are to combine and/or modify the parents by using variation operators to generate new candidate solutions, and to evaluate these new solutions. A multiset of candidate solutions is selected to *survive* for the next *generation*, i.e., a multiset of solutions is selected to comprise the population in the next iteration of the algorithm. In the next generation, the whole procedure from parents selection onward is repeated. This repetition continues until a certain termination condition is met. This could be, for example, a predefined maximum number of generations.

The steps marked with a Star in Figure 24.4 usually contain some selection pressure toward the selection of better solutions. In this way, as generations pass, populations are evolved toward better solutions. As MOEAs aim to optimize two or more possibly conflicting objectives, their selection pressure must consider all these objectives in some way in order to determine which solutions are "better." This is frequently done through the concept of dominance [93], even though there are also MOEAs that operate in different ways [378]. A solution s_1 dominates another solution s_2 if

- s_1 performs at least as well as s_2 in any objective; and
- s_1 performs better than s_2 in at least one objective.

By using the concept of dominance, a solution s_1 that dominates another solution s_2 can be seen as "better" than s_2. Thus, the MOEA looks for solutions that are nondominated by other solutions. The set of optimal solutions nondominated by any other solution in the search space is referred to as *Pareto front*. Even though the true Pareto front is very difficult to find, a MOEA can often find a set of good solutions nondominated by any other solution in the last generation. For simplicity, we will refer to the nondominated solutions in the last generation as *Pareto solutions* in this work.

The components of an EA are the following (please refer to Eiben and Smith [111] for more details):

- Representation: candidate solutions must be represented within the EA in such a way to allow easy manipulation by the EA without restricting areas of the search space that may contain important solutions. Solutions represented within the EA's context are called *genotypes*, whereas solutions in the original problem context are called *phenotypes*. For example, in SEE, the phenotype could be a SEE model such as an MLP, whereas the genotype could be a vector of floating point numbers representing the weights of the MLP.
- Objective/evaluation functions: these are functions that represent the requirements to improve on. In MOEAs, there is more than one objective function. For example, in the case of SEE, Section 24.4.1 shows that we can use different performance measures (e.g., MMRE, PRED(25), and LSD) calculated on the training set as objective functions. In single-objective EAs, the objective function is typically referred to as fitness function.

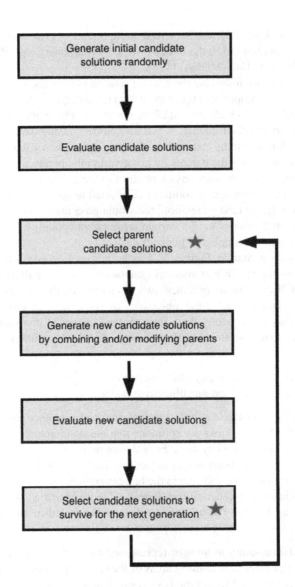

FIGURE 24.4

General scheme of evolutionary algorithms.

- Population: this is a multiset of genotypes maintained by the EA. It typically keeps a constant size as generations pass.
- Parents selection mechanism: in order to create pressure toward better candidate solutions, parents are typically selected through a probabilistic mechanism that gives higher chances for selecting better candidate solutions and smaller chances for selecting lower quality ones. The probabilistic nature of selection helps to avoid the algorithm getting stuck in local optima. An example of parents selection mechanism is binary tournament selection [317]. In this case, two candidate solutions are picked uniformly at random from the population, and the best between them is selected as a parent. This is repeated until the desired number of parents is obtained.
- Variation operators: these are operators to create new candidate solutions based on parent candidate solutions. They are usually applied with a certain probability, i.e., there is some chance that they are not applied. Operators called *crossover/recombination* can be used to combine two or more parents in order to create one or more offspring candidate solutions. The general idea is that combining two or more parents with different but desirable features will result in offspring that combine these features. Even though some offspring will not be better than the parents, it is hoped that some will be. The better solutions will be more likely to survive, contributing to the improvement of the quality of the population as a whole. An example of crossover operator for vectors of floating point numbers is to randomly swap numbers between two vectors. Note that this example is not a good crossover operator when the vector of floating point numbers represents an MLP. This is because it could break the relationship among different weights within an MLP, which is important to define the function that the MLP represents. An example of an operator good for the context of MLPs will be shown in Section 24.4.3. *Mutation* is another type of variation operator. It is applied to single candidate solutions, instead of combining different solutions, and causes random changes in the solution. An example of a mutation operator that can be probabilistically applied to each position of a vector of floating point numbers is to add a random value drawn from a Gaussian distribution.
- Survivor selection/replacement mechanism: as the population usually has constant size, a survivor selection mechanism is necessary to determine which candidate solutions among parents and offspring will be part of the population in the next generation. Survivor selection is usually based on the quality of the solutions, even though the concept of age is also frequently used. For example, solutions may be selected only among the offspring, rather than among parents and offspring. Different from parents selection, survivor selection is frequently deterministic rather than probabilistic. For example, solutions may be ranked based on their quality and the top-ranked ones selected as survivors.

In order to apply a MOEA to a certain problem, the components explained above must be defined. MOEAs (as well as EAs in general) can be used for several different problems. The same population, parents and survivor selection mechanisms can be used for several different problems. Particular care must be taken when choosing the representation, objective functions, and variation operators to be used for a particular problem. Section 24.3 introduces an example of MOEA called HaD-MOEA and its population, parents selection, and survivor selection mechanisms. Specific representation, objective functions, and variation operators to be used for the problem of creating SEE models are explained in Section 24.4.

24.3 HaD-MOEA

HaD-MOEA's [438] pseudocode is shown in Algorithm 5. HaD-MOEA maintains a population of α candidate solutions, which is initialized randomly (line 1). Parents are selected from the population (line 3) to produce offspring based on variation operators (line 4). HaD-MOEA then combines the population of parents and offspring (line 5), and deterministically selects the α "best" candidate solutions of the combined population as survivors (lines 6 to 16). The loop from parents selection to survivors selection is repeated until the maximum number of generations G is achieved.

ALGORITHM 5 HaD-MOEA [438]

Require: population size α, number of generations G.
  1: Initialize initial population $P_1 = \{x_1, x_2, \ldots, x_\alpha\}$
  2: **for** $g \leftarrow 1$ to G **do**
  3:    Select parents from P_g using binary tournament selection
  4:    Generate offspring population Q_g with size α based on the parents and variation operators
  5:    Combine current and offspring population $R_g = P_g \cup Q_g$
  6:    Sort all solutions of R_g to get all nondominated fronts $F = fast\_nondominated\_sort(R_g)$,
       where $F = (F_1, F_2, \ldots)$
  7:    Set $P_{g+1} = \{\}$ and $i = 1$
  8:    **while** the population size $|P_{g+1}| + |F_i| < N$ **do**
  9:       Add the ith nondominated front F_i to P_{g+1}
 10:       $i = i + 1$
 11:    **end while**
 12:    Combine F_i and P_{g+1} to a temporary vector T
 13:    Calculate the harmonic crowding distance of candidate solutions of F_i in T
 14:    Sort F_i according to the crowding distance in descending order
 15:    Set $T = \{\}$
 16:    Fill P_{g+1} with the first $\alpha - |P_{g+1}|$ elements of F_i
 17: **end for**
 18: **return** P_g.

The survivor selection mechanism must determine which solutions can be considered as "best" solutions to survive. HaD-MOEA does so by using the concept of dominance explained in Section 24.2, and the concept of crowding distance. Based on the concept of dominance, solutions are separated into nondominated fronts (line 6). Each front is comprised of candidate solutions that are nondominated by any candidate solution of any subsequent front. So, solutions in the former fronts can be considered as "better" than solutions in the latter fronts. The new population is filled with all the solutions from each nondominated front F_1 to F_{i-1}, where i is the identifier of the front that would cause the new population to have size larger than α (lines 7 to 11).

If the number of solutions from F_1 to F_{i-1} is smaller than α, a certain number of solutions from F_i needs to be chosen to complete the new population. Within a given front, no solution dominates another. Therefore, a strategy must be adopted to decide which solutions to select. HaD-MOEA considers the "best" solutions to survive as the ones in the least crowded region of the objective space, given the solutions from all fronts from F_1 to F_i. In this way, solutions that cover the whole objective space well are selected as survivors. This is a critical step, because it helps to maintain the diversity of the population, which in turn helps the search process to find solutions of better quality. In order to determine how crowded the region of the objective space where a solution is located is, the crowding distance of this solution is calculated. HaD-MOEA defines the crowding distance of a solution as the harmonic distance between this solution and its k-nearest neighbor solutions in the m-dimensional objective space:

$$ d = \frac{k}{\frac{1}{d1} + \frac{1}{d2} + \cdots + \frac{1}{d_k}} $$

where d_i, $1 \leq i \leq k$ are the Euclidean distances between the solution whose harmonic distance is being calculated and each of its k- nearest neighbor solutions. The solutions with the largest harmonic distances are considered to be in the least crowded region of the objective space, and thus selected as survivors (lines 14 to 16).

Those familiar with MOEAs will note that HaD-MOEA is very similar to the well-known NSGA-II. HaD-MOEA was proposed with the aim of improving upon NSGA-II, which is known not to perform well when the number of objectives increases [209]. Wang et al. [438] explained that two key problems in NSGA-II are its measure of crowding distance and the method for selecting survivors based on it. NSGA-II uses the 1-norm distance between the two nearest neighbors of a solution as the crowding distance measure of this solution. Wang et al. [438] showed that this inherently does not reflect well the actual crowding degree of a given solution. In addition, NSGA-II calculates the crowding distance of a given solution based only on the solutions belonging to the same nondominated front as this solution. This obviously does not reflect the crowding distance considering all solutions selected so far, which is the real crowding of the solutions. So, in HaD-MOEA, the crowding distance is calculated based on both the solutions belonging to the same front and all the previously selected solutions. HaD-MOEA has been demonstrated to perform better than NSGA-II in the domain of optimal testing resource allocation when using three objectives [438].

Wang et al. [438] do not restrict HaD-MOEA to a specific parents selection mechanism. However, they use binary tournament selection in their experiments. As explained in Section 24.2, binary tournament selection works by picking two candidate solutions uniformly at random, and then selecting the best between them. A similar mechanism to the one used for survivor selection can be used to determine which of the two randomly picked candidate solutions is the "best." This is repeated until the desired number of parents is obtained. The number of parents selected in this step depends on how the variation operators work, so as to generate the desired number of offspring. For example, if α offspring are to be generated and the crossover of two parents generates two offspring, then α parents must be selected. Note that, as crossover is probabilistic, there is some chance that it is not applied. In this case, the two parents could be cloned to produce two offspring. After crossover (or cloning), each offspring also has some chance to go through mutation.

24.4 USING MOEAS FOR CREATING SEE MODELS

As explained by Harman and Clark [163] ,"[m]etrics, whether collected statically or dynamically, and whether constructed from source code, systems or processes, are largely regarded as a means of evaluating some property of interest." For example, functional size and software effort are metrics derived from the project data. Performance measures such as MMRE, PRED, and LSD are metrics that represent how well a certain model fits the project data, and are calculated based on metrics such as software effort.

Harman and Clark [163] explain that metrics can be used as fitness functions in search-based software engineering, being able to guide the force behind the search for optimal or near optimal solutions in such a way to automate software engineering tasks. In that sense, search-based software engineering is very related to the construction of prediction models [162]. For instance, in the context of software cost/effort estimation, genetic programming has been applied using MSE as fitness function [102, 103, 386]. SEE was then innovatively proposed to be viewed as a multiobjective learning problem where the performance measures that we are interested in can be seen as separate objectives to be optimized by a MOEA in [319, 327], and soon after in [128, 376, 377].

This section explains the problem formulation and approach proposed by Minku and Yao [319, 327] to use MOEAs for creating SEE models. Different performance measures are used as objectives to be optimized simultaneously for generating SEE models. Different from single-objective formulations, that allows us to get a better understanding of different performance measures, to create well performing SEE ensembles, and to emphasize different performance measures if desired, as explained later in Section 24.5.

Once a representation, variation operators, and objective functions are defined, this approach can be used in combination with any MOEA. This chapter does not intend to show that a particular MOEA performs better or worse than another. For that reason, the evaluation of which MOEA is better for evolving SEE models is left as future work. In the current study, we concentrate on the multiobjective formulation of the problem, how to use a multiobjective approach to solve it, and providing a better understanding of different performance measures. Section 24.4.1 explains how we formulate the problem of creating SEE models as a multiobjective optimization problem, defining its objective functions. Section 24.4.2 comments on the type of SEE models generated. Section 24.4.3 explains the representation of the models and the variation operators used. Section 24.4.4 explains how to use the solutions produced by the MOEA.

24.4.1 MULTIOBJECTIVE FORMULATION OF THE PROBLEM

Different performance measures can be used as objectives to be optimized when creating SEE models. In this work, considering a set of T projects, the following measures were used:

- Mean magnitude of the relative error:

$$\text{MMRE} = \frac{1}{T} \sum_{i=1}^{T} \text{MRE}_i,$$

where $\text{MRE}_i = |\hat{y}_i - y_i|/y_i$; $\hat{y}_i$ is the predicted effort; and y_i is the actual effort.
- Percentage of estimations within 25% of the actual values:

$$\text{PRED(25)} = \frac{1}{T} \sum_{i=1}^{T} \begin{cases} 1, & \text{if } \text{MRE}_i \leq \frac{25}{100} \\ 0, & \text{otherwise} \end{cases}.$$

- Logarithmic standard deviation:

$$LSD = \sqrt{\frac{\sum_{i=1}^{T}\left(e_i + \frac{s^2}{2}\right)^2}{T-1}},$$

where s^2 is an estimator of the variance of the residual e_i and $e_i = \ln y_i - \ln \hat{y}_i$.

MMRE and LSD are objectives to be minimized, whereas PRED(25) is to be maximized. In order to avoid possible infinite LSD averages due to negative estimations, any negative estimation was replaced by the value one when calculating $\ln \hat{y}$. MMRE and PRED(25) are popular metrics in the SEE literature, as illustrated by Table 2 of Dejaeger et al.'s [94] work, whereas LSD was recommended by Foss et al. [133] as being more reliable, especially for multiplicative models. These measures were chosen because, even though all of them were initially designed to represent how well a model performs, they are believed to behave very differently from each other, as confirmed in Section 24.6. This is potentially very useful for maximizing diversity among ensemble members, as explained in Chapter 20. Other measures can be investigated as future work.

During the MOEA evolving procedure, the objective values are calculated using a set of projects with known effort, which will be referred to as the training set. When evaluating the results of the approaches, the performance measures are calculated over the test set.

Several different performance measures for SEE can be found in the literature. Most of them are calculated over the prediction error $(y_i - \hat{y}_i)$ [297]. The mean absolute error (MAE) is the mean of the absolute prediction error, providing an unbiased measure that does not favor under- or overestimates. Sometimes median measures are used to avoid influence of extreme values. For these reasons, the evaluation analysis of our approach also considers its MAE, median absolute error (MdAE) and median MRE (MdMRE), which are defined as follows:

- $MAE = \frac{1}{T}\sum_{i=1}^{T}|\hat{y}_i - y_i|$;
- $MdAE = \text{Median } \{|\hat{y}_i - y_i| \,/\, 1 \le i \le T\}$; and
- $MdMRE = \text{Median } \{MRE_i \,/\, 1 \le i \le T\}$.

24.4.2 SEE MODELS GENERATED

The models generated by the MOEA in this work are MLPs [32]. As explained in Section 24.1, MLPs can improve over conventional linear models when the function being modeled is not linear [422]. Even though we evolve MLPs in this work, MOEAs could also be used to generate other types of models for SEE, such as RBFs, RTs and linear regression equations. As the key point of this work is to analyze the multiobjective formulation of the creation of SEE models, and not the comparison among different types of models, the experimentation of MOEAs to create other types of models is left as future work.

24.4.3 REPRESENTATION AND VARIATION OPERATORS

The MLP models were represented by a real value vector of size $n_i \cdot (n_h + 1) + n_h \cdot (n_o + 1)$, where n_i, n_h, and n_o are the number of inputs, hidden neurons, and output neurons, respectively. This real value vector is manipulated by the MOEA to generate SEE models. Each position of the vector represents a weight or the threshold of a neuron. The value one summed to n_h and n_o in the formula above represents the threshold. The number of input neurons corresponds to the number of project input features and the number of output neurons is always one for the SEE task. The number of hidden neurons is a parameter of the approach.

The variation operators were inspired by Chandra and Yao's [69] work, which also involves evolution of MLPs. Let w^{p1}, w^{p2}, and w^{p3} be three parents. One offspring w^c is generated with probability p_c according to the following equation:

$$w^c = w^{p1} + N(0, \sigma^2)(w^{p2} - w^{p3}),$$

where w is the real value vector representing the candidate solutions and $N(0, \sigma^2)$ is a random number drawn from a Gaussian distribution with mean zero and variance σ^2.

An adaptive procedure inspired by simulated annealing is used to update the variance σ^2 of the Gaussian at every generation [69]. This procedure allows the crossover to be initially explorative and then become more exploitative. The variance is updated according to the following equation:

$$\sigma^2 = 2 - \left(\frac{1}{1 + e^{(\text{anneal\_time} - \text{generation})}} \right),$$

where *anneal_time* is a parameter meaning the number of generations for which the search is to be explorative, after which σ^2 decreases exponentially until reaching and keeping the value of one.

Mutation is performed elementwise with probability p_m according to the following equation:

$$w_i = w_i + N(0, 0.1),$$

where w_i represents a position of the vector representing the MLP and $N(0, 0.1)$ is a random number drawn from a Gaussian distribution with mean zero and variance 0.1.

The offspring candidate solutions receive further local training using backpropagation [32], as in Chandra and Yao's [69] work.

24.4.4 USING THE SOLUTIONS PRODUCED BY A MOEA

The solutions produced by the MOEA are innovatively used for SEE in two ways in this work. The first one is a *Pareto ensemble* composed of the *best fit Pareto solutions*. Best fit Pareto solutions are the Pareto solutions with the best train performance considering each objective separately. So, the ensemble will be composed of the Pareto solution with the best train LSD, best train MMRE, and best train PRED(25). The effort estimation given by the ensemble is the arithmetic average of the estimations given by each of its base models. So, each performance measure can be seen as having "one vote," providing a fair and ideal trade-off among the measures when no emphasis is given to a certain measure over the others. This avoids the need for a software manager to decide on a certain measure to be emphasized.

It is worth noting that this approach to create ensembles focuses not only on accuracy, but also on diversity among base learners, which is known to be a key issue when creating ensembles [61, 244]. Accuracy is encouraged by using a MOEA to optimize MMRE, PRED, and LSD simultaneously. So, the base models are created in such a way to be generally accurate considering these three measures at the same time. Diversity is encouraged by selecting only the best fit Pareto solution according to each of these measures. As shown in Section 24.6, these measures behave very differently from each other.

So, it is likely that the MMRE of the best fit Pareto solution according to LSD will be different from the MMRE of the best fit Pareto solution according to MMRE itself. The same is valid for the other performance measures. Models with different performance considering a particular measure are likely to produce different estimations, being diverse.

The second way to use the solutions produced by the MOEA is to use each best fit Pareto solution by itself. These solutions can be used when a particular measure is to be emphasized.

It is worth noting that a MOEA automatically creates these models. The Pareto solutions and the best fit Pareto solutions can be automatically determined by the algorithm. There is no need to invole manual/visual checking.

24.5 **EXPERIMENTAL SETUP**

The experiments presented in this chapter were designed to answer research questions RQ1-RQ3 explained in the beginning of the chapter. In our experiments, HaD-MOEA (Section 24.3) has been used as the MOEA algorithm for generating MLP SEE models, due to its simplicity and advantages over NSGA-II (see Section 24.3). Our implementation of HaD-MOEA was based on the meta-heuristic optimization framework for Java Opt4J [273]. MLP SEE models were generated according to Section 24.4.

In order to answer RQ1, we show that plots of the Pareto solutions can be used to provide a better understanding of the relationship among different performance measures. They can show that, for example, when increasing the value of a certain measure, the value of another measure may decrease and by how much. Our study shows the very different and sometimes even opposite behavior of different measures. This is an indicator that these measures can be used to create diverse ensembles for SEE (Section 24.6).

In order to answer RQ2, the following comparison was made (Section 24.7):

- Pareto ensemble versus backpropagation MLP (single MLP created using backpropagation). This comparison was made to show the applicability of MOEAs to generate SEE ensemble models. It analyzes the use of a MOEA, which considers several performance measures at the same time, against the nonuse of a MOEA.

The results of this comparison show that the MOEA is successful in generating SEE ensemble models by optimizing different performance measures explicitly at the same time. These ensembles present performance similar to or better than a model that does not optimize the three measures concurrently. Furthermore, the similar or better performance is achieved considering all the measures used to create the ensemble, showing that these ensembles not only provide a better trade-off among different measures, but also improve the performance considering these measures.

In order to answer RQ3, the following comparison was made (Section 24.8):

- Best fit Pareto MLP versus Pareto ensemble. This comparison allows us to check whether it is possible to increase the performance considering a particular measure if we would like to emphasize it. This is particularly useful when there is a certain measure that we believe to be more appropriate than the others.

The results of this comparison reveal that MOEAs are flexible in terms of providing SEE models based on a multiobjective formulation of the problem. They can provide both solutions considered as having a good trade-off when no measure is to be emphasized and solutions that emphasize certain measures over the others if desired. If there is no measure to be emphasized, a Pareto ensemble can be used to provide a relatively good performance in terms of different measures. If the software manager would like to emphasize a certain measure, it is possible to use the best fit Pareto solution in terms of this measure.

Additionally, the following comparisons were made to test the optimality of the choice of best fit MLPs as models to be used (Section 24.9):

- Best Pareto MLP in terms of test performance versus backpropagation MLP, and Pareto ensemble composed of the best Pareto MLPs in terms of each test performance versus backpropagation MLP. This comparison was made to check whether better results could be achieved if a better choice of solution from the Pareto front was made. Please note that choosing the best models based on their test performance was done for analysis purposes only and could not be done in practice.

The results of this comparison show that there is still room for improvement in terms of Pareto solution choice.

The comparisons to answer the research questions as outlined above show that it is possible and worth considering SEE models generation as a multiobjective learning problem and that a MOEA can be used to provide a better understanding of different performance measures, to create well-performing SEE ensembles, and to create SEE models that emphasize particular performance measures.

In order to show how the solutions generated by the HaD-MOEA to evolve MLPs compare to other approaches in the literature, an additional round of comparisons was made against the following methods (Section 24.10):

- Single learners: MLPs [32]; RBFs [32]; RTs [459]; and estimation by analogy (EBA) [390] based on log transformed data.
- Ensemble learners: bagging [46] with MLPs, with RBFs and with RTs; random [156] with MLPs; and negative correlation learning (NCL) [263, 264] with MLPs.

These comparisons do not evaluate the multiobjective formulation of the problem by itself, but a mix of the HaD-MOEA to the type of models being evolved (MLP). According to very recent studies [223, 321, 326], REPTrees, bagging ensembles of MLPs, bagging ensembles of REPTrees, and EBA based on log transformed data can be considered to be among the best current methods for SEE. The implementation used for all the opponent learning machines but NCL was based on Weka [156]. The RTs were based on the REPTree model. We recommend the software Weka should the reader wish to get more details about the implementation and parameters. The software used for NCL is available upon request.

The results of these comparisons show that the MOEA-evolved MLPs were ranked first more often in terms of MMRE, PRED(25), MdMRE, MAE, and MdAE, but performed less well in terms of LSD. They were also ranked first more often for the International Software Benchmarking Standards Group (ISBSG) (cross-company) data sets, which are likely to be more heterogeneous. It is important to emphasize, though, that this additional comparison is not only evaluating the MOEA and the multiobjective formulation of the problem, but also the type of model being evolved (MLP). Other types of models could also be evolved by the MOEA and could possibly provide better results in terms of LSD.

The experiments were based on the PROMISE data sets explained in Section 20.4.1.1, the ISBSG subsets explained in Section 20.4.1.2, and a data set containing the union of all the ISBSG subsets (orgAll). The union was used in order to create a data set likely to be more heterogeneous than the previous ones.

Thirty rounds of executions were performed for each data set from Section 20.4.1. In each round, for each data set, 10 projects were randomly picked for testing and the remaining were used for the MOEA optimization process/training of approaches. Holdout of size 10 was suggested by Menzies et al. [292] and allows the largest possible number of projects to be used for training without hindering the testing. For the data set sdr (described in Section 20.4.1.1), half of the projects were used for testing and half for training, due to the small size of the data set. The measures of performance used to evaluate the approaches are MMRE, PRED(25), and LSD, which are the same performance measures used to create the models (Section 24.4.1), but calculated on the test set. It is worth noting that MMRE and PRED using the parameter 25 were chosen for being popular measures, even though raw values from different papers are not directly comparable because they use different training and test sets, besides possibly using different evaluation methods. In addition, we also report MdMRE, MAE, and MdAE.

The absolute value of the Glass's Δ effect size [373] was used to evaluate the practical significance of the changes in performance when choosing between the Pareto ensemble and an opponent approach:

$$\Delta = \frac{|M_a - M_p|}{SD_p},\tag{24.1}$$

where M_p and M_a are the performances obtained by the Pareto ensemble and an opponent approach, and SD_p is the standard deviation obtained by the Pareto ensemble. As the effect size is scale-free, it was interpreted based on Cohen's [80] suggested categories: small (≈ 0.2), medium (≈ 0.5), and large (≈ 0.8). Medium and large effect sizes are of more "practical" significance.

The parameters choice of the opponent approaches was based on five preliminary executions using several different parameters (Table 24.1). The set of parameters leading to the best MMRE for each data set was used for the final 30 executions used in the analysis. MMRE was chosen for being a popular measure in the literature. The experiments with the opponent approaches were also used by Minku and Yao [321].

The MLP's learning rate, momentum, and number of hidden neurons used by HaD-MOEA were chosen so as to correspond to the parameters used by the opponent backpropagation MLPs and are presented in Table 24.2. These parameters were tuned to provide very good results for the opponent backpropagation MLPs, but were not specifically tuned for the MOEA approach described in this chapter. The number of generations, also shown in Table 24.2, is the number of epochs used by the opponent backpropagation MLPs divided by the number of epochs for the offspring backpropagation. This value was chosen so that each MLP at the end of the evolutionary process is potentially trained with the same total number of epochs as the opponent backpropagation MLPs. The remaining evolutionary parameters were fixed for all data sets and were not intended to be optimal. In summary, these are

- Tournament size: 2 (binary tournament selection). Tournament is a popular parent selection method. A tournament size of 2 is commonly used in practice because it often provides sufficient selection pressure on the most fit candidate solutions [248].
- Population size: 100. This value was arbitrarily chosen.

Table 24.1 Parameter Values for Preliminary Executions

Approach	Parameters
MLP	Learning rate = {0.1, 0.2, 0.3, 0.4, 0.5} Momentum = {0.1, 0.2, 0.3, 0.4, 0.5} # Epochs = {100, 500, 1000} # Hidden neurons = {3, 5, 9}
RBF	# Clusters = {2, 3, 4, 5, 6} Minimum standard deviation for the clusters = {0.01, 0.1, 0.2, 0.3, 0.4}
REPTree	Minimum total weight for instances in a leaf = {1, 2, 3, 4, 5} Minimum proportion of the data variance at a node for splitting to be performed = {0.0001, 0.001, 0.01, 0.1}
Ensembles	# Base learners = {10, 25, 50} All the possible parameters of the adopted base learners, as shown above
NCL	Penalty strength = {0.3, 0.4, 0.5}

Note: *From [327].*

Table 24.2 Parameter Values Used in the HaD-MOEA

Data Set	Learning Rate	Momentum	# Generations	# Hidden Neurons
Cocomo81	0.3	0.5	200	9
Sdr	0.5	0.2	20	9
Nasa	0.1	0.1	100	9
Desharnais	0.1	0.1	100	9
Nasa93	0.4	0.5	20	5
Org1	0.1	0.2	200	9
Org2	0.1	0.1	100	5
Org3	0.1	0.3	100	5
Org4	0.2	0.3	200	9
Org5	0.2	0.3	200	9
Org6	0.1	0.1	20	3
Org7	0.5	0.3	20	5
OrgAll	0.1	0.5	20	9

Note: *From [327].*

- Number of epochs used for the backpropagation applied to the offspring candidate solutions: 5. This is the same value as used by Chandra and Yao [69].
- Anneal_time: number of generations divided by 4, as in Chandra and Yao's [69] work.
- Probability of crossover: 0.8. Chosen between 0.8 and 0.9 (the value used by Wang et al. [438]) so as to reduce the MMRE in five preliminary executions for cocomo81. We decided to check whether 0.8 would be better than 0.9 because 0.9 can be considered as a fairly large probability.
- Probability of mutation: 0.05. Chosen between 0.05 and 0.1 (the value used by Wang et al. [438]) so as to reduce the MMRE in five preliminary executions for cocomo81. We decided to check whether 0.05 would be better than 0.1 because the value 0.1 can be considered large considering the size of each candidate solution of the population in our case.

A population size arbitrarily reduced to 30 and number of epochs for the offspring backpropagation reduced to zero (no backpropagation) were used for additional MOEA executions in the analysis. Unless stated otherwise, the original parameters summarized above were used.

The analysis presented in this chapter is based on five data sets from the PRedictOr Models In Software Engineering Software (PROMISE) Repository [300] and eight data sets based on the ISBSG Repository [271] Release 10, as in [321]. The data sets were the same as the ones used in Chapter 20 (cocomo81, nasa93, nasa, sdr, desharnais, org1-org7 and orgAll) and chosen to cover a wide range of problem features, such as number of projects, types of features, countries and companies.

24.6 THE RELATIONSHIP AMONG DIFFERENT PERFORMANCE MEASURES

This section presents an analysis of the Pareto solutions with the aim of providing a better understanding of the relationship among MMRE, PRED(25), and LSD (RQ1). All the plots presented here refer to the execution among the 30 runs in which the Pareto ensemble obtained the median test MMRE, unless its test PRED(25) was zero. In that case, the nonzero test PRED(25) execution closest to the median MMRE solution was chosen. This execution will be called *median MMRE run*.

Figure 24.5 presents an example of Pareto solutions plot for nasa93. We can see that solutions with better PRED(25) do not necessarily have better MMRE and LSD. The same is valid for the other performance measures. For example, a solution with relatively good MMRE may have very bad LSD, and a solution with good LSD may have very bad PRED(25). This demonstrates that model choice or creation based solely on one performance measure may not be ideal. In the same way, choosing a model based solely on MMRE when the difference in MMRE is statistically significant [292] may not be ideal.

In order to better understand the relationship among the performance measures, we plotted graphs LSD versus MMRE, LSD versus PRED(25), and MMRE versus PRED(25) for the median MMRE run, for each PROMISE data set and for ISBSG orgAll. Figure 24.6 shows representative plots for cocomo81 and orgAll. Other figures were omitted due to space restrictions and present the same tendencies. It is worth noting that, even though some Pareto solutions have worse performance than other solutions considering the two measures in the plots, they are still nondominated when all three objectives are considered. All the three objectives have to be considered at the same time to determine whether a solution is (non)dominated.

Considering LSD versus MMRE (Figure 24.6a and b), we can see that as MMRE is improved (reduced), LSD tends to get worse (increased). This tendency is particularly noticeable for cocomo81, which contains more solutions in the Pareto front.

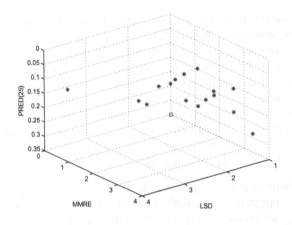

FIGURE 24.5

An example plot of "Pareto solutions" (nondominated solutions in the last generation) for nasa93. The red (dark gray in print versions) square represents the best position that can be plotted in this graph. From [327].

Considering LSD versus PRED(25) (Figure 24.6c and d), we can see that solutions with similar PRED(25) frequently present different LSD. The opposite is also valid: solutions with similar LSD frequently present different PRED(25). As PRED(25) is the percentage of estimations within 25% of the actual effort, one would expect several solutions with different LSD to have the same PRED(25), as a big improvement is necessary to cause impact on PRED(25). The opposite is somewhat more surprising. It indicates that average LSD by itself is not necessarily a good performance measure and may be affected by a few estimations containing extreme values.

A similar behavior is observed in the graphs MMRE versus PRED(25) (Figure 24.6e and f), but it is even more extreme in this case: Solutions with even more different MMRE present the same PRED(25).

Overall, the plots show that, even though a certain solution may appear better than another in terms of a certain measure, it may be actually worse in terms of the other measures. As none of the existing performance measures has a perfect behavior, the software manager may opt to analyze solutions using several different measures, instead of basing decisions on a single measure. For instance, s/he may opt for a solution that behaves better considering most performance measures. The analysis also shows that MMRE, PRED(25), and LSD behave differently, indicating that they may be useful for creating SEE ensembles. This is further investigated in Section 24.7.

Moreover, considering this difference in behavior, the choice of a solution by a software manager may not be easy. If the software manager has a reason for emphasizing a certain performance measure, s/he may choose the solution more likely to perform best for this measure. However, if it is not known what measure to emphasize, s/he may be interested in a solution that provides a good trade-off among different measures. We show in Section 24.7 that MOEA can be used to automatically generate an ensemble that provides a good trade-off among different measures, so that the software manager does not necessarily need to decide on a particular solution or performance measure. Our approach is also robust, allowing the software manager to emphasize a certain measure should s/he wish to, as shown in Section 24.8.

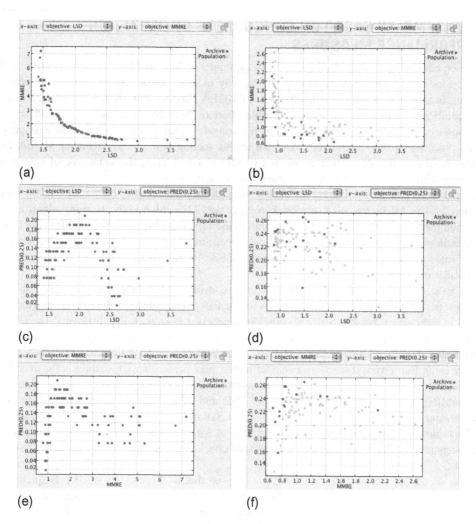

FIGURE 24.6

Plot of solutions in the last generation according to two of the three objectives. Points in red (dark points in print versions) represent the Pareto solutions. Points in light gray represent the other solutions in the population. From [327]. (a) Cocomo81 LSD versus MMRE, (b) OrgAll LSD versus MMRE, (c) Cocomo81 LSD versus PRED(25), (d) OrgAll LSD versus PRED(25), (e) Cocomo81 MMRE versus PRED(25), (f) OrgAll MMRE versus PRED(25).

24.7 ENSEMBLES BASED ON CONCURRENT OPTIMIZATION OF PERFORMANCE MEASURES

This section concentrates on answering RQ2. As explained in Section 24.6, different measures behave differently, indicating they may provide a natural way to generate diverse models to compose SEE ensembles. In this section, we show that the best fit MOEA Pareto solutions in terms of each objective can be combined to produce an SEE ensemble (Pareto ensemble) that achieves good results in comparison to a traditional algorithm that does not consider several different measures explicitly. So, the main objective of the comparison presented in this section is to analyze whether MOEA can be used improve the performance over the nonuse of MOEA considering the same type of base models. Comparison with other types of models is shown in Section 24.10.

The analysis is done by comparing the Pareto ensemble of MLPs created by the MOEA as explained in Section 24.4 to MLPs trained using backpropagation [32], which is the learning algorithm most widely used for training MLPs. Each best fit solution used to create the Pareto ensemble is the one with the best train performance considering a particular measure. The Pareto ensemble represents a good trade-off among different performance measures, if the software manager does not wish to emphasize any particular measure.

First, let's analyze the test performance average considering all data sets. Table 24.3 shows the average test performance and standard deviation for the Pareto ensemble and the backpropagation MLP. The cells in light gray represent better averages (not necessarily statistically different). The table also shows the overall average and p-value of the Wilcoxon test used for the statistical comparison of all runs over multiple data sets. p-Values less than 0.0167 (shown in dark gray) indicate statistically significant difference using Bonferroni corrections considering the three performance measures at the overall level of significance of 0.05. As we can see, the two approaches are statistically the same considering the overall MMRE, but different when considering LSD and PRED(25). In the latter case, the Pareto ensemble wins in 7 out of 13 data sets considering LSD and PRED(25), as shown by the light gray cells. This number of wins is similar to the number of losses, so additional analysis is necessary to better understand the Pareto ensemble's behavior and check if it can be improved, as shown in the next paragraphs.

Hence, second, if we take a closer look, we can see that backpropagation MLP frequently wins for the smallest data sets, whereas the Pareto ensemble tends to behave better for the largest data sets. Considering LSD, the Pareto ensemble wins in 6 out of 8 large data sets. Considering MMRE, it wins in 5 out of 8 large data sets. Considering PRED(25), it wins in 7 out of 8 large data sets. So, we performed additional statistical tests to compare the behavior of all the runs considering the data sets with less than 35 projects (sdr, org2, org5, org6, org7) and with 60 or more projects (cocomo81, nasa93, nasa, desharnais, org1, org3, org4, orgAll) separately.

Table 24.4 shows the overall averages and p-values for these two groups of data sets. We can see that there is statistically significant difference considering all performance measures for the large data sets, including MMRE. That, together with the fact that the Pareto ensemble wins in most cases for these data sets, indicates that it is likely to perform better than backpropagation MLPs for large data sets. That is a very good achievement, especially considering that the backpropagation MLPs were very well tuned for providing good MMRE. For the small data sets, the two approaches obtained were statistically significantly different LSD and the Pareto ensemble was worse in 4 out of 5 small data sets. The two approaches were statistically equal in terms of MMRE and PRED(25) for the small data sets.

Table 24.3 Pareto Ensemble vs Backpropagation MLP—Test Performance Average and Standard Deviation

Data Set	Pareto Ensemble			Backpropagation MLP		
	LSD	MMRE	PRED(25)	LSD	MMRE	PRED(25)
Cocomo81	1.9193 ± 0.7709	4.2374 ± 5.3865	0.1600 ± 0.1354	2.8237 ± 1.5270	2.7914 ± 1.6687	0.1300 ± 0.1179
Sdr	2.0944 ± 0.8367	8.6331 ± 19.0015	0.0833 ± 0.1295	1.5782 ± 0.4282	1.9254 ± 0.9617	0.1444 ± 0.1217
Nasa	1.4005 ± 0.9419	1.1140 ± 0.8244	0.3200 ± 0.1606	1.6676 ± 1.0735	1.0805 ± 0.9497	0.4267 ± 0.1530
Desharnais	1.1515 ± 1.3872	0.4701 ± 0.1903	0.4200 ± 0.1846	1.0291 ± 1.2157	0.4986 ± 0.1712	0.3333 ± 0.1373
Nasa93	1.2518 ± 0.4061	1.8031 ± 1.2951	0.1848 ± 0.1318	2.6262 ± 1.4871	1.7866 ± 0.8316	0.1970 ± 0.0927
Org1	1.1560 ± 1.3867	0.8739 ± 0.4551	0.2967 ± 0.1564	1.8601 ± 2.2647	1.2233 ± 0.9439	0.2600 ± 0.1653
Org2	0.8120 ± 0.2751	1.6575 ± 3.5308	0.2633 ± 0.1402	1.2455 ± 1.0130	1.0554 ± 0.3322	0.2200 ± 0.1186
Org3	0.7076 ± 0.2120	0.9449 ± 1.4016	0.2909 ± 0.1338	1.8770 ± 2.3732	3.2484 ± 9.6361	0.2333 ± 0.1485
Org4	1.1074 ± 1.1572	0.8596 ± 0.2613	0.2121 ± 0.1271	2.0374 ± 2.6682	1.1014 ± 0.6457	0.1848 ± 0.1157
Org5	6.4777 ± 5.4380	5.4348 ± 14.5110	0.2033 ± 0.0964	3.0275 ± 4.1660	1.2569 ± 0.7010	0.2133 ± 0.1106
Org6	1.4703 ± 1.5488	1.1507 ± 0.6037	0.1833 ± 0.1053	0.8470 ± 0.1909	1.0493 ± 0.4745	0.2067 ± 0.0944
Org7	2.1753 ± 1.5659	4.3080 ± 5.2502	0.1633 ± 0.1129	1.9786 ± 3.2286	1.3280 ± 0.8346	0.1833 ± 0.0913
OrgAll	1.1025 ± 0.9509	0.7313 ± 0.2866	0.2641 ± 0.1350	2.6782 ± 2.7064	2.0317 ± 2.5790	0.1744 ± 0.1068
Average	1.7559	2.4783	0.2343	1.9443	1.5675	0.2236
p-Value	0.0076	0.2168	0.0036			

Notes: The p-values of the Wilcoxon tests for the comparison over multiple data sets are also shown. p-Values less than 0.0167 indicate statistically significant difference using Bonferroni corrections at the overall level of significance of 0.05 and are in dark gray. The cells in light gray represent better averages (not necessarily statistically different). From [327].

Table 24.4 Pareto Ensemble vs Backpropagation MLP Considering Large and Small Data Sets Separately—Test Performance

Data Set	Pareto Ensemble			Backpropagation MLP		
	LSD	MMRE	PRED(25)	LSD	MMRE	PRED(25)
Large	1.2246	1.3793	0.2686	2.0749	1.7202	0.2424
p-Value	0.0000	0.0012	0.0003			
Small	2.6059	4.2368	0.1793	1.7354	1.323	0.1936
p-Value	0.0001	0.0444	0.8449			

Notes: *The p-values of the Wilcoxon tests for the comparison over multiple data sets are also shown. p-Values less than 0.0167 indicate statistically significant difference using Bonferroni corrections at the overall level of significance of 0.05 and are in dark gray. From [327].*

A possible reason for the worse behavior for the smallest data sets is overfitting. To make this hypothesis more well-grounded, we checked the MMREs obtained by each MLP of the Pareto ensemble for the median MMRE run of org5. Org5 was chosen for being the data set in which the Pareto ensemble obtained the worst test MMRE, but not the one with the smallest number of projects, as only 12 projects may be too little for a significant analysis. The test MMREs were 1.9396, 1.9217, and 1.9613, whereas the corresponding train MMREs were 0.0998, 0.0976, and 0.1017, respectively. We can see that the test MMREs were drastically larger than the train MMREs. On the other hand, the three runs on and around the median test MMRE for the backpropagation MLPs obtained 1.0403, 1.0433, and 1.1599 test MMRE, whereas the train MMREs were 0.3183, 1.0857, and 0.1176. So, the train MMREs were higher (worse) for the backpropagation MLPs than for the best fit Pareto MLPs. That indicates that the MOEA may indeed be overfitting when the data sets are too small. Besides the fact that learning is inherently hard due to the small number of training examples, a possible cause for that is the parameters choice, as the parameters were not so well-tuned for the MOEA.

So, third, additional MOEA runs were performed in such a way to use the essence of the early stopping strategy to avoid overfitting [131]. This was done by reducing the population size from 100 to 30 and the number of epochs for the offspring backpropagation from 5 to 0 (no backpropagation). The results are shown in Table 24.5. As we can see, the Pareto ensemble obtained similar LSD and MMRE to backpropagation MLPs. PRED(25) was statistically significantly different and the Pareto ensemble won in 3 out of 5 data sets. The improvement in the overall average was of about 0.79 for LSD, 2.44 for MMRE, and 0.04 for PRED(25). The test MMREs for the median MMRE run of the Pareto ensemble for org5 were 0.8649, 0.8528, and 1.4543, whereas the corresponding train MMREs were 0.3311, 0.3116, and 0.5427. These train MMREs are closer to the corresponding test MMREs than when using the previous parameters configuration, indicating less overfitting.

Last, in order to check the performance of the Pareto ensemble for outlier projects, we have also tested it using test sets comprised only of the outliers identified in Section 20.4.1. The MMRE and PRED(25) obtained for the outlier sets were compared to the original test sets. It is not possible to compare LSD because the number of outliers is too small and LSD's equation is divided by the number of projects minus one. So, even if the error obtained for the outlier sets is potentially smaller, the small number of examples increases LSD.

Table 24.5 Pareto Ensemble Using Adjusted Parameters (Reduced Population Size and No Backpropagation) vs Backpropagation MLP for Small Data Sets—Test Performance and Standard Deviation

Data Set	Pareto Ensemble			Backpropagation MLP		
	LSD	MMRE	PRED(25)	LSD	MMRE	PRED(25)
Sdr	2.1160 ± 0.7330	4.1618 ± 2.7773	0.0944 ± 0.1132	1.5782 ± 0.4282	1.9254 ± 0.9617	0.1444 ± 0.1217
Org2	0.9022 ± 0.7834	0.5966 ± 0.2501	0.2833 ± 0.1416	1.2455 ± 1.0130	1.0554 ± 0.3322	0.2200 ± 0.1186
Org5	3.4037 ± 4.1020	1.5130 ± 1.6793	0.2833 ± 0.1234	3.0275 ± 4.1660	1.2569 ± 0.7010	0.2133 ± 0.1106
Org6	0.8075 ± 0.2065	0.7688 ± 0.3216	0.2800 ± 0.1126	0.8470 ± 0.1909	1.0493 ± 0.4745	0.2067 ± 0.0944
Org7	1.8411 ± 1.2749	1.9268 ± 1.7951	0.1700 ± 0.1088	1.9786 ± 3.2286	1.3280 ± 0.8346	0.1833 ± 0.0913
Average	1.8141	1.7934	0.2222	1.7354	1.3230	0.1936
p-Value	0.1170	0.7166	0.0004			

Notes: The p-values of the Wilcoxon tests for the comparison over multiple data sets are also shown. p-Values less than 0.0167 indicate statistically significant difference using Bonferroni corrections at the overall level of significance of 0.05 and are in dark gray. The cells in light gray represent better averages (not necessarily statistically different). From [327].

The results show that PRED(25) was always worse for the outlier sets than for the original test sets. That means that these outliers are projects to which the Pareto ensemble has difficulties in predicting within 25% of the actual effort. However, the MMRE is actually better for 3 out of 9 data sets that involve outliers. So, in about a third of the cases, the outliers are not projects to which the Pareto ensemble obtains the worst performances. For the other cases, the MMRE was usually less than 0.27 higher.

The analysis performed in this section shows that the use of MOEA for considering several performance measures at the same time is successful in generating SEE ensembles. The Pareto ensemble manages to obtain similar or better performance than backpropagation MLP across data sets in terms of all the measures used as objectives by the MOEA. So, it is worth considering the creation of SEE models as a multiobjective problem and the Pareto ensemble can be used when none of the performance measures is to be emphasized over the others.

24.8 EMPHASIZING PARTICULAR PERFORMANCE MEASURES

This section concentrates on answering RQ3. As shown in Section 24.7, MOEA can be used to automatically generate an ensemble that provides an ideal trade-off among different measures, so that the software manager does not need to decide on a particular solution or performance measure. The main objective of the comparison presented in the present section is to analyze whether we can further increase the test performance for each measure separately if we wish to emphasize this particular measure. This section provides a better understanding of the solutions that can be produced by the MOEA and shows that our approach is robust in the case where the manager wishes to emphasize a certain measure. In order to do so, we check the performance of the best fit solution considering each objective separately. The best fit solution is the one with the best train performance considering a particular measure.

Table 24.6a and b shows the results of the comparisons between the best fit Pareto MLP in terms of each objective versus the Pareto ensemble for large and small data sets, respectively. The MOEA parameters for the small data sets are the ones with population size 30 and no backpropagation. Dark gray color means statistically significant difference using Wilcoxon tests with Bonferroni corrections at the overall level of significance of 0.05 (statistically significant difference when p-value $< 0.05/(3 *$ 3)). The number of times in which each approach wins against the Pareto ensemble is also shown and is in light gray when the approach wins more times.

The results of these comparisons indicate that using each best fit Pareto MLP considering a certain objective can sometimes improve the test performance considering this objective. Even though the test performance to be emphasized becomes equal or better than the Pareto ensemble, as shown by the statistical test and the number of wins, the performance considering the other measures gets equal or worse. It is worth noting, though, that the best fit Pareto MLPs are still nondominated solutions, providing acceptable performance in terms of all the measures in comparison to other solutions generated by the MOEA.

In addition to the statistical comparison, we are also interested in the effect size Δ (Equation (24.1), Section 24.5) of each best MLP in comparison to the Pareto ensemble, in terms of the performance

Table 24.6 Test Performance Average of Best Fit Pareto MLPs Against the Pareto Ensemble

Data Set	LSD	MMRE	PRED(25)
(a) For large data sets			
Pareto ensemble	1.2246	1.3793	0.2686
Best LSD MLP avg.	1.1356	2.1518	0.2587
Wins vs Pareto ens	6	0	3
p-Value	0.0034	0.0000	0.3062
Best MMRE MLP avg.	2.0070	0.8256	0.1974
Wins vs Pareto ens	0	7	0
p-Value	0.0000	0.0000	0.0000
Best PRED MLP avg.	1.4775	1.5084	0.2680
Wins vs Pareto ens	2	1	4
p-Value	0.0000	0.0000	0.9240
Data Set	**LSD**	**MMRE**	**PRED**
(b) For small data sets			
Pareto ensemble avg.	1.8141	1.7934	0.2222
Best LSD MLP avg.	1.8432	2.5741	0.1913
Wins vs Pareto ens	3	0	2
p-Value	0.1326	0.0000	0.0075
Best MMRE MLP avg.	2.1598	1.3511	0.2113
Wins vs Pareto ens	0	5	3
p-Value	0.0000	0.0000	0.5068
Best PRED MLP avg.	2.0739	1.9623	0.2178
Wins vs Pareto ens	0	1	1
p-Value	0.0000	0.0037	0.5438

Notes: *The adjusted MOEA parameters were used for the small data sets. The p-values of the Wilcoxon tests for the comparison over multiple data sets are also shown. p-Values less than 0.0056 (in dark gray) indicate statistically significant difference using Bonferroni corrections at the overall level of significance of 0.05. When the best fit Pareto MLP wins more times than the Pareto ensemble, its number of wins is highlighted in light gray. From [327].*

measure for which the MLP performs best. Table 24.7 presents the minimum, maximum, average, and standard deviation of the effect size Δ, as well as the number of data sets for which the effect size was small, medium, or large. Even though using each best MLP separately can provide some improvement in performance, the improvements are usually small. Nevertheless, as it would be very easy to configure an approach to use the best MLPs instead of the Pareto ensemble, one may wish to use the best MLPs to emphasize a certain performance measure even considering that the improvement in performance is small.

Table 24.7 Effect Size for Each Best MLP Against the Pareto Ensemble, in Terms of the Performance Measure for Which the MLP Performs Best

	Min. Δ	Max. Δ	Avg. Δ	Std Δ	# Small	# Medium	# Large	# Medium + Large
(a) Large data sets								
Best LSD MLP	0.0257	0.3221	0.1395	0.0993	8	0	0	0
Best MMRE MLP	0.0046	0.7983	0.3462	0.3035	4	3	1	4
Best PRED MLP	0.0542	0.2953	0.1699	0.0987	8	0	0	0
(b) Small data sets								
Best LSD MLP	0.0294	0.4468	0.2009	0.1687	4	1	0	1
Best MMRE MLP	0.0567	0.5913	0.2665	0.2080	4	1	0	1
Best PRED MLP	0.0235	0.9502	0.4050	0.3977	2	1	2	3

Note: From [327].

24.9 FURTHER ANALYSIS OF THE MODEL CHOICE

The main objective of the comparison presented in this section is to analyze whether our approach still has room for improvement in terms of model choice. If so, as future work, other methods for choosing models for the Pareto ensemble should be investigated with the aim of improving this approach further. In order to make this analysis, we used the best Pareto MLPs according to each test performance. These MLPs represent the best possible choice of solutions generated by the MOEA considering each objective separately. A Pareto ensemble comprised of these MLPs was also formed. Table 24.8a and b shows the results of the comparisons for large and small data sets, respectively. Again, the parameters used by the MOEA for the small data sets here are the ones with population size 30 and no backpropagation. Wilcoxon tests with Bonferroni corrections at the overall significance level of 0.05 (statistically significant difference when p-value $< 0.05/(3 * 4)$) were used to aid the comparison.

We can see that there are test performance improvements in almost all cases, both when using the best Pareto MLPs by themselves and when combining them into a Pareto ensemble. In particular, for most results with statistically significant difference in the average LSD, MMRE, or PRED(25), the best test performance approach wins more times than the backpropagation MLPs. This analysis shows that, even though our approach can significantly reduce overfitting by reducing the population size and eliminating offspring backpropagation for smaller data sets, simply choosing the best fit Pareto MLPs according to the train performance still does not necessarily lead to the best achievable performance. As future work, other strategies to chose models among the Pareto solutions should be investigated to improve the performance even further.

24.10 COMPARISON AGAINST OTHER TYPES OF MODELS

The main objectives of RQ2 and RQ3 were to show that MOEAs can be used to evolve models considering different performance measures at the same time, being able to produce solutions that achieve good results in comparison to a traditional algorithm that does not use several different

Table 24.8 Test Performance Average of Best Test Performing Pareto MLPs Against Backpropagation MLP

Data Set	LSD	MMRE	PRED(25)
(a) For large data sets			
Backprop MLP	2.0749	1.7202	0.2424
MLP Best LSD	0.8651	1.363	0.2994
Wins vs Backprop MLP	8	6	7
p-Value	0.0000	0.0004	0.0000
MLP Best MMRE	1.4759	0.6423	0.31
Wins vs Backprop MLP	7	8	7
p-Value	0.0031	0.0000	0.0000
MLP Best PRED	1.241	1.0735	0.437
Wins vs Backprop MLP	8	6	8
p-Value	0.0000	0.0000	0.0000
Pareto ensemble	0.9951	0.9649	0.3272
Wins vs Backprop MLP	7	5	6
p-Value	0.0000	0.0000	0.0000
(b) For small data sets			
Backprop MLP	1.7354	1.323	0.1936
MLP Best LSD	1.3761	1.4272	0.2267
Wins vs Backprop MLP	5	2	4
p-Value	0.0001	0.0812	0.0001
MLP Best MMRE	1.8198	1.0558	0.2496
Wins vs Backprop MLP	1	4	4
p-Value	0.3141	0.0000	0.0000
MLP Best PRED	1.785	1.4286	0.3489
Wins vs Backprop MLP	2	2	5
p-Value	0.5729	0.0043	0.0000
Pareto ensemble	1.5671	1.2636	0.2482
Wins vs Backprop MLP	3	2	3
p-Value	0.1653	0.0011	0.0000

Notes: *The adjusted MOEA parameters were used for the small data sets. The p-values of the Wilcoxon tests for the comparison over multiple data sets are also shown. p-Values less than 0.0042 (in dark gray) indicate statistically significant difference using Bonferroni corrections at the overall level of significance of 0.05. When the best test performing Pareto MLP wins more times than the backpropagation MLP, its number of wins is highlighted in light gray. From [327].*

measures explicitly to generate the same type of models, besides being flexible to allow emphasizing different performance measures. The analyses explained in Sections 24.7, 24.8 answer RQ2 and RQ3. Nevertheless, even though it is not the key point of this work, it is still interesting to know how well HaD-MOEA to evolve MLPs behaves in comparison to other types of models. Differently from the previous analyses, this comparison mixes the evaluation of the MOEA to the evaluation of the underlying model being evolved (MLP).

In this section, we present a comparison of the Pareto ensemble to several different types of model besides MLPs: RBFs, RTs, EBA with log transformed data, bagging with MLPs, bagging with RBFs, bagging with RTs, random with MLPs, and NCL with MLPs, as explained in Section 24.5. For this comparison, the parameters used by the MOEA on the small data sets were adjusted to population size of 30 and no offspring backpropagation. The performance measures used to evaluate the models are LSD, MMRE, PRED(25), MdMRE, MAE, and MdAE.

The first step of our analysis consists of performing Friedman tests [96] for the statistical comparison of multiple models over multiple data sets for each performance measure. The null hypothesis is that all the models perform similarly according to the measure considered. The tests rejected the null hypothesis for the six performance measures with Holm-Bonferroni corrections at the overall level of significance of 0.05. The Friedman tests also provide rankings of the approaches across data sets, which show that Pareto ensemble, bagging + MLPs, log + EBA, and RTs have the top half average ranks considering all measures but LSD. Models based on MLPs, including the Pareto ensemble, tend to be lower ranked considering LSD. A closer analysis of the MLPs revealed that they can sometimes make negative estimations, which have a strong impact on LSD. RTs, on the other hand, can never give negative estimations or estimations close to zero when the training data does not contain such effort values. So, learners based on RTs obtained, in general, better LSD. Bagging + RTs was the highest ranked approach in terms of both LSD and MAE.

It is important to note that MOEAs could also be used to evolve other types of structure than MLPs. However, the key point of this work is the investigation of the multiobjective formulation of the problem of creating SEE models and obtaining a better understanding of the performance measures. The use of MOEA to evolve other types of models such as RTs, which could improve LSD, is proposed as future work.

It is also interesting to verify the standard deviation of the Friedman ranking across different performance measures. The Pareto ensemble and log + EBA presented the median standard deviation, meaning that their average ranking across data sets does not vary too much when considering different performance measures, even though they are not the approaches that vary the least. Bagging + MLPs presented the lowest and bagging + RTs presented the highest standard deviation.

Nevertheless, simply looking at the ranking provided by the Friedman test is not very descriptive for SEE, as the models tend to behave very differently depending on the data set. Ideally, we would like to use the approach that is most suitable for the data set in hand. So, as the second step of our analysis, we determine what approaches are ranked first according to the test performance on each data set separately. This is particularly interesting because it allows us to identify on what type of data sets a certain approach behaves better. Table 24.9 shows the approaches ranked as first considering each data set and performance measure. Table 24.10a helps us to see that the Pareto ensemble appears more often as the first than the other approaches in terms of all measures but LSD. Table 24.10b shows that the Pareto ensemble is never ranked last more than twice considering all 13 data sets and it is only ranked worse twice in terms of MMRE. For the reason explained in the previous paragraphs, approaches based

Table 24.9 Approaches Ranked as First per Data Set

Approach	LSD	MMRE	PRED(25)	MdMRE	MAE	MdAE
Cocomo81	RT	Bag + MLP	Bag + MLP	Bag + MLP	Bag + MLP	Bag + MLP
Sdr	RT	RT	Bag + RT	RT	RT	RBF
Nasa	Bag + RT	RT	Bag + MLP	Bag + MLP	Bag + RT	Bag + RT
Desharnais	Bag + RT	Bag + MLP	Pareto Ens	Pareto Ens	Pareto Ens	Pareto Ens
Nasa93	RT	RT	RT	RT	RT	RT
Org1	Bag + RBF	Pareto Ens	Pareto Ens	Pareto Ens	Pareto Ens	Pareto Ens
Org2	Bag + RT	Pareto Ens	Pareto Ens	Pareto Ens	Pareto Ens	Pareto Ens
Org3	Pareto Ens	Pareto Ens	Log + EBA	Log + EBA	Log + EBA	Log + EBA
Org4	Bag + RBF	Pareto Ens	RT	RT	Pareto Ens	Pareto Ens
Org5	Bag + RT	Log + EBA	Bag + RBF	Rand + MLP	Bag + RT	RT
Org6	Bag + RBF	Pareto Ens	Pareto Ens	Pareto Ens	Bag + RBF	Pareto Ens
Org7	Bag + RT	Log + EBA	Log + EBA	Log + EBA	Bag + RBF	Pareto Ens
OrgAll	RT	Pareto Ens	Pareto Ens	Pareto Ens	Pareto Ens	Pareto Ens

Note: *From [327].*

on MLPs are rarely ranked first in terms of LSD, whereas bagging + RTs and RTs are the approaches that appear most often as first in terms of this measure.

Table 24.9 also reveals that the Pareto ensemble was first more often for the ISBSG data sets than for the PROMISE data sets. ISBSG data sets are considered as very heterogeneous. So, MOEAs might be particularly useful for more heterogeneous data. A possible reason for that is that the Pareto ensemble uses a global optimization algorithm, which is usually better at identifying the most promising regions of the search space than local algorithms such as backpropagation. More heterogeneous data sets may present search surfaces with several peaks, more difficult to tackle by local search algorithms.

As a third step of our analysis, the absolute value of the effect size Δ (Equation (24.1), Section 24.5) using MAE as the performance measure were calculated (Table 24.11). We report Δ based on MAE because this performance measure is symmetric/unbiased. As we can see, many of the effect sizes are medium or large. So, the choice of a certain approach instead of the Pareto ensemble can have a big impact on the performance of the SEEs.

Finally, it is also worth noting that, in terms of computational time, some approaches such as log + EBA are faster than the MOEA. However, we do not consider the differences as of practical significance, because our approach did not present high running time. The reasons for the low running time are (1) SEE data sets are usually small in comparison to other ML applications and (2) our results were obtained without running the MOEA for too many generations. As an example, one run for the largest, the second largest, and the third largest data sets, which use 20, 100, and 200 generations, respectively, takes less than 1 minute to finish.

In summary, this section shows that MOEA-evolved MLPs are able to achieve competitive results in comparison to other approaches in the literature. The Pareto ensemble usually obtained comparatively good results in terms of all measures but LSD. Whether this is acceptable is problem (project) dependent

Table 24.10 Approaches Ranked as First—Summary

Approach	LSD	MMRE	PRED(25)	MdMRE	MAE	MdAE
(a) Total number of times ranked as first per approach: approaches never ranked as first are omitted						
Pareto Ens	1	6	5	5	5	7
RT	4	3	2	3	2	2
Bag + RT	5	0	1	0	2	1
Bag + MLP	0	2	2	2	1	1
Log + EBA	0	2	2	2	1	1
Bag + RBF	3	0	1	0	2	0
Rand + MLP	0	0	0	1	0	0
RBF	0	0	0	0	0	1
Total	13	13	13	13	13	13
(b) Total number of times ranked as last per approach: approaches never ranked as last are omitted						
Bag + MLP	0	0	0	0	1	0
MLP	1	0	1	0	0	0
RT	0	0	0	1	1	0
Bag + RT	0	1	1	0	0	1
Pareto Ens	1	2	0	1	1	1
Rand + MLP	2	1	1	2	1	1
Bag + RBF	0	3	3	2	0	2
RBF	1	2	4	3	4	3
NCL	8	4	3	4	5	5
Total	13	13	13	13	13	13

Note: *Values higher than 3 are highlighted in gray. From [327].*

Table 24.11 Effect Size for Each Approach Against the Pareto Ensemble

Approach	Min. Δ	Max. Δ	Avg. Δ	Std Δ	# Small	# Medium	# Large	# Medium + Large
Bag + MLP	0.0296	0.9194	0.3775	0.2839	7	4	2	6
Bag + RBF	0.0046	1.3072	0.5007	0.4233	6	3	4	7
Bag + RT	0.0518	1.3383	0.4842	0.4195	7	3	3	6
Log + EBA	0.0199	1.4054	0.5333	0.4839	7	2	4	6
MLP	0.0202	1.5049	0.4155	0.4034	7	3	3	6
NCL	0.0170	2.4236	0.7194	0.6534	5	3	5	8
Rand	0.0720	1.5655	0.4615	0.4444	7	3	3	6
RBF	0.0393	1.5730	0.6207	0.5299	6	2	5	7
RT	0.0392	1.8151	0.5614	0.5203	4	6	3	9

Note: *From [327].*

and also depends on the magnitude of loss in terms of LSD compared to the gain in other measures. Moreover, the Pareto ensemble seems to perform better for more heterogeneous data sets such as ISBSG.

24.11 SUMMARY

This chapter demonstrates how to view the problem of creating SEE models through a different perspective, by tackling it as a multiobjective problem that considers different performance measures explicitly and simultaneously. Using a MOEA to solve this problem allows us to better understand different performance measures and to produce SEE models with good overall performance in comparison to a model that does not consider these measures explicitly.

As an answer to RQ1, we show that LSD and MMRE are performance measures with somewhat opposite behavior. Moreover, models with similar LSD/MMRE are likely to present different PRED(25) and vice versa. So, one may wish to choose a model that does not behave particularly bad for any intended performance measures. This is one of the motivations for our approach to use MOEAs, as MOEAs consider all these performance measures at the same time. This difference in behavior also provides the second motivation for our approach: it can produce diverse ensembles, which are more likely to have increased performance.

The results above indicate that considering different performance measures explicitly when creating a model may be used to produce good ensembles. As an answer to RQ2, we show that indeed a MOEA can be used to create models by explicitly considering different performance measures at the same time. Pareto ensemble of MLPs produced by a MOEA generally obtained similar or better performance than backpropagation MLPs considering both LSD, MMRE, and PRED(25). The average performances were generally better for the data sets with 60 or more projects.

As an answer to RQ3, we show that MOEAs are also flexible, allowing the software manager to choose models that emphasize certain performance measures over the others, if s/he desires to do so. A MOEA can be used to produce and choose models that emphasize a particular measure without completely ignoring the performance using other measures, whereas the Pareto ensemble can be used as a good trade-off among measures, if the software manager does not wish to emphasize any particular measure.

As shown in our comparison of the Pareto ensemble against backpropagation MLPs, which produce the same type of model as the MOEA, the Pareto ensemble has shown to be useful for both single and multicompany data sets. Our comparison against models of a different type than the base models evolved by the MOEA further shows that MOEAs may be particularly useful for more heterogeneous data sets. They can make types of models that would usually not be ranked first in terms of performance become ranked first through the Pareto ensemble.

In addition to the results reported in this chapter, Minku et al. [325] also show that a diverse set of objective performance measures S_d can lead to a diverse Pareto ensemble able to outperform Pareto ensembles generated based on a set of nondiverse performance measures S_{nd}, in terms of test performance on several measures, including the ones in S_{nd}. For instance, using the set {MMRE, PRED(25), LSD} obtained similar or better test performance than using {MAE, RMSE, Corr}, {MAE, RMSE, StdDev} and {MdAE, MdMRE, RMSE} in terms of LSD, MMRE, PRED(25), MAE, RMSE, Corr, StdDev, MdAE, and MdMRE, where RMSE is the root mean squared error, Corr is the Pearson correlation between the desired and obtained output, and StdDev is the standard deviation of the absolute errors.

A FINAL WORD

This book has been about *sharing ideas* and how *data mining can help that sharing*. As we have seen

- Sharing can be very useful and insightful.
- But sharing ideas is not a simple matter.

The bad news is that, usually, ideas are shared very badly. The good news is that, based on much recent research, it is now possible to offer much guidance on how to use data miners to share:

1. Although not all shared data from other sites is relevant, *some of it is*. The trick is to have the right *relevancy filter* that shares just enough of the correct data.
2. Although not all models move verbatim from domain to domain, it is possible to automatically build many models, then *assess what models work best* for a particular domain.
3. It is possible and useful to automatically form committees of models (called ensembles) in which *different models can debate and combine their recommendations*.

We have also explored methods to make best use of the available data: For example, *privacy algorithms* let organizations share more data without divulging important secrets. Also, *data repair* operators can compensate for missing data. Further, *active learners* can make most use of existing data, thus avoiding needless further data collection.

The key problem in all of this has been to provide *insights* into the behavior of software companies and their processes, rather than just predictions about the future. Such insights can be used by software engineers to better understand the achievements and failures of their companies, helping them to improve their companies.

The practical problems facing software engineering (as well as the practicalities of real-world data sets) often require a deep understanding of the data and tailoring the right learners and algorithms to it. In every tailoring scenario, a practitioner will need to justify his decisions and choices of algorithms. Hence, rather than an elementary knowledge, a deeper understanding of the algorithms (as well as having on-the-field-experience notes through books like this one) is a must for a successful practitioner in data science.

Another point that the practitioner may want to pay attention to is the nature and size of the available data to process. In the age of the Internet, we now have access to an enormous gateway of different kinds and sizes of data sets; let it be social network data, online search data, or advertisement data that targets monetizing the prior two. One of the main challenges with such data is the fact that it may come unlabeled and labeling may be associated with high costs or not possible at all. Therefore, finding quick and effective ways of labeling the data (through active learning solutions) or mining the right clusters out of this data (through scalable clustering algorithms) will be of high value.

There is one other aspect of data science for software engineering that is now ripe for a paradigm shift. Software engineering tasks rarely involve a single goal. For example, when a software engineer is testing a software, he/she may be interested in finding the highest possible number of software defects at the same time as minimizing the time required for testing. Similarly, when a software engineer is planning the development of a software, he/she may be interested in minimizing the number of defects, the effort required to develop the software, and the cost of the software. The existence of *multiple goals* and *multiobjective optimizers* thus profoundly affects data science for software engineering. So far, the existence of multiple goals/objectives has been studied more in search-based software engineering than in data science for software engineering. We think that will change, very soon. In the very near future, we foresee a stronger emphasis on multiple goals in data science for software engineering.

Bibliography

[1] Aggmakarwal K, Singh Y, Kaur A, Malhotra R. Empirical analysis for investigating the effect of object-oriented metrics on fault proneness: a replicated case study. Softw Process Improv Pract 2009;14 (January (1)).

[2] Aha DW, Kibler D, Albert MK. Instance-based learning algorithms. Mach Learn 1991;6(January (1)): 37-66.

[3] Al Khalidi N, Saifan AA, Alsmadi IM. Selecting a standard set of attributes for cost estimation of software projects. In: International conference on computer, information and telecommunication systems (CITS); May 2012. p. 1-5.

[4] Albrecht A, Gaffney J. Software function, source lines of code and development effort prediction: a software science validation. IEEE Trans Softw Eng 1983;9:639-48.

[5] Ali K. On the link between error correlation and error reduction in decision tree ensembles. Technical report, Dept. of Information and Computer Science, Univ. of California, Irvine; 1995.

[6] Alpaydin E. Techniques for combining multiple learners. Proc Eng Intell Syst 1998;2:6-12.

[7] Alpaydin E. Introduction to machine learning. 2nd ed. Cambridge, MA: MIT Press; 2010.

[8] Arisholm E, Briand L. Predicting fault prone components in a JAVA legacy system. In: 2006 ACM/IEEE international symposium on empirical software engineering; 2006. p. 17.

[9] Arisholm E, Briand L. Predicting fault-prone components in a JAVA legacy system. In: 5th ACM-IEEE international symposium on empirical software engineering (ISESE), Rio de Janeiro, Brazil, September 21-22; 2006. Available from: http://simula.no/research/engineering/publications/Arisholm.2006.4.

[10] Arnold A, Nallapati R, Cohen WW. A comparative study of methods for transductive transfer learning. In: ICDM'07: seventh IEEE international conference on data mining workshops; 2007. p. 77-82.

[11] Arthur JD, Groner MK, Hayhurst KJ, Holloway CM. Evaluating the effectiveness of independent verification and validation. IEEE Computer; October 1999. p. 79-83.

[12] Arun Kumar S, Arun Kumar T. State of software metrics to forecast variety of elements in the software development process. In: Nagamalai D, Renault E, Dhanuskodi M, editors. Advances in parallel distributed computing. Communications in computer and information science, vol. 203. Berlin/Heidelberg: Springer; 2011. p. 561-9.

[13] Atkinson K, Shepperd M. The use of function points to find cost analogies. In: European software cost modelling meeting, Ivrea, Italy; 1994.

[14] Atzori M, Bonchi F, Giannotti F, Pedreschi D. Anonymity preserving pattern discovery. VLDB J 2008;17(July (4)):703-27.

[15] Azhar D, Riddle P, Mendes E, Mittas N, Angelis L. Using ensembles for web effort estimation. In: IEEE 2013 ACM/IEEE international symposium on empirical software engineering and measurement; 2013. p. 173-82.

[16] Azzeh M. Software effort estimation based on optimized model tree. In: Proceedings of the 7th international conference on predictive models in software engineering, Promise '11. New York, NY: ACM; 2011. p. 6:1-6:8.

[17] Bacchelli A, Dal Sasso T, D'Ambros M, Lanza M. Content classification of development emails. In: Proceedings of the 34th international conference on software engineering, ICSE '12; 2012. p. 375-85.

[18] Baena-García M, Del Campo-Ávila J, Fidalgo R, Bifet A. Early drift detection method. In: Proceedings of the 3rd international wokshop on knowledge discovery from data streams (IWKDDS), Berlin, Germany; 2006. p. 77-86.

[19] Baker D. A hybrid approach to expert and model-based effort estimation. Master's thesis, Lane Department of Computer Science and Electrical Engineering, West Virginia University; 2007. Available from: https://eidr.wvu.edu/etd/documentdata.eTD?documentid=5443.

[20] Bakir A, Turhan B, Bener A. A comparative study for estimating software development effort intervals. Softw Qual J 2011;19(September (3)):537-52.

[21] Bakir A, Turhan B, Bener AB. A new perspective on data homogeneity in software cost estimation: a study in the embedded systems domain. Softw Qual J 2010;18(March):57-80.

[22] Barbaro M, Zeller T, Hansell S. A face is exposed for aol searcher no. 4417749. New York Times 2006;9(August (2008)):8.

[23] Vic Basil. Personnel communication; 2008.

[24] Basili V, Briand L, Melo W. A validation of object-oriented design metrics as quality indicators. IEEE Trans Softw Eng 1996;22(10):751-61.

[25] Baskeles B, Turhan B, Bener A. Software effort estimation using machine learning methods. In: Proceedings of the 22nd international symposium on computer and information sciences (ISCIS'07), Ankara; 2007. p. 1-6.

[26] Bauer E, Kohavi R. An empirical comparison of voting classification algorithms: bagging, boosting, and variants. Mach Learn 1999;36:105-39.

[27] Begel A, Zimmermann T. Analyze this! 145 questions for data scientists in software engineering. In: Proceedings of the 36th international conference on software engineering (ICSE 2014), ACM; June 2014.

[28] Bettenburg N, Nagappan M, Hassan AE. Think locally, act globally: improving defect and effort prediction models. In: 9th IEEE working conference on mining software repositories (MSR); 2012. p. 60-9.

[29] Bezdek JC, Kuncheva LI. Nearest prototype classifier designs: an experimental study. Int J Intell Syst 2001;16(12):1445-73.

[30] Bezdek JC, Kuncheva LI. Some notes on twenty one (21) nearest prototype classifiers. In: Ferri FJ, Inesta JM, Amin A, Pudil P, editor. Advances in pattern recognition. Lecture notes in computer science, vol. 1876; 2000. p. 1-16.

[31] Bird C, Gourley A, Devanbu P, Gertz M, Swaminathan A. Mining email social networks. In: Proceedings of the 2006 international workshop on mining software repositories, MSR '06; 2006. p. 137-43.

[32] Bishop CM. Neural networks for pattern recognition. United Kingdom: Oxford University Press; 2005.

[33] Bishop CM, Hinton G. Neural networks for pattern recognition. Oxford: Clarendon Press; 1995.

[34] Boehm B. Software engineering economics. Englewood Cliffs, NJ: Prentice-Hall; 1981.

[35] Boehm B. Safe and simple software cost analysis. IEEE Software; 2000. p. 14-7.

[36] Boehm B. Safe and simple software cost analysis. IEEE Software; September/October 2000. p. 14-7. Available from: http://www.computer.org/certification/beta/Boehm_Safe.pdf.

[37] Boehm B, Abts C, Brown AW, Chulani S, Clark BK, Horowitz E, et al. Software cost estimation with COCOMO II. Englewood Cliffs, NJ: Prentice-Hall; 2000.

[38] Boehm B, Abts C, Chulani S. Software development cost estimation approaches—a survey. Ann Softw Eng 2000;10:177-205.

[39] Boehm B, Papaccio P. Understanding and controlling software costs. IEEE Trans Softw Eng 1988;14 (October (10)):1462-77.

[40] Boehm BW. Software engineering. IEEE Trans Comput 1976;25(December):1226-41.

[41] Boehm B. Boehm, quoting Dijkstra, in his 2004 keynote address to the international conference on Automated Software Engineering, Linz, Austria, http://goo.gl/mxgjv; 2004.

[42] Boehm B, Horowitz E, Madachy R, Reifer D, Clark BK, Steece B, et al. Software cost estimation with COCOMO II. Englewood Cliffs, NJ: Prentice-Hall; 2000.

[43] Boehm BW, Abts C, Brown AW, Chulani S, Clark BK, Horowitz E, et al. Software cost estimation with COCOMO II. Englewood Cliffs, NJ: Prentice-Hall; 2000.

[44] Bowring JF, Rehg JM, Harrold MJ. Active learning for automatic classification of software behavior. ACM SIGSOFT Softw Eng Notes 2004;29(July (4)):195.

[45] Braga PL, Oliveira ALI, Ribeiro GHT, Meira SRL. Bagging predictors for estimation of software project effort. In: Proceedings of the international joint conference on neural networks (IJCNN'07), Orlando; 2007. p. 1595-600.

[46] Breiman L. Bagging predictors. Mach Learn 1996;24(2):123-40.

[47] Breiman L. Heuristics of instability and stabilization in model selection. Ann Stat 1996;24(6):2350-83.

[48] Breiman L, Friedman JH, Olshen RA, Stone CJ. Classification and regression trees. Technical report, Wadsworth International, Monterey, CA; 1984.

[49] Breiman L. Random forests. Mach Learn 2001;45:5-32.

[50] Breiman L, Spector P. Submodel selection and evaluation in regression. The x-random case. Int Stat Rev 1992;60(December (3)):291-319.

[51] Breimann L. Random forests. Mach Learn 2001;45(October):5-32.

[52] Briand L, Wieczorek I. Resource modeling in software engineering. Encyclopedia of software engineering. 2nd ed. New York: Wiley; 2002.

[53] Briand L, Wust J, Daly J, Victor Porter D. Exploring the relationships between design measures and software quality in object-oriented systems. J Syst Softw 2000;51(3):245-73.

[54] Briand L, Wust J, Lounis H. Replicated case studies for investigating quality factors in object-oriented designs. Empir Softw Eng 2001;6(1):11-58.

[55] Briand LC, El Emam K, Surmann D, Wieczorek I, Maxwell KD. An assessment and comparison of common software cost estimation modeling techniques. In: ICSE '99: proceedings of the 21st international conference on software engineering. New York, NY: ACM; 1999. p. 313-22.

[56] Briand LC, Melo WL, Wst J. Assessing the applicability of fault-proneness models across object-oriented software projects. IEEE Trans Softw Eng 2002;28(7):706-20.

[57] Brickell J, Shmatikov V. The cost of privacy: destruction of data-mining utility in anonymized data publishing. In: Proceeding of the 14th ACM SIGKDD international conference on knowledge discovery and data mining, KDD '08. New York, NY: ACM; 2008. p. 70-8.

[58] Brighton H, Mellish C. Advances in instance selection for instance-based learning algorithms. Data Min Knowl Discov 2002;6:153-72. doi: 10.1023/A:1014043630878.

[59] Brooks FP. The mythical man-month, Anniversary edition. Reading, MA: Addison-Wesley; 1995.

[60] Brown D. Next nasa mars mission rescheduled for 2011; 2009. http://www.nasa.gov/mission_pages/mars/news/msl-20081204.html.

[61] Brown G, Wyatt J, Harris R, Yao X. Diversity creation methods: a survey and categorisation. Inform Fusion 2005;6:5-20.

[62] Brown G, Wyatt JL, Ti no P. Managing diversity in regression ensembles. J Mach Learn Res 2005;6:1621-50.

[63] Budi A, Lo D, Jiang L, Lucia. kb-anonymity: a model for anonymized behaviour-preserving test and debugging data. In: Proceedings of the 32nd ACM SIGPLAN conference on programming language design and implementation, PLDI '11. New York, NY: ACM; 2011. p. 447-57.

[64] Buse RPL, Zimmermann T. Information needs for software development analytics. In: Proceedings of the 2012 international conference on software engineering. IEEE Press; 2012. p. 987-96.

[65] Cartwright M, Shepperd M. An empirical investigation of an object-oriented software system. IEEE Trans Softw Eng 2000;26(8):786-96.

[66] Cartwright MH, Shepperd MJ, Song Q. Dealing with missing software project data. In: Proceedings of the 9th international software metrics symposium (METRICS'03), Sydney; 2003. p. 154-65.

[67] Castro M, Costa M, Martin J-P. Better bug reporting with better privacy. In: Proceedings of the 13th international conference on architectural support for programming languages and operating systems, ASPLOS XIII. New York, NY: ACM; 2008. p. 319-28.

[68] Catlett J. Inductive learning from subsets or disposal of excess training data considered harmful. In: Australian workshop on knowledge acquisition for knowledge-based systems, Pokolbin; 1991. p. 53-67.

[69] Chandra A, Yao X. Ensemble learning using multi-objective evolutionary algorithms. J Math Model Algorithms 2006;5(4):417-45.

[70] Chang C-L. Finding prototypes for nearest classifiers. IEEE Trans Comput 1974;C(11).

[71] Chang C-L. Finding prototypes for nearest neighbor classifiers. IEEE Trans Comput 1974;C-23(November (11)):1179-84.

[72] Chen B-C, LeFevre K, Ramakrishnan R. Privacy skyline: privacy with multidimensional adversarial knowledge. In: Proceedings of the 33rd international conference on very large data bases, VLDB '07, VLDB Endowment; 2007. p. 770-81.

[73] Chen H, Yao X. Regularized negative correlation learning for neural network ensembles. IEEE Trans Neural Netw 2009;20(12):1962-79.

[74] Chen Z, Menzies T, Port D, Boehm B. Finding the right data for software cost modeling. IEEE Software; November 2005.

[75] Chen Z, Menzies T, Port D. Feature subset selection can improve software cost estimation. In: PROMISE'05; 2005. Available from: http://menzies.us/pdf/05/fsscocomo.pdf.

[76] Chin A, Klinefelter A. Differential privacy as a response to the reidentification threat: the facebook advertiser case study. N C Law Rev 2012;90(5).

[77] Chulani S, Boehm B, Steece B. Bayesian analysis of empirical software engineering cost models. IEEE Trans Softw Eng 1999;25(July/August (4)).

[78] Chulani S, Boehm B, Steece B. From multiple regression to Bayesian analysis for calibrating COCOMO II. J Parametrics, 1999;15(2):175-88.

[79] Clause J, Orso A. Camouflage: automated anonymization of field data. Proceeding of the 33rd international conference on software engineering; 2011. p. 21-30.

[80] Cohen J. A power primer. Psychol Bull 1992;112:155-9.

[81] Conte SD, Dunsmore HE, Shen VY. Software engineering metrics and models. Menlo Park, CA: Benjamin Cummings Publishing; 1986.

[82] Corazza A, Di Martino S, Ferrucci F, Gravino C, Sarro F, Mendes E. How effective is Tabu search to configure support vector regression for effort estimation? In: Proceedings of the 6th international conference on predictive models in software engineering, PROMISE '10; 2010. p. 4:1-4:10.

[83] Certified parametric practitioner tutorial; 2006.

[84] Craw S, Sleeman D, Boswell R, Carbonara L. Is knowledge refinement different from theory revision? In: Wrobel S, editor. Proceedings of the MLNet familiarization workshop on theory revision and restructuring in machine learning (ECML-94); 1994. p. 32-4.

[85] Cruz AEC, Ochimizu K. Towards logistic regression models for predicting fault-prone code across software projects. In: ESEM; 2009. p. 460-3.

[86] Czerwonka J, Das R, Nagappan N, Tarvo A, Teterev A. Crane: failure prediction, change analysis and test prioritization in practice—experiences from windows. In: IEEE fourth international conference on software testing, verification and validation (ICST); March 2011. p. 357-66.

[87] Dabney JB, Barber G, Ohi D. Predicting software defect function point ratios using a Bayesian belief network. In: Proceedings of the PROMISE workshop; 2006. Available from: http://promisedata.org/pdf/phil2006DabneyBarberOhi.pdf.

[88] Dai W, Xue G-R, Qiang Y, Yong Y. Transferring naive bayes classifiers for text classification. In: AAAI'07: proceedings of the 22nd national conference on artificial intelligence; 2007. p. 540-45.

[89] Dalenius T. Towards a methodology for statistical disclosure control. Statistik Tidskrift; 1977.

[90] Dasgupta S. Analysis of a greedy active learning strategy. In: Advances in neural information processing systems, vol. 17; 2005.

[91] Dawkins R. Redundancy reduction and pattern recognition; 2012. Available from: http://edge.org/response-detail/10369.

[92] de Aquino RRB, Ferreira AA, Carvalho MA, Neto ON, Santos GSM. Combining multiple artificial neural networks using random committee to decide upon electrical disturbance classification. In: Proceedings of the 2007 international joint conference on neural networks (IJCNN'07), Orlando, Florida; 2007. p. 2863-8.

[93] Deb K, Pratap A, Agarwal S, Meyarivan T. A fast and elitist multiobjective genetic algorithm: Nsga-II. IEEE Trans Evol Comput 2002;6(April (2)):182-97.

[94] Dejaeger K, Verbeke W, Martens D, Baesens B. Data mining techniques for software effort estimation: a comparative study. IEEE Trans Softw Eng 2012;38(2):375-97.

[95] DeMarco T, Lister T. Peopleware: productive projects and teams. New York, NY: Dorset House Publishing Co., Inc.; 1987.

[96] Demšar J. Statistical comparisons of classifiers over multiple data sets. J Mach Learn Res 2006;7:1-30.

[97] Denaro G, Lavazza L, Pezze M. An empirical evaluation of object oriented metrics in industrial setting. In: The 5th CaberNet plenary workshop, Porto Santo, Madeira Archipelago, Portugal; 2003.

[98] Desharnais J. Analyse statistique de la productivitie des projets informatique a partie de la technique des point des fonction. Master's thesis, Univ. of Montreal; 1989.

[99] Devnani-Chulani S. Bayesian analysis of software cost and quality models. PhD thesis; 1999. Available from: http://citeseer.ist.psu.edu/devnani-chulani99bayesian.html.

[100] Dietterich T. An experimental comparison of three methods for constructing ensembles of decision trees: Bagging, boosting and randomization. Mach Learn 2000;40:1-22.

[101] Dinur I, Nissim K. Revealing information while preserving privacy. In: Proceedings of the twenty-second ACM SIGMOD-SIGACT-SIGART symposium on principles of database systems. New York, NY: ACM; 2003. p. 202-10.

[102] Dolado JJ. A validation of the component-based method for software size estimation. IEEE Trans Softw Eng 2000;26:1006-21.

[103] Dolado JJ. On the problem of the software cost function. Inform Softw Technol 2001;43:61-72.

[104] Domingo-Ferrer J, Gonzalez-Nicolas U. Hybrid microdata using microaggregation. Inform Sci 2010;180 (August (15)):2834-44.

[105] Dougherty J, Kohavi R, Sahami M. Supervised and unsupervised discretization of continuous features. In: International conference on machine learning; 1995. p. 194-202. Available from: http://www.cs.pdx.edu/~timm/dm/dougherty95supervised.pdf.

[106] Du W, Teng Z, Zhu Z. Privacy-maxent: integrating background knowledge in privacy quantification. In: Proceedings of the 2008 ACM SIGMOD international conference on management of data; SIGMOD '08. New York, NY: ACM; 2008. p. 459-72.

[107] Duda RO, Hart PE, Stork DG. Pattern classification. New York: John Wiley & Sons; 2012.

[108] Dwork C. Differential privacy: a survey of results. In: Theory and applications of models of computation; 2008. p. 1-19.

[109] Dwork C. Differential privacy. In: Bugliesi M, Preneel B, Sassone V, Wegener I, editors. Automata, languages and programming. Lecture notes in computer science, vol. 4052. Berlin/Heidelberg: Springer; 2006. p. 1-12.

[110] Easterbrook SM, Singer J, Storey M, Damian D. Selecting empirical methods for software engineering research. In: Shull F, Singer J, editors. Guide to advanced empirical software engineering. London: Springer; 2007.

[111] Eiben AE, Smith JE. Introduction to evolutionary computing. Berlin: Springer-Verlag; 2003.

[112] El-Emam K, Benlarbi S, Goel N, Rai S. A validation of object-oriented metrics. National Research Council of Canada, NRC/ERB 1063; 1999.

[113] El-Emam K, Benlarbi S, Goel N, Rai S. The confounding effect of class size on the validity of object-oriented metrics. IEEE Trans Softw Eng 2001;27(7):630-50.

[114] El-Emam K, Melo W, Machado J. The prediction of faulty classes using object-oriented design metrics. J Syst Softw 2001;56(1):63-75.

[115] El-Rawas O, Menzies T. A second look at faster, better, cheaper. Innov Syst Softw Eng 2010;6(4):319-35. Available from: http://menzies.us/pdf/10bfc.pdf.

[116] English M, Exton C, Rigon I, Cleary B. Fault detection and prediction in an open-source software project. In: Proceedings of the 5th international conference on predictor models in software engineering; 2009. p. 1-11.

[117] Shull F, Mendoncca MG, Basili V, Carver J, Maldonado JC, Fabbri S, et al. Knowledge-sharing issues in experimental software engineering. Empir Softw Eng 2004;9(1-2).

[118] Fagan M. Design and code inspections to reduce errors in program development. IBM Syst J 1976;15(3).

[119] Fagan M. Advances in software inspections. IEEE Trans Softw Eng 1986;July:744-51.

[120] Faloutsos C, Lin K-I. Fastmap: a fast algorithm for indexing, data-mining and visualization of traditional and multimedia datasets. In: Proceedings of the 1995 ACM SIGMOD international conference on management of data, San Jose, California, May 22-25; 1995. p. 163-74.

[121] Farnstrom F, Lewis J, Elkan C. Scalability for clustering algorithms revisited. SIGKDD Explor 2000;2:51-7.

[122] Fayyad UM, Irani IH. Multi-interval discretization of continuous-valued attributes for classification learning. In: Proceedings of the thirteenth international joint conference on artificial intelligence; 1993. p. 1022-7.

[123] Fayyad U, Piatetsky-Shapiro G, Smyth P. From data mining to knowledge discovery in databases. AI Magazine; Fall 1996. p. 37-54.

[124] Feather MS, Fickas S, Razermera-Mamy N-A. Model-checking for validation of a fault protection system. In: Sixth IEEE international symposium on high assurance systems engineering; 2001. p. 32-41.

[125] Feather MS, Menzies T. Converging on the optimal attainment of requirements. In: IEEE joint conference on requirements engineering ICRE'02 and RE'02, September 9-13, University of Essen, Germany; 2002. Available from: http://menzies.us/pdf/02re02.pdf.

[126] Ferens D, Christensen D. Calibrating software cost models to Department of Defense Database: a review of ten studies. J Parametrics 1998;18(November (1)):55-74.

[127] Ferens D, Christensen D. Calibrating software cost models to Department of Defense Database: a review of ten studies. J Parametrics 1998;18(November (1)):55-74.

[128] Ferrucci F, Gravino C, Sarro F. How multi-objective genetic programming is effective for software development effort estimation? In: International symposium on search-based software engineering (SSBSE); September 2011. p. 274-5.

[129] Ferrucci F, Mendes E, Sarro F. Web effort estimation: the value of cross-company data set compared to single-company data set. In: International conference on predictive models in software engineering (PROMISE), Lund, Sweden; 2012. p. 29-38.

[130] Finnie GR, Wittig GE, Desharnais J-M. A comparison of software effort estimation techniques: using function points with neural networks, case-based reasoning and regression models. J Syst Softw 1997;39(3): 281-9.

[131] Finnoff W, Hergert F, Zimmermann HG. Improving model selection by nonconvergent methods. Neural Netw 1993;6:771-83.

[132] Fioravanti F, Nesi P. A study on fault-proneness detection of object-oriented systems. In: Fifth European conference on software maintenance and reengineering; 2001. p. 121-30.

[133] Foss T, Stensrud E, Kitchenham B, Myrtveit I. A simulation study of the model evaluation criterion MMRE. IEEE Trans Softw Eng 2003;29(11):985-95.

[134] Foster G, Goutte C, Kuhn R. Discriminative instance weighting for domain adaptation in statistical machine translation. In: EMNLP '10: conference on empirical methods in natural language processing; 2010. p. 451-9.

[135] Frank E, Trigg L, Holmes G, Witten IH. Technical note: naive bayes for regression. Mach Learn 2000;41: 5-25.

[136] Freund Y, Schapire R. A decision-theoretic generalization of on-line learning and an application to boosting. J Comput Syst Sci 1997;55(1):119-39.

[137] Freund Y, Schapire RE. A decision-theoretic generalization of on-line learning and an application to boosting. J Comput Syst Sci 1997;55.

[138] Fung BCM, Wang K, Chen R, Yu PS. Privacy-preserving data publishing: a survey of recent developments. ACM Comput Surv 2010;42(June (4)).

[139] Gama J, Pinto C. Discretization from data streams: applications to histograms and data mining. In: SAC '06: proceedings of the 2006 ACM symposium on applied computing. New York, NY: ACM Press; 2006. p. 662-7.

[140] Gao J, Fan W, Jiang J, Han J. Knowledge transfer via multiple model local structure mapping. In: International conference on knowledge discovery and data mining, Las Vegas, NV; 2008.

[141] Gay G, Menzies T, Davies M, Gundy-Burlet K. Automatically finding the control variables for complex system behavior. Autom Softw Eng 2010;December(4). Available from: http://menzies.us/pdf/10tar34.pdf.

[142] Giannella C, Liu K, Kargupta H. On the privacy of Euclidean distance preserving data perturbation. CoRR; abs/0911.2942; 2009.

[143] Gigerenzer G, Goldstein DG. Reasoning the fast and frugal way: models of bounded rationality. Psychol Rev 1996;103:650-69.

[144] Glasberg D, El-Emam K, Memo W, Madhavji N. Validating object-oriented design metrics on a commercial JAVA application. NRC 44146; 2000.

[145] Gordon DF. Apt agents: agents that are adaptive, predictable, and timely. In: First international workshop on formal approaches to agent-based systems, FAABS 2000, Greenbelt, MD, USA, April 5-7, 2000, Revised Papers; 2000. p. 278-93.

[146] Grechanik M, Csallner C, Fu C, Xie Q. Is data privacy always good for software testing? In: Proceedings of the 2010 IEEE 21st international symposium on software reliability engineering; ISSRE '10. Washington, DC: IEEE Computer Society; 2010. p. 368-77.

[147] Green P, Menzies T, Williams S, El-Rawas O. Understanding the value of software engineering technologies. In: ASE 2009, 24th IEEE/ACM international conference on automated software engineering, Auckland, New Zealand, November 16-20; 2009. p. 52-61.

[148] Gruska N, Wasylkowski A, Zeller A. Learning from 6,000 projects: lightweight cross-project anomaly detection. In: Proceedings of the 19th international symposium on software testing and analysis; ISSTA '10; 2010. p. 119-30.

[149] Günter S, Bunke H. Feature selection algorithms for the generation of multiple classifier systems and their application to handwritten word recognition. Pattern Recogn Lett 2004;25(11):1323-36.

[150] Guo PJ, Zimmermann T, Nagappan N. Characterizing and predicting which bugs get fixed: an empirical study of Microsoft Windows. In: Proceedings of the 32nd international conference on software engineering; 2010. p. 495-504.

[151] Gurney K. Introduction to neural networks. United Kingdom: Taylor and Francis; 2005.

[152] Gyimothy T, Ferenc R, Siket I. Empirical validation of object-oriented metrics on open source software for fault prediction. IEEE Trans Softw Eng 2005;31(10):897-910.

[153] Habib-Agahi H, Malhotra S, Quirk J. Estimating software productivity and cost for NASA projects. J Parametrics; November 1998. p. 59-71.

[154]   Hall MA, Smith LA. Practical feature subset selection for machine learning. In: Proceedings of the 21st Australasian computer science conference (ACSC'98), Perth, Australia; 1998. p. 181-91.

[155]   Hall MA, Holmes G. Benchmarking attribute selection techniques for discrete class data mining. IEEE Trans Knowl Data Eng 2003;15(6):1437-47. Available from: http://www.cs.waikato.ac.nz/~mhall/HallHolmesTKDE.pdf.

[156]   Hall M, Frank E, Holmes G, Pfahringer B, Reutemann P, Witten IH. The WEKA data mining software: an update. SIGKDD Explor Newsl 2009;11(November):10-8.

[157]   Hall T, Beecham S, Bowes D, Gray D, Counsell S. A systematic review of fault prediction performance in software engineering. IEEE Trans Softw Eng; 2011 (pre-print).

[158]   Hall T, Beecham S, Bowes D, Gray D, Counsell S. A systematic review of fault prediction performance in software engineering. IEEE Trans Softw Eng 2011;99 (pre-prints).

[159]   Hamerly G. Making k-means even faster. In: Proceedings of the SIAM international conference on data; 2010. p. 130-40.

[160]   Han S, Dang Y, Ge S, Zhang D, Xie T. Performance debugging in the large via mining millions of stack traces. In: Proceedings of the 34th international conference on software engineering; ICSE '12; 2012. p. 145-55.

[161]   Hand DJ. Protection or privacy? Data mining and personal data. In: Ng WK, Kitsuregawa M, Li J, Chang K, editor. Advances in knowledge discovery and data mining. Lecture notes in artificial intelligence, vol. 3918; 2006. p. 1-10.

[162]   Harman M. The relationship between search based software engineering and predictive modeling. In: International conference on predictive models in software engineering (PROMISE); 2010. p. 2492-9.

[163]   Harman M, Clark J. Metrics are fitness functions too. In: Proceedings of the 10th international software metrics symposium (METRICS'04), Chicago; 2004. p. 172-83.

[164]   Harman M, Jia Y, Zhang Y. App store mining and analysis: MSR for app stores. In: MSR,12; 2012. p. 108-11.

[165]   Hartigan JA. Clustering algorithms. New York: John Wiley & Sons; 1975.

[166]   Hassan AE, Xie T. Software intelligence: the future of mining software engineering data. In: Proceedings of the FSE/SDP workshop on future of software engineering research. New York, NY: ACM; 2010. p. 161-6.

[167]   Hastie T, Tibshirani R, Friedman J. The elements of statistical learning: data mining, inference and prediction. 2nd ed. Berlin/Heidelberg: Springer; 2008.

[168]   Hatton L. Does oo sync with how we think? IEEE Software; May/June 1998. p. 46-54.

[169]   Hayes JH, Dekhtyar A, Sundaram SK. Advancing candidate link generation for requirements tracing: the study of methods. IEEE Trans Software Eng 2006;32(1):4-19.

[170]   He Z, Shu F, Yang Y, Li M, Wang Q. An investigation on the feasibility of cross-project defect prediction. Autom Softw Eng 2012;19:167-99.

[171]   Heiat A. Comparison of artificial neural network and regression models for estimating software development effort. Inform Softw Technol 2002;44:911-22.

[172]   Herraiz I, Robles G, Gonzalez-Barahona JM, Capiluppi A, Ramil JF. Comparison between slocs and number of files as size metrics for software evolution analysis. In: CSMR06: proceedings of the 10th European conference on software maintenance and reengineering; 2006. 8 p.

[173]   Hihn J. personnel communication; 2012.

[174]   Hindle A. Green mining: a methodology of relating software change to power consumption. In: Proceedings, MSR'12; 2012.

[175]   Hintogdlu AA, Saygin Y. Suppressing microdata to prevent classification based inference. VLDB J 2010;19(June (3)):385-410.

[176]   Health information privacy; August 2007.

[177] Ho TK. Random decision forests. In: ICDAR '95: proceedings of the third international conference on document analysis and recognition, vol. 1. Washington, DC: IEEE Computer Society; 1995. p. 278.

[178] Ho TK, Hull JJ, Srihari SN. Decision combination in multiple classifier systems. IEEE Trans Pattern Anal Mach Intell 1994;16(1):66-75.

[179] Holschuh T, Pauser M, Herzig K, Zimmermann T, Premraj R, Zeller A. Predicting defects in SAP Java code: An experience report. In: Software engineering—companion volume, 2009. ICSE-companion 2009. 31st international conference; 2009. p. 172-81.

[180] Hornik K. Approximation capabilities of multilayer feedforward networks. Neural Netw 1991;4(2): 251-7.

[181] Huang J, Smola A, Gretton A, Borgwardt KM, Scholkopf B. Correcting sample selection bias by unlabeled data. In: Proceedings of the 19th annual conference on neural information processing systems; 2007. p. 601-8.

[182] Huang L. Software quality analysis: a value-based approach. PhD thesis, Department of Computer Science, University of Southern California, 2006. Available from: http://csse.usc.edu/csse/TECHRPTS/PhD_Dissertations/files/Huang_Dissertation.pdf.

[183] Huang L, Boehm B. How much software quality investment is enough: a value-based approach. IEEE Softw 2006;23(September-October (5)):88-95.

[184] Jalali O, Menzies T, Feather M. Optimizing requirements decisions with keys. In: Proceedings of the PROMISE 2008 workshop (ICSE); 2008. Available from: http://menzies.us/pdf/08keys.pdf.

[185] Janes A, Scotto M, Pedrycz W, Russo B, Stefanovic M, Succi G. Identification of defect-prone classes in telecommunication software systems using design metrics. Inform Sci 2006;176(24):3711-34.

[186] Jiang Y, Cukic B, Ma Y. Techniques for evaluating fault prediction models. Empir Softw Eng 2008;13: 561-95.

[187] Jiang Y, Cukic B, Menzies T. Cost curve evaluation of fault prediction models. In: ISSRE '08: proceedings of the 2008 19th international symposium on software reliability engineering; 2008. p. 197-206.

[188] Jodpimai P, Sophatsathit P, Lursinsap C. Estimating software effort with minimum features using neural functional approximation. In: International conference on computational science and its applications (ICCSA); March 2010. p. 266-73.

[189] John GH, Langley P. Estimating continuous distributions in Bayesian classifiers. In: Proceedings of the eleventh conference on uncertainty in artificial intelligence; UAI'95. San Francisco, CA: Morgan Kaufmann Publishers Inc.; 1995. p. 338-45.

[190] Jorgensen M. A review of studies on expert estimation of software development effort. J Syst Softw 2004;70(1-2):37-60.

[191] Jørgensen M, Gruschke TM. The impact of lessons-learned sessions on effort estimation and uncertainty assessments. IEEE Trans Softw Eng 2009;35(May-June (3)):368-83.

[192] Jorgensen M, Shepperd M. A systematic review of software development cost estimation studies; January 2007. Available from: http://www.simula.no/departments/engineering/publications/Jorgensen.2005.12.

[193] Jorgensen M, Shepperd M. A systematic review of software development cost estimation studies. IEEE Trans Softw Eng 2007;33(1):33-53.

[194] Jørgensen M. Contrasting ideal and realistic conditions as a means to improve judgment-based software development effort estimation. Inform Softw Technol; 2011 (in press).

[195] Jørgensen M, Moløkken-Østvold K. How large are software cost overruns? a review of the 1994 chaos report. Inform Softw Technol 2006;48(4):297-301.

[196] Jureczko M, Madeyski L. Towards identifying software project clusters with regard to defect prediction. In: Proceedings of the 6th international conference on predictive models in software engineering; PROMISE '10. New York, NY: ACM; 2010. p. 9:1-9:10.

[197] Jureczko M, Madeyski L. Towards identifying software project clusters with regard to defect prediction. In: Proceedings of the 6th international conference on predictive models in software engineering; PROMISE '10. New York, NY: ACM; 2010. p. 9:1-9:10.

[198] Jureczko M, Madeyski L. Towards identifying software project clusters with regard to defect prediction. In: Proceedings of the 6th international conference on predictive models in software engineering; PROMISE '10. New York, NY: ACM; 2010. p. 9:1-9:10.

[199] Kadoda G, Cartwright M, Shepperd M. On configuring a case-based reasoning software project prediction system. UK CBR Workshop, Cambridge, UK; 2000. p. 1-10.

[200] Kampenes VB, Dybå T, Hannay JE, Sjøberg DIK. A systematic review of effect size in software engineering experiments. Inform Softw Technol 2007;49(11-12):1073-86.

[201] Kamvar SD, Klein D, Manning CD. Spectral learning. In: IJCAI'03; 2003. p. 561-6.

[202] Kapser C, Godfrey MW. "Cloning considered harmful" considered harmful. In: 13th working conference on reverse engineering, 2006. WCRE '06; October 2006. p. 19-28, .

[203] Kelly GA. The psychology of persona constructs. Volume 1: a theory of personality. Volume 2: clinical diagnosis and psychotherapy. Norton; 1955.

[204] Kemerer CF. An empirical validation of software cost estimation models. Commun ACM 1987;30(May (5)):416-29.

[205] Kemerer CF. An empirical validation of software cost estimation models. Commun ACM 1987;30(May (5)):416-29.

[206] Keung J. Empirical evaluation of analogy-x for software cost estimation. In: ESEM '08: proceedings of the second international symposium on empirical software engineering and measurement. New York, NY: ACM; 2008. p. 294-6.

[207] Keung J, Kocaguneli E, Menzies T. Finding conclusion stability for selecting the best effort predictor in software effort estimation. Autom Softw Eng 2012;1-25. doi: 10.1007/s10515-012-0108-5.

[208] Keung JW. Theoretical maximum prediction accuracy for analogy-based software cost estimation. In: 15th Asia-Pacific software engineering conference; 2008. p. 495-502.

[209] Khare V, Yao X, Deb K. Performance scaling of multi-objective evolutionary algorithms. In: Fonseca CM, Fleming PJ, Zitzler E, Deb K, Thiele L, editors. 2nd international conference on evolutionary multi-criterion optimization (EMO'03). Lecture notes in computer science, vol. 2632. Berlin/Heidelberg: Springer-Verlag; 2003. p. 376-90.

[210] Khoshgoftaar TM, Rebours P, Seliya N. Software quality analysis by combining multiple projects and learners. Softw Qual Control 2009;17(1):25-49.

[211] Kim SW, Oommen BJ. A brief taxonomy and ranking of creative prototype reduction schemes. Pattern Anal Appl 2003;6(December (3)):232-44.

[212] Kirsopp C, Shepperd M. Case and feature subset selection in case-based software project effort prediction. In: Proc. of 22nd SGAI international conference on knowledge-based systems and applied artificial intelligence, Cambridge, UK; 2002.

[213] Kirsopp C, Shepperd M, House RL. Case and feature subset selection in case-based software project effort prediction. In: Research and development in intelligent systems XIX: proceedings of ES2002, the twenty-second SGAI international conference on knowledge based systems and applied artificial intelligence; 2003. p. 61.

[214] Kitchenham B, Pfleeger SL, McColl B, Eagan S. An empirical study of maintenance and development estimation accuracy. J Syst Softw 2002;64:57-77.

[215] Kitchenham B, Pickard LM, MacDonell SG, Shepperd MJ. What accuracy statistics really measure. IEE Proc Softw 2001;148(3):81-5.

[216] Kitchenham BA, Mendes E, Travassos GH. Cross versus within-company cost estimation studies: a systematic review. IEEE Trans Softw Eng 2007;33(5):316-29.

[217] Kitchenham BA, Dyba T, Jørgensen M. Evidence-based software engineering. In: ICSE '04: proceedings of the 26th international conference on software engineering. Washington, DC: IEEE Computer Society; 2004. p. 273-81.

[218] Kitchenham BA, Mendes E, Travassos GH. Cross versus within-company cost estimation studies: a systematic review. IEEE Trans Softw Eng 2007;33(5):316-29.

[219] Kittler J, Hatef M, Duin RPW, Matas J. On combining classifiers. IEEE Trans Pattern Anal Mach Intell 1998;20:226-39.

[220] Kocaguneli E, Gay G, Menzies T, Yang Y, Keung JW. When to use data from other projects for effort estimation. In: Proceedings of the 25th IEEE/ACM international conference on automated software engineering (ASE), Antwerp, Belgium; 2010. p. 321-4.

[221] Kocaguneli E, Menzies T, Bener A, Keung J. Exploiting the essential assumptions of analogy-based effort estimation. IEEE Trans Softw Eng; 28:425-38, 2012. Available from: http://menzies.us/pdf/11teak.pdf.

[222] Kocaguneli E, Menzies T, Keung J. How to find relevant data for effort estimation? 2011.

[223] Kocaguneli E, Menzies T, Keung J. On the value of ensemble effort estimation. IEEE Trans Softw Eng 2011;PP(99):1.

[224] Kocaguneli E, Menzies T, Mendes E. Transfer learning in effort estimation. Empir Softw Eng 2014 (to appear).

[225] Kocaguneli E, Menzies T, Keung J. On the value of ensemble effort estimation. IEEE Trans Softw Eng 2012. Available from: http://menzies.us/pdf/11comba.pdf.

[226] Kocaguneli E, Cukic B, Menzies T, Lu H. Building a second opinion: learning cross-company data. In: PROMSE'13; October 2013.

[227] Kocaguneli E, Gay G, Yang Y, Menzies T, Keung J. When to use data from other projects for effort estimation. In: ASE '10: to appear in the proceedings of the twenty-second IEEE/ACM international conference on automated software engineering, New York, NY; 2010.

[228] Kocaguneli E, Kultur Y, Bener A. Combining multiple learners induced on multiple datasets for software effort prediction. In: International symposium on software reliability engineering (ISSRE); 2009 (Student Paper).

[229] Kocaguneli E, Menzies T, Bener A, Keung JW. Exploiting the essential assumptions of analogy-based effort estimation. IEEE Trans Softw Eng 2012;38(March-April (2)):425-38.

[230] Kocaguneli E, Menzies T, Hihn J, Kang BH. Size doesn't matter?: on the value of software size features for effort estimation. In: Proceedings of the 8th international conference on predictive models in software engineering, PROMISE '12, Lund, Sweden, September 21-22, 2012. p. 89-98.

[231] Kocaguneli E, Menzies T, Keung J, Cok D, Madachy R. Active learning and effort estimation: finding the essential content of software effort estimation data. IEEE Trans Softw Eng; 2013 (pre-print).

[232] Kocaguneli E, Zimmermann T, Bird C, Nagappan N, Menzies T. Distributed development considered harmful? In: ICSE'13; 2013. p. 882-90.

[233] Kohavi R. A study of cross-validation and bootstrap for accuracy estimation and model selection. In: Proceedings of the 14th international joint conference on artificial intelligence, vol. 2, San Francisco, CA, USA; 1995. p. 1137-43.

[234] Kohavi R, John GH. Wrappers for feature subset selection. Artif Intell 1997;97(1-2):273-324.

[235] Kolodner JL. Improving human decision making through case-based decision aiding. AI Magazine; Summer 1991. p. 68.

[236] Kolter JZ, Maloof MA. Using additive expert ensembles to cope with concept drift. In: Proceedings of the 30th ACM international conference on machine learning (ICML), Bonn, Germany; 2005. p. 449-56.

[237] Kolter JZ, Maloof MA. Dynamic weighted majority: an ensemble method for drifting concepts. J Mach Learn Res 2007;8:2755-90.

[238] Korte M, Port D. Confidence in software cost estimation results based on mmre and pred. In: Proceedings of the 4th international workshop on predictor models in software engineering; PROMISE '08. New York, NY: ACM; 2008. p. 63-70.

[239] Koru AG, El-Emam K, Zhang D, Liu H, Mathew D. Theory of relative defect proneness. Empir Softw Eng 2008;13(October (5)):473-98.

[240] Kotsiantis S Kanellopoulos D. Discretization techniques: a recent survey. GESTS Int Trans Comput Sci Eng 2006;32(1):47-58.

[241] Krogh A, Vedelsby J. Neural network ensembles, cross validation, and active learning. In: Advances in neural information processing system (NIPS), vol. 7; 1995. p. 231-8.

[242] Kultur Y, Turhan B, Bener A. Ensemble of neural networks with associative memory (ENNA) for estimating software development costs. Knowl Based Syst 2009;22:395-402.

[243] Kultur Y, Turhan B, Bener AB. ENNA: software effort estimation using ensemble of neural networks with associative memory. In: SIGSOFT '08/FSE-16: proceedings of the 16th ACM SIGSOFT international symposium on foundations of software engineering. New York, NY: ACM; 2008. p. 330-8.

[244] Kuncheva L, Whitaker CJ. Measures of diversity in classifier ensembles and their relationship with the ensemble accuracy. Mach Learn 2003;51:181-207.

[245] Laurenz Eveleens J, Verhoef C. The rise and fall of the chaos report figures. IEEE Softw 2010;27(January (1)):30-6.

[246] Lee S-I, Chatalbashev V, Vickrey D, Koller D. Learning a meta-level prior for feature relevance from multiple related tasks. In: ICML '07: proceedings of the 24th international conference on machine learning; 2007. p. 489-96.

[247] LeFevre K, DeWitt DJ, Ramakrishnan R. Workload-aware anonymization techniques for large-scale datasets. ACM Trans Database Syst 2008;33(August (3)).

[248] Legg S, Hutter M, Kumar A. Tournament versus fitness uniform selection. In: Proceedings of the 2004 congress of evolutionary computation (CEC); 2004. p. 2144-51.

[249] Lessmann S, Baesens B, Mues C, Pietsch S. Benchmarking classification models for software defect prediction: a proposed framework and novel findings. IEEE Trans Softw Eng 2008;34(July-August (4)):485-96.

[250] Levene H. Contributions to probability and statistics: essays in honor of harold hotelling. 1st ed. USA: Stanford University Press; 1960.

[251] Levina E, Bickel PJ. Maximum likelihood estimation of intrinsic dimension. In: NIPS; 2004.

[252] Lewis D. Naive (bayes) at forty: the independence assumption in information retrieval. In: Ndellec C, Rouveirol C, editors. Machine learning: ECML-98. Lecture notes in computer science, vol. 1398. Berlin/Heidelberg: Springer; 1998. p. 4-15.

[253] Li J, Ruhe G. Analysis of attribute weighting heuristics for analogy-based software effort estimation method AQUA+. Empir Softw Eng 2008;13(1):63-96.

[254] Li M, Zhang H, Wu R, Zhou Z-H. Sample-based software defect prediction with active and semi-supervised learning. Autom Softw Eng 2012;19(2):201-30.

[255] Li N, Li T. t-Closeness: privacy beyond k-anonymity and l-diversity. In: Proc. of IEEE 23rd int'l conf. on data engineering (ICDE'07); 2007.

[256] Li T, Li N. Injector: mining background knowledge for data anonymization. In: IEEE 24th international conference on data engineering. ICDE 2008; 2008. p. 446-55.

[257] Li T, Li N, Zhang J. Modeling and integrating background knowledge in data anonymization. In: IEEE 25th international conference on data engineering. ICDE '09; 2009. p. 6-17.

[258] Li X-B, Sarkar S. Against classification attacks: a decision tree pruning approach to privacy protection in data mining. Oper Res 2009;57(November-December (6)):1496-509.

[259] Li Y, Xie M, Goh T. A study of project selection and feature weighting for analogy based software cost estimation. J Syst Softw 2009;82:241-52.

[260]   Li Y, Xie M, Goh T. A study of the non-linear adjustment for analogy based software cost estimation. Empir Softw Eng 2009:603-43.

[261]   Li YF, Xie M, Goh TN. A study of mutual information based feature selection for case based reasoning in software cost estimation. Expert Syst Appl 2009;36(3):5921-31.

[262]   Lipowezky U. Selection of the optimal prototype subset for 1-nn classification. Pattern Recogn Lett 1998;19:907-18.

[263]   Liu Y, Yao X. Ensemble learning via negative correlation. Neural Netw 1999;12:1399-404.

[264]   Liu Y, Yao X. Simultaneous training of negatively correlated neural networks in an ensemble. IEEE Trans Syst Man Cybern B: Cybern 1999;29(6):716-25.

[265]   Liu Y, Khoshgoftaar TM, Seliya N. Evolutionary optimization of software quality modeling with multiple repositories. IEEE Trans Softw Eng 2010;36(6):852-64.

[266]   Lokan C, Mendes E. Investigating the use of chronological splitting to compare software cross-company and single-company effort predictions. In: Proceedings of the 12th international conference on evaluation & assessment in software engineering (EASE'08), Bari, Italy; 2008. p. 151-60.

[267]   Lokan C, Mendes E. Investigating the use of chronological split for software effort estimation. IET Softw 2009;3(5):422-34.

[268]   Lokan C, Mendes E. Using chronological splitting to compare cross- and single-company effort models: further investigation. In: Proceedings of the 32nd Australasian computer science conference (ACSC'09), Wellington, New Zealand; 2009. p. 35-42.

[269]   Lokan C, Mendes E. Applying moving windows to software effort estimation. In: ESEM'09: proceedings of the 3rd international symposium on empirical software engineering and measurement; 2009. p. 111-122.

[270]   Lokan C, Mendes E. Using chronological splitting to compare cross- and single-company effort models: further investigation. In: Proceedings of the thirty-second Australasian conference on computer science. ACSC '09, vol. 91; 2009. p. 47-54.

[271]   Lokan CJ, Wright T, Hill PR, Stringer M. Organizational benchmarking using the ISBSG data repository. IEEE Softw 2001;18(5):26-32.

[272]   Lu H, Cukic B. An adaptive approach with active learning in software fault prediction. In: Proceedings of the 8th international conference on predictive models in software engineering; PROMISE '12; 2012. p. 79-88.

[273]   Lukasiewycz M, Gla M, Reimann F, Helwig S. Opt4j: the meta-heuristic optimisation framework for java; 2011. http://opt4j.sourceforge.net.

[274]   Lum K, Powell J, Hihn J. Validation of spacecraft software cost estimation models for flight and ground systems. In: ISPA conference proceedings, software modeling track; May 2002.

[275]   Lum K, Menzies T, Baker D. 2cee, a twenty first century effort estimation methodology. In: International society of parametric analysis conference (ISPA/SCEA); May 2008.

[276]   Lumpe M, Vasa R, Menzies T, Rush R, Turhan R. Learning better inspection optimization policies. Int J Softw Eng Knowl Eng 2011;21(45):725-53.

[277]   Ma Y, Luo G, Zeng X, Chen A. Transfer learning for cross-company software defect prediction. Inf Softw Technol 2012;54(March (3)):248-56.

[278]   Machanavajjhala A, Kifer D, Gehrke J, Venkitasubramaniam M. L-diversity: privacy beyond k-anonymity. ACM Trans Knowl Discov Data 2007;1(March).

[279]   Madachy RJ, Boehm BW, Clark B, Tan T, Rosa W. Us dod application domain empirical software cost analysis. In: Empirical Software Engineering and Measurement, ESEM 2011, Banff; 2011. p. 392-5.

[280]   Mair C, Shepperd M. The consistency of empirical comparisons of regression and analogy-based software project cost prediction. In: International symposium on empirical software engineering; November 2005. 10 p.

[281]   Mann HB, Whitney DR. On a test of whether one of two random variables is stochastically larger than the other. Ann Math Stat 1947;18(1):50-60.

[282] Martin DJ, Kifer D, Machanavajjhala A, Gehrke J, Halpern JY. Worst-case background knowledge for privacy-preserving data publishing. In: IEEE 23rd international conference on data Engineering. ICDE 2007; 2007. p. 126-35.

[283] Mashiko Y, Basili VR. Using the GQM paradigm to investigate influential factors for software process improvement. J Syst Softw 1997;36:17-32.

[284] Maxwell K, Van Wassenhove L, Dutta S. Performance evaluation of general and company specific models in software development effort estimation. Manag Sci 1999;45(6):787-803.

[285] McCabe TJ. A complexity measure. IEEE Trans Softw Eng 1976;2(December (4)):308-20.

[286] McCabe TJ. Mccabe QA®; 2005. http://www.mccabe.com.

[287] McCallum A, Nigam K, Ungar LH. Efficient clustering of high-dimensional data sets with application to reference matching. In: Proceedings of the sixth ACM SIGKDD international conference on knowledge discovery and data mining; KDD '00; 2000. p. 169-78.

[288] Mendes E, Lokan C. Investigating the use of chronological splitting to compare software cross-company and single-company effort predictions: a replicated study. In: Proceedings of the 13th international conference on evaluation & assessment in software engineering (EASE'09), Durham, UK; 2009. 10 p.

[289] Mendes E, Mosley N. Bayesian network models for web effort prediction: a comparative study. IEEE Trans Softw Eng 2008;34:723-37.

[290] Mendes E, Watson ID, Triggs C, Mosley N, Counsell S. A comparative study of cost estimation models for web hypermedia applications. Empir Softw Eng 2003;8(2):163-96.

[291] Menzies T, Butcher A, Cok D, Marcus A, Layman L, Shull F, et al. Local vs. global lessons for defect prediction and effort estimation. IEEE Trans Softw Eng 2012:1. Available from: http://menzies.us/pdf/12localb.pdf.

[292] Menzies T, Chen Z, Hihn J, Lum K. Selecting best practices for effort estimation. IEEE Trans Softw Eng 2006;32(11):883-95.

[293] Menzies T, Elwaras O, Hihn J, Feathear M, Boehm B, Madachy R. The business case for automated software engineering. In: IEEE ASE; 2007. Available from: http://menzies.us/pdf/07casease-v0.pdf.

[294] Menzies T, Greenwald J, Frank A. Data mining static code attributes to learn defect predictors. IEEE Trans Softw Eng 2007;33(January (1)):2-13.

[295] Menzies T, Hu Y. Data mining for very busy people. In: IEEE computer; November 2003. Available from: http://menzies.us/pdf/03tar2.pdf.

[296] Menzies T, Port D, Chen Z, Hihn J, Stukes S. Validation methods for calibrating software effort models. In: Proceedings, ICSE; 2005. Available from: http://menzies.us/pdf/04coconut.pdf.

[297] Menzies T, Shepperd M. Special issue on repeatable results in software engineering prediction. Empir Softw Eng 2012;17:1-17.

[298] Menzies T, Bird C, Zimmermann T, Schulte W, Kocaganeli E. The inductive software engineering manifesto: principles for industrial data mining. In: Proceedings of the international workshop on machine learning technologies in software engineering; MALETS '11. New York, NY: ACM; 2011. p. 19-26.

[299] Menzies T, Brady A, Keung J, Hihn J, Williams S, El-Rawas O, et al. Learning project management decisions: a case study with case-based reasoning versus data farming. IEEE Trans Softw Eng 2013;39(12):1698-713.

[300] Menzies T, Caglayan B, Kocaguneli E, Krall J, Peters F, Turhan B. The promise repository of empirical software engineering data; June 2012.

[301] Menzies T, Chen Z, Hihn J, Lum K. Selecting best practices for effort estimation. IEEE Trans Softw Eng 2006;32(11):883-95.

[302] Menzies T, Chen Z, Port D, Hihn J. Simple software cost estimation: safe or unsafe? In: Proceedings, PROMISE workshop, ICSE 2005; 2005. Available from: http://menzies.us/pdf/05safewhen.pdf.

[303] Menzies T, Dekhtyar A, Distefano J, Greenwald J. Problems with precision: a response to "comments on 'data mining static code attributes to learn defect predictors'". IEEE Trans Softw Eng 2007; 33(September (9)):637-40.

[304] Menzies T, El-Rawas O, Hihn J, Boehm B. Can we build software faster and better and cheaper? In: PROMISE'09; 2009. Available from: http://menzies.us/pdf/09bfc.pdf.

[305] Menzies T, Elrawas O, Hihn J, Feather M, Madachy R, Boehm B. The business case for automated software engineering. ASE; 2007. p. 303-12.

[306] Menzies T, Hu Y. Just enough learning (of association rules): the TAR2 treatment learner. In: Artificial intelligence review; 2007. Available from: http://menzies.us/pdf/07tar2.pdf.

[307] Menzies T, Jalali O, Hihn J, Baker D, Lum K. Stable rankings for different effort models. Autom Softw Eng 2010;December(4). Available from: http://menzies.us/pdf/10stable.pdf.

[308] Menzies T, Port D, Chen Z, Hihn J, Stukes S. Validation methods for calibrating software effort models. In: ICSE '05: proceedings of the 27th international conference on software engineering. New York, NY: ACM; 2005. p. 587-95.

[309] Menzies T, Raffo D, Setamanit S-o, Hu Y, Tootoonian S. Model-based tests of truisms. In: Proceedings of IEEE. ASE 2002; 2002. Available from http://menzies.us/pdf/02truisms.pdf.

[310] Menzies T, Shepperd M. Special issue on repeatable results in software engineering prediction. Empir Softw Eng 2012;17(1-2):1-17.

[311] Menzies T, Turhan B, Bener A, Gay G, Cukic B, Jiang Y. Implications of ceiling effects in defect predictors. In: Proceedings of the 4th international workshop on predictor models in software engineering, PROMISE '08. New York, NY: ACM; 2008. p. 47-54.

[312] Menzies T, Williams S, El-Rawas O, Boehm B, Hihn J. How to avoid drastic software process change (using stochastic stability). In: ICSE'09; 2009. Available from: http://menzies.us/pdf/08drastic.pdf.

[313] Menzies T, Zimmermann T. Goldfish bowl panel: software development analytics. In: ICSE; 2012. p. 1032-3.

[314] Meyer B. Object-oriented software construction. Hemel Hempstead: Prentice-Hall; 1988.

[315] Mihalkova L, Huynh T, Mooney RJ. Mapping and revising markov logic networks for transfer learning. In: AAAI'07: proceedings of the 22nd national conference on artificial intelligence; 2007. p. 608-14.

[316] Miller A. Subset selection in regression. 2nd ed. London: Chapman & Hall, 2002.

[317] Miller BL, Goldberg DE. Genetic algorithms, tournament selection, and the effects of noise. Complex Syst 1995;9(3):193-212.

[318] Minku L, Yao X. How to make best use of cross-company data in software effort estimation? In: International conference on software engineering (ICSE); Hyderabad, India; 2014 (accepted). doi: 10.1145/2568225.2568228.

[319] Minku LL. Machine learning for software effort estimation. The 13th CREST open workshop future internet testing (FITTEST) & search based software engineering (SBSE); May 2011. http://crest.cs.ucl.ac.uk/cow/13/slides/presentation_leandro.pdf; http://crest.cs.ucl.ac.uk/cow/13/videos/M2U00270Minku.mp4.

[320] Minku LL, White A, Yao X. The impact of diversity on on-line ensemble learning in the presence of concept drift. IEEE Trans Knowl Data Eng 2010;22(5):730-42.

[321] Minku LL, Yao X. A principled evaluation of ensembles of learning machines for software effort estimation. In: Proceedings of the 7th international conference on predictive models in software engineering (PROMISE'11), Banff, Canada; 2011. 10 p.

[322] Minku LL, Yao X. Can cross-company data improve performance in software effort estimation? In: Proceedings of the 8th international conference on predictive models in software engineering (PROMISE'12), Lund, Sweden; 2012. p. 69-78.

[323] Minku LL, Yao X. DDD: a new ensemble approach for dealing with concept drift. IEEE Trans Knowl Data Eng 2012;24(4):619-33.

[324] Minku LL, Yao X. Using unreliable data for creating more reliable online learners. In: Proceedings of the 2012 international joint conference on neural networks (IJCNN'12), Brisbane, Australia; 2012. 8 p.

[325] Minku LL, Yao X. An analysis of multi-objective evolutionary algorithms for training ensemble models based on different performance measures in software effort estimation. In: Proceedings of the 9th international conference on predictive models in software engineering (PROMISE'13), Baltimore, USA; 2013. 10 p.

[326] Minku LL, Yao X. Ensembles and locality: insight on improving software effort estimation. Inform Softw Technol 2013;55(8):1512-28.

[327] Minku LL, Yao X. Software effort estimation as a multi-objective learning problem. ACM Trans Softw Eng Methodol 2013;22(4, Article No. 35):32.

[328] Mitchell ML, Jolley JM. Research design explained. 7th ed. USA: Cengage Learning; 2010.

[329] Miyazaki Y, Terakado M, Ozaki K, Nozaki H. Robust regression for developing software estimation models. J Syst Softw 1994;27(1):3-16.

[330] Mockus A, Anda B, Sjoberg D. Experiences from replicating a case study to investigate reproducibility of software development. In: First international workshop on replication in empirical software engineering research, ICSE'09; 2009.

[331] Molokken K, Jorgensen M. A review of surveys on software effort estimation. In: ISESE '03: proceedings of the 2003 international symposium on empirical software engineering. Washington, DC: IEEE Computer Society; 2003. p. 223.

[332] Montgomery DC. Design and analysis of experiments. 6th ed. UK: John Wiley & Sons; 2004.

[333] Murphy B. The difficulties of building generic reliability models for software. Empir Softw Eng 2012;17:18-22.

[334] Muthukrishnan S. Data streams: algorithms and applications. Hanover, MA: Now Publishers Inc.; 2005.

[335] Myrtveit I, Stensrud E, Shepperd M. Reliability and validity in comparative studies of software prediction models. IEEE Trans Softw Eng 2005;31(May (5)):380-91.

[336] Nakano R, Ueda N. Generalization error of ensemble estimators. In: Proceedings of international conference on neural networks, Washington; 1996. p. 90-5.

[337] Nagappan N, Ball T. Static analysis tools as early indicators of pre-release defect density. In: ICSE 2005, St. Louis; 2005.

[338] Nam J, Pan SJ, Kim S. Transfer defect learning. In: ICSE'13. Piscataway, NJ: IEEE Press; 2013. p. 802-11.

[339] Nelson A, Menzies T, Gay G. Sharing experiments using open-source software. Software Pract Exper 2011; 41(March):283-305.

[340] Nguyen V, Huang LG, Boehm B. An analysis of trends in productivity and cost drivers over years. In: Promise '11: proceedings of the 7th international conference on predictive models in software engineering; 2011. p. 3:1-3:10.

[341] Noll J, Seichter D, Beecham S. Can automated text classification improve content analysis of software project data? In: 2013 ACM/IEEE international symposium on empirical software engineering and measurement; 2013. p. 300-3.

[342] Novak PK, Lavrač N, Webb GI. Supervised descriptive rule discovery: a unifying survey of contrast set, emerging pattern and subgroup mining. J Mach Learn Res 2009;10(June):377-403.

[343] Olague H, Etzkorn L, Gholston S, Quattlebaum S. Empirical validation of three software metrics suites to predict fault-proneness of object-oriented classes developed using highly iterative or agile software development processes. IEEE Trans Softw Eng 2007;33(6):402-19.

[344] Oliveira ALI, Braga PL, Lima RMF, Cornalio ML. Ga-based method for feature selection and parameters optimization for machine learning regression applied to software effort estimation. Inform Softw Technol 2010;52(11):1155-66 (Special Section on Best Papers PROMISE 2009).

[345] Arturo Olvera-López J, Ariel Carrasco-Ochoa J, Francisco Martínez-Trinidad J, Kittler J. A review of instance selection methods. Artif Intell Rev 2010;34(August):133-43.

[346] Arturo Olvera-Lpez J, Ariel Carrasco-Ochoa J, Francisco Martnez-Trinidad J. A new fast prototype selection method based on clustering. Pattern Anal Appl 2010;13(2):131-41.

[347] Orrego AS. Sawtooth: learning from huge amounts of data. Master's thesis, Computer Science, West Virginia University; 2004.

[348] Ostrand TJ, Weyuker EJ, Bell RM. Where the bugs are. In: ISSTA '04: proceedings of the 2004 ACM SIGSOFT international symposium on software testing and analysis. New York, NY: ACM; 2004. p. 86-96.

[349] Ostrand TJ, Weyuker EJ, Bell RM. Programmer-based fault prediction. In: Proceedings of the 6th international conference on predictive models in software engineering; PROMISE '10; 2010. p. 19:1-19:10.

[350] Osuna E, Freund R, Girosit F. Training support vector machines: an application to face detection. In: IEEE computer society conference on computer vision and pattern recognition; June 1997. p. 130-6.

[351] Palma F, Farzin H, Gueheneuc Y, Moha N. Recommendation system for design patterns in software development: an DPR overview. In: Recommendation systems for software engineering (RSSE); June 2012. p. 1-5.

[352] Pan SJ, Yang Q. A survey on transfer learning. IEEE Trans Knowl Data Eng 2010;22(10):1345-59.

[353] Park H, Shim K. Approximate algorithms with generalizing attribute values for k-anonymity. Inform Syst 2010;35(December (8)):933-55.

[354] Passos C, Braun AP, Cruzes DS, Mendonca M. Analyzing the impact of beliefs in software project practices. In: ESEM'11; 2011.

[355] Peters F, Menzies T. Privacy and utility for defect prediction: experiments with morph. In: 34th international conference on software engineering (ICSE), June 2012; p. 189-99.

[356] Peters F, Menzies T, Gong L, Zhang H. Balancing privacy and utility in cross-company defect prediction. IEEE Trans Softw Eng 2013;39:1054-68.

[357] Peters F. Cliff: finding prototypes for nearest neighbor algorithms with application to forensic trace evidence. Copyright ProQuest, UMI Dissertations Publishing 2010. Master's thesis; 2010.

[358] Petersen K, Wohlin C. Context in industrial software engineering research. In: 3rd international symposium on empirical software engineering and measurement. ESEM 2009; October 2009. p. 401-4.

[359] Platt J. FastMap, MetricMap, and landmark MDS are all nystrom algorithms. In: Society for Artificial Intelligence and Statistics; 2005. p. 261-8.

[360] Platt JC. Fast training of support vector machines using sequential minimal optimization. In: Advances in kernel methods. Cambridge, MA: MIT Press; 1999. p. 185-208.

[361] Posnett D, Filkov V, Devanbu P. Ecological inference in empirical software engineering. In: Proceedings of ASE'11; 2011.

[362] Praditwong K, Yao X. A new multi-objective evolutionary optimisation algorithm: the two-archive algorithm. In: International conference on computational intelligence and security (CIS'2006), Guangzhou, China, vol. 1; 2006. p. 286-91.

[363] Quinlan R. C4.5: programs for machine learning. San Francisco, CA: Morgan Kaufmann; 1992. ISBN: 1558602380.

[364] Rachlin Y, Probst K, Ghani R. Maximizing privacy under data distortion constraints in noise perturbation methods. In: Bonchi F, Ferrari E, Jiang W, Malin B, editors. Privacy, security, and trust in KDD. Lecture notes in computer science, vol. 5456. Berlin/Heidelberg: Springer; 2009. p. 92-110.

[365] Agrawal R, Imeilinski T, Swami A. Mining association rules between sets of items in large databases. In: Proceedings of the 1993 ACM SIGMOD conference, Washington, DC, USA; 1993. Available from: http://citeseer.nj.nec.com/agrawal93mining.html.

[366] Rahman F, Posnett D, Devanbu PT. Recalling the "imprecision" of cross-project defect prediction. In: Foundations of software engineering (FSE-20); 2012. p. 61.

[367] Rakitin SR. Software verification and validation for practitioners and managers. 2nd ed. Norwood, MA: Artech House; 2001.

[368] Reed R. Pruning algorithms—a survey. IEEE Trans Neural Netw 1993;4(5):740-7.

[369] Robles G. Replicating MSR: a study of the potential replicability of papers published in the mining software repositories proceedings. In: MSR'10; 2010.

[370] Rodríguez D, Carreira MR, Riquelme J, Harrison R. Multiobjective simulation optimisation in software project management. In: GECCO; 2011. p. 1883-90.

[371] Roh S-B, Oh S-K, Pedrycz W. Design of fuzzy radial basis function-based polynomial neural networks. Fuzzy Sets Syst 2011;185(1):15-37 (Theme: Systems Engineering).

[372] Rosenblatt F. The perceptron—a perceiving and recognizing automaton. Technical report, Cornell Aeronautical Laboratory; 1957.

[373] Rosenthal R. The handbook of research synthesis, vol. 236. New York: Sage; 1994.

[374] Boehm B, Chulani S, Clark B, Steece B. Calibration approach and results of the cocomo ii post-architecture model. In: Proceedings ISPA, 98; 1998.

[375] Samarati P, Sweeney L. Protecting privacy when disclosing information: k-anonymity and its enforcement through generalization and suppression; 1998.

[376] Sarro F. Genetic programming for effort estimation. The 14th CREST open workshop—genetic programming for software engineering; July 2011. http://crest.cs.ucl.ac.uk/cow/14/slides/Sarro_14thCrestOW.pdf, http://crest.cs.ucl.ac.uk/cow/14/videos/M2U00285Federica.mp4.

[377] Sarro F, Ferrucci F, Gravino C. Single and multi objective genetic programming for software development effort estimation. In: ACM SAC'12, Riva del Garda (Trento), Italy; 2012. p. 1221-6.

[378] Sayyad AS, Menzies T, Ammar H. On the value of user preferences in search-based software engineering: a case study in software product lines. In: Proceedings of the 2013 international conference on software engineering; ICSE '13; 2013. p. 492-501.

[379] Sayyad AS, Ingram J, Menzies T, Ammar H. Scalable product line configuration: a straw to break the camel'FS back. In: ASE'13, Palo Alto, CA; 2013.

[380] Schank R, Abelson R. Scripts, plans, goals and understanding: an inquiry into human knowledge structures. Hillsdale, NJ: Lawrence Erlbaum Associates; 1977.

[381] Sculley D. Web-scale k-means clustering. In: Proceedings of the 19th international conference on World Wide Web; WWW '10; 2010. p. 1177-8.

[382] Selman B, Kautz HA, Cohen B. Local search strategies for satisfiability testing. In: Trick M, Johnson DS, editors. Proceedings of the second DIMACS challenge on cliques, coloring, and satisfiability, Providence, RI; 1993.

[383] Seni G, Elder J. Ensemble methods in data mining: improving accuracy through combining predictions. San Rafael: Morgan and Claypool Publishers; 2010.

[384] Sentas P, Angelis L, Stamelos I, Bleris G. Software productivity and effort prediction with ordinal regression. Inform Softw Technol 2005;47(1):17-29.

[385] Seo Y-S, Yoon K-A, Bae D-H. An empirical analysis of software effort estimation with outlier elimination. In: Proceedings of the 4th international workshop on predictor models in software engineering (PROMISE'08), Leipzig; 2008. p. 25-32.

[386] Shan Y, McKay RJ, Lokan CJ, Essam DL. Software project effort estimation using genetic programming. In: Proceedings of the 2002 international conference on communications, circuits and systems and west sino expositions (ICCCAS & WESINO EXPO), Chengdu Sichuan, China, vol. 2; 2002. p. 1108-12.

[387] Shatnawi R. A quantitative investigation of the acceptable risk levels of object-oriented metrics in open-source systems. IEEE Trans Softw Eng 2010;36(2):216-25.

[388] Shatnawi R, Li W. The effectiveness of software metrics in identifying error-prone classes in post-release software evolution process. J Syst Softw 2008;81(11):1868-82.

[389] Shepperd M, McDonell S. Evaluating prediction systems in software project estimation. Inform Softw Technol 2012;54:820-7.

[390] Shepperd M, Schofield C. Estimating software project effort using analogies. IEEE Trans Softw Eng 1997;23(November (12)). Available from: http://www.utdallas.edu/~rbanker/SE_XII.pdf.

[391] Shepperd M. It doesn't matter what you do but does matter who does it!; 2011. Available from: http://goo.gl/JbXcL.

[392] Shepperd M, Kadoda G. Comparing software prediction techniques using simulation. IEEE Trans Softw Eng 2001;27(11):1014-22.

[393] Shepperd M, MacDonell S. Evaluating prediction systems in software project estimation. Inform Softw Technol 2012 (pre-print).

[394] Shepperd M, Schofield C, Kitchenham B. Effort estimation using analogy. In: ICSE '96: proceedings of the 18th international conference on software engineering. Washington, DC: IEEE Computer Society; 1996. p. 170-8.

[395] Shin Y, Meneely A, Williams L, Osborne JA. Evaluating complexity, code churn, and developer activity metrics as indicators of software vulnerabilities. IEEE Trans Softw Eng; 2011;37(November (6)):772-87.

[396] Shull F, Basili VR, Boehm B, Brown AW, Costa P, Lindvall M, et al. What we have learned about fighting defects. In: Proceedings of 8th international software metrics symposium, Ottawa, Canada; 2002. p. 249-58. Available from: http://fc-md.umd.edu/fcmd/Papers/shull_defects.ps.

[397] Shull F, Lanubile F, Basili VR. Investigating reading techniques for object-oriented framework learning. IEEE Trans Softw Eng 2000;26(11):1101-18.

[398] Shull F, Rus I, Basili VR. How perspective-based reading can improve requirements inspections. IEEE Comput 2000;33(7):73-9. Available from: http://www.cs.umd.edu/projects/SoftEng/ESEG/papers/82.77.pdf.

[399] Silver N. The signal and the noise: why most predictions fail—but some don't. New York, NY: Penguin; 2012.

[400] Simons DJ, Chabris CF. Gorillas in our midst: sustained inattentional blindness for dynamic events perception. Perception 1999;28:1059-74.

[401] Singh Y, Kaur A, Malhotra R. Empirical validation of object-oriented metrics for predicting fault proneness models. Softw Qual J 2010;18(1):3-35.

[402] Spareref.com. Nasa to shut down checkout & launch control system, August 26, 2002. http://www.spaceref.com/news/viewnews.html?id=475.

[403] Srivasan K, Fisher D. Machine learning approaches to estimating software development effort. IEEE Trans Softw Eng 1995;21(2):126-37.

[404] The Standish Group Report: Chaos; 1995. Available from: http://www4.in.tum.de/lehre/vorlesungen/vse/WS2004/1995_Standish_Chaos.pdf.

[405] Storkey A. When training and test sets are different: characterizing learning transfer. In: Candela J, Sugiyama M, Schwaighofer A, Lawrence N, editors. Dataset shift in machine learning. Cambridge, MA: MIT Press; 2009. p. 3-28.

[406] Strutzke R. Estimating software-intensive systems: products, projects and processes. Boston, MA: Addison Wesley; 2005.

[407] Stukes S, Apgar H. Applications oriented software data collection: software model calibration report, TR-9007/549-1, management consulting and research; March 1991.

[408] Stukes S, Ferens D. Software cost model calibration. J Parametrics 1998;18(1):77-98.

[409] Subramanyam R, Krishnan MS. Empirical analysis of CK metrics for object-oriented design complexity: implications for software defects. IEEE Trans Softw Eng 2003;29(April (4)):297-310.

[410] Succi G. Practical assessment of the models for identification of defect-prone classes in object-oriented commercial systems using design metrics. J Syst Softw 2003;65(January (1)):1-12.

[411] Sweeney L. Achieving k-anonymity privacy protection using generalization and suppression. Int J Uncertainty Fuzziness Knowl Based Syst 2002;10(October (5)):571-88.

[412] Sweeney L. k-anonymity: a model for protecting privacy. IEEE Secur Priv 2002;10(5):557-70.

[413] Taneja K, Grechanik M, Ghani R, Xie T. Testing software in age of data privacy: a balancing act. In: Proceedings of the 19th ACM SIGSOFT symposium and the 13th European conference on foundations of software engineering; ESEC/FSE '11. New York, NY: ACM; 2011, p. 201-11.

[414] Tang EK, Suganthan PN, Yao X. An analysis of diversity measures. Mach Learn 2006;65:247-71.

[415] Tang M, Kao M, Chen M. An empirical study on object-oriented metrics. In: Proceedings of sixth international software metrics symposium; 1999. p. 242-9.

[416] Thapaliyal M, Verma G. Software defects and object oriented metrics-an empirical analysis. Int J Comput Appl 2010;9/5.

[417] Thongmak M, Muenchaisri P. Predicting faulty classes using design metrics with discriminant analysis. Softw Eng Res Pract; 2003. p. 621-7.

[418] Torra V, Endo Y, Miyamoto S. On the comparison of some fuzzy clustering methods for privacy preserving data mining: towards the development of specific information loss measures. Kybernetika 2009;45(3): 548-60.

[419] Tosun A, Bener A, Turhan B. Practical considerations of deploying Ai in defect prediction: a case study within the Turkish telecommunication industry. In: PROMISE'09; 2009.

[420] Tosun A, Bener AB, Turhan B, Menzies T. Practical considerations in deploying statistical methods for defect prediction: a case study within the Turkish telecommunications industry. Inform Softw Technol 2010;52(11):1242-57.

[421] Tresp V. Handbook of neural network signal processing. Chapter 5: Committee machines. USA: CRC Press; 2001.

[422] Tronto IFB, Silva JDS, Sant'Anna N. Comparison of artificial neural network and regression models in software effort estimation. In: Proceedings of the 2007 international joint conference on neural networks (IJCNN'07), Orlando; 2007. p. 771-6.

[423] Turhan B, Kutlubay O, Bener A. Evaluation of feature extraction methods on software cost estimation. In: First international symposium on empirical software engineering and measurement. ESEM 2007; 2007. p. 497.

[424] Turhan B, Menzies T, Bener AB, Di Stefano J. On the relative value of cross-company and within-company data for defect prediction. Empir Softw Eng 2009;14(5):540-78.

[425] Turhan B. On the dataset shift problem in software engineering prediction models. Empir Softw Eng 2012;17:62-74.

[426] Turhan B, Bener AB, Menzies T. Regularities in learning defect predictors. In: Ali Babar M, Vierimaa M, Oivo M, editors. PROFES. Lecture notes in business information processing, vol. 6156. Berlin/Heidelberg: Springer; 2010. p. 116-30.

[427] Turhan B, Menzies T, Bener A, Di Stefano J. On the relative value of cross-company and within-company data for defect prediction. Empir Softw Eng 2009;14:540-78.

[428] Turner J. A predictive approach to eliminating errors in software code; 2006. Web page, Office of the NASA Chief Technologist, http://www.sti.nasa.gov/tto/Spinoff2006/ct_1.htm.

[429] Vaidya J, Clifton C. Privacy-preserving data mining: why, how, and when. IEEE Secur Priv 2004;2 (November (6)):19-27.

[430] Valerdi R. Convergence of expert opinion via the wideband Delphi method: an application in cost estimation models. In: Incose international symposium, Denver, USA; 2011. Available from: http://goo.gl/Zo9HT.

[431] Valerdi R. Heuristics for systems engineering cost estimation. IEEE Syst J 2011;5(1):91-8.

[432] Vargha A, Delaney H. A critique and improvement of the CL common language effect size statistics of mcgraw and wong. J Educ Behav Stat 2000;25(2):101-32.

[433] Verykios VS, Bertino E, Fovin IN, Provenza LP, Saygin Y, Theodoridis Y. State-of-the-art in privacy preserving data mining. SIGMOD Record 2004;33(March (1)):50-7.

[434] Walkerden F, Jeffery R. An empirical study of analogy-based software effort estimation. Empir Softw Eng 1999;4(2):135-58.

[435] Wallace BC, Small K, Brodley CE, Trikalinos TA. Active learning for biomedical citation screening. In: Proceedings of the 16th ACM SIGKDD international conference on knowledge discovery and data mining. New York, NY: ACM; 2010. p. 173-82.

[436] Wang S-L, Maskey R, Jafari A, Hong T-P. Efficient sanitization of informative association rules. Expert Syst Appl 2008;35(July-August (1-2)):442-50.

[437] Wang S-L, Parikh B, Jafarl A. Hiding informative association rule sets. Expert Syst Appl 2007;33 (August (2)):316-23.

[438] Wang Z, Tang K, Yao X. Multi-objective approaches to optimal testing resource allocation in modular software systems. IEEE Trans Reliab 2010;59(3):563-75.

[439] Wettel R, Lanza M, Robbes R. Software systems as cities: a controlled experiment. In: Proceedings of the 33rd international conference on software engineering; ICSE '11; 2011. p. 551-60.

[440] Weyuker EJ, Ostrand T, Bell RM. Do too many cooks spoil the broth? using the number of developers to enhance defect prediction models. Empir Softw Eng 2008;13(5):539-59.

[441] White T. Hadoop: the definitive guide. O'Reilly Media; 2009.

[442] Wilcoxon F. Individual comparisons by ranking methods. Biometrics 1945;1(6):80-3.

[443] Wilkes M. Memoirs of a computer pioneer. Cambridge, MA: MIT Press; 1985.

[444] Witten IH, Frank E. Data mining. 2nd ed. Los Altos, CA: Morgan Kaufmann; 2005.

[445] Wittig GE, Finnie GR. Estimating software development effort with connectionist models. Inform Softw Technol 1997;39:469-76.

[446] Wu P, Dietterich TG. Improving SVM accuracy by training on auxiliary data sources. In: Proceedings of the twenty-first international conference on machine learning; ICML '04. New York, NY: ACM; 2004. p. 110.

[447] Würsch M, Ghezzi G, Reif G, Gall HC. Supporting developers with natural language queries. In: Proceedings of the 32Nd ACM/IEEE international conference on software engineering; ICSE '10, vol. 1; 2010. p. 165-74.

[448] Wyatt P. Whose bug is this anyway?!? December 2012. http://www.codeofhonor.com/blog/whose-bug-is-this-anyway.

[449] Xie T, Notkin D. Mutually enhancing test generation and specification inference. Formal approaches to software testing; 2004. p. 1100-01.

[450] Xie T, Thummalapenta S, Lo D, Liu C. Data mining for software engineering. Computer 2009;42 (August (8)):55-62.

[451] Xu J, Ho D, Capretz L. An empirical validation of object-oriented design metrics for fault prediction. J Comput Sci 2008;July:571-7.

[452] Yang Y, He Z, Mao K, Li Q, Nguyen V, Boehm BW, et al. Analyzing and handling local bias for calibrating parametric cost estimation models. Inform Softw Technol 2013;55(8):1496-511.

[453] Yang Y, Webb GI. Discretization for naive-bayes learning: managing discretization bias and variance. Mach Learn 2009;74(1):39-74.

[454] Yu P, Systa T, Muller H. Predicting fault-proneness using oo metrics an industrial case study. In: Sixth European conference on software maintenance and reengineering; 2002. p. 99-107.

[455] Zhang H, Sheng S. Learning weighted naive bayes with accurate ranking. In: ICDM '04. Fourth IEEE international conference on data mining; 2004. p. 567-70.

[456] Zhang N, Zhao W. Privacy-preserving data mining systems. Computer 2007;40(April (4)):52+.

[457] Zhang X, Dai W, Xue G-R, Yu Y. Adaptive email spam filtering based on information theory. In: Web information systems engineering WISE 2007. Lecture notes in computer science, vol. 4831. Berlin/Heidelberg: Springer; 2007. p. 159-170.

[458] Zhao H, Ram S. Constrained cascade generalization of decision trees. IEEE Trans Knowl Data Eng 2004;16:727-39.

[459] Zhao Y, Zhang Y. Comparison of decision tree methods for finding active objects. Adv Space Res 2008;41:1955-9.

[460] Zhou Y, Leung H. Empirical analysis of object-oriented design metrics for predicting high and low severity faults. IEEE Trans Softw Eng 2006;32(10):771-89.

[461] Zhu D, Li X-B, Wu S. Identity disclosure protection: a data reconstruction approach for privacy-preserving data mining. Decis Support Syst 2009;48(December (1, Sp. Iss. SI)):133-40.

[462] Zimmermann T, Menzies T. Software analytics: so what? IEEE Softw 2013;30(4):31-7.

[463] Zimmermann T, Nagappan N, Gall H, Giger E, Murphy B. Cross-project defect prediction: a large scale experiment on data vs. domain vs. process. In: van Vliet H, Issarny V, editors. ESEC/SIGSOFT FSE. New York, NY: ACM; 2009. p. 91-100.

[464] Zitzler E, Kunzli S. Indicator-based selection in multiobjective search. In: Parallel problem solving from nature (PPSN); 2004. p. 832-42.

[465] Zitzler E, Laumanns M, Thiele L. SPEA2: improving the strength pareto evolutionary algorithm. In: Evolutionary methods for design, optimization and control with applications to industrial problems (EUROGEN'2002); 2002. p. 95-100.

[466] Žliobaitė I. Learning under concept drift: an overview. CoRR; abs/1010.4784; 2010.

[467] Zorkadis V, Karras DA. Efficient information theoretic extraction of higher order features for improving neural network-based spam e-mail categorization. J Exp Theor Artif Intell 2006;18(4):523-34.

[468] Zorkadis V, Karras DA, Panayoto M. Efficient information theoretic strategies for classifier combination, feature extraction and performance evaluation in improving false positives and false negatives for spam e-mail filtering. Neural Netw 2005;18(5-6):799-807.

Printed in the United States
By Bookmasters